Britain's Imperial Century
1815–1914

Britain's Imperial Century 1815–1914

A Study of Empire and Expansion

Ronald Hyam

BOOKS
10 East 53d St. New York 10022
(a division of Harper & Row Publishers, Inc.)

© 1976 Ronald Hyam
Published in the U.S.A. 1976 by
HARPER & ROW PUBLISHERS, INC.
BARNES & NOBLE IMPORT DIVISION
ISBN 0–06–493099–8
Printed in Great Britain

Blind, fooled, and staggering from her throne, I saw her fall,
Clutching at the gaud of Empire;
And wondering, round her, sons and daughter-nations stood –
What madness had possessed her;
But when they lifted her, the heart was dead,
Withered within the body, and all the veins
Were choked with yellow dirt.

Edward Carpenter,
Towards Democracy Pt IV, "Empire" [1902]

Wider still and wider,
Shall thy bounds be set;
God who made thee mighty,
Make thee mightier yet.

A. C. Benson *Land of Hope and Glory* (1902)

By the same author

Elgin and Churchill at the Colonial Office 1905–1908 (Macmillan 1968)

A History of Isleworth Grammar School (1969)

The Failure of South African Expansion 1908–1948 (Macmillan 1972)

With Ged Martin: *Reappraisals in British imperial history* (Macmillan 1975)

Contents

List of Maps and Tables

PREFACE

The aim of this book is to provide suitable reading for people who, having an outline knowledge of conventional British imperial history, need a point of departure into the vast range of monographic studies, and who wish to see how, within the covers of a single book, regional examples of British activity can be fitted into a world-wide pattern, and how areas of formal territorial control can be related to those of informal influence. It is in fact an attempt, and I think the first of its kind, to produce a full-scale book based on the framework put forward in 1953 by Robinson and Gallagher in their famous essay 'The imperialism of free trade'. Although basing myself on that methodological break-through in imperial history, I have at the same time tried to re-examine the whole concept of the British empire afresh, uncluttered by much in the way of historiographical commentary upon existing studies.* The result tends to present the British empire as a by-product of British global expansion and as part of the history of race relations. Following the sound but seldom heeded injunctions of Hancock and Ashton, I have written this book without using the contentious and emotive words 'imperialism', 'colonialism' and 'capitalism', though unavoidably they sometimes appear in quotations. This procedure has held in check the quantity of abstract theorising, though I do nevertheless present a new hypothesis about the underlying dynamics of empire and expansion.

The subject predicates an ambivalent attitude, and some readers may find my tone slightly flippant in places. If so, I would remind them of Kipling's response to such a charge:

> I have written the tale of our life
>   For a sheltered people's mirth,
> In jesting guise – but ye are wise,
>   And ye know what the jest is worth.

* *Reappraisals in British imperial history* by Ged Martin and myself (Macmillan 1975) does, however, deal with problems of interpretation, and may be regarded as a companion volume to the present study; while W. R. Louis (ed.) *Imperialism: the Robinson & Gallagher controversy* (1976) covers a central area of modern debate.

My foremost debt is to Ronald Robinson and it is only a little less to Jack Gallagher and Nicholas Mansergh. It was 'Robbie' who, at St John's College, Cambridge in 1959, first interested me in this subject, and I have since then received continual stimulus and unobtrusive kindness from each of them. More recently, my closer colleagues in the Cambridge History Faculty have also included John Lonsdale, Christopher Platt, Anil Seal and Eric Stokes. They have all influenced me; several of them have scrutinised my drafts, in whole or part, with great care. For Ged Martin I reserve a special word of thanks, first as enthusiastic pupil, then as helpful colleague, always as friendly critic. Valuable suggestions have also come from the Earl of Elgin, Hilary Beattie (Yale), Rodney Davenport (Rhodes, Grahamstown), and Wm. Roger Louis (Texas).

Although it is a good and well-understood convention that no blame for the shortcomings of the text attaches to those acknowledged in the preface, this caveat is the more necessary in a work of this scale and compression, where it is peculiarly difficult to attain balance, up-to-dateness and accuracy. The global gymnastics of this exercise will doubtless seem unsatisfactory to regional specialists. I have not, however, tried to provide potted histories either of imperial evolution as a whole or of individual countries, but merely to record and comment upon some general, some interlocking and some rather neglected aspects of the imperial relationship and British world influence. In Part I this is mainly done chronologically – in Part II regionally, but regional development is sketched only in relation to the Victorian cosmoplastic process.

I have omitted a separate bibliography, since my list of references is in effect a running bibliography and as such, I hope, a more effectual way of fulfilling the aim stated in my opening sentence above.

The way in which my family and friends have provided hospitality, advice, encouragement and diversion has left me much in their debt. Among those who more particularly put themselves out on my behalf when they need not have done, were Adrian Bush, David Pountney and Josephine Turner. And I have received much kindness in various parts of the world from Bombay to Mbabane.

Jane Cooke typed the crucial first draft in such a way as to win my admiration. Nigel Hancock, of that great institution the Cambridge University Library, solved all my hardest bibliographical problems. Joan Pocock drew the maps which so enhance this volume. Geoffrey Barraclough suggested to Batsford many years ago that I should write this book, and Samuel Carr has been an infinitely patient publisher.

Magdalene College   RONALD HYAM
& St John's College,
Cambridge,
December 1974

PART ONE

1 The Foundations of Power, 1815–1870

When you come to think of it, there was no such thing as Greater Britain, still less a British empire – India perhaps apart. There was only a ragbag of territorial bits and pieces, some remaindered remnants, some pre-empted luxury items, some cheap samples. All that red on the map represented in truth at best only a dominion of opinion[1] and a grand anomaly,[2] and at worst a temptation to illusions of grandeur and a gross abuse. There was always a fundamental hiatus in the imperial bureaucratic process: the impossibility, in the last resort, of translating the democratic political decisions of one society into the totally different political realities of another, the problem of producing any kind of real relation between policy determined in London and the practice of government on the spot. Before the coming of the telegraph, even the imperfect translation of will into act could in many places be a matter of years, or perhaps decades. There was also the problem of getting public support at home for the effective maintenance of the empire, for it was the public, not the policy-makers, who behaved with a 'fit of absence of mind' about the empire for much of the century. As the 15th Earl of Derby shrewdly remarked, 'Kings and aristocracies may govern empires, but one people cannot rule another'.

British empire and expansion was a set of aspirations and activities only loosely held together, chiefly by the defining limits and overshadowing realities of the American Republic and the Indian Empire. Between the challenge of the United States and the problem of India was hammered out all that was constructive in Britain's imperial century: for example, its insistent resort constitutionally to a federal panacea and its fitful concern morally for humanitarian trusteeship. Insofar as imperial Britain operated a system, its economic centre was the Atlantic Ocean with the United States an integral part; and its strategic centre was the Indian Ocean based on the continental powerhouse of the Indian Army. British interests throughout the nineteenth century hinged upon two necessities. One was to contain or accommodate to the rival expansion generated by the Great Experiment in North America. The other was to defend the Pax Britannica in India from internal subversion and external pressure from rival European expanding powers. The history of Britain as an imperial power can only be written in the light of the challenge of the United States, which had freed itself politically from the mother country in the eighteenth century, and the problem of India which was being prepared or preparing to do so in the twentieth, and meanwhile might collapse into anarchy at any time. The record of the British empire is strewn with so much red-tape, so much irrationality and so many mad-cap programmes, such as Wakefield's colonisation scheme or 'imperial federation', all of which were merely attempts to impose a system where no system was, or even could be. Martin's words, 'to clothe with illusion that which lacked reality', go straight to the heart of the essential vacuum.[3]

As Palmerston rightly observed, 'British interests encircled the globe' – but this is far from saying that there was a global imperial system. Tests of central control (administrative or legislative) or comparisons of colonial problems fail to reveal any all-embracing or monolithic empire – only a congeries of individual attempts by a large power to impose its will on diverse and unique weaker territories. 'The "man on the spot" came to feel himself less a subordinate in a great Empire than a ruler of an empire of his own.'

The empire was unified by no coherent philosophy, nor by any coercive policy. Local administrators defined the strength of imperial rule. The authority of the imperial government seldom existed at the local level. For example in South Africa in the early nineteenth century the crucial matter of land policy was framed and implemented in an amateurish and sluggish way; 'systematic colonisation' was never applied, and governors could completely disregard directives from London. In the 1820s it was said in the Cape that they knew no law but the will of the autocratic governor, Lord Charles Somerset.[4]

There was constant talk of *creating* an empire from Adderley in 1854 to Lyttelton in 1910. Adderley wrote, 'This little island wants not energy, but only territory and basis to extend itself; its sea-girt home would become the citadel of one of the greatest of the empires . . .'[5] The historian J. A. Froude in 1869 spoke of the possibility that Britain 'might become the metropolis of an enormous and coherent empire'. Joseph Chamberlain spoke of the dream of 'creating an empire,' his son Austen of the fact that until the very end of the nineteenth century the empire was little more than an aspiration. Both noted the difficulty of trying to turn it into something more tangible. Lyttelton described the empire as 'a confederation of independent nations' without unifying force.[6] F. S. Oliver writing in 1906 stated that the empire rested solely on sentiment, influence and management: it was not, he added, 'a political fact, but only a phrase, an influence or a sentiment', a 'voluntary league of states, terminable upon a breath'. He hoped this 'loose confederation' might be converted into a firm union – as the American states had converted themselves in the eighteenth century against much harder obstacles.[7]

Adam Smith described how the British had amused themselves with the idea that they had really possessed a great empire in America. But, he pointed out, it had hitherto existed in the imagination only; it had been, not an empire, but a project for an empire, not a gold-mine but a project for a gold-mine, which if pursued would cost much and bring no likely profit. And so it proved to be. The empire *always* remained a project, and existed only in the imagination.[8] Even that apparently most solid portion, India, when really· examined in depth begins to look nearly a hollow sham: it certainly no longer bears the interpretation of having been ruled by omniscient 'guardians'. Lord William Bentinck (governor-general 1828–35) recognised 'we are in fact strangers in the land', and Fort St George was so self-contained a British enclave that he went out to Madras with all his requirements bought in London, including 'Indian pickled gherkins' and 'melon mangoes'. As late as the 1860s land settlement work fell a long way short of official theory; many returns were based on guesswork. There simply wasn't the manpower or technical resources for adequate land surveys, and Indian subordinates and village communities could mislead and obstruct. The men who ruled India always took vital decisions on the basis of inadequate information, and so, it has been said, 'the Indian empire in the last analysis rested upon their ability to make an educated guess'. Historians studying administration at the village level have suggested how 'silent combinations of local influence' acted to corrode the impact of directives handed down from higher levels. The traditional resistant and rejective process of silent corrosive local indigenous power has been called the 'principle of the white ant' by Frykenberg, drawing the analogy from a tiny creature of tremendous energy and science, devouring the inner structure of the stoutest kind, leaving only a hollow shell without necessarily destroying the outward form. This, he suggests, typifies what happened in South India when these local forces, the Indian service castes, 'made a hollow mockery of the stout administrative structures of successive systems of regal and imperial power' – of which the British administrative invasion was only one. This picture swings rather too far in underplaying the imperial role. Nineteenth-century Indian government functioned rather by a 'balancing of relative weakness' between those occupying premier positions at different levels (local, provincial, all-India), with the British shifting their patronage between competing local élites – a technique which used to be called 'divide and rule'. Bargains were struck to the mutual advantage of imperial guardians and local Indian élites because their interests were not the same: imperial power did not want to intervene in the local power struggles which formed the focus of local concern. The British imperial yoke was light. Thus, as Anil Seal observes, the eventual contest between the Indian nationalist movements and the British was 'a strange struggle between impotent rivals', a duel between hollow statues 'locked in motionless and simulated combat'.[9]

Frykenberg pointed out how from the earliest years of East India Company activity in India, local Indian participation in government had been recognised as essential and inescapable, as the very key to power, since a mere handful of Britons unaided from within could never really have governed so many millions. In general, empire and expansion were simply not practicable without the collaboration of elements – they can be called mediating élites – within non-European societies. Indigenous help and co-operation, whether voluntary or enforced, was continuously needed to promote British interests and to avert resistance or hold it down. Robinson has made an irrefutable case for this thesis. The amenable Indian sepoy, who in effect conquered India for the British, remained indispensable to imperial control. He had few equivalents in China or Japan, which goes a long way towards explaining why the foreigner was held at bay in those countries. Only a tiny fraction of British power was ever actually committed on a regular basis to Asian or African empire, and none at all to Latin America, and yet in all these areas the expansive forces generated by industrial Britain combined with elements in the agrarian-based economies of the underdeveloped world to make a mutually advantageous bargain. In trade, the intermediaries came in a variety of guises, the mulattos in the West Indies and West Africa, the Levantine Christians in the Ottoman empire, the compradors in China. Their role was vital. Thus as Richard Graham writes:

The force of the imperial power is to be measured not only or even primarily by the overt acts of political control but by the degree to which the values, attitudes and institutions of the expansionist nation infiltrate and overcome those of the recipient one. In this process the native collaborator or sepoy is indispensable.

It was a precarious mechanism, and far from being one which gave an automatic upper-hand to the British. The indigenous élite could dictate the terms of the bargain until well into the nineteenth century in West Africa; there and elsewhere they could sometimes divert the agents of expansion to serve the needs of their own traditional societies. Missionaries were especially vulnerable, and there were many African chiefs (such as Moshweshwe of Basutoland, Kgama of the Ngwato, Lewanika of Barotseland and the Tonga chiefs of Nyasaland) who used them as commercial and diplomatic agents, agricultural and military advisers, secretaries and gun-repairers. The British were thus sometimes exploited for indigenous ends and their objectives frustrated.

Nevertheless there was a strength in the British position which transcended its institutional structure, political and economic. This was the ability of many of its representatives to understand the realities of the local situation and to evoke admiration, support and co-operation by their courage, integrity and sympathy.[10]

There was a considerable intellectual difficulty in holding all the parts of the empire and the expansive processes in the mind; this afflicted contemporaries and has frustrated all historians until Robinson and Gallagher showed how it might be done. At least six government departments were integral to the operation of British overseas interests: the foreign office, the India office, the war office, the admiralty, the board of trade and the colonial office – and for much of the nineteenth century the last was almost the least important. Contemporary ignorance was often startling. Even Palmerston had to look at the map to see where the colonies were, and Gladstone, though four times prime minister, never travelled further afield than the Ionian Isles. At least one astute commentator felt he ought never to have been prime minister of all 'because he is so invincibly ignorant of British duties and interests outside Britain'. He never displayed much concern about India and was only once aroused to any enthusiasm about it – by the possibility of arranging Cook's tours there. Joseph Chamberlain never visited India and he seldom spoke about it.[11] India was at one and the same time so basic a part of the empire that it could be taken for granted, and so much an entity in itself that it was often regarded as a thing apart, an empire in its own right, with a secretary of state in the cabinet sometimes working at cross-purposes with wider imperial interests. The importance of the United States in the British scheme of things was, however, obvious to contemporaries, and it was only historians who lost sight of this fact, assuming that because it had fallen outside the formal part of the empire it no longer had any imperial significance.[12]

In 1815 it was to America and India that men chiefly looked. The challenge of the independent republic in the west had to be faced. The burden of having become a paramount power in the eastern hemisphere had to be shouldered. Specific parallels between the two were drawn. Bentinck wanted a kind of American India, with settlers leading 'civilisation' forward to an ultimate independence on the American model: in Rosselli's striking phrase, 'a tropical America haloed with the glory of a regenerated Mughal Empire'. Charles Trevelyan and Rammohan Roy drew similar parallels, and Macaulay had something similar in mind. And yet Bentinck could still decline to read a report on Central Asia on the ground that 'civilisation alone interests me, and I would rather see the improvement and happiness of America than all the rest of the world beyond the limits of Europe'.[13]

The late eighteenth century saw the first beginnings of massive industrialisation and an unprecedented Protestant missionary movement. The former cemented relations with the erstwhile American rebels. The latter turned first in a frenzy of evangelical fervour to India and the Pacific islands.

The eighteenth-century aristocracy had found outlet enough for eccentric energies in Britain itself: in subjugating the Scottish highlands (compensating peasants by making them servants to grouse-shooting Englishmen), in improving their estates, embellishing their country seats and building their extravagant 'follies'. In the nineteenth century wider fields were needed for expertise, eccentricity and evangelical piety. The result was a diaspora of younger sons and the spread of a globally conspicuous consumption. Many there were who discovered that pig-sticking in India or Kenya was more exciting than grouse-shooting in Scotland or Yorkshire, or that being a district officer responsible for millions was more satisfying than being a country magistrate in Berkshire. Governing the empire was literally seen in terms of the principles of estate management writ large. Bentinck, after 15 years improving Norfolk farms, saw Bengal as 'almost a facsimile upon a gigantic scale of the Great Level of the Fens'; he regarded India as 'a great estate of which I am the chief agent'. The civilising mission walked hand-in-hand with the indulgence of whim, duty with dottiness.

Until the joyous confidence snapped after mid-century, the decades between 1838 and 1858 were 'great ones in which to be alive and British'. As William Cory* described it, the period was Britain's Golden Age, 'beyond compare the happiest': 'To have lived in the flow of life, not in the backwaters or swamps, as a Briton from 1810 to 1860 was, I am sure, the last, the consummate blessing. Since then our educated people have been less happy . . .' In that period British activity was, Cory believed, 'far-reaching, elastic, productive, fearless, rational'.[14]

SEA POWER AND GUNBOAT DIPLOMACY

'The British Empire is pre-eminently a great Naval, Indian and Colonial power'. These are the words of the official report inaugurating the Committee of Imperial Defence in 1904. And according to Admiral John Fisher in 1903: 'The British Empire floats on the British Navy'. Without command of the sea there would have been no British empire in the form which it had assumed by 1815. It was superiority at sea which had enabled Britain to win the eighteenth-century Anglo-French struggle for empire. The elder Pitt declared in his speech on the peace preliminaries in 1762 (during the Seven Years' War) that the 'great fundamental principle' of British policy was that France was 'chiefly if not solely to be dreaded by us in the light of a maritime and commercial power'.[15] British superiority at sea, however, meant that France could not successfully defend her colonies because large expeditions and reinforcements were never allowed to reach them. Thus Britain won the contest for dominance in India and Canada. Until 1815 Britain concentrated her fleet in the western squadron off south-west England in order to intercept at its point of departure any hostile expedition from European rivals.[16] The English Channel was the pivot of naval strategy, and India's attachment to the empire was a direct consequence of British naval command of the English Channel. By 1815 Britain emerged from the Napoleonic Wars 'unchallenged

* William Johnson, changed his name to Cory in 1872; 1823-92, Fellow of King's, assistant master at Eton, mentor of Lord Rosebery and very nearly Regius Professor of Modern History at Cambridge.

and almost unassailable' at sea. As a consequence of her overwhelming naval superiority, in the nineteenth century phrases such as 'the struggle for command of the sea' lost all meaning. Naval supremacy owed its potency to the pursuit of no doctrine or theory. It was a fact of life resulting from the French wars. East of the Cape of Good Hope after 1824 there was no foreign port from which an enemy squadron could effectively challenge British command of the Indian Ocean. Thereafter, and until 1905, British routes to India and China were never threatened by a major foreign naval incursion. At no time did the fragments of other empires (the Portuguese in Mozambique and Goa, the Dutch in Java, the Arabs in Zanzibar, the French in Bourbon, Madagascar and ultimately Indo-China) affect British control of the Indian Ocean. The presence of only two or three ships cruising in the Malacca Straits or off the west coast of Malaya was enough to discourage major pirate operations and gave confidence to trading communities. When Labuan was acquired in 1846 it closed the 1,500-mile gap in the chain of harbours circling the globe (it was 707 miles from Singapore, 1009 from Hong Kong). Naval superiority significantly increased from the 1840s with the coming of ships built with iron and powered by steam, since British iron and coal supplies were so much better than her timber ones had been. Ships with wooden walls had been built cheaper in Norway, Sweden and Prussia. American ships had dominated the Atlantic in the 1840s and were not only faster than their British rivals but also cheaper to run. But Britain could build iron ships cheaper than any competitor.[17] British maritime ascendancy also owed much to the damage suffered by the American merchant marine in the American Civil War (1861–65). In 1870 the mercantile tonnage of the British empire nearly equalled that of all non-British countries, and by 1880 it exceeded it: the figure of 2,950,000 tons was more than twice that for all other countries.[18]

The famous P. and O. line (Peninsular and Oriental Steam Navigation Company) was incorporated by royal charter in 1840, and in the course of the next few years it successfully extended its service across half the world. In 1854 it secured the Aden–Bombay service, and thus gained a virtual monopoly of British communications with the east. It became the largest and most successful steamship company in the world, paying an average dividend of nine per cent in the 1850s and ten per cent in the 1890s. It pulled together all British interests east of Suez, and converted the Red Sea into a British lake. It was in short 'the unofficial fleet of the empire'.

Oddly enough, the prestige of the royal navy was low and its development as a fighting service was heavily circumscribed financially. There was continual reduction of naval force in the 1830s and 1840s, largely because there was no serious military or commercial competition. It was possible to have naval supremacy on the cheap.[19] Its morale and discipline rested upon crude but effective foundations. 'The Royal Navy', Churchill once declared, 'has for long been founded upon Nelson, rum, buggery and the lash; and so founded it shall continue'.[20]

Because of the improved command of communications established after 1815, the navy was much more dispersed over the world than it had been in the eighteenth century. A long chain of harbours and coaling stations now existed to maintain a dispersed fleet. During the French wars Britain had acquired, and at the Peace of Vienna retained, Malta and Heligoland in Europe, ports in India, Penang (a Malay off-shore island), Ceylon (from the Dutch), the Seychelles, Mauritius, Cape Colony, and Sierra Leone; together with Trinidad, Tobago and St Lucia in the West Indies. Gibraltar had been hers since 1704 (and formally recognised as such in 1713). During the nineteenth century many other key points in the chain of naval communications were added: Aden in 1839, Hong Kong in 1842, Labuan in 1846, Lagos in 1861, Mombasa in 1890.

The navy's function was two-fold: first to deny rivals new naval bases or the spread of their influence to important areas; and second, to protect British interests where respect for the British citizen and his property was not automatic or where conceptions of justice differed from European conventions. This secondary duty expanded to a point where it embarrassed the performance of its more strictly naval and political duties. There was much to be done in protecting commerce by the suppression of piracy, especially in the Persian Gulf and the East Indian archipelago. In the former area (where activity spread even to the coasts of India) a great deal had been achieved by the 1830s. An important subsidiary service rendered to commerce by the navy was the coastal and harbour surveying it undertook.[21]

The period from 1835 to 1860 is often thought of as an era of gunboat diplomacy and naval intervention.[22] It is certainly true that there were gunboats making regular patrols and that their presence assisted the objectives of British policy. A squadron of cruisers patrolled the West African coast to intercept foreign slave-carrying ships every year from 1819; by 1850 there were two dozen cruisers engaged in this work. The cost rose by 50 per cent between 1829 and 1841, to somewhere between £100,000 and £200,000 a year in the 1840s. At this time it became more militant, releasing captives, destroying slave factories and warehouses, and coming closer to the coast. Nevertheless, against the statistical yardstick of the numbers of slaves it diverted from their destination it would not seem to have been very successful. In its best year, 1837, the royal navy had been able to capture and liberate only 8,652 slaves in transit – probably less than ten per cent of the total. The average figure intercepted annually was about eight per cent, but the navy's presence had a deterrent effect much greater than this figure suggests. Perhaps 43 per cent more slaves might otherwise have been shipped between 1811 and 1870. From 1850 Brazil began enforcing her own anti-slave trade legislation and this by 1852 broke the back of the Atlantic slave trade. But the admission of duty-free sugar into Britain from 1846 increased the objections to the squadron, because more slaves were needed in Cuba and Brazil if Britain was to import their cheaper sugar: British consumer interests seemed to lie in the growth of Central and Latin American production.[23] The presence of the naval squadron also helped marginally to enforce British policy towards the coastal African states, because it could threaten naval bombardment. Palmerston reminded the king of Lagos in the crisis of 1851: 'Lagos is near the sea, and ... on the sea are the ships and cannon of England'.[24]

There was also a Latin American squadron, but although it made some displays of strength, much restraint and understanding was shown by officers on that station. The well-known episodes in the River Plata between 1843 and 1846 were perhaps the least successful of gunboat diplomacy operations. The story is confused, but the essence of it was that British forces with some French assistance tried to prop up a weak Uruguayan regime against Argentinian-supported forces, and they also tried to open the River Paraná to trade against the opposition of the Argentinian strong man General Rosas. Militarily both operations had some shortlived success, but economically results were unfortunate. Trade with Montevideo declined, and British merchants in Buenos Aires found these actions detrimental to their interests. Palmerston withdrew the gunboats from 1846.

Gunboat diplomacy in fact was never more than a useful instrument in certain special conditions. All external pressures had to be carefully controlled lest they precipitated total internal collapse. The reactions of local sentiment repeatedly reduced the effectiveness of naval action. The cost of some naval squadrons was hardly justified by the profits of the trade they protected. But to argue, as the Manchester School did, that the United States' trade flourished without the aid of a great navy was to overlook the American debt to British naval power, especially in the China seas. Moreover, the action of other European powers undoubtedly could be constrained by British naval power. It is certain that they would not have remained so inactive in the wars of Latin American independence but for the British naval veto on intervention. As Bolivar said, 'Only England, mistress of the seas, can protect us against the united force of European reaction'.[25]

To a remarkable extent, early and mid-Victorian expansion was a strategy based on rivers and sea power. It was well understood that England's writ ran no further than the range of her ships' guns. There was an instinctive dislike of advancing imperial land frontiers in Asia and Africa beyond the protective reach of British sea power.[26] The growth of commerce in North America by way of the St Lawrence and the Mississippi had made it a primary assumption of the Victorians that great rivers flowing out of vast continents might be the means of comparable developments elsewhere. Palmerston wrote to the board of trade in 1841 about Latin America, noting that so far the Plata, the Amazon and Orinoco and the rivers which fell into them had 'not been rendered available for commercial intercourse with the interior of the country', but adding that surely in time 'the use of them may render those great water communications ... available for the purposes of commerce'. By contrast, the lack of inland waterways in Australia helps to explain the long neglect of the interior by the British and the concentration on acquiring strategic harbours.[27]

Some of the Latin American railways (almost entirely British-built) were simply feeders to the river steamship system or coastal trade. The first Argentinian railways were mere tributaries of the steamer in the days when steamers were supreme. This is why Chile with its long coast developed precociously, and why the Amazon was opened to international trade in 1866, though the river led only into equatorial forest. Railways were short and not very efficient, connecting places on the high plateau to coastal ports.[28]

People looked upon rivers as one of the best means of diffusing civilisation. Some of the most celebrated events in Victorian exploration and expansion were expeditions up the world's great rivers, such as Elgin's trip up the Yangtse in 1858 through Taiping-held China, the Niger expeditions of 1841–42, 1854 and 1857, and Baker's Nile expedition of 1869. By 1878 companies and individuals were pushing up the Niger with the aid of 14 steamers. The government made occasional efforts to provide protection for the expanding commerce of the Niger valley – there were military expeditions in 1871–79, destroying the towns of the Delta and hinterland which had attacked British life and property. So long as the warships remained in the vicinity of trading posts a thriving trade was done; but Africans resumed their attacks when the ships could not ascend the river, which was for seven months in the dry season. In 1879 Onitsha was bombarded for three days, and Yamaha (another important inland trading station) was destroyed for attacking British traders. The advantage of going up-river was that palm oil (which Britain was trying to develop as a staple product) was cheaper there – it could be had for £13 per ton rather than £24 in the Delta in 1856. Thus trading-post enclaves were extended into the interior under the cover of sea power along 600 miles of navigable waterway.[29] A similar penetration occurred on the Yangtse river in China in the 1890s.

Naval supremacy was the basis on which industrial supremacy was reared. In considering Britain's pre-eminence or world hegemony between 1815 and 1860 it is vitally important to remember the parlous, disunited and confused state of European powers during this period. French and Dutch power had been contained, while Russian and German threats had not yet successfully emerged. Industrialisation everywhere lagged behind Britain's. What happened from the 1860s onwards, when rivals emerged, only gives point to the fact of the dependence of British power upon a period of unusual European weakness. As soon as effective European and American competitors began to emerge after they had sorted out their domestic problems, British world power immediately began relatively to decline. This is not to say that all was calm confidence before the 1860s. Alarm was caused by the Russian Baltic fleet in the 1830s, and then there were Anglo-French war scares in 1844, 1852–53 and 1858–60. In 1844 it was feared that steamers would bring

30,000 French invaders across the channel in one night. There was prolonged cabinet debate on defence between 1844 and 1848, having some resemblance to the excitement produced by the rise of the German navy from 1898. But by and large there was an unusual degree of confidence in the security provided by naval superiority.[30]

ECONOMIC HEGEMONY 1815–1870

The peace treaty of 1815 set the seal on a pre-industrial formal empire, of which the major components were in India, British North America (Canada), the West Indies and Australia (New South Wales), together with the Cape Colony. All these acquisitions had been made before, or in the earliest stages of, the industrial revolution. The year 1815 is therefore an excellent starting-point for our study, since it was the first time that a modernising industrial economy was able to operate in peacetime conditions. Britain was not yet a free-trading power: indeed, free trade came only surprisingly late in the day. Until well into the nineteenth century all expansionist activity from 1763 had been based on the merchants' interest in the distribution of goods rather than on the manufacturers' interest in the production of more of them, and merchants had never felt able to dispense with government assistance and territorial acquisition. Free trade was thus adopted when the pattern of the formal empire had been largely shaped. But without the capture of the Indian, Chinese and South-east Asian inter-port trade in the 30 years before 1815, without the position built up in the 'carrying trades' in Asian primary products (tea, opium, raw cotton, spices and tin), Britain would not have been able so rapidly later to develop the sale of her manufactured textiles in the east as she did.[31]

From the expansionist point of view, after 1815 the industrial revolution involved the movements of manufactures, men and money overseas on a scale without precedent. Since Britain was the only industrial power in the world, this gave her unique opportunities to try to develop trade without territorial possession.

Britain became 'the workshop of the world' and this largely meant being the supplier of the world's textiles, both woollen and cotton. The 'declared value' of exports increased from £38.9 million in 1825 to £60.1 million in 1845 and £190 million in 1869. The increase in the export of cotton was remarkable:

EXPORT OF COTTON MANUFACTURED PIECE GOODS

1815 – 253   million yards
1825 – 336   million yards
1855 – 1938   million yards
1875 – 3562   million yards

Even in the 1860s in the whole world there was virtually only one industrial economy, the British, which probably accounted for more than one-third of the world's entire output of manufactured goods. By 1851 Britain was producing about two-thirds of the world's coal and more than half of its iron and its cotton cloth.[32]

Britain continuously sent artisans, entrepreneurs, engineers, foremen and operatives to found and work industries overseas, first in Europe, and then throughout the world. Britain built the railways of the world from Belgium to India, though the United States was an exception (even so it was estimated in 1857 that fully £80 million in American railway securities were held in Britain).[33]

Migration on a world-wide scale was in some respects an extension of an established practice of seasonal migration within the United Kingdom or Europe. The difference between those migrant labourers and the 'proletarian globe-trotters' was one of degree only. In Europe, in the United States, in Canada and Australia, the role of the migrating British technician was important. Thistlethwaite has shown how all kinds of workers took part: workers in iron and steel, in pottery and textiles. Their seasonal migrations were sometimes remarkable in their scope. For example, there were miners who spent half the year in Scotland and half in the Appalachian coal-mines of the United States. Or again, there were English house-painters who worked in the United States in the spring, in Scotland in the summer before the English families went north, and in England in the autumn while the shooting season was in progress. Such Atlantic movements have their parallel in the Pacific interchange of goldminers who switched impartially between Sydney, San Francisco and Auckland with the altering prospects of gold discoveries.[34]

It is estimated that between 1815 and 1912 some 21½ million people emigrated from the British Isles, of whom more than half went to the United States, especially in the earlier part of the period, despite six separate experiments in state-aided emigration within the empire between 1815 and 1826. Between 1843 and 1913 an average of 65 per cent every decade went to the United States. Even in 1852, after the discovery of gold, and in Australia's peak year for immigrants, three times as many people left the United Kingdom for the United States as for Australia. And this was despite the efforts of the Colonial Land and Emigration Commission (1840) which set out to meet the American challenge by offering an attractive programme of emigration within the empire. Thus, as Dilke wrote, 'Our colonies are no more an outlet for our surplus population than they would be if the Great Mogul ruled over them'.[35]

Why did so many make for the United States? One obvious reason was its relative proximity, which meant an easier and cheaper journey than to anywhere else. The fare to Australia was five times as great. Equally important, however, was probably the attraction, especially for the Irish, of an egalitarian and less hierarchical society based, moreover, on rebellion.

DESTINATION OF EMIGRANTS FROM BRITAIN[36]

Date	U.S.A.	Empire	Elsewhere
1843–52	70.1%	29.0%	0.9%
1853–60	61.0	38.4	0.6
1861–70	72.0	26.1	1.9
1871–80	64.9	31.5	3.6
1881–90	67.2	29.3	3.5
1891–1900	65.5	28.2	6.3
1901–10	44.4	47.9	7.7
1911–13	26.5	65.1	8.4

These percentages suggest that the class structure, real or supposed, was one reason why on balance the empire was losing population.[37] There were, however, more important practical reasons inhibiting empire emigration: the native troubles of New Zealand and South Africa, the poor farming opportunities in South Africa, the proverbial coldness of Canada. Land regulations after 1831 and Wakefield's policies tended to force the price of land up compared with the United States. Wakefield regarded the Americans as uncivilised. Yet three-quarters of Irish emigrants went to the United States.[38] The one type of family which unfailingly had relatives overseas was that of the Irish peasant.[39] The factors of 'push' were probably more important in motive than the factors of 'pull'.[40] Of course the discovery of gold could exercise a tremendous positive attraction, but generally migration was caused by social misery and discomfort; Highland clearance accounted for heavy Scottish emigration in the late eighteenth century. Movement was greatest at times when there was famine, as among the Irish peasants after the potato crop failures in 1822 and 1846, or among the Scottish crofters in 1836–37. The volume of emigration in the wretched years of the 1830s was almost treble what it had been in the 1820s. The period of industrial and commercial prosperity between 1850 and 1878 caused a lull in emigration, even though transport improved.[41] The migrations of the nineteenth century were major historical episodes; as Hancock says, in the last four centuries, and especially during the last century, the 'greatest migrations of man since the Neolithic age have taken place'.[42] One of the main features of nineteenth-century world history was the populating by Europeans of large territories; Australia, the Mississippi Valley, Brazil, the Canadian prairies. By 1900 two-thirds of the English-speaking peoples lived outside Europe.[43]

The new scale of capital movement in the nineteenth century was essentially dependent on industrial wealth. Britain was not merely workshop of the world, but banker too. Already in 1800 London had replaced Amsterdam as the commercial-financial capital of Europe.[44] 'Export of

Capital' is a misleading term – conceptually the process is best understood as one of buying things abroad – companies, railways, and so forth. It was the prospect of profitable markets which induced investment in items necessary to operate the market. The strongest attraction was to railways and mining. Capital went primarily to those lands from the development of which the British people hoped for benefits, in the way of new sources of raw materials and foodstuffs, as well as new markets, and it was used to develop the facilities which increased the capacity of primary producers to export and thus ultimately to import.[45] From the figures available for publicly-issued capital, it would seem that over half of this investment went outside the formal empire. Analysing the long-term publicly-issued British capital investment made overseas by 1913, Feis concludes that 47 per cent, or £1,780 million went to countries inside the empire, with £754.6 million of the remainder to the United States alone.[46] The amounts built up steadily during the course of the century:[47]

ACCUMULATING BALANCE OF CREDIT ABROAD

1816	£24.6	million
1831	£113.1	million
1851	£217.9	million
1871	£763.6	million
1891	£2,004.5	million
1913	£3,989.6	million

Source: Imlah

All previous estimates have been completely recalculated fairly recently by M. Simon on the basis of new British portfolio foreign investment between 1865 and 1914, and his conclusions may be set out diagramatically (opposite).[48]

By and large the recalculation confirms older estimates: his figure for 1913 is £3,879, compared with Imlah's £3,989.6 and Feis's £3,763.3. But, like theirs, it perpetuates one defect of unknown size. They all underestimate the amount of investment in the empire, since so much of the transfer of British funds to the empire consisted of the buying of land, plantations, factories and ships by private individuals, often soldiers or civil servants on the spot, the investment of mercantile capital in industrial enterprises, mines and so forth, and the construction of branch plants by British manufacturers. Investments of this kind never appeared in the statistics for public issues, and they absorbed so much more of British resources within the empire than outside it. Nevertheless the quantity of investment going outside the empire remains impressive.[49]

The great movement of capital lessened after 1875. For the 20 years ending

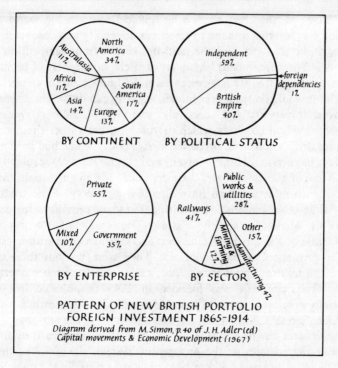

BY CONTINENT — North America 34%, Australasia 11%, Africa 11%, Asia 14%, Europe 13%, South America 17%

BY POLITICAL STATUS — Independent 59%, foreign dependencies 1%, British Empire 40%

BY ENTERPRISE — Private 55%, Mixed 10%, Government 35%

BY SECTOR — Railways 41%, Public works & utilities 28%, Other 15%, Mining & Farming 12%, Manufacturing 4%

PATTERN OF NEW BRITISH PORTFOLIO
FOREIGN INVESTMENT 1865–1914
Diagram derived from M. Simon, p. 40 of J. H. Adler (ed)
Capital movements & Economic Development (1967)

in 1874 Britain had been exporting an average annual surplus of capital of about £15 million, in addition to re-investing abroad all the earnings upon foreign investment already made. Then the export of a capital surplus came to an end, and there was simply re-investment of earnings.[50] This movement of capital was of great importance to developing regions overseas.[51]

Although various moves for freer trade had taken place before Peel's ministry (1841–46), it was chiefly he who began the free trade era. Peel's latest biographer emphasises the 'condition of England' as being decisive in forming his view that change was necessary. He stresses Peel's concern with economic policy as a piece of domestic social engineering.[52] There must be a great deal of truth in this interpretation. Peel was a man much moved by human suffering. But, if we can judge from Peel's speeches early in 1842, there were wider questions at least kept in view. Peel observed how in the Napoleonic wars Britain had 'commanded the supply of the nations'. Now Britain was encountering difficulties, and the longer peace was maintained, the more extensive and formidable competition from foreign manufacturers would become. The continuance of her long-enjoyed 'manufacturing and commercial pre-eminence' might be ensured by cheap and abundant food, since this would promote the increase of British capital, by which in turn pre-eminence could be retained. 'Advance', he said, must be taken as the imperial motto and Britain must fully take up her God-ordained destiny.

Britain stood as 'the chief connecting link between the old world and the new'. She was inferior to none in resources, ingenuity and character, as well as in maritime strength, and she need not shrink from competition. Surely Britain could flourish outside 'the sickly artificial atmosphere of prohibition'? In short, Peel saw free trade as essential to Britain's position as workshop of the world: it would do 'whatever human sagacity can do for the promotion of commercial prosperity'. It certainly was not Cobden's vision of a cosmopolitan world economy which moved him, but rather the necessity of preserving British industrial predominance, a policy which had been urged by Macaulay, Palmerston, Hume, Torrens and others. It was Macaulay who said in 1842 that if the Corn Laws were repealed, 'we might supply the whole world with manufactures and have almost a monopoly of the trade of the world', while other nations 'were raising abundant provisions for us on the banks of the Mississippi and the Vistula'. The repealers felt a new need for haste because of the threat of American and German competition, especially after the formation of the Zollverein. They were anxious to secure and preserve the immense markets of America by means of more liberal trade policies. The *Economist* was founded in 1843 to promote free trade.[53] Restrictions were being removed in order to build British greatness on a surer foundation: 'stretching her dominion over the wants of the universe'.[54]

In the debates on the abolition of the corn laws comparatively little was said about the colonies or the preferential system, since, unlike the sugar duties, the taxes on grain had not been designed primarily to protect colonial interests. But a few M.P.s did think that abandonment of this principle of protection would destroy the whole basis on which the 'colonial system' rested.[55] The imperial preference which existed before 1846 meant tariff discrimination in favour of colonial as against foreign products in the mother country, and discrimination in favour of British (and British colonial) as against foreign products in the colonies. The Montreal Board of Trade said the repeal of the corn laws was equivalent to the subversion of 'an entire system of government', and Canada has never lacked historians to represent the British unilateral initiative, especially when viewed in conjunction with the repeal of the Navigation Laws in 1849, as the 'British declaration of economic independence', and a 'major catastrophe' for the old commercial empire of the St Lawrence.[56] Canadian reaction was to turn almost instinctively towards the United States, towards the idea of trading reciprocity, and even towards political annexation, in order to promote her economic interests. The year 1846 was also marked by a big reduction in foreign timber duties, at which Canadian lumber interests protested. The disadvantage to Canada of the change of policy was obvious. The earl of Elgin (governor-general 1847–54) thought the proper course to follow was a yet further development of free trade by the repeal of the navigation laws and the extension of Canadian commercial intercourse with the United States. Repeal of the navigation laws was something which the colonies wanted, and so from 1849 it was no longer necessary in law for British merchandise to be carried in British-built ships. It thus enabled greater interchange of goods to take place between Canada and the United States on their inland waterways. Sugar duties had afforded the British West Indian colonies a virtual monopoly of the British market. In 1846 Russell, in order to avoid a sugar famine, equalised the duties on colonial and foreign sugar (that is to say he abolished preference), arguing that both Britain and the colonies would be better off by the 'abolition of useless restrictions; ... the affection felt reciprocally will be all the stronger when neither party is subject to any restrictions imposed by the other'. The last remaining preferential duties were removed by an unrepentent Gladstone in the 1860 budget: the flourishing condition of the Canadian colonies made him impervious to the echoes of gloomy predictions which had accompanied previous measures unshackling trade.[57]

Political frontiers were thus no longer reinforced with economic barriers, and something very like the Great Commercial Republic envisaged by Adam Smith was brought into being.[58] The old economic privileges of the colonies had conflicted with the vision of Britain becoming the workshop of the world. Manufacturers became impatient of established monopolies which imposed restrictions in return for a tariff protection which they no longer needed. All monopolies were attacked, not least that of the East India Company, which lost its monopoly of eastern trade in 1813 and ceased to be a trading concern in 1833.[59]

THE PROBLEM OF IMPERIAL ORGANISATION

It may be stated quite categorically that, despite what many historians have believed,[60] no minister of the Crown between 1815 and 1914 wished, as a settled policy, to be rid of all colonies. It was certainly not the view of Palmerston[61] or Russell or Disraeli[62] that Britain should abandon them. It is scarcely less true to say that no other man in public life held any contrary view either. The British frequently disliked *colonists,* but they had in principle no animus against *colonies.*[63] Goldwin Smith, often regarded as 'against colonies' in fact said he was no more against them than the solar system, but he was opposed to withholding independence from them when they were fit for it; but, he added, even independent nations did not necessarily cease to be colonies of Britain.[64] There was well-nigh universal agreement with J. S. Mill's view that colonies added to British 'moral influence and weight in the councils of the world'.[65] Colonial separation, he thought, would be disadvantageous to the world in general and England in particular: it would greatly diminish the prestige of Britain, which he believed (in 1862) to be 'in the present state of the world, a very great advantage to mankind'. For a governor's view, we may cite Sir William Denison. He believed that colonies added to Britain's strength as well as her political importance; colonies assured her citizens a friendly welcome in every corner of the globe, and guaranteed to British ships assistance and protection in every colonial harbour, instead of the cold treatment of a neutral, or the active hostility of a trade competitor.[66] Russell, as a politician, expressed himself similarly in 1849, particularly stressing the value of colonies, commercially and militarily, in time of war. As far as Canada and Australia were concerned, he declared, 'The British race in these colonies form in time of war one Nation with us, as much as Aberdeen or Cork, though divided by a larger space of the world. But in point of communication Halifax is now almost as near as Inverness was a century ago'. The flag also helped to ensure fair play for merchants. The loss of any large portion of the colonial empire would, wrote Russell, 'diminish our importance in the world, and the vultures would soon gather together to despoil us of other parts of our Empire, or to offer insults to us which we could not bear'.[67]

The question was not whether to get rid of colonies, but how to organise them so as to make the best use of them with a minimum of effort and expense. In the mid-1840s there were a great many scattered and disconnected colonies and it was obvious to the British that there ought to be more links between them. This feeling became stronger in the mid-1850s when the Crimean War demonstrated the equation between Russia's size and her power.[68]

As early as 1652 there had been a suggestion that Barbados should send M.P.s to Westminster. The plan of representing the colonies in the House of Commons was widely discussed before the American war of independence. Franklin and Adam Smith favoured it, but Burke was more sceptical. When the Americans set up their own federation this was observed with close interest. If one part of the old empire could run itself as a federal organisation, could not the remainder? Round about 1830 Nova Scotians in particular were urging British ministers to recognise 'a vast confederacy of kingdoms, islands and provinces' spread throughout the world, and to 'endeavour to comprehend the whole dominions of Great Britain as one society, and the colonies for its integral parts, as much as if they adjoined Valentia or the Land's End . . .'[69] The Canadian rebellions of 1837 caused a more serious look to be taken at the idea of colonial representation at Westminster. By a strange coincidence three companies made their first transatlantic steamship crossings in 1838 between London and Halifax, and the *Annual Register* was able to point out that as a result one considerable obstacle had been removed by the speed and certainty of communication. Howe of Nova Scotia supported the idea of colonial representation strongly in 1846. Arguing that the colonies would no more declare war on anyone by themselves than the corporations of Glasgow, Liverpool or Hull would, Howe claimed that the colonies did not enjoy as much power as those municipalities did. From this he concluded that they should be represented in parliament.[70] Russell was inclined to agree. The flaring up of dissidence in Canada again in 1849 had the same effect as the 1837 rebellions had done: to bring the idea to the forefront again. As a result Russell, Disraeli and Molesworth all discussed the possibility and it became a familiar one. The example of the United States was powerful. The empire might be converted into a quasi-federal unit, roughly modelled on the United States, but deriving greater strength from its adherence to the monarchical bond. As Molesworth expressed it: 'The United States is a system of States clustered round a central republic. Our colonial empire ought to be a system of Colonies clustered round the hereditary monarchy of England'.[71] J. S. Mill also saw the parallel: self-governing colonies were more free than a state in the United States; 'their union with Great Britain is the slightest kind of federal union; but not a strictly equal federation' since they were compelled to join Britain in war without being consulted.[72] Disraeli in 1849 was concerned about the alarming state of Europe and the consequent instability introduced into much of Britain's foreign trade. He talked about a possible 'consolidation of our colonial empire' and in 1851 suggested to Derby that the time was ripe for 'a great push ... to reconstruct our Colonial system'. If the colonies had 'as it were their Ambassadors sitting in our Senate, their hearts would be with us in a struggle'. The American system was not one he would willingly appeal to as a model for domestic and foreign affairs, but there was, he thought, 'nearly a complete analogy between the two countries as regards their Colonies'. If California, accessible mainly by voyage round Cape Horn, could be represented in Washington, why not Canada in London? It might help to prevent Canada too from seeking a voice in Congress.

From 1837 until 1855 hardly a year passed without some attempt to give intelligent discussion to the idea of parliamentary representation for the colonies. Russell, Disraeli and Newcastle had all favoured it. As the colonies grew in stature this no longer seemed appropriate, and other schemes were put forward, principally for an advisory council of the empire. The weakness of this idea was the impossibility of agreement as to the powers it should have.

At about this point in time, there also appeared schemes of what can only be called 'Imperial Federation'. (The term seems to have been coined in 1853 by the *London Quarterly Review*.) Colonial representation was seen as a device to stave off independence and one suited to small, scattered colonies. But by 1850 the Canadian colonies at least were in fact independent and all the colonies were growing in size. Thus any future link would have to be on an extra- or supra-parliamentary federal basis. A further reason for the transition from schemes of parliamentary representation to imperial federation was that the issue of parliamentary reform in Britain revived from 1852 and token representation of the colonies ran contrary to the increasing demand for equal constituencies. An analogy from the Chinese empire was also drawn at this point. Consul Meadows suggested in 1856 that there were two very good leaves Britain could take out of the Chinese book. One was competitive examinations for the civil service. The other was the possibility of holding a vast united empire together on the basis of agreed moral principles.

The Chinese had done it for 4,000 years, and they did not have the added advantage now possessed by Britain, namely the help given by steamships and electric telegraphs. A union of the empire would constitute and perpetuate overseas a 'great united homogeneous British people under their present mixed institutions' and it would check the idea that the emigrant deserted England and aided in establishing a separate and possibly hostile state. If Britain could thus turn British North America, South Africa, Australia, New Zealand into 'integral portions of one great British Empire' alongside Cornwall and Cumberland, Inverness and Londonderry, 'then we shall have little difficulty in holding British India' and the smaller stations (Hong Kong, the Bermudas, etc) against any aggression. All that Meadows suggested they might learn from America was a more civilised way of treating women.[73]

The attempt to draw a federal scheme out of analogy with the United States remained weak, however, since from the mid-1850s the prospects of the American union began to appear doubtful. The outbreak of the American Civil War tended to silence proposals of this nature. The possibility of federal institutions and the existence of the United States were regarded as identical questions.[74] As the power of the United States increased, so did the urgency with which the debate was pursued, and this of course was a major reason for its revival after the Civil War.

'Imperial federation' has traditionally been dated from 1868,[75] but, as Martin has shown, this is to confuse origins and revival. Many of those who gave their opinion thereafter had made their minds up on the question long before 1868: Gladstone from 1855, Grey from 1849, Merivale from 1842, Tupper from 1860, and all of them were against it. Disraeli's advocacy in 1872 harked back to his views of 20 years before. Goldwin Smith's view in 1891 was the same as it had been in 1863. Traditionally also, the later imperial federation movement has been seen as a response to a supposedly new fear: the rise of an era of big states. There was, however, little new in this. The United States had *always* been a subject of apprehension, less rather than more after 1867, at least for the next 30 years. Russophobia dated from 1837 at least and was intensified by the Crimean War.[76] It is true that German unification introduced an entirely new competitor and made the sense of insecurity greater than before, but the response to this was an old-fashioned one, since insecurity had long been felt. Herman Merivale was quite unequivocal in an article he published in 1870. The idea of admitting colonial members to the House of Commons, he wrote,

> has been familiar to political thinkers ever since our first American dissensions a hundred years ago ... No plan of a great public reform has ever been more thoroughly ventilated than this has by the discussions of a century, since the time of Burke.

These discussions, he concluded, had shown insoluble difficulties and he regarded the project as not only debated but dismissed.[77]

The problem which schemes of colonial representation and imperial federation were attempting to answer was how to hold the allegiance of colonies. From 1850 they stood little chance of success, since an alternative had been found in responsible self-government. The reason why responsible government was conceded was partly that prolonged consideration had failed to present colonial representation as a viable alternative. Mill favoured self-government but failed to see 'any practicable mode of federal government for communities so widely scattered over the world'.[78] Lord Durham in 1839 had perhaps been one of the first clearly to realise this after considering colonial representation, but it was above all Elgin who shaped the answer to the problem of imperial organisation, and found a solution which proved enduring, despite all the later machinations of Chamberlain and the Imperial Federation League. This is why in 1920 J. X. Merriman denounced the League of Nations as a concept disruptive of 'the loose hung Commonwealth that has lasted for the last seventy years ever since Lord Elgin's day'.[79]

RESPONSIBLE GOVERNMENT AND COLONIAL FEDERATIONS IN THE 1850s

The decisions between 1846 and 1856 to allow colonies self-government were clearly the major developments in nineteenth-century imperial organisation. Once Earl Grey and Lord Elgin (influenced by Robert Baldwin and Joseph Howe) had decided in favour of responsible government in British North America there was a tendency to hope the system might be more widely applied, partly because it relieved the British taxpayer of expense and the government of responsibility, and partly because it would forestall a conflict provoked by larger demands than had so far been made. Colonies were in future to have responsible government forced upon them for these reasons. It was urged upon a reluctant New South Wales élite in 1856, and instituted in Cape Colony in 1872.[80] Grey planned a constitution for New Zealand implying the right of responsible government, which was eventually achieved in 1856. Even for the Gold Coast, he wrote, Britain ought 'to keep constantly in sight the formation of a regular government on the European model, and the establishment of a civilised polity, as the goal ultimately to be attained'. The real interest of Britain was gradually to train Africans in government until they were 'capable of protecting themselves and of managing their own affairs'.[81]

This does not mean, however, that the British did not apply tests before conceding responsible government. They had to satisfy themselves that new states would be economically viable and capable of self-defence; imperial strategic interests must not be endangered; there must be obvious collaborating groups who could be trusted to uphold British interests; and preferably there must be no risk of deterioration in the treatment of native peoples. Doubts on any one of these scores could preclude the grant of responsible government. Nor was progress along this path automatic or irreversible. Following smaller steps of constitutional regression from 1859, progress to self-government was brought to a sharp halt in the West Indies after 1865. Many proud and ancient legislatures there accepted death. Jamaica was the first; then in 1876 Grenada, Tobago and St Vincent voluntarily surrendered their independence. 'In a society so divided political rights for the few appeared inequitable, oppressive and dangerous; political rights for the masses, had anybody demanded them, would have appeared plain suicide'.[82]

The most striking example of the way in which a changed economic situation made responsible government feasible was in Australia 'after the gold' – or rather, made possible the first step towards it, representative government*.[83]

Meanwhile Earl Grey and Stephen in the late 1840s had advocated local federations and in the 1850s there were proposals for local federations in Australia, Canada and South Africa. All of them failed. In South Africa the colonial office was hardly likely to be enthusiastic about a scheme from Sir George Grey by which he sought to remove restrictions on his freedom of manoeuvre.[84] In Australia the proposals reflected more than anything the memories of Earl Grey's long and hard effort to promote federation for reasons of commercial and administrative advantage, but the institution of four responsible governments increased the centrifugal tendencies which were already strong. Australians did not want federation. It was regarded as unsuitable and uninteresting, and in parliament it was attacked as unwarranted, unwanted and unsafe. Lowe said it would be an absurdity: dual governments were immensely expensive, and any community of feeling the Australians had was directly with the mother country and not with their neighbours.[85] Sir William Denison, governor of Van Diemen's Land (as Tasmania was known until 1856) was also strongly opposed. He could see nothing for a federal government to do in Australia. Problems like tariffs, posts and lighthouses had been settled, and it could not be worth while to establish a complicated federal system just to determine the character and powers of a court of appeal. Land ought to be dealt with regionally, and a federal system would require men to sacrifice their new power and dignity. He believed the colonies to differ much in their origins and antecedents.[86] As far as Canadian moves towards federation were concerned, the colonial office would not support these, regarding them as 'premature and unwise'.[87] Federation would come eventually, but it must not be forced. Events in America were already casting doubts on the wisdom of federal constitutions. The New Zealand federal constitution adopted in 1853, five years after Earl Grey had planned it, was witheringly described by Denison as no more than 'a wretched parody of the constitution of the United States'; it was never a success.[88]

* Under 'responsible government' the executive council is responsible to the elected representatives in the legislative assembly; under a 'representative' system it is not (and is usually nominated by the governor).

2 The Motives and Methods of Expansion 1815–1860

RACIAL ATTITUDES

During the eighteenth century, European racial attitudes were made up of four main elements: belief in the homogeneity of mankind, disbelief that skin colour had any special significance, romantic idealisation of the 'noble savage' and respect for non-European civilisations, especially the Chinese and Indian. Eighteenth-century urbanity gave way to nineteenth-century arrogance and censoriousness as a result of several influences: accumulating experience of closer contact with non-European peoples, industrialisation, the evangelical revival and the rise of utilitarian doctrines. Industrialisation enormously increased the disparity in power between Britain and the rest of the world, and induced contempt for those regions which did not experience it. This led in particular to a decline in the prestige of China, which the French Revolution only underlined, since it showed that government could be improved by popular involvement as well as by élitist enlightenment.[1] Thus Tennyson could write, 'Better fifty years of Europe than a cycle of Cathay'. And even so sensitive a man as the eighth earl of Elgin declared before the Royal Academy in 1861 that 'the distinguishing characteristic of the Chinese mind' was 'occasionally to have caught glimpses of a heaven far beyond the range of its ordinary ken and vision': it caught glimpses of the paths which lead to military, maritime and literary supremacy when it invented gunpowder, the compass and printing-press, but in their hands:

> the invention of gunpowder has exploded in crackers and harmless fireworks. The mariner's compass has produced nothing better than the coasting junk. The art of printing has stagnated in stereotyped editions of *Confucius,* and the most cynical representations of the grotesque have been the principal products of Chinese conceptions of the sublime and the beautiful.

He was nevertheless disposed to believe that 'under this mass of abortions and rubbish there lie hidden some sparks of a diviner fire, which the genius of my countrymen may gather and nurse into a flame'.[2]

British cultural arrogance was accompanied by a brash cultural aggression inspired with a passion to 'improve' other peoples, an idea unknown in the early eighteenth century.[3] The evangelical revival after the 1790s produced a whole crop of fanatics determined to impose the Christian religion on Buddhists and Hindus, so that the British were no longer content, as Warren Hastings had been, to leave the religious system of India 'to the Being who has so long endured it and who will in his own time reform it'. There had always been Britons who found things wrong in Indian society. But evangelicals believed it to be in a degraded and perverse state. They were apt to think of Hindu gods as real devils and of Indians as subject people under a divinely ordained penalty for spiritual wickedness.[4] The earliest missionary in India, William Carey (1793), first secretary of the Baptist Missionary Society, supposed that 'no people can have more completely surrendered their reason than the Hindus'. The utilitarians with their zeal for reform quickly found much to condemn from the secular point of view in the social organisation of Asian societies. They regarded them as corrupt, sunk in misery and shackled in slavery. And they had considerable influence on shaping the attitudes of the government of India.[5] Evangelicals and utilitarians found themselves bound together in their abhorrence of superstitious and idolatrous Indian society, and in their confidence in the power of English education to accomplish a moral reformation. Both revealed religion and political science held the door open to improvement.

James Mill's *History of British India* (1817) was a utilitarian text of importance in shaping attitudes, if only because it was standard reading on the voyage out to India for those joining the Indian Civil Service. 'Exactly in proportion as *Utility* is the object of every pursuit [wrote Mill] we may regard a nation as civilised. Exactly in proportion as its ingenuity is wasted on contemptible or mischievous objects . . . the nation may safely be denominated barbarous'. According to this rule, be found 'conclusive evidence against the Hindus', especially since they had perverted mathematics to the purposes of astrology, 'one of the most irrational of all imaginable pursuits'. Their religious ideals he described as barbarous because 'the attention of the Hindu is much more engaged by frivolous observances than by objects of utility'. The epithets flowed grandly from his pen: Hindu religion was mean, ridiculous, gross, disgusting, grovelling and base. He was convinced that Britons had hitherto placed the Hindus too high in the scale of civilisation. He could find no evidence supporting the claims of eminent scholars such as Sir William Jones that the Hindus were 'once in a high state of civilisation'.[6]

Although these industrial and intellectual developments punctured the respect and idealisation once lavished on oriental civilisation, eighteenth-century beliefs in the homogeneity and perfectibility of mankind persisted for the time being. Deficiency in 'civilisation' was ascribed to an unfavourable but rectifiable environment. Palmerston in the mid-1850s still accepted the Indians as 'human beings like ourselves', amenable to the same general principles as regulated the conduct of all mankind.[7] It seldom occurred to early Victorians that human characteristics might be the result of inherited rather than environmental influences. If there was inferiority it might easily be removed.[8] Not until the 1860s did the sympathetic and optimistic basic belief in the equality and perfectibility of mankind disappear. Not until the 1860s did 'efficiency' replace 'improvement' as the keynote of good administration. Not until the 1860s did the dreaded bogey become fear of a total dissolution of society rather than distaste for its merely corrupt hideousness.[9]

Reared in a strongly hierarchical society, the British arranged the races of the world in a hierarchy too. According to the Victorian world picture, all nations could be assigned to a place on the ladder of progress, could be fixed at a point on the moral scale.[10] Assuming that ' a scale of civilisation can be formed, on which the relative position of nations may be accurately marked', it was Mill's object in his *History of British India* 'to ascertain the true state of the Hindus in the scale of civilisation', by which he meant of course measuring them by what he supposed to be the accurate and universally valid British standard:

> The nations in the western parts of Asia, the Persians, the Arabians, and even the Turks possessed an order of intellectual faculties rather higher than the nations situated beyond them towards the East; were rather less deeply involved in the absurdities and weaknesses of a rude state of society; had in fact attained a stage of civilisation in some little degree higher. . . . This is a statistical fact. . . .[11]

Rank was measurable by the extent of conformity to the dictates of utility in the organisation of society; hence the Muslims were reckoned by James Mill to be higher than the Hindus. His son John Stuart Mill also subscribed to the 'scale of civilisation' concept, with the 'striving, go-ahead' British and Americans, the 'self-helping and struggling Anglo-Saxons' at the top.[12] The Victorians thought the Americans were nearest to the British at the top of the ladder of progress, followed by Germans, because they showed the right spirit of enterprise, had the right religion; behind the Anglo-Saxon leaders came the Roman Catholic French; then the other Latin nations. Palmerston said 'The plain truth is that the Portuguese are of all European nations the lowest in the moral scale'.[13] Much lower came the Asian and African communities, with the Irish about on a par with them. All Orientals from Cairo to Canton were despised as barbarians, ignorant and insolent.[14]

E. B. Tylor claimed that ethnographers were able to set up 'at least a rough scale of civilisation' and that few would dispute that he had arranged the following races in approximate order of cultural level: Australian, Tahitian, Aztec, Chinese. Darwin's doctrine of the survival of the fittest lent further pseudo-scientific authority to the notion of a racial hierarchy.

As late as 1913 Conan Doyle's story *The Poison Belt* implied a table of racial rank in order of fitness to survive. Africans and Australian aborigines were speedily extinguished by a mysterious etheric poison, followed by Indians and Persians, while in Europe the Slavs collapsed sooner than the Teutons, the southern French before the northern.[15] The idea of a 'hierarchy of races' was still enshrined as a Liberal party doctrine in 1900,[16] and later Nehru had a clear idea of the twentieth-century British order of preference.[17]

ANTI-SLAVERY AND THE HUMANITARIAN IMPULSE

Two of the greatest achievements of the empire came early in the century – the abolition of the slave trade in 1807 and the emancipation of the slaves in 1833. By 1807 Britain had probably been responsible for exporting more than $2\frac{1}{2}$ million Africans into slavery – an annual average of 28,310 in the period 1751–1807, or 32,550 between 1791 and 1800. Accounts of these decisions divide themselves into those which give primacy to the humanitarian motive and those which give it to a change in economic self-interest.[18] It would be difficult to argue that the humanitarian element was a mere charade. British abolition probably made little difference to the total size of the trade; the peak levels of the 1780s and 1790s were never reached again between 1810 and 1840, but demand was high and steady until the 1840s. Demand was growing in Brazil, Cuba and the American cotton south, none of which abolished slavery until the 1860s. Nineteenth-century demand was about one-third less than the peak; say 40,000 as against 60,000 a year. The number of slaves arriving in the West Indies between 1811 and 1870 was 1,898,400, and would have been more but for about 15 per cent mortality on the Atlantic crossing. In short there was still plenty of business to be done between 1807 and 1870.

By the 1840s a slave bought for £4 in West Africa could be sold for £150 in Brazil. Moreover, no amount of economic self-interest on the part of the taxpayer could have justified payment of the £20,000,000 compensation voted in 1833 to the slave owners. This was a huge sum of money, especially when placed beside the government expenditure in the same year on aid to education, which was a mere £20,000. The leaders of the anti-slavery campaign certainly thought themselves primarily moved by moral, even religious, considerations.[19]

On the other hand, although intellectual opinion was solidly against slavery by the 1780s,[20] appeal on humanitarian grounds alone had not proved efficacious by 1806, and the campaign had collapsed on the outbreak of war with France. The position was not greatly different from what it had been a generation before: a belief that slavery was wrong but necessary.[21] Only in 1807 could economic self-interest be shown to point in the same direction. The more hard-headed sections of society, including parliament, needed persuading on political and economic grounds. Since people had long been ready to be persuaded on humanitarian grounds, economic changes may be

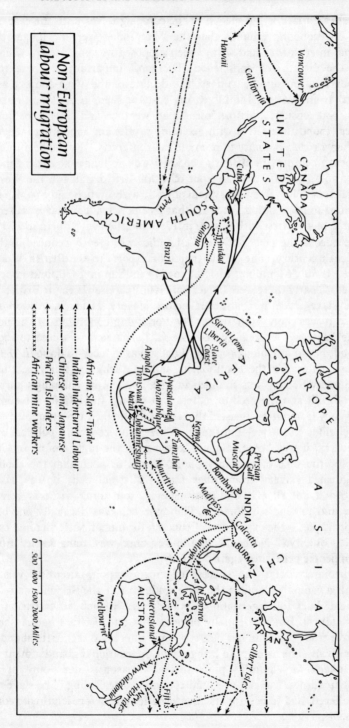

Non-European labour migration

African Slave Trade
Indian Indentured Labour
Chinese and Japanese
Pacific Islanders
African mine workers

0 500 1000 1500 2000 Miles

deemed essential for the success of the campaign. Not until the case could be made on economic grounds that the West Indies were no longer the vital national interest they had always been supposed was parliament willing to act upon the dictates of conscience. The most important of these economic grounds may be summed up as 'the decline of the West Indies', a decline marked from 1760 by the increasing costs of sugar production, rising slave prices, soil erosion, wartime losses, bad weather and slave rebellions. The planters found themselves with declining profits and mounting indebtedness, and thus a reduced ability to promote their interests.[22] By the beginning of the nineteenth century the Atlantic economy was no longer so dependent on the slave trade. By 1804 only 150 out of 1,000 British ships in the West Indies were slavers.[23] The free port system of trade with French and Spanish colonies continued to grow despite the fact that free port trade in slaves ceased on the outbreak of war, first with France in 1793 and then with Spain in 1796.[24]

The purchasing power of the West Indies was greatly reduced in the early nineteenth century. The official value of exports to the British West Indies dropped from £6¼ million in 1814 to £3¾ million in 1830, and imports also declined. Clearly there were bigger opportunities elsewhere for British trade.

The slave trade was attacked before slavery as an institution perhaps because it was more vulnerable. The horrifying conditions of the notorious Middle Passage were readily understood. Parliament was used to regulating trade but not to touching property. That it was induced to do so in 1833 was a striking victory for the abolitionists and one achieved fairly speedily. The Anti-Slavery Society was founded in 1823, and in its campaign played on a sense of guilt and the need to redress past wrong. In 1831 its sub-committee, the Agency Committee, insisted that it was dealing with 'a question essentially of a religious character' and though it was connected with political economy and liberty, it was 'important not to abandon the high ground of Christian duty' for the sake of getting support. It was as a sin that the abolitionists distinguished slavery from other forms of social evil; it was as Buxton described it, 'of all evils the monster evil', something wickedly contrary to nature and to God's ordinance. The approach was decidedly one based on high principles – the expression of concern for human suffering had rather an abstract quality.[25] Nevertheless the response was remarkable. About 1½ million people petitioned against slavery.

Immediately after the success of emancipation, attention was turned towards a campaign against the slave trade outside the British empire. Evil, it was held, knew no international boundaries, so such an extension was no doubt natural. But it is equally obvious that once Britain had rid herself of the slave trade it was in her best economic interest to secure its abandonment by her rivals. The attempt to bring about international abandonment was not undertaken for purely philanthropic reasons, nor out of simple self-righteousness but out of sound commercial reasoning. The slave trade, it was believed, had to be suppressed internationally before legitimate commerce could develop in its stead. With hindsight it is now possible to demonstrate that suppression did not make such good economic sense as was supposed and that legitimate commerce could co-exist with it. It has also been argued that since the costs of the African naval squadron were disproportionate to the results, and to the value of African legitimate commerce, it must have been maintained for strictly humanitarian reasons. However these facts were not understood in the 1830s, and when in the following decade they became plain there was much criticism of the policy. Fowell Buxton declared 'our great argument surely is that the slave trade kills all other trade.'[26] This was a Victorian orthodoxy, but it was wrong.

The Agency Committee became the Society for the Universal Abolition of Slavery and the Slave Trade in 1834. The British and Foreign Anti-Slavery Society was founded by Joseph Sturge. The two societies overlapped a good deal and both tapped traditional Quaker support.

Because the path of humanity was realised to be equally the path of economic wisdom, British policy should not be written off as simply hypocritical, for as Palmerston said in explaining his desire to secure international abolition:[27]

Let no man imagine that those treaties for the suppression of the slave trade are valuable only as being calculated to promote the great interests of humanity, and as tending to rid mankind of a foul and detestable crime. Such is indeed their great object and their chief merit. But in this case, as in many others, virtue carries with it its own reward; and if the nations of the world could extirpate this abominable traffic, and if the vast population of Africa could by that means be left free to betake themselves to peaceful and innocent trade, the greatest commercial benefit would accrue, not to England only, but to every civilised nation which engages in maritime commerce. These slave trade treaties therefore are indirectly treaties for the encouragement of commerce.

The Niger expedition of 1841-42 was one of a number of government exertions in the early 1840s intended to contribute to the suppression of slavery in West Africa. A network of territorial footholds on the coast had been established; Sierra Leone in 1808, the Gambia in 1816, the Gold Coast in 1821. Buxton wished to bend these more directly into agencies for suppression, and he also took up the positive policies advocated years earlier by Wilberforce. Russell accepted the necessity of some new large move. The result was the Niger expedition, and its failure (55 out of 149 Europeans died) was severely discrediting to the humanitarians.[28]

Palmerston was particularly active in trying to bring an end to the trade in the Persian Gulf. After Britain emerged strongly from the Near East crisis of 1839-41, Palmerston decided to launch a full-scale assault on the Arab slave trade, and to do so without being deflected by political misgivings. He did not feel it necessary any longer to be over-solicitous for the feelings of petty Arab rulers. With typical Palmerstonian presumption he let it be known that Britain was 'the main instrument in the hands of Providence' for the ending of the slave trade, and it was 'vain for these Arabs to endeavour to resist the consummation of that which is written in the Book of Fate'. Instead they should 'betake themselves to the cultivation of their soil and to lawful and innocent commerce'. His policy of treaties backed by naval patrols was insufficient to root out so well-established a system. Sultan Saiyid Said was disinclined as well as unable to honour his obligation of 1845 to do his best to prevent the traffic in slaves being carried on between his African and his Arabian dominions, Zanzibar and Muscat. Exports from Zanzibar at this time were of the order of 15,000 a year. Perhaps as a result of the failure of the Niger expedition, Palmerston was unwilling to tackle the Arab slave trade at its source. This was, however, the only effective way to tackle it, and once it was attempted from 1871 it rapidly yielded results which even intensive naval patrols of the Gulf had failed to bring.[29]

Much of the Victorian thinking about Africa centred on a belief that Britain had a guilt to expiate. African peoples had suffered more than any other from white rapacity, wrote Livingstone in 1855, and 'we did not wipe out all our obligations when we paid twenty millions'. His contribution to the crusade against the slave trade was of great importance, and he inspired many followers.[30] Even in the 1890s Lugard regarded his main work in Africa as having been the checking of the slave trade, and he 'strongly declined to be tied', or to shut his mouth, on any question connected with slavery; his employers must take him as they found him on this subject.[31]

If there ever was a time when the humanitarian impulse influenced government it was in the decade after 1831. Two well-known humanitarians ran the colonial office: Lord Glenelg as colonial secretary 1835 to 1839 and James Stephen as permanent under-secretary from 1836. Public interest was indicated by the foundation of the British and Foreign Aborigines Protection Society, and Buxton's report of the select committee on aborigines 1837 provided a possible policy document. An age which found ethical considerations hard to refute, and which was extremely ignorant of the empire, was one peculiarly susceptible to persuasion by argument from moral principles, although humanitarians were adept at promising material benefits too. The Buxton report asserted the imperial duty to safeguard native rights, and it proposed that a share of colonial revenues should be set aside for native education and religious instruction. After two years spent investigating an appropriate policy for Africa and the Pacific Islands it concluded that in future Britain's main concern should be 'to carry civilisation and humanity, peace and good government, and above all the knowledge of the true God to the uttermost ends of the earth'. But it also noted that converts desired the advantages of civilised life, with the result that commercial interests would be bound to benefit from such a programme. Virtue would be its own reward.[32]

Glenelg was a man of intellectual power (he had held a fellowship at a Cambridge College) but he was dilatory. He was idealistic but also indecisive. His period of office is significant in that it saw a real attempt to base an imperial policy on moral considerations. This attempt was not successful, and once this became clear, the experiment was not repeated. He felt it would be a calamity if South Africa were added 'to the list of the regions which have seen their aboriginal inhabitants disappear under the withering influence of European neighbourhood', and, objecting to the aspersions cast on missionary endeavour by governor D'Urban's description of the inhabitants as 'irreclaimable savages', Glenelg ordered the abandonment of Queen Adelaide province. In Australia he insisted that the rights of the aborigines as British subjects should be fully acknowledged: hence he ordered an inquest to be held whenever any were killed by British officers. In 1838 a committee was set up at Port Phillip, charged with protecting aborigines from encroachments on their property, from cruelty and injustice; it was also to represent their wants, wishes and grievances to the governor. Glenelg hoped that there would be severe punishments for every European convicted of injustice or violence towards natives; nothing could be regarded as trifling. 'It cannot be too stongly impressed on every European', he wrote in 1837, 'that the lives of the natives must be considered as equally valuable and entitled to the same protection as those of any European settlers'. He also kept a close watch on the situation of the Amerindians in Canada, urging the necessity of taking care not to offend their national habits and prejudices, and proclaiming himself anxious to 'protect and cherish this helpless race, to raise them in the scale of humanity, and to extend and consolidate the advantages which they possess as the dependents of the British Crown'. There was a commission of enquiry into the state of British North American Indian affairs in 1843–44. [33]

Such were the ascendant principles at the time when the future position of New Zealand required a decision. The fundamental problem of law and order, affecting traders and missionaries as well as settlers, of whom there were 2,000, was behind its reluctant annexation. Humanitarians, it has been suggested, were as anxious to guide British policy to New Zealand as they were a little earlier to abolish slavery throughout the empire. [34] Under the treaty of Waitangi in 1840 the Maoris in the North Island were to be guaranteed full and undisputed possession of their lands and fisheries and to receive the rights and privileges of British subjects. Once again it was Glenelg who, before leaving office, had indicated the main lines of policy. Regular government was established which would acquire sovereignty for British settlers by negotiation. It was hoped that New Zealand would be better than previous colonies of settlement, that Maoris would not suffer the fate of Red Indians, or aborigines. The British government accepted the country as belonging to its native inhabitants and hoped the treaty of Waitangi would lay a basis for a just society in which two races could live in amity. [35]

However, humanitarian influence declined after 1842. Its heyday was over.

Officials were irritated by the increasingly emotional distortion and exaggeration of facts put before them. The operation of the treaty of Waitangi pleased nobody. White settlers had never been moved by the humanitarian impulse, and the colonial office found itself more and more disliking disputes with colonials. Responsible government meant restraint and co-operation in dealing with them. A humanitarian policy required strong imperial control and this was expensive; the treasury had no desire to finance moral crusades. Humanitarians continued to put forward plans for the development of the African interior, but increasingly arguments of humanity proved not to be enough. As ideals broke on the hard facts of reality, so government became more hard-headed.[36] The Buxton report was of little use as a guide to policy and it was virtually ignored. The primary concern in South African policy was economical administration. The entire cabinet approved Glenelg's withdrawal from Queen Adelaide province and many of its members were certainly not moved by humanitarian considerations: they approved the policy because it saved money. Glenelg's policy achieved little in South Africa. Humanitarian pronouncements infuriated the Boers without bringing improvements to the Bantu. The wars of the 1840s and 1850s were waged against the Bantu and not for their protection. Nor is the general power and cohesion of the humanitarians to be exaggerated. At times the Wesleyan Missionary and the London Missionary societies were openly hostile to each other, and the advice they tendered to the government was at variance.[37] By abolishing the sugar duties in 1846 the government openly repudiated humanitarian advice. This reversal of policy meant opening the British market to foreign slave-grown sugar in order to bring down British prices.[38] From 1835 to 1841 it was estimated that the British consumer paid annually for sugar £5½ million more than he would have done if not compelled to buy from the British West Indies, and more than any other European nation paid for the same quantity. Faced with this enormous discrepancy in price between foreign and colonial sugar, and with mounting popular clamour for the removal of preferential tariffs, the government abolished the sugar duties. This episode provides further evidence of the difficulty humanitarians experienced in trying to hold governments to a policy which was not also the policy of economic self-interest.

The settled attitude of Victorian government towards humanitarian pressure was slightly scornful. It regarded itself as adequately humanitarian, without falling into the trap of becoming sentimental. Its access to information was infinitely superior to that of any pressure group or private individual, and it regarded the sources of humanitarian information as often suspect and inaccurate. There were still some notable examples of government action for humanitarian reasons, but the most spectacular of these had a distinct tendency to be in territories outside the British empire, such as the campaign against the red rubber scandals in the Congo or the Putumayo region of Peru. It is beyond doubt that there were no clandestine economic motives behind these campaigns.[39] They were perhaps exceptional in being scandals reported and investigated by men whom the government respected: E. D. Morel was almost unique in being a private individual whose views the government and colonial office were prepared to listen to. Generally speaking, however, they found humanitarians eccentric, moved by sentiments divorced from full knowledge, impartial responsibility and a cool comprehension of realities.

ECONOMIC AND IDEOLOGICAL MOTIVES FOR EXPANSION

Victorian motives for expansion may be broadly divided into economic and ideological. The economic impulse was to find markets and outlets for the new manufacturing potential set in motion by industrialisation, together with an increased need to find the raw materials to feed it. Britain became the 'workshop of the world' and entrepreneurs looked well beyond the confines of their homeland. From the middle of the eighteenth century interest was steadily growing in the Far East and India, in Latin America, China and the Pacific, based upon the supposition that there must be a limitless potential demand for cheap goods, just those most suitably mass-produced by machines. It is important, however, not to pre-date the movement into many overseas regions: some did not feel the impact before the 1850s.[40] The industrial revolution, initially a revolution based on cotton exports, proceeded by a process of anticipating potential demand overseas. Where demand did not exist, as among the unclothed inhabitants in Africa, it could be created. Until well after 1850 blankets were almost unknown among Africans, but by the end of the century were worn so widely throughout southern Africa that the term 'blanket Kaffir' was a common designation.[41] What interested entrepreneurs such as Matthew Boulton, of Boulton and Watt's steam engine firm,[42] or Huntley and Palmer of biscuit fame,[43] or Josiah Wedgwood the potter, was to sell their products to the whole world. Josiah Wedgwood in 1769 called himself 'Vase-Maker General to the Universe' and had the words inscribed above the entrance to his works. He defined his aim in 1775 as being 'to astonish all the world at once', contemplating the possibilities of Turkey, Mexico and China with an excitement which McKendrick has called 'purely ceramic lust'.[44] As Dundas, Pitt's lieutenant, alleged in 1790, 'the spirit of commercial adventure in this country was unbounded'. This spirit grew.[45]

Without a doubt the products of Manchester and Birmingham spread widely, and sources of supply were also remarkably diffused. W. S. Jevons in *The Coal Question* (1865) rhapsodised:

The plains of North America and Russia are our corn fields; Chicago and Odessa our granaries; Canada and the Baltic are our timber forests; Australasia contains our sheep farms, and in Argentina and on the western prairies of North America are our herds of oxen; Peru sends her silver, and the gold of South Africa and Australia flows to London; the Hindus and the Chinese grow tea for us, and our coffee, sugar and spice plantations are in all the Indies. Spain and France are our vineyards and the Mediterranean our fruit garden; and our cotton grounds, which for long have occupied the Southern United States, are now being extended everywhere in the warm regions of the earth.

Unfettered commerce, he concluded, had made 'the several quarters of the globe our willing tributaries'.[46] Here we see the intoxication of a sense of world mastery, the exciting feeling of having organised the entire world for the purpose of satisfying the needs of the expanding British economy.

Earl Grey wrote that if only Africa could be made peaceful and order be maintained there, 'it was not doubted that trade, with its civilising influences would quickly spring up'; if the Africans were made civilised they would be a source of urgently needed labour and would demand European manufactures – the improvement of the natives was therefore a matter of vital importance.[47] Above all, it was Palmerston who led the movement into exotic new regions. He pointed out in 1842 that a considerable portion of foreign office correspondence dealt with grievances of merchants in places where central authority was weak and local authorities abused their power; in almost every case the British had got satisfaction. 'Another way in which a government may assist the commerce of the country is by opening new markets for our trade', he added, and announced that merchants had just established themselves at Tadjoura on the coast of Ethiopia and at Aden. The Opposition, he continued, talked sneeringly of attempts to extend commerce into the wilds of Ethiopia and the deserts of Arabia, but he pointed out that:

the finest coffee in the world . . . grows in the greatest abundance in those Abyssinian wilds and in those Arabian deserts; and that those wilds and those deserts are inhabited by a numerous population, wanting many things which we can supply, and able to give us valuable commodities in return . . . I am sure that in process of time they will lead to a considerable increase of our commerce.

The foundations of a vast new opening for commerce had, he hoped, been laid in China. Securing so big a market for British manufacturers, was, he claimed, a matter of the highest importance. The solution to domestic distress, said Palmerston, was the extension of foreign trade: hence 'We must look again to Africa, and we must look especially to India and China', since the world was large enough and mankind sufficiently numerous 'to consume all that the most industrious manufacturers could possibly produce'.[48] As he said, his 'restless activity encircled the globe'; 'the sun never sets upon the interests of this country . . . '.[49] The dynamic vision which drove exertions forward was based for example on the expectation of British manufacturers in the 1840s that all the mills of Lancashire could not make stocking stuff sufficient for one of the provinces of China. A market of over 300 million people was a tempting prospect. Industrial transformation seemed destined to proceed indefinitely and thus Britain could indulge in long-term calculations even in marginal areas. Not unnaturally, some of them were misconceived.

The Victorians had a tremendous sense of being in some way in harmony with the progressive forces of the universe. God was on their side. Prince Albert regarded the 1851 Exhibition as a festival of *Christian* civilisation. As Kingsley entered the Crystal Palace 'he was moved to tears; to him it was like going into a sacred place'. In *Yeast* he wrote (1851):

> The spinning jenny and the railroad, Cunard's liners and the electric telegraph, are to me ... signs that we are, on some points at least, in harmony with the universe; that there is a mighty spirit working among us ... the Ordering and Creating God.[50]

The whole human race seemed destined to bear the indelible impress of British science. Restless, diligent and determined pursuit of knowledge was very characteristic of Victorian intellectuals; the whole of life to them consisted in learning, and in knowledge was power. It was a sense of power bred by education which underlay their solid achievements and sustained their further efforts.[51] Macaulay began his *History of England* with words reflecting the magisterial confidence of the mid-1850s.

> ... the history of our country during the last hundred and sixty years is eminently the history of physical, of moral, and of intellectual improvement ... no man who is correctly informed as to the past will be disposed to take a morose or desponding view of the present.[52]

There was a general conviction that the British had reached the top of the ladder of progress, and that it was their duty to improve the lot of others. The usual British attitude to foreigners was that expressed by Dickens's Mr Podsnap, that other countries were a 'mistake'. In *In Memoriam* Tennyson denounced the French as given to 'schoolboy heat' and the Celts as prone to 'blind hysterics'. Upon England alone had Providence lavished the brightest constellations of its bounty.[53]

More important still were the views of Palmerston. His rejoicing in nature's favours, the people's virtue and the blessings of British freedom was reiterated. Pre-eminently, he declared,

> Our duty – our vocation – is not to enslave, but to set free; and I may say without any vainglorious boast, or without great offence to anyone, that we stand at the head of moral, social and political civilisation. Our task is to lead the way and direct the march of other nations.[54]

There is the ideological mainspring of British expansion, in – to mix metaphors – a nutshell. Upon what facts did this confidence rest? Upon four, mainly. First, upon economic pre-eminence – Britain, 'the workshop of the world', able to produce more goods of better quality and cheaper price than any competitor. Second, upon the unchallengeable power of the British navy. Third, upon internal stability and social balance. British institutions seemed superior to those of other nations, and, in particular, the avoidance of revolution in 1848 when almost every throne in Europe was emptied or shaken, was a notable fact in promoting the sense of stability.[55] Palmerston claimed in the Don Pacifico Debate in 1850 that Britain had shown the example of a nation 'in which every class of society accepts with cheerfulness the lot which Providence has assigned to it'. He exaggerated, but the point had some substance. After all, Bagehot said much the same, though more cautiously.[56] Underpinning everything there was a deep religious sanction and driving force. J. H. Newman, speaking in 1852, said that western civilisation 'has a claim to be considered as the perfect representative society and civilisation of the human race, as its perfect result and limit, in fact.' To a remarkable extent the ideological motive for expansion was religious. All authorities are agreed on the fundamentally religious nature of the Victorian age. Outside the urban poor it was one of the most religious societies the world has known, and its doctrine was a Protestant one which, moreover, believed largely in salvation by works. Two evangelical revivals and the Oxford movement made mid-Victorian society a religious society in a deeper and more complete sense than any country in the West since the Reformation.[57] The attempt to re-convert Britain was one of the major preoccupations of the age; the amount spent in this work, both in terms of effort, sacrifice and money, is one of the really important facts of the nineteenth century. Between 1840 and 1876, the Church of England restored 7,144 churches and built 1,727 at a cost of £25½ million, mostly raised by voluntary subscription. The Methodists had 11,007 chapels in 1851. All this church building probably commanded more of the disinterested enthusiasm of Victorians than any other of their achievements.[58] Nor was the overseas missionary side ignored. Diagnosis of and propaganda for the springs of missionary expansion were clearly set forth in the missionary hymns of *Hymns Ancient and Modern*.[59] The Bishop of Calcutta's famous 'From Greenland's icy mountains' (1819) contains the central supposition, that from all over the world,

> 'They call us to deliver
> Their land from error's chain'.

The hymn writers convinced themselves that evangelisation was really wanted by the whole world, even if non-Europeans never consciously realised it. Most of the chief British missionary societies were founded at the end of the

eighteenth century and in the early nineteenth century: the English Baptist
Missionary Society in 1792, the London Missionary Society in 1795, the
Scottish Missionary Society in 1796, the Church Missionary Society in 1799,
the British and Foreign Bible Society in 1804, and the Wesleyan Methodist
Missionary Society in 1814. The United Presbyterian Church of Scotland
Mission Society was founded in 1835, the Edinburgh Medical Missionary
Society in 1841. The University Mission to Central Africa dates from 1860,
the China Inland Mission from 1862. As Livingstone himself said, missionary
activity was one of the central characteristics of the age.[60] It was a
phenomenon which did not pre-date the 1790s. Earlier societies – the Society
for the Propagation of the Gospel and also the Society for Promoting
Christian Knowledge – had ministered chiefly to Anglican colonists in exile.
Even as late as 1813 the church establishment created in India was supposed
to do no more. A completely new departure was heralded by William Carey's
pamphlet, *Christian obligation to the heathen* (1788) and his foundation of
the Baptist Mission. Evangelical Protestants were in the grip of an abounding
vitality and a daring unequalled in Christian history. Never before had the
followers of any faith formulated comprehensive plans covering the entire
surface of the earth. It was the American Student Volunteer Missionary
Union, founded in 1886, which actually adopted as its watchword the
'evangelisation of the world in this generation', but the motto perfectly fits
the early Victorian attitude. Following John Wesley's famous phrase literally,
missionaries took the whole world as their parish, and aimed at 'an entire
moral revolution in the entire human race':

'Go to the conquest of all lands
   All must be His at length'.

By 1870 the Victorians were delighting in Ellerton's hymn, 'The day Thou
gavest, Lord, is ended', reflecting another kind of global intoxication, 'the
imperial mind of the Victorian missionary':

As o'er each continent and island
   The dawn leads on another day,
The voice of prayer is never silent
   Nor dies the strain of praise away.

The missionary motive was made up of many complex elements. A sense of
being 'constrained by Jesus' love', and gratitude for the gospel, was mingled
with a sterner sense of duty; for some (like Henry Martyn) there was an
ascetic appeal, for others, a romantic one (Carey was influenced by his
reading of Captain Cook's voyages). In some, zeal was combined with more
secular considerations: Claudius Buchanan in 1812 said that religion
'attaches the governed to their governors'. Reparation for the slave trade

became an important motive, and it certainly dominated Josiah Pratt of the C.M.S., the most influential publicist for the missionary cause in the first 25 years of the nineteenth century.[61]

We may sum up by saying that ideologically the Victorian desire was to improve the rest of the world by a programme of Christian regeneration to spread civilisation on the British model, since this was the only – and God-ordained – perfection open to mankind.

The regeneration of the world did not necessarily or permanently require territorial possession. The essential insight may be discerned early, in the theories of Castlereagh and Raffles.[62] The theory was nobly expounded by Macaulay in debate on 10 July 1833:

> The mere extent of empire is not necessarily an advantage . . . It would be, on the most selfish view of the case, far better for us that the people of India . . . were ruled by their own kings, but wearing our broadcloth, and working with our cutlery, than that they were performing their salaams to English collectors and English magistrates. . . . To trade with civilised men is infinitely more profitable than to govern savages . . .

The sceptre might of course pass away from Britain:

> But there are triumphs which are followed by no reverse. There is an empire exempt from all natural causes of decay. Those triumphs are the pacific triumphs of reason over barbarism; that empire is the imperishable empire of our arts and our morals, our literature and our laws.[63]

Later apologists have similarly designated an imperishable empire of railways, canals and bridges, of cattle and wheat. Long after British rule was over, these things would be left behind as a permanent mark.[64] Crucial to this distinction between moral ascendancy and territorial dominion, or, to use modern terms, between informal and formal empire, was the inclusion of the United States of America within the sphere of Greater Britain.[65] Sir Charles Dilke in his book *Greater Britain* (1868) wrote the classical statement of this view:

> In America, the peoples of the world are being fused together, but they are run into an English mould . . . She [England] has imposed her institutions upon the offshoots of Germany, of Ireland, of Scandinavia, and of Spain. Through America, England is speaking to the world . . . The development of the England of Elizabeth is to be found, not in the Britain of Victoria, but in half the habitable globe. If two small islands are by

courtesy styled 'Great', America, Australia, India must form a 'Greater Britain'.

In his memoirs he referred to this explanatory and justifying preface, which he believed to be 'the best piece of work of my life':

As will be seen from it, I included in my 'Greater Britain' our Magna Graecia of the United States ... It is contracting an idea, which, as its author, I think lofty and even noble, to use 'Greater Britain' only of the British Empire, as is now done.

Dilke also wrote: 'America offers the English race the moral dictatorship of the globe, by ruling mankind through Anglo-Saxon institutions and the English tongue'. And again:

common institutions, common freedom, and common tongue have evidently far more to do with trade than union has: and for purposes of commerce and civilisation, America is a truer colony of Britain than is Canada.[66]

Gibbon Wakefield in his *A View of the Art of Colonisation* (1849) on three occasions wrote of the United States as 'still colonies of England', in the sense that they took the bulk of British trade and emigrants.[67] Later in the century Cecil Rhodes determined in his youth to work for 'the recovery of the U.S.A. as an integral part of the British Empire, for the making of the Anglo-Saxon race into one Empire'. He reserved many of his Rhodes Scholarships for Americans, hoping that one day the United States would rejoin the imperial community.[68] It was a widespread idea. H. P. Hughes, the leading Methodist of the 1890s, also hoped that the United States might re-enter the English-speaking brotherhood.[69]

Macaulay was right, of course. 'The mere extent of empire is not necessarily an advantage.' It led to enormous contingent liabilities, particularly of defence, as the case of India amply demonstrated.[70] The sophisticated, ideal method of control was influence exercised informally, from outside. Palmerston insisted that trade was better than territory, and he castigated Russia for not yet having reached

that point of civilisation at which the government of a powerful country discovers that there are other objects deserving of attention and other sources of glory ... besides augmentation of territory and foreign conquest.[71]

Palmerston refused to take possession of Ethiopia:

I do not see any advantage in our getting land in these quarters. All we want is trade and land is not necessary for trade; we can carry on commerce on ground belonging to other people. Possession of land involves civil and military establishments and responsibility, and the Red Sea is not a good place for a settlement to be made by Government.[72]

The splendidly near-monosyllabic phrase, 'all we want is trade and land is not necessary for trade', embodies a key Victorian doctrine. Palmerston also refused to take territory in Egypt. Napoleon III made overtures to Britain for the partitioning of North Africa. Palmerston replied:

We want to trade with Egypt and to travel through Egypt but we do not want the burden of governing Egypt ... Let us try to improve all these countries by the general influence of our commerce, but let us abstain from a crusade of conquest ...

A couple of years later he said the same thing to Cowley, in homely terms which leave no doubt of the way in which the British aristocracy viewed world problems as those of estate-management writ large:

We do not want Egypt or wish it for ourselves, any more than any rational man with an estate in the north of England and a residence in the south [for which read India] would have wished to possess the inns on the north road. All he could want would have been that the inns should be well kept, always accessible, and furnishing him when he came with mutton chops and post-horses.[73]

British policy, said Palmerston, ought to be to assist peoples 'starving for freedom', by which he meant 'rational government', and to extend 'as far and as fast as possible civilisation all over the world'. He was sure that this was in the British interest, and equally sure it would 'redound to our honour'.[74] The Victorians had a clear theory of how the level of the rest of the world could be 'improved' and hoisted up the ladder of civilisation. There were five main methods of 'regenerating rotten empires':[75] by constitutional and legal provisions, by free trade, by conversion to Christianity, by education, and by technology. The exact weight given to any one of these elements varied with the general philosophical standpoint of the person concerned, but everyone believed that each element would help the others, and each had behind it the same underlying principle of removing the shackles and inhibitions to progress. These five elements in spreading civilisation may be analysed as follows.

Constitutional and legal provisions were widely regarded as basic. The establishment of the reign of law and civil order was believed by Wilberforce to be the beginning of civilisation in any country. Then, 'from law arises security; from security, curiosity; from curiosity, knowledge', and as security gave rise to accumulation of property, so a 'taste for new gratification is formed'.[76] Cases of governmental institutions impeding movement up the ladder of progress were, said John Stuart Mill, frequent, and 'among the most melancholy facts in history'. He argued, for example, that the despotic rulers of Egypt and China had brought their peoples so far and then no further: 'they were brought to a permanent halt for want of mental liberty and individuality ... as the institutions did not break down and give place to others, further improvements stopped'.[77] The experience of mankind, declared Palmerston, showed that only a constitution could produce good government, fully develop the natural resources of a country, and ensure security for life, liberty and property. Despotic governments could not achieve these objects. Liberty was the goal, but, said Palmerston, 'I cannot conceive liberty without two houses of parliament and a free press', in other words, liberty in the British conception.[78] It was of course the utilitarians who placed most emphasis on the efficacy of a code of laws, or education in what would later have been called 'citizenship'. James Mill thought ordinary schooling a subordinate influence forming the individual mind, but political education was 'the keystone of the arch', and the vital influences were the form of government and laws. Upon these the tone and temper of society depended. Thus: 'The most effectual step which can be taken by any government to diminish the vices of the people is to take away from the laws every imperfection'. Moreover, it was therefore necessary, 'before education can operate to any great result, that the poverty of the people should be redressed; that their laws and government should operate beneficently'. James Mill stressed the efficacy of law reform as the engine of moral improvement. Likewise Macaulay in 1833 declared his belief that no country ever stood so much in need of a code of laws as India. The difference between them was that while Macaulay placed great faith in English education, James Mill looked first to good government, just law and scientific taxation.[79]

There were many who regarded free trade, commerce and economic improvement as the most efficacious instruments, including Munro who invoked it for India, Buxton for Africa, Alcock for China and Cobden and Bright for Ireland, where they believed free trade in land would introduce solvent, improving proprietors.[80] Free trade was of quintessential importance. Palmerston was convinced that commerce was the best pioneer for civilisation and described free trade as 'the dispensation of Providence'. God meant man to be dependent on man: the world was made as it was so as to encourage the exchange of commodities, accompanied by 'the extension and diffusion of knowledge – by the interchange of mutual benefits engendering mutual kind feelings – multiplying and confirming friendly relations'. Commerce was intended to go forth freely, 'leading civilisation with one hand, and peace with the other, to render mankind happier, wiser, better':

This is the dispensation of Providence – this is the decree of that power which created and disposes the universe; but in the face of it, with arrogant, presumptuous folly, the dealers in restrictive duties fly, fettering the inborn energies of man, and setting up their miserable legislation instead of the great standing laws of nature. [81]

This passage is striking enough, but John Bright surpassed it in 1864 speaking of his fight for free trade and of his consciousness that he had 'laboured to expound and uphold laws, which, though they were not given amid the thunders of Sinai, are not less the commandments of God and not less intended to promote and secure the happiness of man'. [82] In more prosaic vein Cobden, in 1862, described commerce as 'the grand panacea which, like a beneficent medical discovery, will serve to inoculate with the healthy and saving taste for civilisation all the nations of the world', [83] but he too regarded the repeal of the corn laws as the most important event since the coming of Christ, calculated to promote the enduring interests of humanity; free trade was a principle which he hoped would act on the moral will as gravitation in the physical, drawing men together. [84] For Sir Richard Burton commercial intercourse was the 'strongest instrument of civilisation in the hand of Providence' – thus, in his view, it was rather the merchant than the missionary who would produce regeneration in Africa by the development of her resources. [85]

As to conversion to Christianity, Charles Grant in 1812 said Christianity would restore to the Hindus 'the use of their reason' and help them to rise in the scale of civilisation. On handing the kabaka of Buganda a bible in 1881 a C.M.S. missionary declared it to be 'the key to the secrets of England's greatness and glory'. Missionary commitment to this interpretation and this method is obvious, but it was widely shared by the secular world. Queen Victoria told two African chiefs: 'England has become great and happy by knowledge of the true God and Jesus Christ'. This was exactly in line with the theory of Sir Harry Smith (who was chief of staff in Cape Colony and later governor), when he addressed African chiefs on 7 January 1836. The British, he said, were now:

the most powerful nation, whose laws, manners, customs and institutions are the wonder of the world . . . Years ago the English were as naked as you, and ignorant as you, as cruel as you . . . ; but the bright day which has opened upon you, dawned upon them; they first learnt to believe in the omnipotent power of Almighty God . . .

Then gradually advancing in civilisation on this foundation, by habits of daily industry, 'by avoiding the evils of yesterday, striving to improve ourselves today', by avoiding theft, murder, witchcraft, perjury, arson, rape and especially treason 'we have become the great, powerful and enlightened and happy nation you see, going about the world teaching others to imitate us, and we are now instructing you'.[86] The report of Buxton's committee in 1837 recognised that 'all attempts to induce natives to adopt civilistion by merely educational instruction have failed', but no sooner did they become converts to Christianity than they seemed to exhibit a desire for the 'advantages of civilised life'.[87] The high Victorian doctrine was stated by W. E. Forster in 1869:

> that the knowledge of cause and effect can never replace the motive to do right and avoid wrong; that our clergymen and ministers are more useful than our schoolmasters; that Religion is the motive power, the faculties are the machines: and the machines are useless without the motive power.[88]

In India the British found that all the practices which most appalled them and inhibited development were, as Charles Trevelyan said, so mixed up with the Hindu religious system that 'nothing short of the conversion of the natives to Christianity would effect any real moral change'.[89] For the Ottoman Empire, Stratford Canning, ambassador to Constantinople, had the same theory – its only chance was 'an approach to the civilisation of Christendom'.[90] Nobody envisaged for a moment that Christianity could co-exist with material poverty or technological backwardness.[91]

The spread of education was credited with almost miraculous powers to create a prosperous and enlightened community. In Britain shorter hours for children in factories were not argued because the hours were thought too long but because they left too little time for education.[92] Even Mill and Bright did not found their expectations of improvement on scientific innovations or economic growth so much as on education and social change.[93] Raffles established schools at Singapore and Benkulen for the education of natives and regarded them as by far his most important achievements, since education would effect 'the grand object of Christian civilisation and improvement'.[94] Sir John Malcolm in 1818 declared: 'I must ever think that to impart knowledge is to impart strength to a community'.[95] Bentinck propounded the theory that education was the primary method of regeneration. On 1 June 1834 he wrote: 'General education is my panacea for the regeneration of India. The ground must be prepared and the jungle cleared away before the human mind can receive, with any prospect of *real* benefit, the seeds of improvement'. Just before his retirement he said:

> Examine the whole scheme of this Indian system, and you will find the same result: poverty, inferiority, degradation in every shape. For all these evils, knowledge! knowledge! knowledge! is the universal cure.

He advocated regenerative education not simply as an Anglicising mechanism: higher education in English he wished to combine with elementary education in the vernacular. On the principle of higher education in English he let Macaulay fire the big guns of rhetorical publicity: but the rhetoric distorted the total scheme.[96] Charles Trevelyan in 1853 expected education to fit Indians 'to co-operate with us in every purpose of improvement'.[97]

Finally, there was the technological regenerator. At a time of such remarkable technological developments it is hardly surprising that much faith came to be placed in them. Railways would break down caste barriers and prove, many thought, to be the 'greatest missionary of them all'. Bentinck said he looked upon 'steam navigation as the great engine of working the moral improvement', particularly by enabling Indians to study in Europe, and he devoted 20 years of hard work to establishing the steam link between Europe and India.[98] Bishop Wilson of Calcutta agreed: he hailed steam navigation in 1833 as 'the entrance and forerunner of all missions, education, commerce, agriculture, science, literature, policy, legislation, everything'. Dalhousie as governor-general, appointed in 1848 at the age of 35, singled out 'three great engines of social improvement' – railways, uniform postage and electric telegraphs.[99] Looking at the weak and disordered state of the Ottoman empire on his journey to Cairo in 1845, W. M. Thackeray counted on steam, 'the civilising paddle-wheel', to sweep the old rottenness away.[100] Elgin believed that railways in India would, 'by calling forth native talent in the form of skilled labour', impart the kind of education which would 'do more for the elevation of the masses than any other which we can provide'.[101] Livingstone welcomed the improved communications, and echoing him, R. Mackenzie wrote in *The 19th century: a history* (1880) that 'God was breaking down the barriers between all nations by railways, steamers and telegraphs', in order that mankind should be one, but Manchu obstructiveness to the providential design had led to the Anglo-Chinese wars.[102]

In practice all the five elements fused together, as is indicated in an abundance of contemporary catchphrases: 'the Bible and the Plough', 'Christianity and Commerce', 'Philanthropy plus Five per cent'. Such blithe equations produced what in retrospect seem to be comic manifestations. Marsden started his New Zealand mission with a grocer, a blacksmith, a carpenter and a gunsmith rather than ordained clergy; they made no converts. A Manchester businessman, Dr John Bowring,* asserted baldly that 'Jesus Christ is Free Trade and Free Trade is Jesus Christ'. A Scots opium captain was, it may be supposed, sublimely unconscious of the incongruity of his journal entry of 2 December 1832: 'Employed delivering opium briskly, No time to read my Bible'.[103] The Rev. S. Annear took polite African participation in a tea party as 'the evident token of civilisation'. The Society for the Abolition of Inhuman and Superstitious Customs and For Promoting Civilisation in Calabar included amongst its compulsory reforms the

* Later Sir John Bowring, (1792-1872) governor of Hong Kong.

observance of the Sabbath as well as Victorian dress fashions, reinforced by pressure from Consul Beecroft.[104]

In short, the means to regeneration was the adoption of the British way of life in every particular, institutional, political, scientific, and even social: the God-fearing, deferential, -liberal-minded, free-trading, self-helping, hard-working, tea-drinking, manly, prudish Victorian way of life. As Sir Harry Smith said, 'As you wish to be real Englishmen, you must observe their manners and customs in everything'. African women must not do 'men's work'. Not the smallest concession to local circumstances, traditions, nor even climates could be allowed. Said Sir Harry:

> It was one of my great endeavours to make them regard appearing naked as a grievous sin, now that they were British subjects; and no one was ever permitted in my camp, much less in my presence, but dressed in his karosse.

The karosse was a bullock skin loin-cloth.[105]

The political, legal, economic, commercial, religious, educational and technological were fused together in an integrated relationship.[106] Civilisation and Christianity had been associated since the days of medieval Christendom, but a new dimension was now added. As Sir Samuel Baker, intrepid explorer of Lake Albert put it: 'True Christianity cannot exist apart from civilisation; thus, the spread of Christianity must depend upon the extension of civilisation; and that extension depends upon commerce'.[107] Livingstone's 'Christianity and Commerce' motto assumed the inseparability of these two pioneers of civilisation. It must be clearly understood that Livingstone's advocacy of commerce was in part specifically meant to combat slave trading: in other words 'commerce' meant 'legitimate commerce' replacing the slave trade. Livingstone's slogan was not a cynical 'Christianity for the African' and 'Commerce for the European'. He wished to promote commerce in the interests of local inhabitants, not for the sake of British traders. Starting from the assumption 'The Africans are all deeply imbued with the spirit of trade', Livingstone (while not ceasing to believe that Christianity was the more beneficial) conceded: 'Commerce has the effect of speedily letting the tribes see their mutual dependence. It breaks up the sullen isolation of heathenism'.[108] In 1855 he wrote in his diary, 'There seems an utter hopelessness in many cases of the Interior except by a long-continued discipline and contact with superior races by commerce'. He was at this time despairing over his work among Sekeletu's people. In a remarkable passage he reminded himself that:

> we are forwarding that great movement which God is carrying on for the renovation of the world. We are parts of [the] machinery he employs, but not exclusive parts, for all who are engaged in ameliorating the condition of our race are fellow-workers, co-operators with God – sanitary reformers

and clergy of all sorts, the soldiers at Sebastapol and sailors on the coast of Africa, inventors of telegraphs and steam engines, promotors of emigration and of prison reform.

Two phrases stand out in this passage: 'co-operators with God' and the 'renovation of the world'.[109] The president of the Church Missionary Society assured the rulers of Abeokuta on behalf of Queen Victoria that 'the commerce between nations in exchanging the fruits of the earth is blessed by God'.[110] Livingstone noted that wherever the missionary lived, traders were sure to come: 'they are mutually dependent, and each aids the work of the other'.[111] Livingstone was a medical missionary who did not hesitate to include immigration schemes in his work. The majority of the early missionaries in the South Pacific were artisans. The Moravian missions always included craftsmen.[112] F. D. Maurice felt he acknowledged as clearly as anyone could that 'commerce is an instrument in the Divine education, and that if there is, lying at the root of Society, the recognition of the unity of men in Christ, the actual intercourse of men in different countries will bring out that belief into clearness and fullness'. For him, however, commerce in itself was not separate from the bond of brotherhood and not a 'more uniting principle than theology'.[113] Henry Venn (1796–1873), secretary of the Church Missionary Society from 1841 till 1873, encouraged missionaries in the field to send him samples of African cotton, ginger, dyes, arrowroot, pepper and coffee, and tried to find merchants willing to market them in Britain. He corresponded regularly with the director of Kew Gardens, whose advice he sought on the possibility of introducing new economic crops into West Africa and on the training of young Africans in economic botany. He tried to develop model cotton farms at Abeokuta for export to European markets.

Buxton believed agriculture was not only a basis for future commercial intercourse, but something 'tending to bring the people into a condition of life most favourable for the reception and spread of Christianity'.[114]

Indeed whatever they did seemed to promote religion. Torrens in 1827 considered that by giving effect to extensive and improved plans of colonisation in Australia, they were not only multiplying the British nation, but 'co-operating in the scheme of Providence; and are its favoured instrument in causing Christian civilisation to "cover the earth as the waters cover the sea" '.[115] However much men might disagree about the relative value of the regenerative instruments, nearly all seemed to have agreed that the crucial cement was Christianity. That was the real link between them, and more often than not, the ultimate objective. The sequence was frequently seen to be: the establishment of commerce, leading to 'civilisation' (which often meant no more than wearing textiles manufactured in Britain), leading to a demand for Christian knowledge.[116] Stratford Canning, ambassador at Constantinople, wished to see 'the Bible . . . go forth with the engine and every choice assortment of Manchester stuffs . . . [with] an honest John

Bunyan to distribute them'.[117]

Although the main emphasis in expansion was on private enterprise, the 'man on the spot', the self-helping free-lance individuals, the imperial government was not without a role. But first we must analyse the role cast for individuals acting under the guidance of enlightened self-interest, as Mill called it. Throughout the nineteenth century, it has been said, the vision of Adam Smith guided the economic energies of the British people.[118] That vision was characterised by its universal outlook and its emphasis on individual enterprise. Belief in freedom was central. Adam Smith wrote that the individual seeking to direct industry in order to secure a maximum output 'intends only his own gain', but, 'he is in this as in many other cases led by an invisible hand to promote an end which was no part of his intention'. Believing that it was relatively easy to bring into being a self-acting or self-sustaining mechanism of progress directed by an 'invisible hand', the Victorians found extensive state interference, especially in Britain itself, superfluous, pernicious, and self-frustrating.[119] Private enterprise, moral pressure, prayer and the impetus of expanding trade: these would suffice to carry on the good work of global improvement. The doctrine of self-help received classic formulation in Samuel Smiles's famous book of that title. It began: ' "Heaven helps those who help themselves" is a well-tried maxim, embodying in a small compass the results of vast human experience. The spirit of self-help is the root of all genuine growth in the individual; and exhibited in the lives of many, it constitutes the true source of national vigour and strength'. *Self-Help* was translated into innumerable languages, and quotations from it were inscribed on the walls of one of the palaces of the Khedive of Egypt; it was influential in Meiji Japan.[120]

Gladstone found the Irish singularly lacking in this glorious quality. He always deplored the difficulty of getting local loyalists to act as special constables to aid their own communities. He found in all Irish opinions 'a strong sense of the bad tradition of the country with regard to self-help'.[121]

Rutherford Alcock was a man excited by the possibility of the revolutionary emergence of new states from the Mediterranean to the Pacific, but, with a soberness greater than that of most of his contemporaries, he realised that Britain could not control the process: civilisation was not something which could be transferred wholesale, either by treaty or the sword. It was 'something that must grow in the soil where it is to take root, and from small beginnings'. His Chinese post did not offer much scope for a parade of what he called 'Utopian theories for the regeneration of the world as a principle of government and national policy', or for the advancement of civilisation and Christianity by imposed 'schemes of reconstruction', but he considered that a 'policy dictated by the more tangible interests of commerce and in harmony with the laws of nations' was also the policy most likely to bring about 'the regeneration of China'.[122]

It was believed that once set on to the path of progress, self-sustaining development was automatic. Elphinstone said that by enjoying freedom as understood by the British 'a nation is entirely changed in the course of a few generations without any effort on the part of its members'.[123] Indeed, an injudicious forcing of British doctrines upon Indians could be an obstacle to their improvement and conversion, while unforced they might revitalise the energies now so deficient.[124] And of course Macaulay wrote in 1836 that with English education, idolatry would disappear from the respectable classes of Bengal in thirty years without any efforts to proselytise, without the smallest interference with religious liberty, merely by the natural operation of knowledge and reflection.[125] Earl Grey said in the early 1850s that 'the surest test of the soundness of measures for the improvement of an uncivilised people, is that they should be self-supporting'. Palmerston's technique for handling African and Asian societies was based on the assumption that the main drive was to come from within the non-European society; large-scale and continuing investment from Europe he did not envisage to be necessary. He wanted to utilise emergent political forces and make the fullest possible use of enlightened 'native' authorities.[126] 'Native agency and European superintendence should be fully established as the principle of our government in India', said Charles Trevelyan in 1853; this formula summed up an entire theory of regeneration.

It was chiefly Palmerston who devised the methodological technique for what he called, with reference to Turkey, the 'regeneration of a rotten empire', so that British objectives could be achieved by merely informal and external pressure for internal adaptions. This is a statement which some readers will no doubt find hard to accept.[127] It may be conceded that Palmerston did not possess a subtle mind and that he relied heavily on bombastic repartee and some sheer claptrap to paper over some of the cracks in his reasoning and his old-fashioned ignorance about the formal empire. He probably knew less than he seemed to, and too much ought not always to be read into his expansionist pronouncements. With these provisos in mind, however, there seems no reason why we should not believe Palmerston to be capable of formulating the simplistic and rigorously circumscribed procedures of mid-nineteenth century British policy. In any case, it seems inconceivable that a dynamic man holding office almost continuously (as foreign secretary or prime minister) throughout the great age of British expansion from 1830 to 1865 should have provided no guidelines for this optimistic activity. Palmerston was a man who imposed his own view of things on everything from parliamentary reform to the relationship between government and trade, even if his influence was sometimes negative (Bagehot observed that he had 'great prohibitive power'). He paid close attention to official trade reports, and took great pains to get additional information. John Bowring was his investigator extraordinary (reporting on Egypt, Syria, Turkey, China, the Philippines and Siam) and James Brooke was used in Siam and Vietnam. Palmerston was a typical exponent of the Victorian world picture.

The role of the government overseas was reduced simply to occasional political functions, based on the idea of holding power in reserve and not using it as a routine. The government would provide an initial impetus or leverage to open up trade. It would try to designate and enlist the co-operation of an indigenous, enlightened collaborating group or élite to provide the continuing momentum for change. Its future participation in the process would then be reduced merely to supervising the diplomatic and consular stations who would defend British subjects against outrage and injury, and collect and transmit information about trade, with the aid of improved postal services. (A world-wide network of consuls existed by 1839: there were never less than a hundred after 1850, and their very presence gave protection to merchants.)[128] Government would also indulge in periodical 'gingering up' if necessary in the more recalcitrant cases, and attempt to keep potential rivals out of British spheres of influence.

These four types of government action need elaboration. First, the provision of initial impetus or leverage. The techniques employed to give this varied from the negotiation of 'open door' commercial treaties to gunboat diplomacy or actual war, depending on the degree of opposition encountered. More or less invariably, of course, the government sought to provide the initial leverage on behalf of merchants by the negotiation of a commercial treaty. The government conducted the wearisome negotiations leading to the Anglo-Dutch treaty of 1824. Lord Macartney's embassy to China in 1793 was charged with the task of establishing diplomatic relations and negotiating a treaty of commerce and friendship which would improve the conditions under which British merchants traded at Canton and spread markets more widely in the Far East.[129] A generation later, even Palmerston tried a repetition of the peaceful method, sending Lord Napier to China in 1833 as superintendent of trade. Palmerston instructed him to maintain a peaceful attitude: the use of menacing language and appeals for protection by British forces were to be avoided; no British ship-of-war was to appear; Chinese laws and customs were to be carefully observed by British subjects. Napier was to study the possibility of extending British trade.[130] Dissatisfied with the results, and under the pressure of local provocation, Palmerston found it necessary to resort in 1839 to more drastic methods, and so the first Anglo-Chinese war broke out. When Palmerston took office in 1830, 18 treaties of commerce existed. By the time he left the foreign office in 1841 he had added another 15, and he increased the anti-slave trade treaties from ten to 16. Treaties or agreements were made with Persia in 1836, 1841 and 1857, with Turkey in 1838 and 1861, with China in 1842 and 1858, with Morocco in 1856. Their common aim was to reduce customs duties, and obtain the privileges of extraterritoriality.[131] But Palmerston easily accepted the principle that the government should if necessary use force to provide the initial leverage: 'it is the business of the government to open and to secure the roads for the merchant' (1841).[132] This applied particularly where trade was being pushed as a support for political influence, as in the Ottoman Empire and Afghanistan as part of the great game against Russia. He would use naval power to break up commercial monopolies and restrictions whether European or African 'so that trade could expand through the cracks, carrying with it the essentials of liberal civilisation and British paramountcy'. Palmerston was ready to use force to help African trade: 'It may be true in one sense that trade ought not to be enforced by cannon balls, but on the other hand trade cannot flourish without security'. It was necessary to keep quiet the ill-disposed people whose violence would render trade insecure and thus prevent its operation. Palmerston was nothing if not a realist:

> The fact is that it rarely ever happens that a foreign government gives up its selfish interests, its passions or its prejudices to the force of argument or persuasion ... persuasion seldom succeeds unless there is compulsion of some sort nearer or farther off behind it. (1850)

After being given 'a Palmerstonian blow' it was hoped the ruler would henceforth realise himself to be under the necessity of co-operation.[133]

Second, the important objective was to have mediating friends and collaborators rather than inactive subjects. Macaulay wrote about India: 'It is impossible for us, with our limited means, to attempt to educate the body of the people. We must at present do our best to form a class who may be interpreters between us and the millions whom we govern; a class of persons, Indian in blood and colour, but English in taste, in opinions, in morals, and in intellect'. Such a class would be left to convey knowledge to the great mass of the population.[134] The natural leaders of indigenous society who could promote improvement had to be sought out. But as Earl Grey recognised, this was a problem of extreme difficulty which had nowhere been satisfactorily solved.[135] In China the British studied the Taiping rebels closely to see if they would act as better collaborators than the Manchu mandarins. There was considerable discussion of this possibility. Some early investigators, like Consul Meadows, thought they must enlist Taiping help in containing Chinese anarchy. The Taipings were, said Meadows, 'manifestly a power of some sort', and there was 'a long succession of irrefragable proofs that the Taipings do earnestly desire friendly commercial relations with us'. Their attitude to Britain seemed 'remarkably satisfactory'. But other investigators came to a different conclusion: that the only trade the Taipings encouraged was one in firearms, gunpowder and steamers; that basically they lived by looting, not by trading, and so long as they looted they would neither work nor trade. Mr Bruce by 1862 considered the movement to be 'irreconcilable with the existence of the educated, wealthy and trading classes': it was 'supported by armies collected from the most barbarous and demoralised part of the population'; wherever the Taipings went trade was destroyed.[136] And so, with the Taipings as rejected collaborators, British governments sought to support 'strong men' to take over in China, suppress the rebels, and establish 'law and order' – Tseng Kuo-fan seemed to be the first person to uphold. [137]

Thirdly, Palmerston expressed the theory of periodical 'gingering up' most precisely with respect to China. In 1847 he insisted that the treaties of 1842 must be observed, unless the Chinese chose 'to have their seaports knocked about their eyes'. Britain had given them 'a most exemplary drubbing' but if she permitted the Chinese to resume their former 'tone of affected superiority we shall very soon be compelled to come to blows with them again'. [138] By 1850 this moment was moving closer to hand. In that year, Palmerston said:

I clearly see that the time is fast coming when we shall be obliged to strike another blow in China, and that blow must be the occupation of a position on the Yangtse-Kiang to cut off communication by the Great Canal. But it would not be advisable to give the Chinese any intimation that such would be our measure. They should be left to reflect upon it when and after it was done. These half-civilised governments, such as those of China, Portugal, Spanish America, require a dressing every eight or ten years to keep them in order. Their minds are too shallow to receive an impression that will last longer than some such period, and warning is of little use. They care little for words and they must not only see the stick but actually feel it on their shoulders before they yield to that only argument which to them brings conviction, the *argumentum Baculinum*. [139]

Palmerston did not confine his bombast to the Far East, as may be seen from the following equally extraordinary utterance during the Crimean War:

In dealing with vulgar-minded bullies, and such unfortunately the people of the United States are, nothing is gained by submission to insult and wrong . . . Such people are always trying how far they can venture to go and they generally pull up when they find they can go no further without encountering resistance of a formidable character . . . The United States have no navy of which we need be afraid, and they might be told that if they were to resort to privateering we should, however reluctantly, be obliged to retaliate by burning all their sea coast towns. [140]

Finally, the government accepted responsibility for keeping rivals out of British spheres of influence. Victorian expansion was in part negative and directed towards keeping options open. Britain kept other Europeans out of Morocco, Arabia and Somaliland. Palmerston warned France off New Zealand, Tahiti and Morocco; he warned Russia off a Korean island in the 1860s. France was warned off Tunis in 1836, in 1843 and 1844. Aberdeen prevented foreign pre-emption in Morocco, the South Pacific and China, and he insisted that trade was open to all. Britain had refused to establish many protectorates, but the assumption of them by alternative governments could not be viewed with indifference. The Boers were shut out from the coasts of South Africa: from Natal in 1843, from Delagoa Bay and St Lucia Bay repeatedly in the 1860s.

It proved impossible to prevent formal territorial advance. This advance was in fact extensive in the 20 years after 1838, although it was chiefly associated with areas of strategic importance in India and near or on the routes to India and in South Africa. Between 1839 and 1851 the following territories were acquired by annexation or occupation: Aden, New Zealand, the Gold Coast, Labuan, Natal, Punjab, Sind (with its fine harbour at Karachi) and Hong Kong. By 1877 control was asserted over Perim Island, Berar, Oudh, Lower Burma, Kowloon, Lagos, the neighbourhood of Sierra Leone, Basutoland, Griqualand and the Transvaal; new colonies were formed in Queensland and British Columbia.[141] The policy of pre-empting against rivals was a continuous thread in British expansion. Palmerston was prepared if necessary to take Afghanistan in hand and 'make it a British dependency': 'we have long declined to meddle with the Afghans and have purposely left them independent, but if the Russians try to make them Russian, we must take care they become British'. When he took Lagos he said, 'if we do not take this step, the French will be before hand with us and to our great detriment'.[142]

British attitudes were both arrogant and ignorant. It was automatically assumed that the Chinese, for example, could not be treated as equals. The Duke of Argyll, at the time of the second China war, said: 'it is supreme nonsense to talk as if we were bound to the Chinese by the same rules which regulate international relations in Europe'. And again: 'it would be madness to be bound on our side by that code with a barbarous people, to whom it is unknown, and if known, would not be followed'.[143] There was an unwarranted optimism. Palmerston believed that the Ottoman empire needed only ten years' peace for re-organising itself, and, given that, 'there is no reason whatever why it should not become again a respectable power ... All that we hear every day of the week about the decay of the Turkish empire, and its being a dead body or sapless trunk, and so forth, is pure unadulterated nonsense'.[144] Palmerston made some whopping over-simplifications, acting on the assumption that 'theories founded as general theories were on large and general observation more likely to be correct than theories founded on narrow and particular observation'. He managed to attribute opposition to British activities, whether in China or Afghanistan, or Africa or Brazil, as merely directed by the selfish interests of a few powerful individuals, and not at all the result of a general dislike of foreign interference. He even persuaded himself in 1860 that the majority of Chinese regarded British successes in war with almost as much pleasure as the British themselves.[145] James Mill believed in universally applicable immutable laws: 'The great outlines ... to be drawn, will be found to be the same for every *territory*, for every *race* and for every *time*'.[146] There was little understanding of emergent 'nationalism'. Mill in

1831 considered 'that the feeling of degradation, from being governed by foreigners is a feeling altogether European'. He believed it had 'little or no existence in any part of Asia'. The application of pure theory without consideration of native customs or political consequences can be seen in the utilitarians' land settlement policies, based on Ricardian rent theory and Benthamite doctrines of egality.[147] Sir George Grey believed that he had only to set up suitable institutions for the Maoris for them to find easy acceptance˙ and to spread over the whole country. It was over-facile to believe that once parliamentary institutions had been granted they could be left to work themselves. He underestimated potential resistance to his plans from the Maoris in the interior with whom he had only slight contact. After eight years in New Zealand he spent seven in South Africa. There is something rather pathetic in his naïve hope that in a mere seven years he could change the course of South African history, 'civilise the Kaffirs', humanise the European frontiersmen, unify South Africa and reconcile the British government to a policy contrary to the one it had already decided upon.[148]

The touching faith of politicians in the willingness of the rest of the world to accept European ways was no less than that of the missionaries. In both cases pride was destined to have a terrible fall. Their vague theorising simply bore no relation at all to the facts of human nature. There were two key thematic words in early Victorian attitudes to non-Europeans: Improvement and Regeneration. They were thought to be the keys to all that the world needed. The two words occur over and over again in all these men said and wrote.[149] 'Improvement Societies' existed everywhere by the 1830s. But it was eventually to become plain that the world did not wish to be regenerated in the early Victorian mould. And the Victorians were not prepared to provide the money which alone could ensure some real result.

The prospects of British commerce were sometimes fantastically exaggerated. Some speculators at times of euphoria had an overgenerous view of Britain's ability to swamp the world's markets with British manufactures. But politicians and consuls on the whole were well aware of the limitations of many of these overseas markets. For local handicraft production existed all over China, the Levant, West Africa and Latin America.[150] West Africa had a range of manufactures closely resembling those of pre-industrial societies everywhere: clothing (mostly cotton) was the most important, but there was also leather, metal-working and pottery, together with a corps of construction workers (including carpenters and plasterers); food and drink for local consumption was also processed. At mid-century Kano and Timbuctu were major centres for distributing cloth. Kano, aided by the presence of cotton and indigo nearby and its position in the highly efficient Hausa communications network, produced at least £40,000-worth of cloth a year. As Hopkins shows, foreigners never really replaced domestic craft products in the nineteenth century, with local cotton goods and pottery remaining important The same was true of Latin America. Buenos Aires in 1830 had 5ʹ

independent workshops in everything from hatters to lathe mechanics. The Latin Americans manufactured their own clothes, boots, plate, pots, candlesticks, buckles, chains, earthenware, iron, copper goods, haberdashery, saddles, bridles, furniture and so on. The Ottoman empire was historically well known for its range of good textiles. There were 10,000 looms in Aleppo in the early 1850s and still 5,000 in 1860. Coarse cotton clothes were woven in every village in Asiatic Turkey and the Balkans. In fact Turkey was self-supporting. Diarbekr in Eastern Turkey in 1863 had 30,000 inhabitants. There were 1,400 looms at work and there were over 2,000 shops and workshops. They included workers in the metal trade and horse equipment; there were shoemakers, candlestick-makers and gunsmiths. Every Chinese cottage had its spinning wheel: British woollens were too expensive and silks were preferred. In Canton in the 1840s there were 67,000 engaged in textile manufacture; there were also plenty of firms producing cheap china ware. From the point of view of the British manufacturer, markets in Latin America, China and the Levant all suffered from the same disabilities: they all had entrenched local handicraft industries operating with cheap labour and catering for established tastes and habits; and, with the exception of China tea, they could hold out no prospect of an expanding exchange trade, which meant that ships might have to return home without cargo. Europe, North America and even India offered incomparably better opportunities for two-way traffic. Despite occasional flurries of over-trading and enthusiastic speculation brought about by military action or treaty, the general pattern of commercial houses permanently interested in China, the Levant and Latin America may well have been one of rationalisation and consolidation rather than expansion in the period 1830 to 1860. In the 1840s the entire trade to Latin America averaged £5.7 million a year, to Turkey £2.6 million and to China £1.6 million. Compared with the massive realities of American demand, such markets were seen to be peripheral. No-one, however, could be quite sure that the peripheral might not become central, and ministerial interest in them was closely maintained.

The self-satisfied assurance and misplaced optimism of the early Victorians is easy to sneer at today. Their vision was part noble, part crass. They placed undue faith in 'facile generalisations, iron laws and panaceas'.[151] One thing is certain: to criticise is to criticise not a few eccentric individuals but an entire generation. In defence of that generation it might be said that they were a breed of intrepid earthshaking giants (the like of which has never been seen before or since) who tried to the utmost of their ability to do all sorts of things in all directions which had never been attempted before. Following Dr Arnold of Rugby, they believed that since the whole bias of human weakness was towards inaction, stagnation and selfishness, it was their duty to be improvers, 'world-betterers' in the Cambridge slang of the early 1840s.[152] Words often spoke louder than actions. They were often wrong, sometimes grievously wrong, but the world has never been quite the same since they set the seal of their influence upon it.

Their inner confidence was short-lived, and from the later 1850s the first cracks in it began to appear.

3 The Decline of British Pre-eminence, 1855–1914

When the Crimean War broke out in 1854 it touched off in Britain (wrote John Morley) a 'remarkable exhibition of political heedlessness, administrative incompetency, and personal incoherence ... Never was confidence in public men more profoundly and universally shaken'. This led to the electoral triumph of Lord Palmerston, succeeding Aberdeen as prime minister, despite the attacks of Cobden and Bright. The latter regarded Russophobia as a phantom invented by crackpots and the idea of permanently upholding Turkish rule in Europe as an absurdity. They found some consolation in 'the break-down of our aristocratic rulers, when their energies are put to the stress of a great emergency'. [1]

The war ended at the Congress of Paris in the Spring of 1856. But it had shaken the British ruling élite considerably. Even if she had not put them to devastating use, the fact remained that mighty Russia had mobilised an army of more than 600,000 effective troops. A fundamental re-thinking of strategy on the north-west frontier of India was begun as a result of the war. [2]

Confidence was shortly to be shaken by an even more portentous event: the Mutiny-Rebellion in India.

At first no-one could believe that the Mutiny had really happened. On the very day of the Meerut outbreak the *Times* correspondent wrote of 'perfect tranquillity pervading the whole of India'. [3] The reaction of politicians and army officers to initial reports was exactly the same. Both Palmerston and Garnet Wolseley simply dismissed them as impossible. [4] There had been one universal belief that no danger could ever approach the British in India, that God was on the side of the empire and that everybody loved the British. When the first news arrived in June Palmerston was inclined to treat it lightly and to postpone a decision on whether or not to send military reinforcements. The Queen and Albert urged vigorous action from the start. [5] No mere Palmerstonian hesitation afflicted Sir George Grey at the Cape. Immediately, without waiting for instructions from London, he intuitively grasped both the seriousness of what had happened and the need to act:

The British Empire is so vast and so unwieldy that it is all important that the whole world should see it has not overgrown its strength, but that it possesses quite as much energy, vitality and power of action at its extremities as iat its centre, and that if any vital position of it is seriously endangered all parts of it can, without communicating with the centre, simultaneously stir themselves to meet the emergency, as if each part were the head and centre of action for the whole body, so that the whole weight and force of the Empire can at once be brought to bear from every part upon the menaced point. (7 August, 1857)

He realised all too well how, in so large and disjointed an empire, a moment of great danger could easily be transformed into a crisis of the greatest peril if dangers occurred simultaneously in different parts.[6] By the autumn it was clear the stakes were high. Clarendon wrote:

We have never before played for so great a stake, and the whole world is watching how we conduct the game upon which our national honour and our prestige and position among nations depend. . . . a large proportion of the spectators devoutly hope that we may lose this game, and that England may henceforward take rank as a second or third-rate power, and it is therefore all the more incumbent upon us to win it.[7]

Granville noted rather grandly on 25 July 1857: 'The greatest panic exists in London about the Indian news; why, I cannot tell'.[8] The diarist Greville recorded that the alarm and surprise were very great. The government, he thought, had been living in a fool's paradise, never paying any attention to hints of possible perils: 'I do not think anybody', he added, 'ever foresaw anything like what has occurred . . .' Mails came only at fortnightly intervals: they were looked for with the utmost impatience; every other topic of interest was superseded and gloomy rumours were rife. Greville noted that, unlike the Crimean War, the Indian 'civil war' as he called it, aroused no enthusiasm or pleasure, only anxiety and horror. He realised it must take Britain out of participation in European affairs for a time, and indeed wrote that 'for the present we are reduced to the condition of an insignificant Power'. He became increasingly gloomy. Britain would probably suppress the rebellion, but could she continue to hold the Indian Empire? Twice he noted that Lord Shaftesbury was stirring up all the fanaticism of the country, exciting the 'rage and indignation of the masses to the highest pitch' with extravagant nonsense.[9] Shaftesbury not only countenanced stories of mutilation by the rebels, which proved unfounded, but clamoured for more bloodthirsty details. Many felt as Goldwin Smith felt: that the frenzy of hysterical British opinion, and the horrible 'yellings of literary eunuchs displaying their virility by cries for blood', were a 'terrible lesson on the moral perils of the Empire'.[10] Other intellectuals found themselves thrown into a state of moral confusion. F. D.

Maurice felt that the Indian Mutiny brought back 'all the questions to this age which the Lisbon earthquake forced upon the last'.* Somewhere in these 'unspeakable horrors' God must be speaking to the British – there should be 'no accusations except of ourselves'; it was a call to repentance and to reform India by first reforming Britain.[11] John Bright was thankful that illness prevented him from stepping on to a platform, because he would have found it impossible to know what to say. In August 1858 he described the Indian question as 'a swamp to which there seems neither bottom nor firm shore'. Britain had attempted an impossible task, which now looked more impossible than ever.[12] Cobden agreed, and he saw no future but trouble, loss, disappointment and crime in India:

> There has been nothing in history since the St Domingo revolt to compare in fiendish ferocity with the atrocities by the Sepoys upon the women and children who have fallen into their hands. One stands aghast and dumbfounded at the reflection that after a century of intercourse with us, the natives of India suddenly exhibit themselves greater savages than any of the North American Indians who have been brought into contact with the white race.

For months the news gave him a perpetual shudder. 'The awful atrocities . . . almost give rise to the impious doubt whether this world is under the government of an all-wise and just Providence'. The unparalleled cruelties caused him more amazement than anything else that had occurred in his lifetime.[13] Charles Kingsley could think of nothing else but the massacres. To F. D. Maurice he wrote:

> The moral problems they involve make me half wild. Night and day, the heaven seems black to me, though I never was so prosperous and blest in my life as I am now . . . What does it all mean? Christ is King nevertheless! . . . But I want sorely some one to tell me that he believes it too. Do write to me and give me a clue out this valley of the shadow of death. (3 September 1857)

To another friend, Bullar, he wrote:

> Do not talk to me about India, and the future of India, till you can explain the past – the past six months. O Bullar, no man knows, or shall know, what thoughts they have cost me . . . Meanwhile I feel as if I could dogmatise no more . . . I have no heart, at least, to continue any argument, while my brain is filled with images fresh out of hell and the shambles.

* The Lisbon earthquake occurred in 1755. Between 30,000 and 40,000 people died, and the value of property destroyed was estimated at £20 million.

Show me what security I have that my wife, my children, should not suffer, from some unexpected outbreak of devils, what other wives and children have suffered, and then I shall sleep quiet, without longing that they were safe out of a world where such things are possible . . . I have been in hell many times in my life . . . But I never have looked hell so close in the face as I have been doing of late.[14]

'I feel as if I could dogmatise no more' – a terrible confession for a Victorian, but a just summary of the disorientation into which men were thrown. Over 500 books appeared about the Mutiny between 1857 and 1862. In later memoirs, all possible superlatives abound. The Mutiny was always the most calamitous, the most tremendous catastrophe, the most serious life-and-death struggle, the most hideous occurrence of the century.[15] The impression created often remained deep and lasting. The Ven. A. T. Wirgman recalled how at the age of 11 'the terrible scenes of the Indian Mutiny were deeply impressed upon my mind'.[16] The Duke of Argyll recorded in his autobiography 50 years later:

Well do I remember the morning on which we read of this disastrous event . . . It still comes back to me how sick we felt with anxiety, how alarming the prospect appeared, and how all our flowers had lost their glory.

And why had the flowers lost their glory? Because there was no reason in the Indian action, 'no opportuneness in their conduct. They seemed to go suddenly mad, like shying horses or stampeded mules'. 'The savage slaughter of the officers came at the end of years of sympathy and affection. It was as if some evil spirit were let loose . . . converting them into demons of treachery and destruction'.[17]

The impact of the Indian Mutiny was deepened because it did not happen in isolation. In the eight years following 1857 there was a whole series of wars and protests against European rule and interference. In the same year as the Mutiny a dreadful 'cattle-killing' episode shook the Xhosa people of South Africa, and it was rumoured that some of their anti-white millenarian animus had been fanned by news of the Indian Mutiny.[18] Also in 1857, in Sarawak James Brooke had put down an insurrection of Chinese; in severe punishment more than a thousand people were killed. Then in 1859–60 he faced an Iban rebellion which was the most severe crisis of the whole era of Brooke rule.[19] Elsewhere, Christians were coming under attack. In June 1858 more than 20 were massacred at Jedda. For two days the town was bombarded in gunboat retaliation until the 11 Muslims most deeply implicated were yielded up. They were beheaded, and in recording the event, the *Annual Register* hoped that Muslims had been given a lesson 'of the irresistible power of England, which they are not likely soon to forget'. But in the summer of 1860 it reported 'frightful atrocities' against Christians in Syria. On one day in June at Seraya perhaps 1,100–1,200 were killed; and at Damascus in July another 1,000–2,000 in one day. Such news was received with the 'profoundest sensation', and referred to in the Queen's Speech of 1861. Beirut was threatened, but the presence in the harbour of a British pleasure yacht with one gun aboard is supposed to have had more effect in averting danger there than all the troops of the Turkish pasha.[20] In Nigeria, the Yoruba wars between the Egba and the Ibadan Yoruba, lasting from 1860 until 1865, caused anxiety to traders and missionaries. After riots and a mass attack, missionaries were expelled in 1867[21] the Maori Wars in New Zealand began in 1860 and lasted for the whole decade.[22] The state of the land war was kept in view in successive Speeches from the Throne. So was the situation in China, where the Taiping rebellion was raging between 1850 and 1864. The second Anglo-Chinese war was concurrently fought, 1856–60. Perhaps the most shattering event of these eight years of crisis was the outbreak of the American Civil War in 1861, recognised as 'a revolution of great importance, no less than the disruption of the hitherto United States into two hostile sections', as the *Annual Register* described the first scenes.[23] In 1865 the Morant Bay rising in Jamaica excited another 'profound sensation', eliciting further comparisons with the Indian Mutiny. Meanwhile, Mexico was caught in a protracted social conflict. Juárez's long years of guerilla struggle began while the Indian Mutiny was raging, and to many Europeans it appeared in a similar light – benighted natives fighting against civilised rule.[24]

Relations between New Zealand and the mother country became so embittered that by 1869 the *New Zealand Herald* openly expressed the view that it would have been better if France had been the first to plant its flag in the islands. That British settlers should ever contemplate a preference for the tricolor was most distressing. Events in New Zealand, however annoying and disturbing, were not so dangerous to civilisation as the American Civil War. The simultaneous crises in America and New Zealand were largely responsible for the sense of urgency which occupied the select committee on defence, which reported in 1862.[25]

Meanwhile at home there was the famous 'war scare' of 1859 to contend with, which led to the establishment of volunteer rifle clubs and cadet corps. It was widely believed that Britain was about to be invaded, as practice bullets ricocheted first at Eton, then at Rossall and finally all over the place.[26] The cattle plague of 1866 was another major worry.[27]

The Jamaica crisis of 1865 was one of the few occasions when Britain raised herself to debate issues involving the treatment of other races.[28] Negroes in the West Indies in the 1850s and 1860s were underprivileged rather than oppressed, but the whole government of the islands was amateurish, inefficient and deteriorating. The immediate cause of the 1865 troubles was of slight importance. At Morant Bay in October a band of about 400 Jamaican malcontents approached the court-house to protest against the decisions of the magistrate in his parish; the background to discontent lay not so much in the admitted grievances of the labouring class as in the desire of the free settlers to obtain the so-called 'back land' rent free. In the clash with local volunteers, seven people were killed on each side. 2,000 men then disappeared into the hinterland, and in the next few days sporadic outbreaks occurred in one or two other settlements. It was hardly an organised general conspiracy against British rule, but it was certainly more than a riot – it was a planned resistance to lawful authority. It was compared with the Indian Mutiny and it led ultimately to the revocation of the Jamaican constitution. In all 18 men (half of them white) were killed by the rebels. 35 people were wounded. The governor, Edward Eyre (the Australian explorer), was not popular, and, as a pious Anglican, he disliked the political manipulations of the remarkable Negro leader, G. W. Gordon, a self-ordained Baptist minister, who was also a respected magistrate and ambitious radical politician. Eyre was unjustified in acting on an assumption of Gordon's moral guilt – it was not more than that; Gordon was an avowed constitutionalist but supposed to favour the elimination of white rule and the establishment of a 'New West India Republic'. Gordon took no obvious part in inciting the people – the action was started by Paul Bogle – and when he heard that there was a warrant for his arrest he gave himself up. He was arrested at Kingston. As martial law did not prevail outside Morant Bay, Eyre had Gordon moved from Kingston, hoping this would prevent the spread of the rebellion, and put him before a court martial. This was composed of two young naval lieutenants and an ensign in the West Indian regiment: an inexperienced and totally unsuitable kind of court. Even so, the tribunal refused to sanction the death penalty, and Eyre himself ordered it personally. Rumours of widespread disaffection had been reaching him for months, and it was clearly impossible for him to tell the extent of possible trouble. His own defence was that the rebellion was completely crushed, and that severe punishments were 'a merciful substitute for the much larger measure of punishment' which would have been necessary if it had been allowed 'time to gather head and extend itself'; he felt that he could not punish merely the ignorant followers but must punish the educated 'leader'. Eyre explicitly said he could not regard a 'rebellion' among negro peasantry as on the same footing as protest on an English estate. 'A most savage and cruel butchery', he reported; 'the whole outrage could only be paralleled by the atrocities of the Indian Mutiny'. It was hardly a proper comparison – women and children were, for example, never touched by the Jamaican rebels. But it was his excuse and justification for the punishments inflicted: martial law resulted in the killing or hanging of 439 persons, 354 by court martial sentences (many were shot without trial); at least 600 more were flogged, and a thousand homes were burned. The hangings went on for five weeks after the outbreak. In the floggings men received a hundred lashes, women thirty. Things certainly got out of control. The cat-o'-nine-tails was used upon women on a simple charge of stealing; wire was twisted round the cords of the whip. Some of the troops had served in the Indian Mutiny and perhaps perpetuated their feelings of revenge. Two of the senior officers administering martial law committed suicide not long after.

A royal commission was appointed under Lt-Gen. Sir H. K. Storks (governor of Malta) and submitted a report in 1866 which had all the impartiality and judicious balancing of praise and blame usually associated with such reports. It found the punishments too severe and the floggings 'positively barbarous', but Eyre was praised for containing the disturbances; to that extent he was exonerated. (It was after all Gen. O'Connor and not Eyre who was technically responsible for the conduct of the martial law). The commission found the declaration of martial law justified, but Eyre, though conscientious, it described as 'very obstinate and in no sense a man of the world'. The colonial office mostly accepted these findings, but Forster found it hard to believe Eyre did not put a different value on black and on white life, and therefore that Eyre's 'recall with blame is a mild retribution'. The cabinet, making every allowance for the difficulties and uncertainties, considered martial law to have been continued too long, and they deplored and condemned the trial and execution of Gordon. They had already decided that Jamaica should become a Crown Colony; they did not wish to see Jamaica proceed to negro control, and they believed the best government would be a direct form as in India.

What is our own judgement of this affair to be? The *Times* in fact came to a sensible conclusion. Eyre was neither a hero nor murderer, but a man who acted inadvisedly in very difficult circumstances. In 1870 an appeal court delivered unanimous judgement in Eyre's favour. Undoubtedly he made grave errors of judgement, but he had to face imponderable issues of order and anarchy, and the Indian Mutiny had distorted many an official outlook. C. S. Roundell, the secretary of the royal commission, noted and deplored 'the military spirit which was engendered by the Indian Mutiny', the first fruits of which were witnessed in the 'red anarchy of Jamaica'.[29]

The whole episode created a tornado of public excitement and bitter controversy.[30] John Bright feared that 'the fame of England has never received a deeper wound or a darker stain' than the 'murder of Gordon'. Huxley believed it was the worst case of political murder since Judge Jeffreys' time. F. Harrison said the issue was the rule of law in the empire: the Mutiny had 'called out all the tiger in our race. That wild beast must be caged again'. Whereas those against Eyre feared savage repression, those in favour of him feared the consequences of an unchecked mindless rabble. Great meetings of ordinary people angered at cruelty were held in many towns in the Midlands, also in Yorkshire, in Plymouth, Reading and Brighton. The *Times* declared that it was an issue which came home to the very soul:

Though a flea-bite compared with the Indian Mutiny, it touches our pride more and is more in the nature of a disappointment. . . . Jamaica is our pet institution and its inhabitants are our spoilt children ... It seemed to be proved in Jamaica that the Negro could become fit for self-government ... Alas for the grand triumphs of humanity, and the improvement of races, and the removal of primeval curses, and the expenditure of twenty millions sterling, Jamaica herself gainsays the fact and belies herself ... It is that which vexes us more than even the Sepoy revolt.[31]

Opposed to Eyre (the 'Jamaica Committee') were John Bright, J. S. Mill, Goldwin Smith, A. V. Dicey, T. H. Green, Darwin, Spencer, Huxley, Lyell, and Thomas Hughes. His defenders (the 'Eyre Defence Committee') included Charles Kingsley, Ruskin, Carlyle, Tennyson, Dickens, Murchison and many of the Anglican clergy. The degree of race prejudice revealed and deepened by this event was recognised with shame by sane contemporaries. W. E. Forster said excesses took place because British officers were not free from racial feeling, contempt for inferior negroes – and no-one challenged his opinion. The Church Missionary Society virtually withdrew from its work in Jamaica. It seemed a hopelessly unregenerate place. The attack upon Eyre was perhaps more rooted in post-Mutiny guilt and the illegality of his acts than in concern for Jamaican negroes.* As Mill wrote, taking a purely abstract stance: 'There was much more at stake than only justice to the negroes, imperative as was that consideration. The question was, whether the British dependencies, and eventually, perhaps, Great Britain itself, were to be under the government of law or of military licence'.[32] Never in his whole life did he feel so clear as to the principles he should follow. Without any personal feeling against Eyre, (of whom he knew nothing) he regarded the governor's conduct with 'deepest indignation', felt it humiliating as an Englishman, and was filled with abhorrence and contempt for Eyre's attempt to shield himself against investigation. If there had not been an inquiry 'all the ties of civil society would ... be at the mercy of accident and I should be ashamed of my country'. Eyre's flagrantly lawless conduct involved 'crimes of violence and cruelty which no man of even ordinarily tender conscience or good heart could be capable of'. His actions were calculated to lower the character of Britain in the eyes of all foreign lovers of liberty.[33] Carnarvon spoke of 'grave acts of undoubted cruelty, oppression and injustice'.[34]

On the other hand Charles Kingsley praised Eyre on his arrival back at Southampton in August 1866. Admitting ignorance of the details, Kingsley was prepared to take Eyre 'upon trust', for he represented the 'English spirit of indomitable perseverance, courage and adventure ... good nature, or temper, of the understanding of human beings'. He hailed him as 'the saviour of society in the West Indies', and hoped he would be made a peer for his

---

* In a way which hardly looks consistent with his attack on Eyre, Mill for example in 1868 defended Gen. Napier's action in Ethiopia when, on the way to Magdala to release the British consul, he killed 500 people and wounded 15,000 more.

services.[35] These incredible remarks drew savage newspaper comment and Kingsley never spoke again on the subject – presumably much to Eyre's relief.

THE HARDENING OF RACIAL ATTITUDES

The events of 1865 in Jamaica deepened the belief that the negro was not fit for political power. The constitutional regression of the West Indies was of the first importance. Britain decided in favour of semi-despotic government over millions of coloured peoples at the time when the United States was trying to implement human equality in the South. Jamaica, Fenian outrages and the Maori Wars were linked in some minds; and all needed 'a strong hand' to put them down. Anthropologist James Hunt said human equality was a 'sham and a delusion' and he admired Eyre. While abolitionists looked with pleasure on the results of the Civil War (Mill said it was 'a happiness to have lived to see the termination of slavery'),[36] conservatives took alarm at the coincidence of black agitation in the United States, Haiti and Jamaica.[37]

One of the lessons of experience seemed to be provided by the negro republic of Haiti. The slave rebellion of Saint Dominigue in 1791 created the first independent ex [French] colony ruled by non-Europeans. Saint Dominigue was permanently lost by the French when Haitians defeated a French expeditionary force 1802–03, and converted itself eventually into the Republic of Haiti. Lord Elgin as governor of Jamaica in the 1840s formed a poor opinion of it:

> as respects moral and intellectual culture, stagnation: in all that concerns material development, a fatal retrogression ... a miserable parody of European and American institutions, without the spirit that animates either: the tinsel of French sentiment on the ground of negro ignorance ... a people which has for its only living belief an ill-defined apprehension of the superiority of the white man.*[38]

After the Jamaica Rebellion of 1865, governor Eyre spoke of the 'mighty danger' threatening 'to make Jamaica a second Haiti'.[39]

---

* The historian Froude, 20 years later was even more caustic about Haiti: the alternative before the West Indies was, he thought, either an English administration on the East Indian model, or 'a falling eventually into a state like that of Haiti, where they eat the babies, and no white man can own a yard of land'. The example of Haiti showed the West Indian negroes were 'a half reclaimed race of savages, cannibals not long ago, and capable ... of reverting to cannibalism again'. Those who know Haiti, he wrote, say it is the most ridiculous caricature of civilisation in the whole world (J. A. Froude *The English in the West Indies* (1888) 56, 262). His brother, Hurrell Froude, concluded as early as 1823 that Barbadans and Eskimoes had 'not at all the manner of rational creatures ... An elephant seems a much more intelligent animal and a monkey does not much yield the place to them in beauty' (P. G. R. Brendon *Hurrell Froude and the Oxford Movement* (1974) 36, 153–54).

Scientific and pseudo-scientific writings played a part in increasing the harshness of racial attitudes, strengthening and confirming the worst suspicions derived from actual experience. The most famous of these are frequently labelled 'social Darwinism'.[40] Darwin's *Origin of Species by Means of Natural Selection* was published in 1859 and seemed to cast doubt on the adaptation of organism to environment and thus on the ease with which non-Europeans could respond to an 'improving' environment.[41] The implication in Darwin's theory was that racial variations had existed for millions of years, and if this was so, alteration might not be so easy as it had been thought to be on a time scale which put the date of creation at 4004 B.C. Darwin seemed also to imply that chance rather than divine will had begotten order in the world. The doctrine of the survival of the fittest lent itself easily to political interpretation. Walter Bagehot's book *Physics and Politics* (1872) carried the notable sub-title *Thoughts on the application of the principles of 'natural selection' and 'inheritance' to Political Society.** Whether or not Bagehot was more influenced by Spencer than Darwin is uncertain. But from this kind of approach it was but a short step to using Darwin to justify military aggressiveness and the seizure of territory. These were made to seem natural and scientific by the currency of phrases like 'survival of the fittest', 'man's fighting instincts', and the 'herd instinct'.[42] No blame attaches to Darwin. He himself regarded racial differences as of minor significance. Exponents of racial contempt existed before Darwin, and merely pressed his ideas into service, distorting them in doing so. Much of so-called 'social Darwinism' was mere lip-service or polemical camouflage, not genuine intellectual influence. Its role, in conjunction with the advance of scientific knowledge and thought, was to undermine older political assumptions and beliefs.[43] Moreover, there was a host of other books besides the *Origin of Species* which, by implying that men were influenced by heredity as well as environment, contributed to the hardening of racial attitudes. In 1853, for example, the French count Arthur Gobineau produced a treatise entitled *The Inequality of the Races of Mankind.*[44]

Charles Kingsley, ever a man to focus attention on issues of empire and power, once again provided one of the most articulate expressions of the way in which racialists used science and pseudo-science to justify their attitudes:

---

* A similar link appears in one-time colonial secretary Bulwer Lytton's 24th novel *The Coming Race* (1871) which he described as 'a solemn quiz on Darwin and Radical Politics'. He satirised Darwin with good humour, ridiculed exaggerated American notions of democracy, and parodied Mill's views on the emancipation of women. The secret of the Vril-ya's potential ability to 'supplant all the inferior races now existing' was in their control of *vril*, a fluid, an unlimited vital force. The word vril passed into the English language to denote a vitalising elixir, and lent its name to 'Bovril', an invigorating beef (bov-ine) extract first marketed in the 1880s. (I owe this note to my colleague Andrew Brown who is studying the whole corpus of Bulwer Lytton's over-neglected literary output.)

Physical science is proving more and more the immense importance of Race; the importance of hereditary powers, hereditary organs, hereditary habits, in all organised beings from the lowest plant to the highest animal. She is proving more and more the omni-present action of the differences between races.

For Kingsley, from being *an* important influence on human culture, race was becoming *the* crucial determinant: science was proving

how the more favoured race (she cannot avoid using the epithet) exterminates the less favoured, or at least expels it, and forces it, under penalty of death, to adapt itself to new circumstances; and, in a word, that competition between every race and every individual of that race, and reward according to desserts, is (as far as we can see) an universal law of living things. And she says — for the facts of history prove it — that as it is among the races of plants and animals, so it is been unto this day among the races of men.[45]

Of the *Origin of Species* he wrote to F. D. Maurice in 1863: 'Darwin is conquering everywhere and rushing in like a flood, by the mere force of truth and fact'. In Canada, G. E. Cartier backed Darwin in an 1865 debate.[46]

Not everyone found Darwin so compelling. Governor Sir William Denison considered him and Lyell to have produced baseless hypotheses and was content to believe 'God made us as told in the Bible', but in any case since God was omnipotent it was not impossible he should have decided to make man out of a turnip. But however mistaken he believed Darwin to be, Denison shared Kingsley's stress on the dominance of inherited qualities. He would have nothing of the idea that the Hindus had been made liars by oppression: 'The character is bred in the bone and is indelible'. He despaired of the Maoris: 'a hopeless race, hanging upon our hands as a deadweight'. They seemed incapable of change, and so all 'talk of educating them, of fitting them for liberty, of teaching them to govern themselves, is the veriest twaddle'. He was quite sure that 'education has no action in altering the type of character'.[47]

Changes of attitude went much deeper than the influence of Darwin. It is not possible to trace the influence of technical and esoteric evolutionary theory in the writings of missionaries, nor, even more surprisingly, in those of anthropologists. Most people simply thought of Africans as 'children' and left it at that. Evolutionary theory was thus only a supplementary and not a causal influence in the formation of British attitudes in the later nineteenth century.[48]

Livingstone had little interest in, or knowledge of, evolutionary theories and was content to argue that in examining African society 'we are thrown back in the imagination to the infancy of the world'. Neither Maine, nor

Tylor, nor McLennan – the emerging anthropologists – made much use of the theory of natural selection. 'Social Darwinism' was merely part of the wider intellectual movement surrounding the origins of anthropology in the 1860s, stemming from the breakdown of earlier sociological interpretations of human development, such as social contract and the mechanical conception of society as an artefact transformable almost at will.[49]

In the 1860s anthropological societies were founded in most British cities. Many of the early anthropologists had no previous training and imported ethnocentric prejudices into their work. Prichard, E. B. Tylor and Sir J. Lubbock were exceptions, but Hunt openly said some races could never be civilised, and Knox declared, 'with me race, or hereditary descent, is everything; it stamps the man'.[50] Some of the early and more controversial findings of anthropology undoubtedly exercised an adverse influence on British racial attitudes, and the whole concept of 'race' took on a more categorical meaning.[51] Dr James Hunt, president of the Anthropological Society of London, said there were 'about six races below the negro and six above him', taking the capacity of the cranium as the test. In 1864 Richard Burton commented on Hunt's *The Negro's Place in Nature* which, he said, showed most graphically the gulf between the black and white races resting on a physical cause: the arrested mental development of the negro resulting from the earlier closure of the sutures of the cranium in the 'lower breeds of mankind'.[52]

The swing towards harsher racial attitudes was not, however, simply something for which disillusioned politicians and the theories of scientists and anthropologists were responsible. A more important contribution, perhaps, was made by missionaries and travellers. Missionary letters were selected and published in journals with wide circulation. Publication was essential to mission work, in order to demonstrate the overwhelming need for financial support of it. As propaganda to stimulate subscriptions they naturally stressed the wickedness of non-Christian societies and the immensity of the 'evil' to be eradicated.[53] Because missionary literature was acceptable reading for the Victorian sabbath, it may justly be said that in the formation of harsher racial attitudes the missionaries played a major role. The 1860s were a time of much despair in mission circles. Missionaries in Basutoland were profoundly discouraged as their whole work ground to a standstill by 1866. Indeed the failure to make much impact on the Bantu was general.[54] The results of Livingstone's second expedition, organised in 1858 under government auspices with the professed object of civilising Africans, were disappointing.[55] Missions made almost no progress for nearly thirty years in Nigeria after the expulsion from Abeokuta in 1867.[56] Mission work in Jamaica was also run down, and throughout the West Indies African religious forms revived, reaching a climax in the early 1860s.[57] In New Zealand missionaries were in despair about their loss of influence over the Maoris. In 1863 Bishop Selwyn felt he was watching over the remnant of a decaying people and faith. It was hard for missionaries to avoid a sense of resentment towards the peoples who had failed them. 'Christianity and Commerce' were seen to be opposites – who could believe any longer that commerce was a civilising influence, when the main trade was in gunpowder and alcohol? When Goldie the atheist formed his United African Company in 1879 the C.M.S. sold its shares.[58]

The writings of the missionaries were supported by the reports of the explorers such as Baker and Burton in the 1860s, whose books were also popular reading. Burton frequently compared Africans with animals. This could be seen, he thought, in their stubbornness and in the way in which 'when childhood is passed, the father and son become natural enemies, after the manner of wild beasts'. He gave credit where he could and pointed out that the intelligence of the East African interlacustrine peoples was 'striking when compared with that of an uneducated English peasant'. Nevertheless he declared unashamedly, even if in a footnote: 'I believe in the inferior genesis of the negro, and in his incapability of improvement, individually and *en masse*'. The removal of Africans from Africa was, he felt, like sending boys away to school: it was their only chance of improvement. Differing strongly from the theories of the 1830s, emigration he believed would be a major regenerator, and he advocated organising it. On the African brain his comment was short: 'a very little learning addles it'.[59] Sir Samuel Baker, reporting on Lake Albert and the Nile Basin, wrote in his journal in 1863:

> I wish the black sympathisers in England could see Africa's inmost heart as I do, much of their sympathy would subside. Human nature viewed in its crude state as pictured amongst African savages is quite on a level with that of the brute, and not to be compared with the noble character of the dog.

Equalising the unequal, he added, was 'a grand error' and a harmful one.[60]

The resultant mid-nineteenth-century 'image of Africa' was held with supreme confidence, but the most obvious characteristic of it was its total inability to penetrate to reality.[61]

In these ways and with such words the optimistic eighteenth-century and early Victorian beliefs about the equality and perfectibility of mankind were sharply reversed. The experience of politicians agreed with the experience of missionaries and explorers. The experience of all three seemed to be confirmed by Darwinian pseudo-science and crude anthropology.

Charles Kingsley decided by 1866 that he no longer believed in the equality of mankind. Although he revered Mill, he seemed to Kingsley to look on man too much as the creature of circumstances:

> This it is which makes him disparage, if not totally deny, the congenital differences of character in individuals, and still more in races. He has, if I mistake not, openly denounced the doctrine of difference and superiority in

race . . . [– an inescapable error] as long as human beings are asserted to be congenitally equal, and circumstances the only cause of subsequent inequality. I held that doctrine strongly myself in past years, and was cured of it, in spite of its seeming justice and charity, by the harsh school of facts. Nearly a quarter of a century spent in educating my parishioners, and experience with my own and others' children . . . have taught me that there are congenital differences and hereditary tendencies which defy all education from circumstances, whether for good or evil . . . I have seen also, that the differences of race are so great, that certain races, e.g. the Irish Celts, seem quite unfit for self-government, and almost for the self-administration of justice involved in trial by jury.

He was sure that no Roman Catholic country would ever be fit for constitutional government: 'anyone who knows the difference between a French lycée and an English public school ought to see what I mean'. [62]

Dilke also diverged from Mill's view, so that Mill took him to task for the views expressed in Greater Britain, since Dilke seemed sometimes to say that there were no sources of national character except race and climate, whereas Mill believed education, legislation and social circumstances to be of prodigiously greater efficacy than both combined. [63]

It is extremely interesting to note that in the 1860s there were, parallel to changes in attitude towards non-Europeans, also changes of attitude in domestic affairs. First of all, there was a revision of attitudes to the Irish question. By 1868 Mill and Cairns had abandoned the idea that England formed either a norm or an ideal society, and admitted the validity of the Irish demand for a form of society radically different from that which England would impose. Suddenly Mill declared in favour of granting the Irish peasant demand for fixity of tenure, and he attacked Lowe in the House of Commons on 16 March 1868 for adhering to the immutability and universal relevance of the principles of political economy; no single economic rule would apply in all cases. This revision of approach was a most important landmark. [64] The world was increasingly realised not to be so simple a place as had once been believed. Then again, a hardening of attitudes may also be seen in harsher attitudes towards criminals. T. B. Macaulay had noted that in 1857, feelings of revenge for the Indian mutiny had silenced not only peace societies and the Aborigines Protection Society, but also societies for the reformation of criminals. [65] And in 1862 Cobden commented on 'a great reaction . . . among that which I call the ruling class, against what they are pleased to call humanitarianism'. He complained about the revival of boxing and prize-fighting, the calls for an increase in corporal punishment and the appeals to the 'devilish standard of mere intellectual superiority as a justification for the injustices inflicted on the African race'. [66] There was a vicious Floggings Act in 1863. The Prisons Act of 1865 and the Habitual Criminals Act of 1869 marked the overthrow of the sentimental or reformatory theory of punishment in favour of more coercion and restraint, because it seemed that the number of criminals had increased despite the construction of gaols on ideal principles.[67] Burton wrote – and it is a most significant passage –

The philanthropico-criminal movement that began with Howard, has at last reached, we are told, its limit of exaggeration, and the pendulum begins slowly to swing back. It is the same with the negro, and as travelling becomes more common, and the world knows more about him, he will lose *prestige* every year.[68]

The same hardening of attitudes can be seen in education. It is from the 1860s that the educational ideal of 'godliness and good learning' of the Arnold tradition became superseded by the cult of games and manliness. Patriotic duty became a sentiment which the new system of education sought to inculcate, and organised games the centre of activity. This change in educational ideals, suggested Newsome, was so important and sweeping as to constitute a revolution.[69] It is hardly surprising that Charles Kingsley was 'undoubtedly the first man who united godliness and manliness' and, in Newsome's words, 'the prophet of this revolution in educational ideals'.* Toughening up of discipline and the glorification of physical prowess can be traced in the volunteer rifle clubs and cadet forces after the war scare of 1859, together with the publication of Thomas Hughes's *Tom Brown's Schooldays* (1857), which exalts manliness in 12 key passages. 'Self-help' received its classic exposition in 1859 with Samuel Smiles's book; self-abuse its classic terrifying condemnation in William Acton's *The Functions and Disorders of the Reproductive Organs,* published in 1857. The year 1857 was indeed a year to remember. Symbolic too was the building of the first gymnasium at an English public school (Uppingham) in 1859, and the composition of the Eton Boating Song in 1863.

Thus, if the 1860s saw a hardening of attitudes towards criminals and children, a general growth of more authoritarian attitudes, a fresh recognition of the differences and inequalities between men, and of the inapplicability of the universal principles of political economy, it is hardly surprising that they also saw a hardening of attitudes towards non-Europeans, an insistence on the inferiority of certain races, and the discrediting of the attempt to apply universally the policy of Anglicising non-Europeans.** The tide against Mill

* As a Cambridge undergraduate (1838–42) Kingsley had learned boxing from a negro prize-fighter, but later in life preferred to play leap-frog with Wellington schoolboys and talk with Sandhurst cadets.
** The difference in racial attitude can also been seen by comparing R. M. Ballantyne's *Coral Island* (1857) with his *Gorilla Hunters* (1863). See *Times Literary Supplement* 13 April 1967, 310 and correspondence on 26 April 67.

was rising slowly. In *Liberty Equality and Fraternity* (1874) James Fitzjames Stephen said the great defect of Mill's later writings seemed to be that 'he has formed too favourable an estimate of human nature ... a tacit assumption that the removal of restraints tends to invigorate character. Surely the very opposite of this is the truth'. Human beings were not equal, nor was there in history any continual progress towards the removal of distinctions between man and man. Bagehot in *Physics and Politics* summed up the way in which the new attitude differed from that held in the eighteenth century:

> A modern savage is anything but the simple being which philosophers of the eighteenth century imagined him to be: on the contrary, his life is twisted into a thousand curious habits; his reason is darkened by a thousand strange prejudices, his feelings are frightened by a thousand cruel superstitions. The whole mind of a modern savage is, so to say, tattooed over with monstrous images; there is not a smooth place anywhere about it.

It is almost incredible, but highly symptomatic, that so perceptive an analyser of the English constitution could write such rubbish about human beings.[70]

Politically the overall result was an increased disposition to take territorial control where it did not exist (as in Africa), and to tighten it where it did (as in the West Indies) by maintaining or reverting to Crown Colony government. It was in these unpropitious circumstances that the Irish question flared into crisis.

THE IRISH PROTEST

The Irish question was not seen as a religious one, neither as an agrarian one, although the fact that a Protestant landowning ascendancy ruled over a Catholic peasantry gave it a peculiarly acrimonious character. Whitehall's view of the problem of Ireland was at bottom and traditionally an unashamedly strategic one. Ireland had to be prevented from falling into the hands of an enemy, and the loyalist Protestant community was deliberately planted to guard against its internal subversion. The essential difference between Catholic and Protestant was one between native dispossessed and alien possessor. The Act of Union (1800) was passed during the French wars in order to strengthen Ireland's position within the United Kingdom. It was therefore in the nineteenth century an integral part of the United Kingdom, sending M.P.s to Westminster. Its position was, however, deeply ambivalent, and in some ways a halfway-house between the metropolis and the empire. But the national movement was grounded on the fact that, with the exception of the north-east, Ireland was not a country of colonial settlement, but one of the ancient historic nations of Europe.[71] The ambivalence of its position is indicated by the fact that its greatest leader was a Protestant landowner educated in England.

The leader of the Irish Parliamentary Party 1880 to 1890 was Charles Stewart Parnell. Not much of a political thinker, his genius was to have held the conflicting requirements of Fenians, land radicals, constitutionalists and liberals in temporary suspension. This organisational *tour-de-force* rested on a tightly constructed party discipline, the first of its kind, and prototype of the modern political party. In the House of Commons it made a thorough nuisance of itself in order to compel attention to be given to its demands for a freer Ireland.[72]

Gladstone described Parnell as the most remarkable man he ever met.[73] Such leaders could not be ignored. By the mid-1880s the Irish protest had to be met. It was not an easy challenge for the English establishment to face, and it had been coming to a head for a long time.

The disastrous famine of 1845–46 was a fundamentally and permanently disturbing experience, not least for the English, and in Ireland it imparted a new intensity to a long-standing deep-rooted hatred of the English connection. There was emigration in bitterness. Between 1841 and 1925, $4\frac{3}{4}$ million Irish emigrated to the United States, 670,000 to Canada and over 370,000 to Australia. Disease and massive emigration reduced the population by about two million inside a decade after the famine.[74] A disaster of this magnitude was something the English rulers could perhaps cope with only by trying to forget about it. For some individuals, however, their witness of Irish misery was something which made them alive to suffering in other parts of the world. As a soldier in Ireland in 1830 Sir George Grey, for example, vowed to do something for the empire's helpless poor and prevent the monopoly of land in new countries, seeing the necessity for change and reform.[75] Sir John Pope Hennessy's enthusiastic belief in equal rights for all men (as seen in his sense of shock at the way the Chinese were treated in Hong Kong) owed much to his early sympathy with the Roman Catholics of western Ireland.[76] Irish suffering particularly influenced Liberal policy. 'Through the difficulties of Ireland', said Sir Edward Grey, 'we have learnt more sympathy and caution on being on our guard against oppression than we should have learnt but for that experience'.[77]

The inability of English politicians in the period 1815 to 1914 to solve the Irish question had many causes. Prominent among them was Protestant revulsion against the Roman Church. Peel in 1837 remarked significantly that the English had conspicuously failed to establish a working relationship with the Roman Catholic Church in Ireland.[78] Relations in fact deteriorated steadily in proportion as the Church of Rome tightened its grip. In 1850 there were 5,000 priests, monks and nuns for a population of five million Roman Catholics. By 1900 the number had risen to 14,000 for a population diminished to 3.3 million.[79] Such was the background to the cry that Home Rule would mean Rome Rule, for to the belief of Winston Churchill's nurse that the Pope was behind the Fenians. The reassertion of papal authority made by the Vatican round about 1870 antagonised the English and created an unpropitious atmosphere for meeting Irish demands.[80] There was a widespread and passionately felt belief in England that the roots of her greatness were indissolubly connected with the Reformation. The Reformation was an event which 'liberated humanitarian and altruistic feelings', it was believed to have vitally influenced the development of commercial and industrial expansion, it was venerated for having 'deepened, strengthened and softened the character of the people'.[81]

There was extraordinary complacency about Irish affairs in Britain from the early 1850s to the mid-1860s; only Palmerston seemed alive to the dangers. Sheer ignorance of Ireland was a potent reason for not solving its problems. Those who had actually *seen* the condition of the Irish peasantry never forgot it: it forced a compassionate revision of prejudices. There were innumerable royal commissions and committees of enquiry. But the lack of personal knowledge and the unwillingness of politicians to visit Ireland was an important cause of the English failure to come to grips with its problems. Gladstone visited it only once, Disraeli never – a plain neglect of duty, since packet boats were cheap and comfortable by 1840. English ignorance did not grasp the underlying affinity between the Irish and the European mind, and so attributed to Irish perversity what was at least in part common to a European conception of the supremacy of abstract ideals.[82]

Another difficulty was the fact that many English landowners had estates in Ireland. Fear that concessions to Irish tenants would lead to a general attack on landownership in England was a decisive reason why the English territorial aristocracy threw its influence into the scale against the Irish parliamentary party. Irish leaders were suspected of being in league with English socialist and progressive forces: 'the teaching of the Irish agitators', declared Lord Derby, 'is open, undisguised socialism'.[83] Landlord fears mutilated Gladstone's Land Act (1870) even before it left the cabinet.[84] Gladstone's Irish land legislation was strongly disapproved of by that normally sensible historian W. E. H. Lecky, who gave currency to the view that the 1881 Land Act was an attack on the principle of property rights more radical than anything done in the French Revolution or Terror. The Act of 1881 appeared to him to be 'one of the most questionable, and indeed extreme, violations of the rights of property in the whole history of English legislation'.[85]

If Ireland infuriated the Unionists, it also irritated the Liberals. The insolent rejection of the British way of life right on the doorstep of the temple of God on earth, the Jerusalem of England's green and pleasant land, was, to say the least, ironic. It was difficult to admit error so near to home. In India, Bryce noted in 1889, 'not a dog wags his tail against us among these 260 millions of people', yet Britain could not govern a mere four million Irishmen even with the aid of 'the loyal garrison of one million'.[86] The English found the character of the Irish maddening. 'Paddy' was regarded as childish, emotional, ignorant, unstable, indolent, superstitious, lying, dirty, vengeful and so forth.* On becoming chief secretary for Ireland in 1903 Wyndham called it 'a backwater spawned over by obscene reptiles . . . [and] anaemic children'.[87] Sir Matthew Nathan (as permanent under-secretary at Dublin Castle) received letters from Augustine Birrell which frequently called the Irish 'pigs', and from chief secretary Walter Long comparing them with children. Strong, unflinching government was what they needed, wrote Long in 1914: 'It is not because they really want to do mischief', he added, but, just like 'naughty children, they think it is amusing to give way to their inclinations'.[88] Victorians explained the rise of empire not only in terms of God's will, the Protestant ethic of sober hard work, and good luck. They also saw it in terms of superior racial character. Opponents of Home Rule argued that for reasons of character the Irish could not be trusted with self-government. The crude and inflexible stereotype of Irish Celtic character was fatal to the cause of Home Rule. The debates turned on the question of whether the Irish could be trusted with the lives, properties and liberties of their English enemies. Salisbury said revealingly: 'you would not confide free representative institutions to the Hottentots for instance', a remark heavy with implication. Froude, who had spent more time in Ireland than any Englishman of his day, found the Irish 'unstable as water'. Lecky did not subscribe to purely racial explanations of human behaviour, but was thoroughly certain that the Irish were unfit for self-government: Home Rule would be 'the most perfect of all earthly realisations of Pandemonium'. A couple of other historians, Green and Froude, favoured Home Rule, but only because it would 'shut the Paddies out from Westminster'. Balfour's private view was that the Irish had all the qualities required to destroy free institutions. He noted their lack of *'driving* capacity', conceded that they were clever, but dismissed them as 'voluble, ineffective – not trustworthy in business'. The mythology of a 'masculine' Anglo-Saxon racial superiority was at its peak from the 1860s to the 1890s, just when it could do most damage to an Irish movement emanating from a 'feminine' Celtic race.[89] Parnell attracted particular exasperation among the English partly because he did not fit the stereotype. He was a lapsed Protestant landowner with very little 'Irish' blood. He was also regarded as a renegade from the Anglo-Saxon value system: despite his American mother, his Protestant upbringing and his Cambridge education, he had decided to lead the Irish struggle. English in manners and speech, he loathed England (his experiences at Magdalene College, Cambridge almost certainly contributed to this)[90] but was socially conservative beneath his wild words and knew little of Irish literature.[91] The execration in which his name was held by the English establishment was such that Winston Churchill did himself irretrievable harm even as late as 1906 by

---

* The stereotype may have been unduly influenced by the Liverpool Irish, who were not perhaps Ireland's best ambassadors. It was said that they stopped in Liverpool because they were too drunk to get on to the emigrant ships.

comparing Milner with Parnell,[92] and Parnell's old College, Magdalene, gave him no official commemoration until 1961, when a small copied portrait was hung on a dark landing.*

By reaction, many English politicians from 1886 found it all the harder to abandon the 'loyalists' of Ulster. In an ever-darkening world situation, people loyal to the British flag were becoming thinner on the ground. But against this consideration had to be weighed the damage done to Anglo-American relations. The existence of the Irish question made it almost impossible to achieve the warm understanding so much desired with the Americans.[93] Moreover, prime minister Asquith had concluded by 1913 that Ulster would have to be sacrificed, since an ungovernable Ireland was a much more alarming prospect than rioting in four counties, serious and undesirable as that was.[94] But the Unionists took their stand on 'Ulster will fight, and Ulster will be right'.

In 1869 Kimberley wrote: 'England must for her own safety hold Ireland, come what may'.[95] Certainly one of the major arguments against granting Home Rule to Ireland was that strategic dangers were involved. It was said that an independent Ireland might be hostile in wartime, offering an enemy numerous potential harbours from which vital trade routes might be menaced; furthermore, it supplied recruits for the army out of all proportion to the size of its population; and Britain was absolutely dependent upon its horses for the cavalry regiments. Strategically, said Chamberlain, Britain dare not establish within thirty miles 'a new foreign country animated from the outset with unfriendly intentions towards us'. After a time, he predicted, Ireland would have to be reconquered or England would be ruined.[96]

Nearly all the British politicians before Gladstone, and half of them right down to 1921, dealt with the Irish national movement by denying its validity and authenticity. The conservatives looked at the preceding centuries of conquest and inter-marriage and scoffed at the idea of a pure and undefiled Irish nation. Its racial integrity was dismissed as a myth; the highest culture that the Irish had ever known (they said) was imported from England. Balfour wrote in 1891:

> The Home Rule agitation, properly understood, is a very hollow affair consisting chiefly ... of two elements in conjunction, neither of which separately have anything to do with Home Rule whatever – the old Fenian element, namely, which desires separation, and the agrarian element which desires or did desire spoliation.[97]

---

* In 1910 a Fellow of Magdalene, A. C. Benson, presented a very modest brass plate to place in Parnell's old rooms. It was only $9\frac{1}{4}$-inch by $1\frac{1}{2}$-inch in size and simply bore the inscription 'Charles Stewart Parnell 1865'. There was no objection to a similar plaque for Charles Kingsley, but the Parnell one provoked an undergraduate rebellion. Benson sadly removed it, recording his hope that one day it might be replaced. This was done (without repercussions) in 1967.

His theory was: dissolve the ties that bound the agrarian and the political agitations together by a scheme of land purchase in favour of the tenant peasants and the nationalist movement would collapse. Yet Wyndham as Unionist Irish Secretary in 1903, by an important Land Act, significantly eased, virtually solved, the agrarian problem – while the nationalist agitation continued to increase.[98]

Goschen (Unionist chancellor of the exchequer 1886–92) once described the Home Rule movement as a 'bastard nationalism'.[99] Salisbury believed it was based on a 'wholesale system of fraudulent bankruptcy', its primary objective being to banish landlords without compensation. Anti-Home Rulers continued to regard the Irish national movement as 'a fraud inspired by a combination of agrarian unrest, religious bigotry and socialism'.[100] The fraudulent nature of Irish demands was to Unionists not simply a matter of political opinion, but in effect an almost irreducible article of a fundamentalist political faith, a rigid dogma virtually written into the constitution of the Unionist Party.[101] Gladstone was altogether more perceptive: saying in 1893 that Grattan's parliament (before 1800) 'had a true and genuine sentiment of nationality', and the 'loss of the spirit of nationality is the heaviest and most deplorable and the most degrading loss that any country can undergo'. The main object of the Irish legislative union of 1800 he saw as having been 'to depress and weaken, and, if possible, to extinguish the spirit of Irish nationality'.[102] He was much more courageous and far-sighted than the Conservatives in his interpretation of the problem. He complained that his opponents were treating the external symptoms and never searching out the causes of the malady.[103]

It would be a mistake, however, to assess Gladstone's Home Rule proposals on the basis of his late rhetoric on the subject. It was the great merit of Gladstone that, like Peel, he tried to do something constructive about Ireland – but this is not to say that he had some miraculous insight into the problem. In fact his initial approach to Home Rule was made more from considerations of economy than from a desire to redress historic injustices. After the rectification of relations between landlord and tenant in Ireland, in 1882 Gladstone wrote of the next great problem's being one of relieving Britain 'from the enormous weight of the Government of Ireland unaided by the people'. Local institutions of self-government would provide the 'liberty alone which fits men for liberty'. This proposition, he admitted, like every other in politics, had its bounds, but it was far safer than the counter-doctrine, wait till they are fit.[104] And it would bring relief to England. Gladstone and his followers were negatively pushed towards some plan of Home Rule because of what they conceived to be the impossibility of the Liberals carrying out the measures which would be necessary if Home Rule were not granted to Ireland: there must follow inevitably a large-scale extension of British governmental activity in Ireland, politically in the shape of coercion, economically in the form of land purchase and schemes of economic aid.

Although he mentioned the economical considerations in passing, on the whole this was an aspect which Gladstone suppressed in his speeches introducing Home Rule to parliament.[105] On the first reading of the Government of Ireland Bill on 8 April 1886, Gladstone explained how Home Rule would restore the dignity of parliament, smooth the passage of legislation by removing from Westminster the obstruction of Irish M.P.s, and 'stay the waste of Treasure' involved in the existing system of government. They should apply the experience of the relations of England and Scotland, which taught that the best and surest foundations were 'afforded by the affections, the convictions and the will of the nation'. Gladstone urged a firm and fearless practice of what they had so often preached:

> the doctrine which we have so often inculcated upon others – namely that the concession of local self-government is not the way to sap or impair, but the way to strengthen and consolidate unity. I ask that we should learn to rely less upon merely written stipulations and more upon those better stipulations which are written on the heart and mind of man.[106]

On the occasion of the second reading, Gladstone said that as had been the case in Canada, Ireland was a danger to the unity of the empire. The mass of the Canadian people had, he recalled, habitually been denounced in the House as rebels. Yet the 'great lesson of history' was that self-government had strengthened their allegiance. He quoted approvingly the words of Sir Charles Duffy: 'Canada did not get Home Rule because she was loyal and friendly, but she has become loyal and friendly because she has got Home Rule'.[107] There was no danger in self-government because it called forth the best in those who received it.

The importance of finding suitable collaborators underlay much of the agony of trying to decide whether or not Ireland should have Home Rule. Gladstone at first thought he had found collaborators in the moderate and reasonably well-to-do supporters of Parnell. He wrote to Forster in October 1881:

> Our ... contention always is that a more intelligent and less impassioned body has gradually come to exist in Ireland. It is on this body, its precepts and examples, that our hopes depend, for if we are at war with a nation, we cannot win. If such a body exist, I would call upon it in places, even in single parishes, where it is strong ...[108]

But there were men who disagreed with Gladstone's analysis, and who disbelieved in the possibility of co-operation with Parnell. It was through the Irish question that Chamberlain began to evolve an entirely different concept of who the co-operators were. They did not exist, but they could be created. The people at large might be made into the collaborative element by constructive measures of reform; by interesting the Irish people, their press and their leaders in local affairs, their attention would be diverted from the conflict with England. In Chamberlain's view, 'whatever the leaders may do or say, the people might be brought round to take a kindly view of the British connection, if their natural ambition for local work and local legislation were fully responded to'. Chamberlain envisaged a system of county government and a central board with independent powers of taxation, to deal with 'local national questions', for example, education, public works, lunatic asylums.[109]

It is impossible to say whether Gladstone was right in his predictions, or whether Chamberlain was right in his hopes. In the event the Liberal party split on Home Rule in 1886, and Chamberlain joined the Whigs who moved over to the Conservative side. The first Home Rule bill was defeated in 1886. Parnell's career was ruined when his love life became public knowledge, and Gladstone repudiated him. Parnell died in 1891.[110] A second Liberal Home Rule bill was passed by the House of Commons, only to be overwhelmingly rejected by the Lords in 1894. Home Rule thereafter was shelved by the Liberals for some 15 years. Not to have done so would have prevented them from achieving any other worth-while objective. But by 1910 Ireland could no longer be ignored. A third Home Rule bill was introduced in April 1912 and reached the statute book, but when war broke out in 1914 its operation was suspended for the duration of hostilities.

THE GROWTH OF PESSIMISM

There had always been an aggressive aspect to British expansion, and there had always been pessimists. In the later nineteenth century these aspects became more prominent. Militarist methods began to pervade social life. This is the period of the Church Lads' Brigade, Lord Rodney's Cadets, Forbush's Knights of King Arthur, the Salvation Army (founded 1865, though not known as such until 1878 – with its journal *War Cry*), the Church Army (1882), the Boys' Brigade (1883). Wyndham in 1904 deplored the fact that Bismarck's message to mankind was 'shoot first', though it was Carlyle who first spoke of 'Might is Right'. Whereas Thomas Hughes had praised the fighting instinct in individuals, General Wolseley, commander-in-chief of the army, glorified war in 1897 as beneficial to nations. With all its horrors it exercised 'a healthy influence on all classes of society', and brought out some of the best qualities in man; the training involved in preparing for it was 'the greatest purifier to the race or nation that has reached the verge of over-refinement', 'an invigorating antidote against that luxury and effeminacy which destroys nations as well as individuals'.[111] War, wrote Professor Cramb of London University, was a means of self-fulfilment; the aim was not the destruction of life but its intensification, the pursuit of an ideal, and a testimony to man's 'limitless capacity for devotion to other ends than existence for existence' sake'.[112]

Uncertainty of outlook was on the increase. Kingsley wrote:

> Do not young men think, speak, act just now in a very incoherent, fragmentary way . . . with the various stereotyped systems which they have received by tradition, breaking up under them like ice in a thaw, with a thousand facts and notions . . . pouring in on them like a flood.[113]

Sir Robert Morier (British minister at Lisbon 1876, Madrid 1881, and ambassador to Russia 1885–93) believed in 1878 that Britain was decadent and decaying, drifting about 'like some huge ironclad, rudderless and with her engine fires out'.

The viceroy of India, Lytton, noted bitterly in 1878 that Britain was 'fast losing the instinct and tact of Empire'.[114] Meredith Townsend, a Liberal writing in 1888, already discerned this change, and traced it to the Irish experience:

> For whether for good or evil, a great change is passing over Englishmen. They have become uncertain of themselves, afraid of their old opinions, doubtful of the true teaching of their consciences. They doubt if they have any longer any moral right to rule anyone, themselves almost included.[115]

Late nineteenth-century pessimistic attitudes were deeply influenced by two political crises: the occupation of Egypt in 1882 and the Home Rule crisis of 1886. In Egypt in 1882 the inadequacy of the classical system of informal control from outside, by bluff, gunboats and collaborating élites, was demonstrated on the banks of the Nile, and the acute disillusionment which this produced was reflected in a cabinet memorandum by Harcourt in 1884. Its argument was as follows. The theory on which they originally undertook the management of Egypt was that after the overthrow of Urabi they should be able to set Egypt on its own feet within a comparatively short period, and, having constructed an adequate 'native' government, leave the country to administer itself. This theory, however plausible it may have been, completely broke down. And, what was worst of all, it was discovered that Egypt did not contain the elements out of which civil government or military organisation could be constructed.[116] Here, and the pattern was shortly to be repeated again in Ireland, the dual elements in the classical liberal theory of the mid-Victorians had fallen apart: 'good government and self government, law and liberty, imperial interests and local aspirations, seemed to have become contradictory'.[117]

The Irish 'Home Rule' split in the Liberal party of 1886 was the chief event in late nineteenth-century party politics, and excited passionate debate. In 1886 Goschen went right to the heart of this debate when he said that no sign was 'more dangerous in this Irish controversy than the effect which surrender and defeat in Ireland will have upon our position in the world', moral, material, political and imperial; the task was to defend 'the bonds which hold together the structure of our social fabric'.[118] Gladstonian policy threatened, as it seemed to those who opposed it (who were the bulk of the Victorian intelligentsia), to disrupt the unity of the empire and promote social revolution at home. Stephen thought Gladstone 'the mouthpiece of blind and furious passions'; he was 'positively revolutionary ... on the high road towards a destruction of nearly everything which I ... chiefly like and value in English life and society'.[119] Those intellectuals who left the Liberal party in the Home Rule split – Maine, Stephen, Sidgwick, Seeley, A. V. Dicey, St Loe Strachey, Cromer and Lyall – were principally concerned, says Stokes, to defend the reign of intelligence against the destructive onslaught of blind mass-emotion. They believed in the iron laws of social progress, to flout which in the name of sentimental ideals appeared to threaten the whole edifice of civilised life; Gladstone's decision was 'a fearful portent since it meant the abject surrender of scientific government to the forces of unreason', and they were against any premature abdication of authority.[120]

The Liberal policy of Home Rule, said H. M. Butler, Master of Trinity, in 1887, might well in a few years lead to 'the relinquishment of Gibraltar, the abandonment of India, the repudiation of the Colonies, and the resignation of our duties as a great fighting power in Europe'.[121] Time and time again Gladstone's bill was denounced as a scheme for the disintegration of the empire. A typical contention was: once start the dangerous principle of disruption, once foster destructive centrifugal forces, and no-one could say where the end might be. Goschen believed that without firmness towards the Irish evil-doers 'the result would be that every subject race, that India, that Europe would know that we were no longer able to cope with resistance'.[122] 'One by one', said Salisbury, 'the flowers will be plucked from the diadem of empire'. Henceforth Gladstone was to him an alarming political force – a man of authority who had lost all sense of responsibility.[123] Chamberlain and his followers objected to Home Rule because they feared a war in which Ireland would be supported by America and France, and more particularly because they believed that the future lay with great empires.[124] As Balfour said in 1893 during his attack on the second Home Rule bill, 'it has been by the concentration and not the dissipation of power that empires have been built up'.[125] Gladstone had dared to open up the sacred issues which Tories could not tamper with: the supremacy of the imperial parliament, the maintenance of imperial rule, the rights of loyal British citizens. In a struggle between the forces of law and decency and those of organised robbery and rebellion, argued Balfour, 'to allow the latter to win is simply to give up civilisation'.[126]

Lord Derby declared in 1891:

I do not recognise in the literature or hear in the talk of the present day that tone of confident optimism which distinguished the years ... between 1840 and 1850. Everybody then seemed so very sure that, given a few changes which would come about almost of themselves, the world was going to be a different place; wars were to cease, for democracy was to triumph ... Education would make everybody wise ... I do not think we are so sanguine now. Experience has done its work; we have learnt that ... neither voting powers nor schools have sufficed to make the world an earthly paradise.[127]

As a result, there was increasing scepticism about ability to influence events or even to retain the empire. Kipling's *Recessional* (1897) was written in the spirit that 'the big smash is coming one of these days'.[128] The United States was urged to take up the thankless 'White Man's Burden' because Britain no longer felt strong enough to bear it alone.[129] Curzon would not have 'Onward Christian Soldiers' sung at the Durbar of 1903 because it contained the lines 'Crowns and Thrones may perish, Kingdoms rise and wane'. Such heightened sensitivity is plainly indicative of a deep underlying nervousness. Cromer in 1907 felt the empire to be running a real risk of crashing on the rocks before long – not just yet, maybe, but they were 'already amongst the breakers'.[130] The *Observer* editor, J. L. Garvin, recognised it to be no foregone conclusion in 1905 that the empire would survive another hundred years.[131] Colonial office officials certainly did not think it possible.[132] Out in the field, Charles Brooke in 1907 correctly predicted severe reverses in all colonial empires by mid-century and the certain loss of India. The reason? – Britain had neglected good relations with those she ruled.[133]

How did these pessimistic and defensive attitudes come into being? One cause was the growing strength, actual or supposed, of non-European races and anti-European movements, allied with a realisation that the lesser breeds without the Law did not love the Englishman. Post-Darwinian fears supposed that the white race might be swamped out of existence by non-whites. Graham Wallas referred to this racial fear in his well-known book on *Human Nature in Politics* (1908) – the grim conception of internecine racial conflict 'hung for a generation after 1859 over the study of world politics as the fear of a cooling sun hung over physics'.[134] In the tropics Africans seemed capable of living safely, while Europeans died in even greater proportions than the indigenous inhabitants of America. Some terrifying implications could be drawn from this. Following the theory of the 'survival of the fittest', was it not possible that Europeans might in time be superseded by a superior race of negroes? Some European writers, among them the essayist W. R. Greg, accepted this as the natural course of history. Others pointed to the expulsion of the French from Haiti by negroes, deducing that they might soon expel other Europeans from the whole of the West Indies and Brazil.[135] This kind of fear culminated in the dread of the 'Yellow Peril' in the early twentieth century; fear of Chinese expansion was much talked of between 1905 and 1917.

Morley regarded as familiar enough to anyone who had speculated on such matters the idea that 'civilisation is in real danger, near, sinister and terrible from the uprising of Asiatic power, yellow, brown, and black against all the forces of the West'.[136]

The historian A. F. Pollard noted in 1912 that the 'slumbering East' had awakened. To him the victory of Japan over Russia was an event beside which the Anglo-Boer war sank into insignificance. The empire seemed likely to be civilising itself out of existence 'in competition with races bred with primitive vigour'. Asian peoples 'relieved by the *Pax Britannica* from mutual destruction, are eating [sic] the whites out of the islands of the Pacific and Indian Oceans, and threatening South Africa, Australia, and the western shores of America'. Their myriad peoples, armed with Western morality and guns, might not always be content to refrain from turning against Europe the means of expansion which Europe had used so successfully against them.[137]

The defeat of Russia by Japan in 1905 impressed others besides Pollard. It was so completely unexpected partly because the power of Russia had been over-estimated. The *Times* grudgingly recognised Japanese moral force, but it made Britain feel 'jealous, uncomfortable, almost annoyed'. Beatrice Webb wrote an impressive passage in her diary about this important event, which she diagnosed not only as a shock to British self-esteem but also as productive of a national shamefacedness.[138] In 1916 Lord Cromer wrote that the West still had scarcely even yet recovered from the 'profound astonishment' at the emergence of Japan as a highly civilised and very powerful nation.[139] Great Britain concluded an alliance with Japan in 1902. This in fact played an important part in the actual decline of British power in the Far East. As a consequence of the treaty five British battleships were withdrawn from China in 1905 as part of a concentration of naval strength in home waters. Japan and the United States were drawn into the vacuum. The British position in the Far East was correspondingly weakened; patently the British empire had begun to decline.[140] Europeans were by the end of the nineteenth century on the defensive. 'We have to recognise the fact', colonial secretary Elgin declared in 1906, 'that all over the world there are difficulties arising on the part of white communities'.[141] One of the most remarkable facts about the treatment of the 'native' problem in the early twentieth century is that it was consistently discussed within the context of apprehended risings against Europeans. The preoccupation with keeping peace among Africans and in India, and thus bringing security to European settlers, is unmistakable. At the root of anxiety about white settlement, missionary enterprise and economic development in Africa – in short, about any constructive action – was the fear of provoking violent reactions. The Indian Mutiny and the Taiping Rebellion had not been forgotten, and in Africa there was a continuing history of uprising and disturbance. The Ndebele and Shona rose up in 1896. There were disturbances and revolts in Uganda 1896–1900; Sierra Leone experienced a hut-tax rebellion in 1898; in Somaliland, the so-called 'Mad Mullah' was most troublesome between 1899 and 1904 and again between

1908 and 1920. There was a rising at Sokoto in Nigeria in 1906, disturbances in Natal in the same year. Concurrently there was the Maji-Maji revolt in German East Africa July 1905 to January 1907 and Herero rising in German South-West Africa 1903–07. Some of these uprisings were of quite a formidable character and not easy to put down. Isandhlawana (1879) and Aduwa (1896) were major Zulu and Ethiopian victories. The colonial office expected there would be many more uprisings, however beneficent British rule.[142]

In the early twentieth century there was also extreme pessimism about trouble brewing in India. Sir Edward Grey apparently had an overwhelming sense of an impending storm there.[143] Fitzmaurice wrote to Ripon in 1908: 'We are getting very serious about India in the Cabinet. It seems to me that we may be in face of very great events in the not distant future'.[144] Thus, defensive attitudes were a rational response to the strengthening and increased recalcitrance of non-Europeans, as well as slightly irrational fears of a general racial *bouleversement*.

A second reason for the characteristic late nineteenth-century attitudes was the belief that the future great powers would be those with the largest extent of territory.[145] The frantic attempt to control land rested on a particular diagnosis about the basis on which power was in the future to rest. The famous historian J. R. Green was already in 1880 diagnosing a new perspective of world history. He was wearying, he said, of leaders born seventy years ago,

> longing for younger men who will realise the world of *fifty years to come* and let Europe alone sink into its coming littleness! In that greater world, how odd, how ludicrous will be the spectacle of a Germany and a France, each passed by in the race of nations, and still growling and snarling over their little Alsace! To me all these Bismarcks, and Dizzys and Andrassys are like anachronisms, men living in a world which is passing away and whose mighty schemes and mightier armies are being quietly shoved aside by the herdsmen of Colorado or the sheep-masters of New South Wales ... I gather courage at the sight of another world that is passing away and I look across the Atlantic and the Pacific to a new world and a better.[146]

That America was destined to become in the twentieth century the greatest and most prosperous country in the world had been widely foreseen. Cobden in 1835 expected it. The *Economist* in 1851 regarded it as certain as the next eclipse. Kingsley predicted it in 1866, Froude in 1878, Gladstone in 1878, Lord Derby in 1880. That America might divide world hegemony with Russia appears to have been foreseen first by André Grimm in the eighteenth century. Tocqueville and von Ranke agreed. So did Russell in 1869 and Sir Robert Morier in 1873.[147] And Seeley in 1883 considered that in 50 years the United States and Russia would have depressed France and Germany into second-class states – and Britain too if she did not quickly transform herself into an imperial federation.[148] A few particularly perspicacious persons, taking a somewhat longer view, saw that China, as another great land-based empire, would be one of the three Great Powers. Most of these predictors were Americans, but Wolseley in 1903 recognised the possibility. He was indeed, all unknowing, the prophet of Mao Tse-tung, since he wrote: 'They only want a Chinese Peter the Great or Napoleon to make them so'. The Battle of Armageddon, he added, could well be fought between the United States and China.[149]

The conceptions of the time divided the world into living and dying empires; with their classical education inculcating analogies with the fate of the Roman empire, the British became worried lest they should become one of the dying empires. To Chamberlain this was the critical question, and he summed up his belief about the world of the future with the words: 'The days are for great Empires and not for little states'. But as Seeley pointed out, if you discounted India, Britain was a nation rather than an empire.[150] The problem, therefore, of perpetuating British world power into the twentieth century, where it might co-exist equally with the great land-based powers, seemed to depend on making it more of an integrated empire.

The third fear was of commercial competition threatening the British position as 'workshop of the world'. British apprehensions were of slow growth. The *Annual Register* in 1866 and 1867 sounded a warning note: the British might lose their position 'through the neglect of ordinary precautions'. It was a favourite argument with those who considered no precautions to be necessary, that Britain showed no sign of decay at present:

> To this argument there are two answers; the first, that when the signs become clearly visible, the catastrophe will perhaps have ceased to be avertible; the other, that there may be signs already, though not precisely the same that have appeared before the decadence of other great empires.

Britain, the *Annual Register* continued, owed her influence to her commanding position in industry and commerce; 'if she forgets this, she is lost . . . to the extent of having to give up the lead, and ceasing to be a first-rate power'.[151] A further warning came from that sadly under-rated and neglected politician, the fifteenth earl of Derby, in 1874: though nothing indicated that British industrial supremacy was seriously threatened as yet, they still had no right to expect that the laws suggesting commercial and industrial supremacy passed from one country to another, 'which have hitherto seemed to regulate the course of human society, will be suspended in our favour'.[152] And then Gladstone in 1878 wrote:

> We may hold all the ground we have (or its equivalent) and more than all, and yet America may be the primate nation in trade. That is what I think likely.[153]

The illusion of the inevitability of economic progress was shattered by the so-called 'Great Depression'. Cromer was not satisfied that British employers and workers were thoroughly alive to the new position created for British trade by foreign competition, since loss of trade spelled the 'suicide of that Empire which is the offspring of trade, and which can only continue to exist so long as its parent continues to thrive and flourish'.[154] Lord George Hamilton, secretary of state for India, wrote to his viceroy, Curzon, in 1902:

> Our supremacy in many branches of life and work, which in the past was uncontested, is now going, and it will require men of exceptional capacity resolution and tenacity to bridge over the time in which we shall pass from the old position we occupied in the 19th century to that which . . . the British Empire ought to occupy in the 20th and succeeding centuries.[155]

ECONOMIC RETARDATION

Upon what specific facts and observations did the waning confidence in British economic expansion rest?

The obvious causes of the worsening position of British world trade were foreign protective tariffs and superior competitive power. Salisbury publicly admitted that outlets for the commercial energies of Britain were being gradually closed 'by the enormous growth which the doctrines of protection are obtaining'. They were growing stronger and stronger, animating her three main rivals, France, Germany and America, and they operated to the exclusion of British commerce wherever their power extended. Thus Salisbury was ready in Uganda and other 'new' countries to do something to 'make smooth the paths for British commerce, British enterprise and the application of British capital'.[156] Russia instituted tariffs in 1877, France in 1878, Germany in coal and textiles in 1879 and agriculture in 1885. Curzon described the commercial competition of the 1890s as a hurricane furiously raging throughout the world. In such a situation he considered the loss of a market to be an irreversibly retrograde step and the gain of one a positive addition to national strength.[157]

Chamberlain wanted the information which would enable British manufacturers to take colonial trade from their foreign competitors. For two years an official gathered statistics, and in August 1897 the colonial office issued a 600-page blue book based on his inquiry. It certainly showed that foreigners were getting access to colonial markets by underselling their British counterparts and adapting selling techniques and products to local situations.[158]

In 1870, Britain had 31.8 per cent of the world's manufacturing capacity; in 1906–10, 14.7 per cent. Meanwhile the German share had increased from 13.2 per cent to 15.9 per cent, and the United States from 23.3 per cent to 35.3 per cent. Britain's share of world trade declined from 23 per cent in 1876 to 19 per cent in 1885.[159]

In the early 1870s Britain was making four times as much iron and twice as much steel as the Zollverein. In 1910/14 by contrast, Germany averaged almost twice as much iron, and more than twice as much steel. The points of passing were 1893 for steel and 1903 for pig iron. By 1910 Germany was exporting more iron and steel than Britain, hitherto the world's leading supplier for more than a century. Even more disagreeable, German steel was being sold in Britain itself. Thus Britain lost 'metallurgical hegemony' in the 1890s.[160] Britain had been passed in steel production by the United States by 1890, and by 1900 American production was more than double the British. Upon the outbreak of war in 1914 the British government found to its alarm that all the magnetos in use in Britain came from Stuttgart. And so did all the khaki dye for army uniforms. London's 'Underground' was built between 1900 and 1914 by American expertise, with plenty of American plant, and with more foreign than British investment. In 1914, a third of all motor cars in Britain were imported: most of them were American 'Fords'. J. Pierpont Morgan had gained control of all but two of the largest British transatlantic shipping lines by 1902. Americans owned or dominated 70 firms in Britain – the invasion began with Singer sewing machines in 1867. Britain had fallen badly behind in newer industries (chemical, electrical engineering, cheap motor cars), and so these could not offset the decline in older industries. These older industries (including cotton) were not accepting innovations or investing capital for re-equipping themselves on a large enough scale. Productivity in coalmining fell faster in Britain than elsewhere. Lancashire's investment in new mills between 1895 and 1914 was based on a largely traditional technology. Moreover, the whole tempo of industrial advance was slowing down. Rates of growth in industrial production which had been 4 per cent 1820–40 fell to 1.5 per cent 1875–94. Even when trade values recovered after 1895, the key ratios of productivity, the rate of capital accumulation and rate of growth of industrial production did not respond significantly. Output per man in industry fell from a growth rate of two per cent per annum to just under one per cent after 1870. Meanwhile the growth rates and productivity rates in Germany and America were two or three times faster than in Britain. The export values of the 1870s were not surpassed until the later 1890s. This period of foreign competition, loss of technological leadership and decline in the rate of economic growth, used to be referred to as the 'Great Depression'. But as a label covering the years from 1873 to 1896 it is losing favour, if only because worrying economic crises were not confined to this period. Even more serious was the long-term retardation of the economy which continued after the 'depression' was over.[161]

Economic historians disagree in their judgements both of how serious the economic decline was, and how it is to be explained.[162] Platt has argued that British withdrawal from Latin American markets outside Argentina was not symptomatic of world decline, and sees it not so much as a total defeat as a deliberate, rational transfer of effort away from marginal and difficult markets to the easier, higher quality markets of Britain and the empire, where long-term prospects were better. If British commerce in much of Latin America and in some sectors seemed uncompetitive, Platt argues, this was partly because Britain was not seriously trying to compete in those small, specialised and cheap-grade areas of commerce. Whether or not he is right about the re-routing of effort and trade, many historians share his doubts over the hypothesis of a general failure of entrepreneurial ability as an explanation of British declining performance. Although a conservative entrepreneurial mode of thinking cannot be wholly ruled out, the self-assessment of contemporaries was probably unduly harsh, and British performance looks a great deal better when the decade of recovery before 1914 is taken into account. Serious German competition was checked, while British exports and investments recovered, sometimes to record levels. This revived prosperity was precarious in the long run, however, since it was not grounded in any radically new marketing methods or technological innovations. Moreover, the British never properly recovered from the shock of facing severe competition in the 1880s at a time when home markets were themselves stagnant, and thus they continued to believe themselves threatened even when some of the force went out of German competition before 1914. The lack of home demand for iron and steel and the high cost of transport to overseas markets undoubtedly restricted the comparative performance of that sector of British production, since the United States and Germany by comparison had rapidly growing home markets. Another point to bear in mind is that there was a structural rigidity in many sectors, stemming from early industrialisation and a complex division of labour, and it was this, at least as much as any failing entrepreneurial ability, which inhibited innovation. Slow expansion maybe reinforced the tendency of the ablest products of the professional classes to seek careers outside industry – if there had been more money in the Morris family Nuffield would have become a surgeon not a car-maker. Overall there was a decided patchiness of performance. Electricity seems to have been handled more competently than the internal combustion engine. It can perhaps be misleading to compare isolated parts of British industry with the world's most successful exemplar in each case; and growing points should not be forgotten. The range and diversity of British markets were bound to present problems unknown to more regionally-concentrated foreign competitors. In shipbuilding Britain remained unchallenged. Charles Parsons did well in marine engineering. Alfred Jones had great success in building up Elder Dempster, capturing the West African carrying trade and bringing bananas to Britain. Some armaments firms retained an unsurpassed reputation. Light industry and food processing did well. These were decades of expansion for Beecham, Lever, Cadbury, Fry, Guinness, Bass, and Harmsworth. Lipton, Maypole and Boot pioneered mass retailing in an extremely successful way. The bicycle was a new and sophisticated product which did well. But few of these contributed significantly to exports. And whatever the absolute level of production, Britain was unquestionably falling into relative decline. Perhaps to contemporaries the most alarming sign was the increase of German and United States exports into the empire. Chamberlain noted in 1905 that in the previous three years these two competitors had increased their exports to Australia by £4.5 million, which was greater than the British increase. He commented: 'Our competitors are gaining upon us in that which makes national greatness. We may be richer, and yet weaker'.[163] This trend, as we have noted, was halted almost as Chamberlain was speaking. The conclusion of the whole matter probably is this: that (as Trebilcock puts it) 'if the economy was not in absolute terms depressed, it was certainly, in growth terms, decelerating'.

Several contemporaries felt that Britain's failure was at least as much educational as it was 'third generation entrepreneurial'. In the biological sciences in the 1890s Europeans, Americans, even the Japanese were feared to be shooting ahead. Germany made striking advances as a result of the close connection of her industrial and academic life. In 1870 she exported no beer at all. By the end of the century she exported almost as much as Britain. One of India's chief products – indigo – was also put in jeopardy by German chemistry. In 1886 Germany imported more than a thousand tons of natural indigo. Ten years later she imported none at all, but instead exported 256 tons of synthetically produced indigo. Even by 1902, 80 per cent of the colours used by the Bradford Dyers Association were produced in Germany.[164] For this reason, educational reform was bound to figure prominently among the various measures proposed to stabilise the general situation and counteract Britain's relatively declining world position.

4 The Search for Stability, 1880–1914

The relative decline in world influence and the new pessimism led to a realisation that many changes would have to be made by Britain. The late Victorians did not whine about their problems, but tried to find solutions. It is this courage which has obscured the depth of their underlying pessimism. Territorial acquisitions received more publicity than hitherto, and it was this which created a misleading appearance of a break in continuity. 'The fit of absence of mind', the previous public uninterest in territory, was over. Salisbury, making sophisticated if makeshift and sometimes hesitant responses to new circumstances, lacked the brash optimism of Palmerston, but superintended the same basic system of policy. By the time Elgin became colonial secretary, and Grey foreign secretary, in 1905, the complexity into which the attainment of British interests had been thrown was extreme, and their policies are susceptible of no easy analysis. Renewed weight had to be given to humanitarian considerations once again, partly because of the confusion to which new problems had given rise. Meanwhile, many less rational devices for upholding British prestige and stemming the decline had been tried – a revived campaign for imperial federation, and an attack on free trade. The Americans were being brought in to redress the balance of the British decline in the Anglo-Saxon world, and new allies were being sought wherever they might be found, among Jews perhaps, as well as Japanese, for it is in this period that the British élite first fatally entangled itself with Zionist aspirations for a 'national home'. Changes were also advocated in schooling and the training of the young, the 'imperial race' of the future.

The first and most obvious pessimistic response to the new circumstances was, however, the reluctant participation in the territorial partition of the world which her rivals had set in motion. Foreign competition forced a defensive role upon Britain in this regard; she had a good deal of success in holding on to areas where her interests were already established, but the government did not, in a dynamic, optimistic way, move at all to create new areas of enterprise. If they had attempted to do so, the obvious prize to have worked for would have been Katanga. The British approach lacked a really positive dimension.

Towards the end of the nineteenth century European politicians felt themselves to be living in an era of world delimitation, 'a partition of the world', as Rosebery called it,[1] from which, as Elgin the viceroy of India agreed, Britain could not stand aside, because of her 'mission as pioneers of civilisation'.[2] The *Morning Post* in January 1885 diagnosed a 'scramble for Africa and Oceania'.[3] Rhodes and Chamberlain often spoke with Baron von Eckardstein (counsellor of the German empire) at the Burlington, where they roughed out successive plans for possible 'partitions of the world', and when these were fulfilled, said Rhodes, he would like to annex the planets if that were possible.[4] The phrase 'partition of the world' was also used by the German Carl Peters and the French minister Étienne.[5] New rivalries gave a fresh importance to the future of small independent states like Morocco, Tunis, Tripoli, Egypt, Ethiopia and Siam. There was a partition of the Pacific from about 1880 and nearly one of China and Korea from about 1895. International rivalries proliferated in Turkey's European provinces and in Central Asia, in the Middle East and Persia (culminating in an Anglo-Russian delimitation of spheres of influence in 1907), and in the Caribbean in the 1890s.[6] This global competition had a strong political dimension, with ample emphasis on prestige by all parties to it. Decisions were not generally made at the expense of economic reason, but a remarkable feature was the accent placed on non-economic viewpoints. Geographical societies multiplied. In Britain the Navy Records Society (1893) and the influential Navy League (1895) also helped to associate professional and political discussion.[7]

Between 1874 and 1902 Britain added to her empire 4,750,000 square miles inhabited by nearly 90 million people. Apart from major acquisitions in Africa, she added Baluchistan in 1876, and annexed Upper Burma in 1886. Innumerable little South Pacific islands also came under her control, including the Gilbert and Ellice Islands, Tonga and many of the Solomons; Pitcairn was recognised as a colony in 1898. More and more Malay states accepted British Residents. The determination to hold India became more definite.[8] Britain was no longer able to do much as she pleased, and competition forced her into buttressing her interests by territorial acquisition.[9] Prestige alone would have dictated the necessity for this, but there was also an economic need. The *Times* declared that Britain could not afford 'to allow any section even of the Dark Continent to believe that our imperial prestige is on the wane', and withdrawal from Uganda would, it said, be 'a fatal blow to all the civilising influences which we hope to exert upon Africa'.[10]

While government concern was chiefly with matters of political adjustment in international relations, with peace and prestige and the requirements of the national interest, the situations to which it responded were as much influenced by private economic interests on the spot as by changes in Europe.

Although these motives operated at different levels, and should be distinguished, there were broadly speaking two attitudes of mind which led Britain into her late nineteenth-century territorial acquisitions. One was a political dislike and fear of foreign competition, a feeling that it was, as Chamberlain once minuted, 'cheek' for rivals to trench upon British world-wide interests, a threat to her pre-eminence and an insult to her prestige.[11] The other was a horror of economic stagnation, a conviction that an economic *status quo* was an abomination, and that any peoples on the face of the earth guilty of it were so immoral that they deserved to be expropriated. From the 1860s the chances of African regeneration and modernisation without colonial rule were increasingly thought to be hopeless. These attitudes did not carry as much weight at the governmental level as international political considerations did, but they were certainly not without influence, and they were useful in justifying acquisitions made.

Fear of the foreigner was in particular fear of the French. This operated from the mid-1870s in regions as far apart as West Africa, the Persian Gulf, Burma, Malaya and Borneo.[12] Anglo-French rivalry eventually culminated in a hostile encounter in the remote interior of Africa, at Fashoda on the Nile in 1898.

Some of the earlier acquisitions were altruistic, an acceptance of responsibilities for the consequences of earlier expansionist activity. A duty to protect Basutoland was grudgingly recognised in 1868. Carnarvon announced his new policy for the Gold Coast by declaring that withdrawal was unthinkable. Britain might have no written obligation, but she had a moral one:

A great nation like ours must be sometimes prepared to discharge disagreeable duties; she must consent to bear burdens which are inseparable from her greatness ... it is certainly not a desire of selfish interests or the ambition of larger empire which bids us remain on the West Coast of Africa; it is simply and solely a sense of obligations to be redeemed and of duties to be performed.

Then, as far as the annexation of Fiji in 1874 was concerned, he certainly thought the 'mission of England' involved and invoked 'a spirit of adventure to fill up waste places of the earth'.[13]

This last observation leads us back to the British hatred of economic stagnation or under-development, a theme which gave continuity to British attitudes from Mungo Park to Winston Churchill. Mungo Park in West Africa in the 1790s lamented that such fertile land 'in a country so abundantly gifted and honoured by nature, should remain in its present savage and neglected state'.[14] The industrial entrepreneur W. T. Mulvany looked at a geological map of the Ruhr, said 'these people do not know their own wealth', and set about directing its development in the 1850s.[15] The self-imposed seclusion and 'closed door' of Japan (before it was opened up by Commodore Perry in 1853) was disapproved of in Britain as a 'wrong not only to themselves, but to the civilised world'. The *Edinburgh Review* expressed the belief that the Japanese undoubtedly had an exclusive right to the possession of their territory, but 'they must not abuse that right to the extent of debarring all other nations from a participation in its riches and virtues'; the only secure title to property, 'whether it be a hovel or an empire, is, that the exclusive possession of one is for the benefit of all'.[16] Sir Samuel Baker in the Nile Basin found it difficult to believe that so magnificent a soil and so enormous an extent of territory could forever remain as it was, while Meredith Townsend was disgusted that the whole of the Sudan so far yielded only elephant tusks and female slaves for harems.[17] Charles Kingsley in the late 1850s castigated the people of Paraguay for their immoral unawareness that to let their wonderful country remain in a 'stationary state', while all the nations round them were struggling for the means of existence, was 'a national sin, because a national selfishness', a burying in the earth of the talent allotted to them:

A moral duty lies on any nation, who can produce far more than sufficient for its own wants, to supply the wants of others from its own surplus . . . the human species has a right to demand (what the Maker thereof demands also, and enforces the demand by very fearful methods), that each people should either develop the capabilities of their own country, or make room for those who will develop them . . . [18]

Goldie wrote of the Africans' duty to the world to exploit their resources effectively through trade.[19] Lord Randolph Churchill was disgusted with the Boers, because in their 'stubborn ignorance' they had resolved not to develop the advantages of South Africa, its unequalled climate, soil of 'exuberant fertility' and its mining potential. Benjamin Kidd argued that the tropics would have to be administered from the temperate regions because of the inexpediency of allowing them to remain undeveloped, with 'resources running largely to waste under the management of races of low social efficiency'.[20] Despite British detestation of Leopold's Congo administration, there were nevertheless some who advised Morel not to work for vesting in the Africans the unfettered right to uncultivated land, since they could not turn it to account in the general interests of the whole state. Lever wrote to Morel:

The land of the world in any part of the world, ought to be in the possession of those people who can develop it and its resources. I do not agree . . . with you because I think that whether a man is a Duke or a Nigger he ought to stand the same in the eyes of his fellow men and be judged by his ability and willingness to make use of God's earth . . . [21]

These lines of thought were naturally in harmony with Chamberlain's view of colonies as 'undeveloped estates', and they led on ultimately to Lugard's propositions that 'the tropics are the heritage of mankind' and the races which inhabited them did not have a right to deny their bounties to those who needed them. The value of a people or the quality of their civilisation was measured by their contribution to the world's productive wealth. Lugard's whole *Dual Mandate* treatise was based on these assumptions.[22] Even the Labour Party leader James Ramsay MacDonald early in his career decided that the world was the inheritance of all men; peoples and nations could not separate themselves off from the world, and Britain had a *right* to tropical produce.[23] It was not in Winston Churchill's nature to be moved by the splendours of the Victoria Falls: he would 'much rather use the water sensibly for power than let it splash over in a useless stream'. And the Ripon Falls at Jinja, urged Churchill, should also be dammed and utilised for hydro-electric power, but it took nearly fifty years for his vision to be realised. There was a general horror of leaving the highlands of Kenya unfarmed. And so white settlement was started there against the better judgement of almost every official and politician. Such was the strength of the belief that people could not be allowed to bury their God-given talent in the ground.[24]

Whatever the reasons for wishing to acquire territory, this never took place where non-European resistance was judged likely to succeed. Of all the European powers, only the Italians in Ethiopia misjudged the strength of their opponents. Nowhere else were Europeans repulsed. The decisive determinant in the acquisition of territory by Britain, as of any other expanding country, has obviously been the inequality or disparity of power between it and the conquered people. This disparity became more pronounced in the last quarter of the nineteenth century, and goes a long way towards explaining the tightening political stranglehold over much of the world which then took place.[25] This disparity showed itself most obviously, perhaps, in the remarkable increase in the efficiency of guns. The rifled breech-loading weapons used in the Franco-Prussian war (1870-71) had ranges nearly ten times as great as the muskets and artillery of the Napoleonic wars. By the end of the century small-calibre rifles (firing cartridges charged with smokeless powder) were considered lethal up to 4,000 yards; field-guns had a maximum range of 9,000 yards and an effective range of between 3,000 and 6,000 yards. The Maxim gun was famous.[26] But railways and telegraph cables were also extremely important ingredients in the overall technological superiority of Europe. The first thing any European power tried to do in any newly acquired African country which it valued was to build a railway. For as Winston Churchill, himself an active promoter of railways in Nigeria and Uganda, wrote, it was no use taking hold of 'the jungle' with naked fingers:

> Civilisation must be armed with machinery if she is to subdue these wild regions to her authority. Iron roads, not jogging porters; tireless engines,

not weary men; cheap power not cheap labour; steam and skill not sweat and fumbling: there lies the only way to tame the jungle – more jungles than one.[27]

The British empire has been described as a web of submarine cables,[28] and they so excited Kipling that he wrote a poem about them. The cable, it could be argued, was more important than the steamship or the railway because it carried *information* overseas. It thus facilitated the centralisation of facts and figures and the concentration of economic and military power. It laid the mechanical basis for a world market by providing fast transmission of political news, and intelligence about the trading situation and market prices. It substantially aided the expansion of British economic interests in Asia as well as making possible withdrawal of many garrisons. By 1873 John Pender's companies became the controllers of the largest cable system in the world and were not far short of a world monopoly.[29] By the mid-1890s there were 170,000 nautical miles of ocean cable, 662,000 miles of aerial wire and buried land cable. By 1897 only Fiji, British Honduras, Tobago, St Helena, the Falkland Islands, Turks Islands and Papua were not yet connected by the telegraph. From 1900 the French embarked on an intensive cable-laying programme, believing that Britain owed her world position more to her cable communications than the navy, because cables controlled news and were 'made to serve her policy and commerce in a marvellous manner'.[30]

One of the most striking examples of how the disparity in technological power ensured victory is the battle of Omdurman (September 1898) which secured the reconquest of the Sudan. Numerically the odds were extremely uneven. The Khalifa put 50,000 brave and confident men into the field. The British Expeditionary Force was only 8,200 strong, assisted by 17,600 Egyptians. Yet of the Khalifa's men 9,700 died, some 10,000 to 16,000 were wounded and 5,000 were taken prisoner. On the British side, losses were insignificant: including the wounded, only 20 officers and 462 men. But the British of course had the guns: 80 big guns and 44 Maxims by land and river. They had commissioned Cook's steamers. They had 2,469 horses, 896 mules, 3,524 camels and 229 donkeys; and these figures exclude private animals in the possession of officers. But above all they built a railway, 500 miles of it, and put up 900 miles of telegraph wire: all in order to win the war. As Winston Churchill wrote: 'Fighting the Dervishes was primarily a matter of transport. The Khalifa was conquered on the railway'. When the railway reached Atbara base camp, the fate of the Khalifa was sealed: 'though the battle was not yet fought the victory was won'. Sir Percy Girouard successfully got all his supplies to the 2,000 platelayers in war conditions, and work was never delayed by waiting for even a piece of wire. Then, with the railway completed, gunboats were brought in sections on it and fitted together on the Nile above the second cataract. Although trans-shipped seven times since leaving London, not a single piece was lost. The Khalifa's mastery of technology was decidedly inferior. Twice he tried to mine the river. On the first occasion he only blew up his own men, and on the second he failed to remember Cromwell's advice about keeping his powder dry. Churchill observed: Omdurman was 'the most signal triumph ever gained by the arms of science over barbarians': Within the space of five hours, 'the strongest and best armed savage army yet arrayed against a modern European Power had been destroyed and dispersed, with hardly any difficulty, comparatively small risk and insignificant loss to the victors'.[31]

By 1914 the European powers had by agreement arranged for the destiny of every disputed country in the world, without a war between themselves. The Pax Britannica covered more of the earth's surface than ever before, and in this respect at least, Britain's search for stability in relations with the non-European world was successfully met on paper, and seldom to her disadvantage as a commercial competitor.

IMPERIAL CONFERENCES

The successful assertion of American federal supremacy and the consolidation of the Great Republic after the Civil War gave a rude shock to beliefs that the United States was heading for disintegration and prophecies that the Civil War would result in the replacement of a continental empire with island outposts by a group of independent nations in close analogy to the system contemplated by British colonial policy. The actual result, so contrary to expectation, at once led to a revival of interest in the federal idea and a reconsideration of British policy in the light of the new revelation, which was later strengthened by the example of German and Italian unification.[32]

The Royal Colonial Institute was founded in 1868 to study colonial problems and it reflected some of these reconsiderations. There was no unanimity among federal enthusiasts. This is plain from the history of the Imperial Federation League which began in 1884.[33] W. E. Forster was chairman for the first two years and apologised for the word 'federation', since not all members necessarily looked to that particular form of closer union. They were equally divided about the retention of free trade. The League held together only while its objectives remained vague. The idea of an imperial council of some sort seemed by 1892 to be probably the lowest common denominator of agreement. However, as soon as the League tried to leave rhetoric behind and formulate a programme it promptly disintegrated. Offshoots included the United Empire Trade League (1891), designed to pursue imperial preference, various dining clubs, and the British Empire League (1894), favouring voluntary co-operation and a system of periodical conferences.[34] Most of those interested seemed to look to an imperial council with advisory and perhaps some executive functions, and they pressed Salisbury to hold a conference while colonial premiers were in London for the jubilee of 1887. The same conjunction of royal ceremonial and colonial conference took place with the 1897 jubilee and the 1902 coronation; thereafter colonial premiers agreed to meet at four-yearly intervals.

In other respects the imperial federation movement attracted little interest or success either at home or in the colonies. Although the original league was avowedly a propagandist organisation, and produced a monthly periodical and more than a hundred pamphlets,[35] its arguments remained little more than academic exercises; the idea failed to interest anybody outside a small minority of doctrinaires and academics such as Sir John Seeley, and a few important politicians such as Rosebery and Chamberlain. Their fundamental contention was unsound: that there must be closer union or total disintegration; in fact the 'loose hung Commonwealth' of the early 1850s, supplemented by the conference system, continued to meet reasonable British needs. Richard Jebb rightly concluded in 1905 that federation was an obsolete idea whose very basis had melted away as a result of what he called the growth of 'a sense of common nationality' among Australians and Canadians.[36] Lyttelton's proposal of 1905 (based on recommendations of the Pollock Committee dining club) for an imperial council with a permanent secretariat met with an exceedingly lukewarm response. It was thrown out by the 1907 conference, not least because although Deakin alone seemed to favour it strongly, he did not fully grasp the nature of the scheme.[37] At the 1911 conference, Ward of New Zealand placed a crazy proposal before the premiers and failed to win his point. Colonial secretary Harcourt was however, with a terrible condescension, prepared to make some concession if necessary. They might, he wrote, have to agree to have two permanent under-secretaries, one to deal exclusively with dominion affairs, since it would 'never do to *say* we are too good for them, and they are not good enough for us', but 'these social vanities of the new rich must be reckoned with and pandered to unless and until they can be convinced of the folly of their foibles'. He felt that the proposals had little to do with improving administrative efficiency.[38]

Harcourt's opinion reveals the chief reason for the failure of the conference system to achieve any really significant change in imperial organisation. Contempt for colonials was so great that there was never the slightest intention of admitting them to the seats of power between 1905 and 1915. Their 'impudence' in 1907 stirred Morley's bile, and Deakin's yarns and harangues in particular turned that conference into 'the greatest bore that ever was known'. It was widely rumoured that colonials wanted to take charge of the empire, and what could be more absurd than that?[39]

At the first meeting of the conference in 1887 Salisbury announced ominously that the proceedings would be prosaic, and so they always remained. Discussions were often upon technical subjects. Available time was severely limited, and important subjects, such as Asian immigration, were never discussed at all, because the colonial office pronounced them hopeless subjects for such discussion. Any efficiency the conferences might have had was almost certainly diminished by the social and gastronomic excesses which accompanied them. There were huge lunches and dinners every day. Laurier had a weak digestion, and the 1902 conference nearly killed him. He did not know, he said, whether or not the empire needed a new constitution but the premiers certainly did. Deakin's breakdown in health can no doubt be largely attributed to his exertions, histrionic and gastronomic, at the 1907 conference.[40]

CHAMBERLAIN, THE WEST INDIES AND TARIFF REFORM

'Joe was a great man', remarked an official many years later, 'he woke the [colonial] office up, and it has been going to sleep ever since'. Chamberlain was very much alive to the need to improve Britain's position in every possible way, and particularly by the development of the new tropical estates. This former mayor of Birmingham became interested in the empire as a result of the occupation of Egypt (which he visited) and the struggle for Irish Home Rule. As colonial secretary 1895-1903, before South Africa monopolised his attention, he was full of schemes for reform on the Birmingham municipal model: 'what Uganda needs is what Birmingham has got – an improvement scheme'. There is some evidence that he had increasing doubts about the appropriateness of a policy based on Birmingham municipal standards. Right at the end of his tenure he minuted on a West Indian file: 'I have an idea that we press sanitation and civilisation too strongly on some of these backward communities. If they like bad water or insufficient water it might be well to let them find out the results for themselves'.[41] Chamberlain certainly suffered disillusionment in one of the main new ideas he brought to imperial administration, namely the desirability of interesting businessmen in the empire and getting their advice. He wanted to use his own business contacts rather than legislative or bureaucratic devices to assist economic development. He attached great importance to persuading Sir Thomas Lipton to invest in West Indian sugar factories but did not succeed.[42] But he did personally negotiate for A. L. Jones a contract for a direct mail, fruit and passenger service between Jamaica and Britain in order to get the backing of Jones's resources, business skill and connections in the fruit trade, which Chamberlain regarded as of vital importance to Jamaica.

Chamberlain sometimes over-simplified problems, but he was a tough, energetic, extremely hard-working and masterful administrator who knew his own mind on many issues and made a deep impression on the colonial office. Some of his most important work was done for the West Indies whose condition alarmed him, especially in its dependence on a sugar industry in 'imminent risk of extinction'. He adopted a planned reconstruction of the West Indies based on imperial grants-in-aid to make up revenue deficits.[43] £20,000 a year was paid in the quinquennium 1898-1903. He encouraged and improved the sugar industry, especially by a grant of £250,000 in 1902–03.

He set up the Imperial Department of Agriculture for the West Indies, which did valuable research and stimulated the modernisation of methods. Chamberlain saw the necessity of diversifying the economy, for instance by developing citrus fruits and bananas as an alternative to sugar. He augmented steamer services, improved the roads of Dominica, settled peasant proprietors in St Vincent and Dominica and encouraged the new School of Tropical Medicine at Liverpool. His methods and approach were shaped by a business and municipal experience unique among nineteenth-century colonial secretaries. The idea of a partnership between public and private enterprise was not entirely new but it was not until 1895 that it was officially acknowledged, vigorously pursued and implemented with imperial funds. He tried to set up a Colonial Development Fund out of the profits of the Suez Canal shares but was thwarted by the treasury. Not everything he did even in the West Indies was successful. The Brussels Sugar Convention which he signed in 1902 is not something to which any increase in prosperity can be traced, and Britain withdrew from it six years later. But Chamberlain's reputation would have been higher if he had stuck to development problems. Unfortunately he was not able, or not content to do this, so that he is chiefly remembered for taking Britain into the Anglo-Boer War ('to strengthen the weakest link in the imperial chain') and for his attempts to bring about the reorganisation of the political and economic structure of the empire. He had originally set himself two objectives: to bring the self-governing colonies and Britain closer together, as well as to develop the resources of tropical 'undeveloped estates', especially by increasing their trade with Britain and opening up new markets.

Chamberlain's two biggest projects were imperial federation and tariff reform and the two were closely linked. Hobson observed that political federation and the unity of the empire were Chamberlain's objective, and that tariff reform was an indirect means to this end; when Chamberlain found the front door to federation shut, bolted and barred, he turned to the tradesmen's entrance, and to tariff reform and colonial preference.[44] These preferences were therefore at bottom a constitutional question and not an economic one, though economic interests focussed attention on the issue. Chamberlain himself had small understanding of economics, though he became increasingly an advocate of protection for its own sake. Tariffs he came to believe a way of safeguarding industry from foreign competition, of maintaining a high level of employment and raising revenue to finance social reform. In 1903 he said: 'we can draw closer the growing nations, the sister states, and by a commercial union we can pave the way for that federation'[45] without which Britain would have to accept her fate as one of the dying empires of the world. By free trade Britain was giving up a weapon which Chamberlain felt she needed in order to hit back at her enemies. He saw great advantages in combination, aiming at an empire which would be 'self-sustaining and self-sufficient, able to maintain itself against the competition of all its rivals'.

By imperial consolidation, if future danger threatened, Britain would not have to meet it as an isolated country, but fortified and buttressed by kinsmen all over the world. 'Our future history', he declared,

> depends upon the extent to which we can weld the different parts of the Empire together. What Washington did for the United States of America, what Bismarck did for Germany, it is our business to do for the British Empire.

As early as 1886 Chamberlain aspired to bring all the colonies 'into one supreme and Imperial Parliament, so . . . that all should be equally responsible . . . have a share in the welfare, and sympathise with the welfare of every part'. Political federation of the empire was to him 'within the limits of possibility' and a 'practical object of aspiration'. By 1903 'the great question of imperial unity' was the only thing he cared about. Everything else was 'secondary or consequential'.[46]

Projects of imperial federation were easily frustrated by a combination of opposition both from Britons at home and from the colonies. In Britain Liberals opposed it because it would split the Anglo-Saxon world. Following the argument of Dilke's *Greater Britain,* good relations with the United States were reckoned to be of paramount concern. Although Chamberlain did not share it, there was undoubtedly a great deal of anti-American feeling in the movement for imperial unity. But as Sir Thomas Farrer, permanent secretary to the board of trade, told Chamberlain in 1887, he did not believe British welfare was to be found in 'setting up the Union Jack against the Stars and Stripes, but in a nearer approach amongst all English peoples'.[47] The Liberals also opposed imperial federation because it conflicted with their other major loyalty, to the international community. This loyalty they put before the empire,[48] and although they liked the empire, this was chiefly because they saw in it a model of co-operation and justice which they hoped the whole world would one day emulate. The Liberals in any case had no wish to work more closely with colonials, of whom they were contemptuous.[49]

Colonial opposition to closer imperial unity was mainly led from Canada, where no government could have accepted any reduction of Canadian autonomy for fear of French Canadian upheavals. Sir Wilfrid Laurier objected to the surrender of any autonomy partly because he regarded it as a retrograde step and partly because he regarded Chamberlain's harping upon a united empire, designed to improve the status and condition of the British Protestant race, as a rebuff to the French Canadians. Laurier said in 1902 that as far as he could see it was settled that the empire was a galaxy of free nations 'owing the same allegiance to the same sovereign, but owing paramount allegiance to their respective peoples'. Of all the colonies, New Zealand had the strongest interest in imperial federation, but this seems to have been based on a totally unrealistic hope that it would give her a better platform for making her voice heard in the world. Other white areas were however fast evolving from colonies into nations and diverging further and further from Britain. There was perhaps a strong feeling for the Throne, but this was quite different from a devotion to Britain. At the 1897 conference even Seddon of New Zealand was forced to give a direct 'no' in reply to Chamberlain's question: would any colony delegate to a representative in Britain the right to decide its course?[50]

Chamberlain resigned office in 1903 in order to campaign for tariff reform.[51] The whole idea was decisively rejected by the British people in the election of 1906. A main reason for this was Chamberlain's frank admission that the new policy would impose sacrifice on the British electorate. But as far as he was concerned, imperial preference was not

> primarily a question of money sacrifice, it is primarily a question of the unity of the empire, and I am firmly convinced that unity cannot be effectually secured in the future unless we can improve and extend our inter-commercial relations.

The argument that a greater future would result from a sharing with kinsmen overseas was hardly attractive enough to combat the threat of dearer bread, since small duties on food were necessary in order to give the colonies a preference. Colonies largely depended on food exports, and food taxes were therefore central to his plans.[52] By 1903 he admitted that the cry of the 'dear loaf' had been much more successful than he had supposed it would be. 'If we could kill that we should cut the ground from under our adversaries' feet, but the superstition in the minds of the working classes seems difficult to destroy'.[53] He undoubtedly seriously underestimated the kind of opposition he would have to meet, and had apparently failed to weigh the significance of the belief reputedly entertained by a schoolgirl of the time that it was John Bright who had invented bread.[54] Time and time again, however, he spoke of the necessity of sacrifice. For example, in a key speech in 1903 he said it was the business of statesmen 'to do everything they can, even at some present sacrifice', to keep and promote colonial trade.[55]

The Liberals reacted fiercely and with some glee to Chamberlain's campaign. It would reunite the Liberal party. Asquith said it was 'only a question of time when we shall sweep this country'. The party's elder statesman, Ripon, wrote:

> The abandonment of free trade, the taxation of food ... the dis-organisation of industry and the war of tariffs which are the inevitable features of this policy, render the present crisis by far the gravest of the last fifty years. It is the greatest political struggle even of my long public life ... Everything else [now] sinks into insignificance. This one battle must be fought to the end.[56]

Winston Churchill went to work, cutting his political teeth as a convert to the
Liberal party, and devised some splendid phrases. In 1905 he declared: 'we do
not want to see the British Empire degenerate into a sullen confederacy,
walled off, like a medieval town, from the surrounding country, victualled for
a siege . . . ' At the 1907 conference he enunciated the doctrine that the
empire was a family not a syndicate.[57]

The issue became closely linked with that of Chinese labour on the
Witwatersrand. Behind both were fears of big-business influence in politics
and an increase in corruption. Churchill defined the election issue as 'dear
food for the millions, cheap labour for the millionaire'. Somebody else spoke
of 'trusts for the rich, crusts for the poor'.[58] Yet another election cry was:
protection was a 'sop to capitalists and only capitalists would make anything
out of it'. The Liberals looked with misgivings upon the formation of
wealthier and bigger corporations. They loathed monopoly in all forms. There
were mutterings about the grip Jewish people were getting on London's
West End as well as on Johannesburg ('Jew-hannesburg'). Chamberlain
deliberately subordinated the interests of the British consumer to imperial
interests, but the Liberals were fixedly upon the side of the consumer in all
matters. Even more important than the objection to big business were the
misgivings expressed about possible repercussions on British home politics of a
shift to protection. Churchill's conversion to the Liberal party was based on
the belief that tampering with free trade and setting up a protective system
would involve commercial disaster and the 'Americanisation' of British
politics. By 'Americanisation' he seems to have meant the corruption which
was the hallmark of American politics in its days of high protectionist policy.
Its entire political system seemed geared to providing advantages for specific
interests. The Senate was dominant and known as 'the millionaires club'.[59]
Seely said American experience showed that 'political corruption must come
with protective duties'.[60] To a large section of British public opinion,
protection meant entrenchment of privileged interests, the multiplication of
government officials and corruption, more commitments overseas, higher
taxes and probably war. Some even questioned whether constitutional
government could survive the destruction of free trade. But it was an
emotionally charged issue. Hugh Cecil declared in 1903: 'the fundamental
propositions which were laid down fifty years ago were propositions of a
scientific character and had relation to abiding principles living in human
nature and were not therefore of temporary application'. Were Palmerston's
'great standing laws of Nature', the 'dispensation of Providence', to be thrown
over? To touch the complicated and entrenched fabric of free trade was like a
sacrilegious attempt to meddle with a great organic creation of nature or God.
For Morley the adoption of free trade in 1846 was 'the dawn of higher ideals
of civilisation all over the world'. It was still widely believed that free trade
was a good, a virtue, like 'holiness and righteousness, to be loved, admired,
honoured' for its own sake, whereas restrictions were evils like vice and crime

to be hated and abhorred at all times. The religious conviction sustaining free trade made it seem something that it was wrong to question.[61] Chamberlain knew that people regarded it as a revealed religion but underrated the fanatical devotion to free trade on this basis since he could not see that it was even a fact. Nevertheless he came to view tariff reform as 'above all else a spiritual movement'. God had to be fought with his own weapons.[62]

Unfortunately for Chamberlain almost the whole weight of professional economic orthodoxy was, and no doubt with good reason, against him. Fourteen university professors wrote to the *Times,* and they too mentioned moral evils such as the loss of purity in politics, unequal distribution of wealth and the growth of 'sinister influence'. Marshall described free trade principles as 'economic truths as certain as those of geometry'.[63] A modern economic historian has said that the idea of even partial isolation of the empire into a single economic unit was nonsensical.[64] Tariff reformers failed to see the empire's true role in the world economy from a broad view. They thought a crisis was imminent, whereas in fact, Britain's economic position proved to be on the upswing in 1905. Others, like Cromer, defended free trade on the ground that it smoothed British relations with the European powers by exercising 'a very steadying effect on all the loose Anglophobia current on the Continent'.[65]

To join battle with positions so deeply entrenched needed intellectual planning and practical organisation of a superlative kind. This Chamberlain could not supply. Essentially, to take a charitable view, he was too old. He was in his seventieth year in 1905. Chamberlain did not understand the magnitude and financial intricacies of the question. He had once read Mill and had tried to read Marshall, but had not come to grips with them. He never succeeded in showing how a preference within low tariffs (which were the most Britain could conceivably tolerate on her food and raw materials) could make the difference (as he constantly reiterated) between imperial consolidation and imperial dissolution. For the Opposition, Asquith made mincemeat of him. Chamberlain was foolish enough to make public speeches without having fully planned and pondered his scheme. He had no policy-making assistants as in his earlier radical days. He was largely without comrades and stimulus. From May 1903 he was deluged with questions, requests and suggestions, for all of which he was quite unprepared. He had no personal staff to deal with them. It was this lack of preparation which explains many of the contradictions, inaccuracies, changes of tack, strange turns of argument, which even his devoted biographer admits marred the early presentation of the case for tariff reform. The movement thus developed a wayward dynamic which was never brought properly under control. He seemed to forget about India. Yet India had never before been excluded from any consideration of fiscal policy and its effect. His lack of references to the empire's largest and most powerful unit weakened people's faith in his grasp of his own proposals: it particularly shook the faith of his erstwhile Tory colleagues.[66]

To turn now to colonial opposition, it is possible that some colonial politicians found Chamberlain's talk of 'sacrifice' wounding to their own self-respect, but mostly they saw the scheme as one of unmitigated advantage to Britain.[67] Canada was prosperous and did not need help. The larger colonies wanted to build up their own industries behind tariff barriers. An imperial Zollverein was the last thing they wanted. The governor-general of Australia, Northcota, reported that Australia might be aroused by imperial sentiment in a war, 'but not in matters of business'. 'The difficulty', he added, 'of making these people think Imperially or of aught but securing a maximum of pay for a minimum of work is incredible'.[68] In a speech at Glasgow on 6 October 1903 Chamberlain made a fatal remark implying that the object of his preferential policy was to keep the colonies from pressing on with their own industrial development. He never repeated this mistake, but he never quite lived it down. To the end a suspicion remained, especially in Canada, that the colonies would be kept as primary producers, confined to subordinate positions in a centrally planned economy.[69]

Chamberlain's schemes failed dismally. At the colonial conference of 1902 he appealed for colonial aid in defence of the empire, echoing a phrase of Matthew Arnold:

> The weary Titan staggers under the vast orb of his fate. We have borne the burden for many years. We think it is time that our children should assist us to support it.[70]

There was some response: colonial contributions were made by Australia, New Zealand, the Cape, Natal and Newfoundland – but not by Canada. The conference rejected outright Chamberlain's proposal of 'free trade within the Empire' and refused to have a representative imperial council.[71]

Why was Chamberlain's failure so complete? The contribution of colonial objections is obvious enough, but it is perhaps worth-while to underline the domestic reasons for it. (In 1906 tariff reform went down before the biggest electoral landslide in British history). First of all, Chamberlain was to the Liberals not merely a materialistic and vulgar politician, but an unscrupulous demagogue, the most hated man in British politics, and unredeemed by the kind of brilliance which Disraeli had displayed.[72] And they put the blame on him for the general lapse in political standards occurring in the 1890s. Campbell-Bannerman complained of Chamberlain's intransigence: 'He ensconces himself in his own self-sufficiency and refuses to listen to either fact or reason'.[73] Sir Edward Grey perceptively commented that Chamberlain 'mistakes delusion for inspiration', and feared the empire would never entirely recover from the disturbances he had made.[74]

It is difficult to say that these Liberal judgements were entirely wrong. Chamberlain was not an attractive person, nor was his motto: 'Never apologise, never explain, always attack'.[75] Not really much of a thinker, he repeatedly indulged in plans portentously rooted in theory and prophecy. He liked bold strokes of policy, wanted quick results, and was thus temperamentally unsuited to the patient, steady administrative application which the West Indian and South African problems required.[76] He took liberties in editing blue books.[77] He made many errors of judgement, misunderstood the attitude of the United States and overrated the future importance of the China trade.[78] If he was right that the days had come for 'big empires rather than little states', he was wrong, even anachronistic, in his notions of how Britain could meet this situation.[79]

Liberal hatred of Chamberlain intensified their view of the tariff reform movement as a moral issue, and automatically discredited all his schemes for the empire. They were, as Churchill described them in a typically telling phrase, 'detestably' full of 'morose, sordid and often absurd extravagancies'.[80] Extensive damage was done to all his plans by the Anglo-Boer war: it was bound to cause a severe reaction both at home and in the colonies against Chamberlainite conceptions of empire. Finally, it is worth repeating Sir Edward Grey's judgement that Chamberlain mistook delusion for inspiration. It is a judgement which would equally describe a whole generation and more of Unionist politicians. Chamberlain and his successors, as well as Milner, his Kindergarten and the *Round Table* group, were essentially 'visionaries *in vacuo*' who never grasped the realities of colonial atmosphere. The whole dream of an organic imperial integration was unrealistic, misplaced, narrow and out of touch with the intellectual, political and economic developments of Britain and the empire. Tory persistence in tariff reform after 1906 had demonstrated its vote-losing character has been sharply commented on by the most recent historian of the Conservative Party: 'It almost gives credibility [writes Lord Blake] to the notion that there can be such a thing as a political death wish'.[81] If there is any answer to the question of how politicians could propose such essentially impracticable policies as imperial federation and tariff reform, it lies presumably in the necessity for comfortable delusions and illusions when the need arose to boost waning confidence about the future of the empire. If Chamberlain was deluded as to what form of imperial policy and organisation people would tolerate it was because he was so worried about the empire. In just the same way Churchill, though right about tariff reform in 1905, was grievously wrong about India in 1935, but wrong because he was desperately worried about the future of imperial Britain. They both proposed to deal with impending doom by unworkable methods which were self-defeating.

DEFENCE AND DIPLOMACY

'To a foreigner reading our press the British Empire must appear in the light of some huge giant sprawling over the globe, with gouty fingers and toes stretching in every direction, which cannot be approached without eliciting a scream.' So wrote Sir Thomas Sanderson (permanent under-secretary at the foreign office) in 1907.[82] It is a good indication of Whitehall's nervous temper once it was fully realised that Britain had become an over-extended empire, magnificent but unnatural. As consciousness grew that it would be impossible to defend commitments everywhere, from the 1890s priorities had to be determined. Military thinking was entirely defensive, even defeatist. The Anglo-Boer war exposed sharply the underlying weakness of the imperial structure, but the roots of alarm may be traced to the alliance in 1894 of Britain's two potential enemies, France and Russia, and then, from 1898 to fear of the German programme of naval expansion. The German concession for a Baghdad railway in 1903 caused further anxiety. Three defence commitments were readily seen to be of the first importance: the defence of the United Kingdom, the defence of India against Russia, and the protection of the route to India. The scientific study of imperial resources, and the co-ordinated planning of their allocation on the basis of priorities, had not previously found a place in the British system of government.[83] Balfour, noted St John Brodrick, was the first prime minister to give any real consideration to the problems of national and imperial defence.[84] The problem confronting him was how to reduce the over-extended and ill-supported nature of Britain's world-wide commitments, and how to improve the efficiency of the army and navy which had not seen a major war for half a century. The inadequacy of financial resources and the amateurishness of planning were seen as severe handicaps to effective defence.[85] Wyndham summed up the Unionist view: 'The empire must be defended: the empire must be united: the manhood of the empire must be safeguarded'.[86]

By 1900 Britain was importing four-fifths of her total grain consumption, and the royal navy was crucial for protecting the sinews of British trade. As early as 1890 the Naval Defence Act had laid it down that at all times Britain should be able to match the next two most powerful navies in the world in combination, in terms of the size and efficiency of the fleet. This was the famous 'two-power standard' principle.

It was Rosebery who began the first tentative grappling with strategic defence planning. In 1895 he made a cautious and not very successful attempt to meet the recommendations of the Hartington Commission of 1890, which suggested the establishment of a naval and military council bringing together the heads of political departments and the service chiefs. Also in 1895 an Indian controversy sharply illuminated the new anxieties. Should Britain withdraw from her outposts beyond the northern and north-west frontier? Viceroy Elgin said not. Rosebery overruled him, using the argument that strict concentration of resources was needed in India. He was less concerned with the Russian threat than a possible French one by way of Burma: 'a most unveracious and unscrupulous government is about to establish a conterminous [sic] frontier with you : I mean France'. While France was menacing India, 'and menacing you in strict alliance with Russia, it would take much to make me agree to any such dispersal of force as is involved in the occupation of Chitral' – which was in Kashmiri country.[87] However, the new Conservative government of July 1895 disagreed with Rosebery. The Conservative secretary of state for India, Lord George Hamilton, lamented that 'strategical arguments are capable of indefinite expansion, and our military forces are not'. He noted too the uncertainty occasioned by disagreement between military experts in the interpretation of strategical reasoning. He decided against a total withdrawal but the trans-frontier presence must not be allowed to impose an unbearable strain on resources.[88]

It was above all the Anglo-Boer war which made defence reassessments imperative. Locally, every symptom of muddle was made manifest. Generally, British preoccupation in South Africa, locking up a large portion of a small army, was seen to increase the vulnerability of other parts of the empire, tempting other powers to interfere in China and Afghanistan, and giving France a chance to take revenge for Fashoda.[89]

A war office report on the military needs of the empire if faced with a war against France and Russia underlined the serious deficiency of available reinforcements to the Indian and colonial garrisons. A fatal blow could be dealt in India. 'The loss of India by conquest', it warned, 'would be a death-blow to our prosperity, prestige and power. The damaging effects of even a near approach by hostile forces would be incalculable'. The report concluded that Russia in wartime would make its 'greatest and most determined effort' against India.[90] Balfour agreed. He diagnosed the 'weakest spot in the empire' as the Indian frontier, and 'a quarrel with Russia anywhere, about anything, means the invasion of India'. Thus, for Balfour, India had become an 'inseparable and integral part of the foreign policy of the empire'. The Russian fleet was growing alarmingly from 1898 and her railway system was developing fast in Central Asia. Russia seemed determined to bring the buffer-states of Tibet, Afghanistan and Persia into her sphere of influence.[91] The royal navy could not help India against Russia. India required an army of horrifying size. Kitchener in 1904 estimated that reinforcements approaching 160,000 would be immediately needed if war broke out; in the second year of war a further 300,000 to 400,000 men would be required, together with three million camels.[92]

In 1902 Balfour set up the Elgin Commission to investigate the military preparations for the Anglo-Boer war and various logistical questions relating to its conduct.[93] He also appointed a major committee under the widely trusted and well-connected Lord Esher to investigate the whole organisation of the war office, with the idea of making it 'a first class business machine'.[94] As a result, the Army Council was created and the commander-in-chief's post abolished. Most important of all Balfour firmly established the Committee of Imperial Defence. Indeed this was possibly the most important and enduring contribution to politics and war made by Balfour personally in his entire career.[95] As he explained to parliament, it would 'survey as a whole the strategical military needs of the empire', and consider 'broad and all-important issues'.[96] It was intended to be an advisory committee, flexible enough to call to its meetings visiting colonial statesmen and service chiefs as well as the heads of British non-military departments of state. Balfour recognised the undesirability of keeping national strategy in a compartment separate from considerations of domestic policy.[97] It was to be 'a free association of the amateur and the expert', with service chiefs meeting politicians on an equal footing.[98] Its form was decisively influenced by Esher, who was a member of it from October 1905. He admired the spirit which the Germans had brought to the study of war, and believed in the need to establish in Britain what today would be inelegantly called a 'think tank'. The committee would co-ordinate the planning policies of the two armed services and other relevant departments, as well as suggest schemes which required technical and careful enquiry and careful inter-departmental co-operation.[99] His considered diagnosis of the situation was as follows:[100]

> We have an Army in excess of our requirements for 'small wars' – and wholly inadequate to the demands of a great war . . . We are still living under the conditions which governed British policy in the reign of Queen Anne. We delude ourselves with the idea that we are an Island state. We are an Island *Race* but we have ceased to be an Island state. The King's Empire has great frontiers co-terminous with the land frontiers of some of the greatest military powers on earth. Russia. Turkey. And the United States. In addition, the commercial and naval superiority of Great Britain is threatened by . . . the expansion of Germany to sea frontiers.

Esher persuaded Balfour to attach a 'permanent element' or secretariat to the C.I.D. in order to promote continuity of policy between changes of government and to offset the dangers which would be posed by a premier ignorant of, or indifferent to, defence problems. Campbell-Bannerman's record as secretary of state for war 1892-95 caused nervous apprehension of his accession to power.[101] In practice Campbell-Bannerman accepted the existence of the C.I.D. as a fait accompli,[102] although like his colleague Morley he found it an 'immense innovation on the established conceptions of cabinet government'. He used it sparingly It met only 15 times during his premiership, and it increasingly performed political functions and investigations, so that it never developed effectively as a high-level consultative or strategic planning body. But the Liberal ministers recognised the new facts of the international situation as necessitating a wide and comprehensive survey of the whole field of empire defence. As Morley realised, 'we have hitherto been far too parochial, separate, isolated and divisive in dealing with military and naval organisation; only moved now and then by the temporary whim of this or that autocratic proconsul, like Curzon for example ... ' Asian policy was much the most momentous branch of foreign policy.[103] The C.I.D. was useful in assisting Haldane's army reform, by shielding defence policies from the more pacific section of the cabinet. Campbell-Bannerman's acceptance of the desirability of a General Staff for the army was a small but striking indication of how circumstances had caused a change of opinion. He had opposed such an institution in 1890. Similarly, in 1890 he had also refused to contemplate the possibility of British troops fighting on the continent of Europe, but by 1907 he accepted Haldane's plans for an expeditionary force, and was holding secret military conversations with France. The imperatives provided by the transformation of the international situation were strong. Campbell-Bannerman accepted as sound the principles on which Conservative policy had been based.[104]

Britain withdrew from a competitive posture towards the United States in the New World. Bases at Halifax and Esquimault were abandoned, the Jamaica dockyards were closed and the West Indian and North American squadrons withdrawn. These measures were drastic and controversial, although seemingly unavoidable. Lord Minto (the governor-general of Canada until 1905) expressed apprehension that they were overlooking the 'moral effect ... produced by a withdrawal of forces from localities ... where they have been a visible testimony of British power' for so long. The American withdrawals might have been strategically sound, he added, but the older generation of Canadians bitterly lamented them as 'withdrawals of the flag', and they largely

> removed the possibility of the appeal so often made to the flag in the case of some trading schooner that had got into difficulty ... In considering imperial defence in an Empire such as ours one must not be guided alone by purely practical considerations but must take human influences into account ...[105]

From the defence point of view of course the real value of these withdrawals was to make hostilities with the United States impossible. They should be seen in the context of the remarkable 'diplomatic revolution' of 1902–1907, which successfully reduced the task of British military planners to more manageable size. The three main achievements were the conclusion of the Anglo-Japanese alliance of 1902, the entente with France in 1904, and the 1907 Anglo-Russian agreement. Together these represented a 'remarkable feat of diplomatic pacification'.[106]

It was the imperial expansion of other European powers, and particularly that of Russia in Asia, which made the new policy necessary. The context of reappraisal was one of a steady recognition of the potentialities of Russia and her power for mischief especially in the Far East. Balfour and the C.I.D. were sure that Russia was the most formidable rival, but from 1903 the foreign office increasingly thought it was Germany.[107] Esher by 1906 was convinced that within measurable distance there was a titanic struggle for mastery looming between Germany and Britain, and he was sceptical of the ability of the new alliance policy to cope with it.[108] It was Lansdowne who gave the chief new impetus and direction to British foreign policy, using two complementary ideas: first the necessity of concentrating British resources, and secondly the need to secure by agreement with an ally the joint use of military force in certain eventualities. His main object was to meet Russia in Asia, and he thought the principal task was agreement with Germany.[109] There was also a simultaneous approach to Japan. His readiness to adapt was remarkable, but it would be wrong to suppose Salisbury to have been woodenly isolationist. One of the more consistent threads of Salisbury's policy had been to prepare an agreement with France and Russia.[110]

The Anglo-Japanese alliance was signed in 1902, revised in 1905 and 1911, and ended in 1923.[111] Its object was to meet the grave crisis in the Far East posed by the growth of Russian power. Its prophets had included Valentine Chirol, Charles Dilke and Lord Curzon, all of whom had seen the advantage of friendly relations with Japan, but it was only with Japan's defeat of China that Britain became fully aware of how far her own ascendancy in the Far East had declined, and new urgency was introduced into Far Eastern policy. The immediate cause of the alliance was British distrust of Russian encroachment in Manchuria and Korea, about which Russia was rumoured to be negotiating with Japan. In the foreign office the alliance was promoted by F. L. Bertie. From the admiralty it was powerfully advocated by Selborne because of the help it would give to British naval strength. A naval agreement, he calculated, would give Britain and Japan together, in 1902, eleven battleships as against a Franco-Russian combination of nine. Although Britain generally assumed the leadership in discussions leading to the alliance, Japan was equally keen and took the initiative at times. Britain was certainly worried that Japan might go over to Russia's side, and another consideration was the possibility of restraining Japanese expansion, which was viewed with suspicion. As the alliance was limited geographically to the Far East it could hardly be described as a fully-fledged flight from isolation. But by giving France and Russia something to pause about it probably helped the willingness of those two powers to seek accommodation with Britain. The revision of the alliance in 1905 was considered by the C.I.D., and its new shape was largely suggested by it. Two cruisers were removed from the Far East in 1902, and it was a saving and a relief for Britain to be able to use Japanese-protected bases if necessary for coaling and repairs. In the Russo-Japanese war of February 1904 to August 1905 Britain was officially neutral. Japan's victory in the war transformed the Far Eastern situation, and made the original alliance irrelevant. The idea of extending it to cover India was discussed by the cabinet in March 1905. Balfour's idea was to get Japanese help in defending the status quo in India and Afghanistan, in return for Britain's preserving the status quo for Japan against Russian encroachment on Japanese rights. The C.I.D. hoped both that Japan would move 150,000 troops to the Indian frontier if it was threatened by Russia, and that the plan would of itself deter Russia from attacking India if indeed her plans to do so were serious. Japan explicitly rejected this extension of the alliance. There were, however, new clauses on India and Korea; the main strategic proposals were implicit rather than explicit, military rather than naval: in certain eventualities Britain would obtain Japan's assistance in Indian frontier defence. The interesting point about the plans for the 1905 renewal was the attempt to use the alliance as part of the scheme for imperial defence, since the main problem in 1905 was to defend the Indian frontier without making large increases in the British standing army. After 1905 Japan was much more likely than Russia to alter the balance of power in the Far East, and so the revised treaty was not an alliance for the status quo. Japan had destroyed the Russian squadron, enabling Britain to withdraw her battleships, although Russia never ceased to be an object of suspicion. Harcourt and the government were anxious 'from an educative point of view' that the Dominions should understand how far their comparative immunity from danger rested on the alliance; they wanted the Dominions to confirm the decision to renew the alliance in 1911 which they did unanimously after listening to Grey's skilful and lucid explanation. He told them that the alliance could not be given up simply because it was distasteful to public opinion. If Britain renounced it after it had worked well, Japan would conclude she was no longer in British confidence and would be bound to make whatever other arrangement she could to secure her position and to increase her fleet, which would be tremendous and undesirable changes in the strategic situation. 'I am convinced', he declared, 'that in the interests of strategy, in the interests of naval expenditure, and in the interests of stability, it is essential that the Japanese Alliance should be extended'. He regarded it as contributing to peace in the Far East. The future of the alliance seemed threatened by the vehemence of Dominion hostility but Grey's argument convinced them. From 1911 its chief value was as a restraining influence on the more expansionist tendencies of Japanese policy. Grey was adamant that Japan could not be allowed to encroach on British interests in the Yangtse valley.[112]

The French entente of 1904, like the Japanese alliance, was in origin designed to check the dangers felt to come from Russia and the Franco-Russian alliance. The entente officially ended the prolonged feud with France, freed Britain in Egypt, reduced her dependence on Germany, and cleared up the position in the Newfoundland fisheries dispute. Britain recognised the French position in Morocco, and France accepted the British position in Egypt. The chief hope behind the entente was, as Cromer put it, that it might be a 'stepping stone to a general understanding with Russia'.[113]

Shortly after taking office, Grey concluded that an agreement with Russia was 'the thing most to be desired in our foreign policy'. It would complete and strengthen the entente with France and 'add very much to the comfort and strength of our position'. Grey and Morley were the two ministers most active in arranging it. Morley hoped they could retain the friendship of the Amir of Afghanistan while preventing him from playing off Russia and Britain against each other; an agreement might stop Russia from being manipulated by Germany. A survey by the General Staff of the war office came to a conclusion surpassing in pessimism anything which Kitchener had written: if Russia absorbed Afghanistan (even without designs on India itself), 'it will become a question of practical politics whether or not it is worth our while to retain India or not'. The fundamental argument for an agreement was, in Morley's view, the conclusion that the despatch of 100,000 men to India in the first year of a war with Russia was a military necessity, 'for we have not got the men to spare and that's the plain truth of it'. Thus it was largely considerations relating to India alone which led to the agreement. Grey had hoped that it would get rid of the 'old policy of drift, with its continual complaints, bickerings and dangerous friction'. The results, however, were disappointing, partly because the really contentious matters of China and the Dardanelles were left out. Nevertheless there were three agreements arranged in 1907. It was agreed that both powers should leave Tibet alone. Russia admitted Afghanistan to be in the British sphere of control. Persia was divided into three zones: Russian, neutral and British. This was the most important part of the total agreement, but it did not provide a settlement. Russia continued to be troublesome in Persia, and after 1907 Grey found Persia trying his patience more than any other question. [114]

Simultaneously with all this diplomatic activity, revolutionary changes were being made in the navy. As first sea lord, 1904-10, Admiral Fisher 'fell on the old régime with a devastating fury'. His radical changes were directly stimulated by fear of German naval expansion from 1898. He emphasised the need to prepare for war, by attending more to proficiency than paintwork, encouraging gunnery practice, and aiming at economy. He drastically reduced dockyard expenditure. Five major changes were made in naval organisation. A new scheme of education was introduced for young officers at Osborne, concentrating on modern problems. Obsolete warships, small ships of no great power, were scrapped. A new all-big-gun type of battleship, the dreadnought, was launched in 1906. A nucleus crew system to man the reserve fleet was started. Finally a redistribution and concentration of the fleet was arranged. 'Five strategic keys lock up the world', said Fisher: Singapore, Cape Town, Alexandria, Gibraltar and Dover. He concentrated on these, and withdrew the Pacific, South Atlantic, and North American stations. The Singapore fleet amalgamated the squadrons of Australia, China and the East Indies. Three-quarters of the fleet was thus made available for use against Germany in home waters. Despite considerable resistance to this programme, Fisher's dynamic exertions carried all before him. [115]

No less remarkable was the extent to which the Dominions by 1911 realised that they had an essential community of interest with Britain in defence matters, in the maintenance of sea power and in Britain's commitment to the continent of Europe. As Grey explained in 1911 command of the seas and the European balance were interdependent objectives and not alternatives, because without a European balance British command of the sea would be lost, and this would permanently separate the Dominions from the empire and from each other. By 1912 dreadnoughts had been offered by New Zealand, the Malay States, Australia and Canada. Under the pressure of a deteriorating international situation the Dominions accepted Asquith's contention that 'the only way of carrying on in such an Empire as ours this task of imperial defence is by hearty and spontaneous co-operation in every quarter'. How did he secure agreement? The diminution of distance made it possible to conceive of the empire as an integrated defence unit, but more important was the naval scare of 1909, associated with a less equivocal German threat.[116]

THE CONTRIBUTION OF THE LIBERAL GOVERNMENT 1905–14

Liberal ministers had their own distinctive contribution to make to the search for stability in the empire. They distinguished between a rational, sane, sober and 'true' imperial emotion, and an irrational, insane, hooligan and 'bastard' form of it; they repudiated the latter. On taking office, the Liberal prime minister Sir Henry Campbell-Bannerman declared that the Liberal government would base itself on 'justice and liberty, not privilege and monopoly', a phrase which set the keynote of their administration. The Liberals believed that stability for the empire could be found only through pursuit of a scrupulously 'moral' policy purged of debasing excesses; they did not think it could be constructively forced by political exertions of the Unionist type. They placed their faith in principles and free assent, not size, soldiers and centralisation – though of course they increasingly gave in to practical imperatives.[117]

The basic dilemma confronting them was how to put imperial policy back on a sound basis without repudiating entirely the essential continuity of policy which they as practical politicians knew to be necessary in a world where the range of options open to Britain was visibly diminishing.[118] A large degree of continuity of foreign policy through changes of government was already an established convention of British government, and there were difficulties about making reversals in other fields. The empire, moreover, had to maintain law and order or perish. There was not much the Liberals could do to alter these facts of life. They had to make compromises. They called an immediate halt to the further importation of Chinese labour to work the Rand goldmines, but they had to allow those already there to complete their contracts. They abandoned Lyttelton's representative constitution for the

Transvaal, but retained its fundamental features in their own responsible government system. Conversely, while they allowed Selborne to stay on in South Africa, they reduced him to acting as a mere channel of communication. They made reforms in Indian administration, but coupled them with repression of disorder, while in Egypt they experimented with allowing Egyptians more influence over their own government and then cancelled the experiment.

The Liberals favoured allowing the white Dominions to settle their own affairs, but there were two possible limitations: in foreign policy and native affairs. In foreign policy they accepted the necessity of alliances and commitments to friends. Although they did not think it a good idea to 'unite' the empire, they accepted the necessity of maintaining imperial control of foreign affairs. Colonial secretary Crewe was opposed to allowing Canada to set up her own foreign affairs department.[119] The empire as an internationally recognised unit must, they believed, be maintained, and to this end they held on to as much control of foreign affairs as they possibly could. Until 1911 they did not even trouble to explain to the Dominions what imperial foreign policy was. In resolving the dilemma between supporting international obligations and the claims of the Dominions the Liberal government consistently gave priority to the former. They were especially careful about relations with the United States. In native affairs the right of self-governing colonies to exclude Asian immigrants had to be admitted, but they felt bound to see 'that no needless hardships are inflicted, and to make representations when we are not in a position to give orders'. Although Southern Rhodesia could be kept open to such immigrants, it was impossible to prevent Transvaal restriction of Indian immigration, despite their dislike of it. The essential truth was that colonists could not be coerced: unlike dealing with foreign powers there could be no ultimate appeal to force. The limitation worried them greatly. They searched painfully for better safeguards for Africans in South Africa, but reluctantly came to the conclusion that this was largely an impossible objective. They were, however, able to withhold the High Commission Territories (Basutoland, the Bechuanaland Protectorate and Swaziland) from the Union of South Africa formed in 1910, with the result that while South Africa was united, the geographical area of southern Africa was partitioned, with immense consequences for the whole future of the region.[120] The overriding concern was with Union itself, as a device for further strengthening of what Chamberlain had called 'the weakest link in the imperial chain'. In the dependent parts of the empire they had more freedom of movement, and Morley posed a central question: 'whether the excited corporal and the angry planter are to be the arbiters of policy'. The answer was clear: the government would not yield to the 'passions and violences of a [colonial] public that is apt to take narrow views'. The excesses of settlers, civil and army officers towards Asians and Africans were checked whenever they came to light. Morley felt that showing common politeness and just consideration to the subject population would do more good in India than any quantity of legislative achievements. The colonial office in general, and parliamentary under-secretary Churchill in particular, worked hard in the same spirit.[121]

It was clearly in the national interest to promote the economic development of the empire, and the Liberals were not averse to continuing Chamberlain's policy of developing the 'great estates'. This posed the dilemma of how to achieve it without opening the door to greedy, hated concessionaires who might exploit the natives. The Liberal government and its advisers were almost excessively wary of those individuals who came forward with development schemes. William Lever, M.P., was repeatedly refused an opening in British West Africa, despite the testimonials of E. D. Morel; Lever was a victim of Liberal dislike for 'the soap-boilers of the world', as colonial secretary Lewis Harcourt (with characteristic disdain) called them. Similar caution was exercised throughout Africa, and in Malaya.[122]

The Liberals' achievement for the empire was considerable. Their South African policy soothed away some of the post-war bitterness. In India too, the outraged reaction to Curzon was calmed down. The pretensions of proconsuls were reduced to size, the excesses of bureaucracies trimmed; administrative standards were tightened up, militaristic and monopolistic tendencies were held in check, and trusteeship conscience given wider expression again. Under colonial secretary Elgin in 1907 the establishment of a Dominions' department went some way towards meeting colonial complaints. The colonial service rule-book was given much-needed revisions; the regulations had become almost scandalously obsolete. The colonial office began to equip itself with more regular and sophisticated channels of advice for running and developing tropical possessions. The clamour of left-wing critics of empire was decidedly quietened: the Liberals made the empire harder to bring under genuine doctrinaire attack.[123]

Whilst the Liberals remained cautious in their hopes, the empire's future certainly looked more secure in 1914 than it had in 1904 or 1894. By 1914 the attitude of Britain as a whole towards all parts of the world, whether inside the empire or not, was highly ambivalent. There was no longer a comfortably agreed world picture such as had inspired the early Victorians. The British governing élite in Edwardian times was disorientated, especially in its attitude towards other world powers. Not everybody approved of the new alignments with the French, the Russians, the Americans and the Japanese. As foreign secretary, Edward Grey pursued a policy which the majority of his party distrusted, since it was difficult to persuade them of the gloomy realities; Grey's advisers were mostly, though not exclusively, anti-German. In 1909 the cabinet split over the naval estimates, with Grey, Haldane, McKenna and Asquith arguing for increases, while Harcourt, Lloyd George, Morley, Churchill and Burns wanted reductions. Intensification of the German threat caused Lloyd George and Churchill to change their minds from 1911, and they began working for effective rearmament. When war came, 'the fleet was ready'; but Morley and Burns resigned. Some said that in Germany Britain was fighting the wrong enemy.

Not the least significant aspect of Liberal government policy was the unusual extent to which it was in harmony with the advice given by colonial office officials, and by 1914 the empire was more efficiently and humanely run than ever before. Nevertheless, pessimism remained. The colonial office was worried less by the threat of nationalist uprisings than by its fear that the white colonists would ultimately destroy the empire, not by wilful maliciousness, but by sheer stupidity, brutal insensitivity to the non-European races, and by a parochial inability to see any problem either in its imperial perspective or within the realities of the international context.[124]

SCHOOLING AND SCOUTING

The search for stability was bound to extend to the education and training of the young, in order to 'safeguard the manhood' of the empire. Here the impact was many-sided, with every kind of panacea being advanced to produce a bracing new tone in the community.

Advocates of 'national efficiency' came to the conclusion that the future of the empire would be decided in Britain itself. No amount of 'feverish activity on the confines of the Empire', wrote Charles Masterman, could arrest decline; the answer lay, if anywhere, in improved efficiency at the heart of the empire. Cromer, writing in 1903, regarded the two greatest national dangers as 'backwardness in education and unsound finance'.[125]

Chamberlain agreed with Haldane that the British educational system needed to be brought up to the level of Germany, a level which the United States was also fast approaching. In a speech at Birmingham, Chamberlain declared:

> The more I study this question of higher education the more I am persuaded of its enormous importance to this country, the more I am convinced of our own deficiencies, both absolutely and in comparison with those of other nations which are our competitors in the struggle, I will not say for existence, but at all events, for a foremost place in the rank of the nations of the world ... I am convinced that, unless we ... [make] application of the highest science to the commonest industries and manufactures in our land, we shall certainly fall very far behind in the race.[126]

Speaking on the Education Bill of 1902, Haldane described it as a national question of great urgency: 'It is vital to our interests, essential to our position as a nation, and necessary for the preservation of our commerce, our Navy, and our Empire'. He said that Britain should put herself on the same footing in education and technical training as those with whom she competed.[127] If anything was done at all towards improvement of education – and it is not clear that much in fact was – it owed a good deal to the influence of Michael Sadler and to his acute recognition of British educational backwardness and intellectual inertia. He could see the commercial and material importance of better teaching and improved and more accessible secondary education – 'the very existence of the Empire depends on sea-power and school-power' – but he also raised the question to a higher plane by his recognition that the competition of nations was 'not merely for supremacy in trade but for the supremacy of certain ideals of government and social order'.[128] One of the most serious gaps in the English educational system at all levels was in technical education. Germany and other countries had significantly anticipated her in this, with detrimental results. From the late 1890s some useful improvements were made. Chamberlain himself founded Birmingham University. The London School of Economics was founded in 1895. The 1902 Education Act made it possible for county councils to provide for secondary schools out of the rates; this was probably the most important domestic achievement of Balfour's ministry. Meanwhile voluntary agencies had been trying to tackle the problem. One interesting example is provided by Andrew Pears, head of the famous family soap business, who poured a good deal of money and time in the 1890s into the conversion of the 'upper department' of a local elementary school into a modern grammar school with a strong linguistic and technical bias. This was done in association with the British and Foreign School Society and along lines approved by Sadler. Pears reserved six scholarships at the school for his personal nomination. When the school was opened, within sniffing distance of his soap factory at Isleworth, the Earl of Jersey declared on behalf of Middlesex County Council (who financed the technical side):

There was a remark that Mr Pears made the other day with regard to trade which struck me as being most essentially true and useful. He said he knew that Englishmen had to contend against foreigners in trade and commerce, but he was perfectly convinced that Englishmen could always beat the foreigner when he made up his mind to do it. Now you boys ought . . . [to] determine to do whatever you can to advance not only yourselves but also your country in the great commercial struggle that is going on throughout the world . . . Our schools are really the machinery by which this country must carry on its good work.[129]

Unfortunately, at this critical juncture in English educational history, Morant gained the upper hand over Sadler in Whitehall, and the experimental development of secondary-level scientific and technical education as an extension of local elementary education was obliterated by a reversion to the narrower classical public school model as a basis for refashioning grammar schools, and by opening 'county' schools which were required to ape Winchester, Morant's old school.[130]

Worries about educational qualifications were paralleled by concern over the evidence of 'physical deterioration' revealed by recruitment for the Anglo-Boer war. Alarming symptoms showed a clear danger to the continued existence of Britain as a world power. In 1900 recruitment medicals showed that 565 men per thousand were below the standard army height of 5' 6'', compared with only 105 per thousand in 1845. 44 men in every thousand weighed under 7 st. 2 lbs. At the Manchester recruiting depot in 1899, 8,000 out of 12,000 men examined were rejected as virtual invalids; and only 1,200 of them were found after service in the army to be physically fit in all respects. Three thousand men had to be sent home from South Africa on account of acutely bad teeth. Baden-Powell considered that half the British losses in war from sickness could have been avoided by better personal hygiene. A committee of the Privy Council prepared a report on 'Physical Deterioration'. The *British Medical Journal* commented in July 1903 on the symptoms of physical decline coming to light, just at the very time when Britain required 'stalwart sons to people the colonies and to uphold the prestige of the nation'.

Rosebery declared in 1900:

An empire such as ours requires as its first condition an Imperial Race – a race vigorous and industrious and intrepid. Health of mind and body exalt a nation in the competition of the universe. The survival of the fittest is an absolute truth in the conditions of the modern world.

For the sake of the empire he concluded that there must be social reform in Britain itself. This theme became widely accepted. Earl Grey in 1901 expressed fears that 'our successors will not be able to bear the burden of empire'.[131] Winston Churchill between 1906 and 1911 became a social reformer from anxiety about the stability of society and the empire: 'to keep our empire we must have a free people, an educated and well fed people'. That he said, was 'why we are in favour of social reform'; the degraded condition of the poor was, he argued, 'a serious hindrance to recruiting for the army and navy'; the essential foundation for security was 'a healthy family life for all'.[132] As Bentley B. Gilbert has rightly observed, for many politicians the physical condition of the working class child came to represent the pivot on which turned the fate of British civilisation. The introduction of subsidised school meals in 1906 and of compulsory school medical inspection in 1907 have been seen by another historian 'with only a little exaggeration, as an institutionalised legacy of the anxieties felt in the Boer War period'. The evolution of national insurance has to be seen in the same context.[133]

Concern for military efficiency gave rise also to a hotly debated campaign for national service conscription. Whatever view might be held of this contentious matter, people could agree that shooting clubs provided an acceptable adjunct. Rifle ranges mushroomed, and school clubs eagerly formed and affiliated themselves to the National Rifle Association. By 1912 in one state grammar school one fifth of all the boys took part in the annual shooting competition. There were many such schools preparing to win the next war on their own playing fields.[134]

One symbolic, and far from insignificant, new development was the introduction of routine circumcision among the upper and professional classes of Britain and America. We know less about this ritual British circumcision than we do about the practice of the most obscure African peoples. As befits a mystic ritual, its origin is shrouded in mystery, but the practice seems to have caught on in the 1890s. The most influential publicist of the benefits of circumcision was Dr Remondino, according to whom, evolution might eventually remove the foreskin; meanwhile, war must be waged upon this 'debatable appendage'. In his *History of Circumcision* (1891) the enthusiastic Remondino wrote:

> Circumcision is like a substantial and well-secured life annuity; . . . parents cannot make a better saving investment for their little boys, as it ensures them better health, greater capacity for labour, longer life, less nervousness, sickness, loss of time, and less doctor bills, as well as it increases their chances for an euthanasian death.

Presumably people believed this nonsense. But *symbolically*, the anthropologist (to whom we must turn for guidance) would regard circumcision as a change 'from a state of infantile filthiness to a state of clean maturity', of rebirth into 'masculinity and personality'. Viewed so, the relevance of its potential contribution to the general improvement of the physique and manliness of the future custodians of empire becomes apparent. That this *was* indeed its function is clear from the sharp difference in attitude towards it between classes. Circumcision was chiefly adopted by the upper and professional classes. In the 1930s (there are unfortunately no earlier statistics) it seems to have been carried out on at least two-thirds of public schoolboys, and at the highest levels of the social scale the proportion may even have exceeded four-fifths; whereas in some 'deprived' working class areas, rural and urban, it may never have got beyond one-tenth. Overall, by the 1930s about one-third of the total male population was probably being circumcised.[135]*

* The post-imperial race is decidedly an uncircumcised people. The operation today is carried out on about 2% of infants, and doctors discourage it as unnecessary and potentially dangerous. The British anti-preputial prejudice thus lasted for barely two generations. There is nothing to suggest that Bulwer Lytton in 1871 conceived his *Vril-ya*, the coming master-race, to be circumcised, despite Remondino's speculation upon this very point. It is a curious fact that outside the traditional circumcising communities (Jewish, Muslim, Melanesian, Amerindian and some African) the only Western peoples ever to adopt it as a common practice were the English-speaking peoples.

The history of British circumcision is thus best seen as part of a whole corpus of phenomena and bundle of enthusiasms at the turn of the century: deference to the United States, Zionism, tariff reform, Boy Scouting, prefectorial systems in state schools, school meals, rifle clubs and short trousers. And to the Boy Scout movement – founded 1908 – we now turn.

The Scout movement has a singularly important position in the history of British expansion. It proved to be the most successful youth movement in world history. Throughout the world, in the first 60 years of its existence, 70 million boys became scouts, and 40 million girls became guides. Nearly 100 countries had scouts by the 1960s, with nine million active boys and six million girls. Baden-Powell originally conceived scouting as a means to preserve the British empire against the fate of the Roman empire. In his first 'prospectus' he began by quoting George Wyndham – 'The same causes which brought about the downfall of the Great Roman Empire are working today in Great Britain'. The truth of this, said Baden-Powell, was

> practically admitted by those who have studied and compared the general conditions of both countries.
> The main cause of the downfall of Rome was the decline of good citizenship among its subjects, due to want of energetic patriotism, to the growth of luxury and idleness, and to the exaggerated importance of local party politics, etc . . .

Britain's enemies abroad were 'daily growing stronger and stronger'. British boys must not be disgraced like the young Romans, who lost the empire of their forefathers by being 'wishy-washy slackers without any go or patriotism in them'. Camp Fire Yarn No. 26 ('Our empire: how it grew – how it must be held'), explained how Britain had 'many powerful enemies' wanting very much to get hold of her trade and colonial farmlands, and it exhorted boys to 'Be Prepared' to defend these from attack, by making themselves 'fit and proper men' to help the empire. The basic intention of the whole scheme was 'for helping in the vital work of developing good citizenship in our rising generation'. *Young Knights of the Empire* was the title of a book produced by Baden-Powell in 1916, and his original idea for the name of the movement. The connection between it and the imperial theme is almost self-evident. Baden-Powell defined his original object: 'to help existing organisations in making the rising generation, of whatever class or creed, into good citizens or useful colonists'. Although the movement eventually became internationalised, he was at first exclusively concerned with empire boys, using scouting as a means of 'consolidating our Empire by the development of personal sympathy and sense of comradeship between the manhood of all the different overseas states and the mother country'. His sister wrote a book: *How Girls Can Help Build Up the Empire*. Kipling was closely interested in the movement. The conception of the 'wolf cubs' was based upon his *Jungle* books, with the author's blessing, and Kipling wrote the official Boy Scout song.[136] The movement seemed important to the government of the day – so much so that Haldane, secretary of state for war, agreed to Baden-Powell's resignation from the army in 1910, writing to him as follows:

> I feel that this organisation of yours has so important a bearing upon the future that probably the greatest service you can render to the country is to devote yourself to it.

Even when war broke out in 1914, Kitchener expressly told Baden-Powell that his most important war job was to carry on with scouting. It conceivably paved the way for acceptance of conscription.[137] Baden-Powell's outlook fitted in perfectly with the aggressive racial attitudes of the time. Although he denied being a 'regular nigger-hater', having been in India and South Africa, he knew all about dealing with natives:

> However good they may be, they must, as a people, be ruled with a hand of iron in a velvet glove; and if they writhe under it, and do not understand the force of it, it is of no use to add more padding – you must take off the glove for a moment and show them the hand. They will then understand and obey.

Baden-Powell found Africans infuriating. 'The stupid inertness of the puzzled negro,' he wrote, 'is duller than that of an ox; a dog would grasp your meaning in one half the time. "Men and brothers"! They may be brothers, but they certainly are not men'. He subscribed to stereotyped notions of the black man's laziness and unreliability in word and deed, and defended domestic slavery for 'unintelligent savages'.[138] On the other hand he admired the bush training of the Zulu and Swazi. 'Our friends the Japanese' also came in for repeated praise, and, in discussing the raising of 'moral tone' he drew a parallel between the bushido of the samurai and scouting.

His movement was unashamedly designed to distract or re-channel adolescent sexual energies. It was also emotionally matriarchal, with the leader's call on all scouts to recognise his mother as their universal grandmother. It was highly personal. His beloved friend McLaren was chief administrator, his brother Warrington wrote for the sea scouts, his sister established the girl guides and his wife led them. 'Be Prepared': the motto was taken from his own initials. Nevertheless, he managed to focus some attention on putative 'scout' heroes alternative to himself, and a motley crew they were too: Charlemagne, Richard I, General Gordon, Speke, Baker, F. C. Selous, Mary Kingsley and Lady Lugard.[139]

5 The Dynamics of Empire and Expansion

There used to be a theory that territories came under the British flag as a result of the export of surplus capital. It would be much truer to say that the driving force behind empire-building was rather the export of surplus emotional, or sexual energy. The empire was a boon to the brokenhearted, the misogynist and to the promiscuous alike. The enjoyment and exploitation of black flesh was as powerful an attraction as any desire to develop economic resources. There were emotional opportunities and sexual satisfactions available overseas greater than could be had in inhibited Britain; and for those who denied themselves such possibilities as there were, empire-building provided a sublimating alternative. These hypotheses are not of course easily susceptible of proof, and they involve some speculation, but the subject is irresistibly tempting and the quantity of relevant evidence is surprisingly large.*

Although the bulk of my argument will be concentrated on repression and sublimation, it is perhaps worthwhile to look first at the opportunities available for the promiscuous. Resort to black flesh was not simply a piece of erotic expediency. The fact that black flesh was a positive magnet to the British was pointed out as early as 1774 by the Jamaican judge and historian Edward Long. His countrymen, he wrote, were all too prone to unions with black women not from a shortage of white women (although there were twice as many white men as women in Jamaica) or the supposed burdens and expenses of marriage, but from the sexual attractiveness of Negro women: 'Many are the men, of every rank, quality, and degree, who would much rather riot in these goatish embraces, than share the pure and lawful bliss

---

* Almost every new biography throws fresh light on this subject. We can already, I think, make reasonable assumptions about the nature of the sex lives of many of the key figures in our empire story. What we cannot do is to explain these, or measure their exact effects. I have no wish to follow the biographer of Rhodes, for example, who ascribes all Rhodes's 'strange imperialism', juvenile romanticism and chronic homosexuality to a 'retarded puberty' during which he was unable to sweat out his 'glandular troubles' and 'secretory overflow' in either sport or poetry (F. Gross *Rhodes of Africa* 63, 248).

derived from matrimonial, mutual love'. He hinted, and he was not alone, that the judgment of many planters was swayed by their concubines. He also noted that, given the chance, white women were strongly drawn sexually to Negro men. We know also that coloured concubines were so popular in New Orleans in the 1850s that three-quarters of the houses in one entire section of the city were occupied by kept women; notorious quadroon balls were held for white gentlemen to survey the latest crop of coloured debutantes; and many planters had two families, one white and one coloured. Gilberto Freyre has put forward the dictum: 'There is no slavery without sexual depravity', and slavery was endemic in the world for much of the century. Wherever there were plantations or mines, whether employing slaves or merely indentured labourers, there was prostitution and sexual exploitation. We shall doubtless never know just how much prostitution there was in the nineteenth-century world. But two things are certain: its incidence both male and female was enormous, and merely to set foot outside Europe was to walk whole new vistas of casual sex, and particularly perhaps of a homosexual kind, since there was no shortage of female prostitutes in London (a mid-century estimate gives a figure of 80,000), and because most of the rest of the world did not share the utter abhorrence in which this aspect of sexual behaviour was officially held in the West. Even so, boy prostitution is believed to have flourished among convicts in early Australia, and in San Francisco during (and long after) the gold rushes. Boy brothels were well established in Naples, as well as in Cairo and Karachi; pederasty was endemic among the Persians, the Sikhs and the Pathans, and was elevated into an integral part of Afghanistan culture in the form of the *batsha* troupes of dancing boys. In the early nineteenth century there were reckoned to be more boy prostitutes in Constantinople than women. In China the availability of small boys was regular enough for it to be the subject of an annual warning to the populace by the Chinese superintendent of trade at Canton: don't indulge the western barbarians with all our best favours. By 1900, however, in Tientsin, Europeans were welcome at the 35 boy brothels, housing 800 boys. In 1834 a British traveller in Egypt recorded how well known it was 'with what design young and beautiful boys are purchased' in Cairo, most of them Greeks; he was told that some 10,000 Greek boys were thus enslaved in Egypt.

The pattern of sexual initiation for many Britons may be conjectured with some reasonable certainty. The soldier, clerk or trader stopping at Cairo or Port Said en route eastwards (or later, perhaps, to the Sudan) would there be tempted into the brothels, or get picked up by one of the *terrasiers,* the youths frequenting the hotel terraces – for, as a French historian has laconically observed, 'anything might happen on this suspect fringe between two worlds'. Then the soldier, clerk or trader would proceed east and, in the words of one British army captain who experienced precisely this mode of initiation,

. . . thus encouraged at once began

To explore the amorous realms of Hindustan.

This captain (his name was Kenneth Searight, and he later invented a neutral international language which he called 'Sona') found in Peshawar as late as 1911 to 1914 that 'to get a boy was easier than to pick the flowers by the wayside', and he even seems to have managed at Simla, 'in the midst of her vast proprieties', to break all manner of taboos with three English teenage schoolboys from Christ Church School.[1]

While the rank-and-file empire builder thus had many openings for the export of his sexual tensions, the administrative élite was, by and large, being driven along by frustration. Not all explorers or servants of empire made a conscious choice between private happiness and public usefulness, as Viscount Milner did after the rejection of his proposal on the Nile at Luxor to Margot Tennant. Nursing a bundle of love-letters, Milner (high commissioner in South Africa 1897–1905) did not marry until his retirement from the colonial secretaryship in 1921 at the age of 67. He was not as ardent in South Africa as he had been in Egypt, and women were notably absent from his 'Kindergarten' circle. Beatrice Webb said Milner badly needed a God and a wife. Curzon was less austere than Milner in this matter, but in early life he deliberately forced celibacy upon himself in order to complete the 12-year programme of oriental study and travel which he hoped would qualify him to become viceroy of India. After a hearty friendship with the four Tennant sisters, he somewhat callously kept his future wife waiting a long time. He fell in love with Mary Leiter in 1890, took two years to propose, and three years more to redeem his promise. He took himself off on his travels; meanwhile she had to fend off another suitor. In 1893 he wrote to her that by her faithfulness 'I am spared all the anxieties of what is called a great courtship, and I have merely, when the hour strikes, to enter into possession of my own'.[2]

There were some conspicuously inveterate bachelors among the famous and successful, such as General Charles Gordon, Cecil Rhodes, Kitchener and Sir Matthew Nathan (1862–1939), governor of the Gold Coast, Hong Kong and Natal – a man who was considered by the colonial office to be superior even to Lugard, who himself did not marry until he was 44. According to his biographer Kitchener was a man whose sexual instincts were wholly sublimated in work; he admitted few distractions and 'thereby reaped an incalculable advantage in competition with his fellows'. There is no evidence that he ever loved a woman; his male friendships were few but fervent; from 1907 until his death his constant and inseparable companion was Capt. O. A. G. FitzGerald who devoted his entire life to Kitchener. He had no use for married men on his staff. Only young officers were admitted to his house – 'my happy family of boys' he called them; he avoided interviews with women, worshipped Gordon, cultivated great interest in the boy scout movement, took a fancy to Botha's son and the sons of Lord Desborough, and embellished his rose garden with four pairs of sculptured bronze boys. The founder of the boy scouts, Baden-Powell, idolised his mother and was 55 before he married. In India he met Kenneth McLaren (known as 'The Boy' on account of his youthful looks) who became his closest friend, and for life. While besieged at Mafeking Baden-Powell wrote to him every day, and on his return to England the first thing he did was visit McLaren. 'The Boy' became chief administrator of the Boy Scouts.[3]

The most intimate relationship Cecil Rhodes ever had was his friendship with Neville Pickering, four years his junior, with whom he shared house in Kimberley from 1881 until Pickering's death in 1886. For Rhodes, Pickering was the incarnation of the masculine ideal, and, in the opinion of his latest biographer, 'probably the only person whom Rhodes ever really loved'. In his second will, Rhodes left everything to Pickering. On his own death-bed, Pickering is said to have whispered to Rhodes 'You have been father, mother, brother and sister to me'. Despite his friendship with Alfred Beit, and even more with Dr Jameson (an attachment another friend described as 'fervent'), Rhodes, the homosexual leader of this unmarried trio, was probably, for the remainder of his own short life, a lonely man. Described by Bramwell Booth as 'a great human heart hungering for love', he found little happiness at the peak of his career in the 1890s. When asked if he was happy Rhodes replied, 'Happy? I happy? Good God, no'. And this was the confession of a man who added two provinces to the empire, became prime minister of the Cape, a millionaire in the City of London, the virtual dictator of a chartered company and two mining firms, and the owner of several newspapers. He once said he could not get married because he had too much work on his hands. It may have been true; but it is also the case that he wanted only unmarried male secretaries in his household – as soon as they married he transferred them to one of his companies; he considered their marriage an act of disloyalty, and he told at least one bride that he was jealous of her. Rumours about his homosexual inclinations always pursued him. His dislike of female company and servants was notorious; his high-pitched effeminate voice did not help matters, nor did his openly displayed collection of phallic cult carvings.

It is certainly an extraordinary fact that in the 1890s all those who held the imperial destiny of South Africa in their hands – Rhodes, Milner, Jameson and Beit – were unmarried, and it is perfectly possible, as W. T. Stead observed, that the history of South Africa might have been different if this had been otherwise. No generalisation is possible about them other than that they were all unmarried at this critical time. Beit was certainly not averse to women, but his cynical attitude is indicated by the fact that he took little care to button up his trousers before leaving the brothel. Other lesser folk in this southern African circle were scathing about women. When Benjamin 'Matabele' Wilson arrived in Bulawayo in 1888, he rhapsodised; 'There is no old woman here to tell you "You are looking pale", or "Oh, I am sorry to see you looking so bad", or having people fooling around you with a cup of tea or soup or other things you do not want'.[4]

Sir George Goldie (1846–1925), the creator of Nigeria, left England in 1877 for Nigeria – largely to escape from personal entanglements. As a young man he lived for three years idyllically with an Arab girl in the Egyptian Sudan; he returned to a life of dissipation in Britain, shocked everybody by eloping with the family governess and then hopelessly compromised himself as a result of getting caught up with her in the Paris siege in 1870. He married her in 1871, but it was what the Victorians called an 'unfortunate' marriage and he was not a faithful husband.[5]

The case of F. D. Lugard (1858–1945) is even more instructive. Towards the end of his life he explicitly admitted that 'The real key to the story of a life lies in a knowledge of the emotions and passions which have sometimes disfigured, sometimes built up character, and in every case influenced the actions recorded. Of these the sexual instinct is recognised as the most potent for good or ill and it has certainly been so in my life'. At the age of 29 he abandoned a successfully begun military career and set sail as a deck-passenger to an unknown African destination, all the while contemplating suicide. Three years earlier in India he had fallen in love with a woman who subsequently abandoned him and established herself in a pleasure-seeking circle in London utterly uncongenial to him. Emotional desperation, together with the depressant effects of fever, led him to desire danger and if possible death in some distant place and among strangers – perhaps Ethiopia. Britain must remain barred to him because it contained his unrequited love. He struggled with the longing for self-destruction all the way to Zanzibar, where he recovered himself a little and in 1888 entered the service of the African Lakes Company at Blantyre. Years of constructive effort in Nyasaland, Uganda and Nigeria followed; when at last in his mid 40s he married Flora Shaw (in 1902) his desire to be near his wife led him to devise a preposterous scheme for the administration of tropical colonies – a scheme scornfully received in the colonial office.[6]

The empire was a very masculine affair, women were honoured in their absence, and for better or for worse, servants of the empire endured long separation from wives and families. Livingstone was a case in point: the disruption of his family life drove his oldest son to death and turned his wife into an alcoholic. Not all explorers had wives as intrepid as Sir Samuel Baker did; she always travelled with him, but, significantly, she was Hungarian and not British. Edward Eyre began his heroic exploration along the Great Australian Bight with three aborigine boys, one of whom had been with him for four years; he formed repeated close associations with such boys before his marriage, and brought two of them to Britain in 1844 to be educated at his expense.[7] Deprivation in desert conditions and close contact with sexually highly sophisticated African and Arabian peoples often intensified latent homosexuality in restless explorers. Heinrich Barth joined the British government expedition to 'Central Africa' in 1849 and spent the next five years of his short life swooning over the beauty and affectionateness of Nigerian teenagers, two of whom be brought back to Britain with him in 1855.[8] T. E. Lawrence (Lawrence of Arabia) enjoyed the company of Arabian boys. H. M. Stanley found most relationships difficult, with his illegitimate and workhouse background and an unsatisfied youthful search for affection after rejection by his Welsh mother. He wanted a wife, but he also needed the company of boys. He became attached to 15-year-old Lewis Noe, and then to 13-year-old Edwin Balch, whom he tried to take on his expedition in 1869 to find Livingstone, but the boy's parents refused permission; he then almost literally picked up three working-class companions. At another point he tried to find a workhouse boy to live with him, but failed. In Africa he was presented with little Kalulu in 1871 and became extremely fond of him, but the boy died in 1877 towards the end of the Nile expedition. Meanwhile in 1874 he had fallen in love with a rich American girl called Alice Pike, but she jilted him in 1876 during his Nile expedition. Subsequently he was also turned down by Kate Gough-Roberts, and at the first time of asking, by Dolly Tennant. Dolly however eventually married him, by which time he was 51, and recognised as the greatest explorer in the world and the chief 'discoverer' of Central Africa, albeit a gun-addicted one. During a critical part of his career he deliberately steeled himself against all but platonic love,[9] and became an utterly ruthless conquistador.

In an area of history where much is inference, Roger Casement's sex life is fully documented. Though there will doubtless continue to be those who insist on believing the homosexual entries in his diaries to be forgeries engineered by an unscrupulous British government, there can be no doubt of their authenticity. All the details are there: locations, partner's ages, penile shapes and sizes, positions assumed, amounts paid. Although Casement enjoyed these encounters in Africa and Latin America in the interstices of acting as consul in Lourenço Marques, Angola, the Congo Free State and Brazil, doing important work in reporting and exposing the 'red rubber' slavery scandals in Leopold's Congo and then in Putamayo, Peru, he never revealed his proclivities to any of his friends. The strain of concealment, especially when everyone regarded him as a person of unimpeachable integrity, was severe enough to produce a gradual disintegration of personality. By his forties Casement was probably a manic depressive and prone to sporadic breakdown. He was executed as an Irish patriot in 1916.[10]

If Casement was an archetypal passive homosexual, the prince of pederasts (in the sense of small-boy lover) was unquestionably an even more important figure: General Charles Gordon, hero of campaigns in the Sudan and China. Totally and irredeemably boy-orientated, he was almost certainly too honourable or inhibited ever to succumb to physical temptation, and so this emotion was heavily sublimated into serving God, the Empire and Good Works. He spent six years of his life (from 1865 to 1871) trying to create in London his own little land where the child might be prince, housing ragged urchins (his 'kings' as he called them), until packing them off to sea when the onset of puberty occurred. 'How far better', he wrote, 'to be allowed to be kind to a little scrub than to govern the greatest kingdoms'. Whilst in

Basutoland he confessed to a sympathetic missionary that his one real desire in life was to retire into Mt Carmel monastery and establish there a small refuge or school for poor Syrian boys, whom he would teach the Christian faith and 'something useful to them in the world'.[11]

It would be entirely wrong to suggest that the pantheon of the British empire consisted of nought but homosexuals, most of them repressed. But it seems to remain true that the empire was an exceedingly masculine affair, based on a somewhat cynical view of women, and a particular rejection of the Regency and Victorian female. If there is such a thing as 'bisexuality', Charles Metcalfe may be an illustration of it. In 1803 he wrote of a youthful 'propensity to form romantic attachments' which he was trying to eradicate, presumably without success, since in 1824 he wrote of 'joys . . . in the pure love which exists beweeen man and man, which cannot, I think, be surpassed in that more alloyed attachment between the opposite sexes, to which the name of love is in general exclusively applied'. Meanwhile he lived together with a Sikh woman for eight years after their meeting (probably at the court of Ranjit Singh) in 1809. She bore him three illegitimate 'Eurasian' sons. He acknowledged them, though they brought him no happiness. In 1819 he wrote to his sister to urge her to find a cottage for the two of them to retire to, since he was almost certain he would never marry: 'my singleness does not proceed merely from absence of pretty and engaging girls' – he was 'determined to remain single . . . (till I alter) . . .' Metcalfc might have found a kindred spirit in Rudyard Kipling, poet of the empire, who revealed in his autobiography that, as a child 'the loveliest sound in the world' was 'deep-voiced men laughing together over dinner'. There was a streak of 'persistent puerility' in Kipling, and his love life seems to have been based on a search for a mother substitute to provide him with the kind of affection he was denied in his early youth. After several affairs, he married Caroline Balestier.[12]

Perhaps it may indeed be possible to suggest the rephrasing of another hoary catchphrase. The empire was not acquired in a fit of absence of mind, so much as in a fit of absence of wives.[13] The whole tenor of Victorian teaching on sex was, notoriously, that a man could not combine an energetic love-live and a successful career, that sex in general was a curse stemming from original sin, and that homosexuality was a criminal and unspeakable abomination into the bargain. It is certainly hard to imagine 'Walter' of My Secret Life as an empire builder.[14] And if, as was solemnly believed, masturbation was likely to turn backbones to jelly, and induce blindness and premature death, it was probably better not to risk it, but to go off pig-sticking in India and organise the whole world instead. The penalties of extra-marital affairs and sexual deviations in British society were severe. Two important political careers were wrecked by divorce scandals: those of Charles Dilke and C. S. Parnell. And two successful careers terminated in suicide for fear of homosexual imputations: those of foreign secretary Castlereagh and colonial secretary 'Loulou' Harcourt.

Overseas, for those who wanted them, liaisons with non-European women were easy to arrange, at least before improved communications and conditions lead to the growth of the expatriate white female community. Provided there was no interference with married native women, the taking of mistresses or concubines was never something which posed any threat to British prestige, although by the early twentieth century it might attract the condemnation of the colonial office and public opinion at home. The colonial service was always regarded officially as unsuitable for married men. Cases of concubinage (as it was officially labelled) were exceedingly common even in 1910 in the lonelier districts of Africa. The situation in North-east Rhodesia was subject to investigation. It was alleged to be the almost universal practice amongst unmarried Europeans, both officials and settlers, in Nyasaland, Kenya, Uganda and in West Africa too; the Administrator of Barotseland was said to have kept a veritable harem of native women. Pressed by the colonial under-secretary, Col. J. E. B. Seely (who had himself had an affair with a Maori lady), the government attempted to take an understanding view: the real difficulty was that the isolated posts at which temptation was strongest were precisely those at which life would have been most difficult for white women; the colonial office thus preferred to try to deal with the matter by moral persuasion rather than by a crusade of holy inquisition, if only because to make dismissals on this score in Rhodesia would have led to the loss of a great many officers. The habit of keeping black mistresses died out as the Zambian copperbelt was opened up.[15]

Planters in the West Indies, and at least one governor of Barbados, in the eighteenth century had taken negro or mulatto mistresses and often accorded them many of the privileges of legitimate wives. The keeping of mistresses was also a well-established tradition in India from the eighteenth century. In the 1790s a governor of Bombay and members of his council publicly kept Mahratta women. Sir David Ochterlony, Resident of Delhi (1803–25), is said to have had 13 mistresses among Indian ladies. Lord Teignmouth, a bible society founder, had such a liaison. These women were sometimes euphemistically called 'sleeping dictionaries', though the linguistic competence of British officers was not noticeably improved by such liaisons. The practice was, however, defended on the grounds that it increased knowledge of native affairs, and some superior officers recommended the custom quite openly. The future Sir Garnet Wolseley, in India just after the Mutiny, confessed to his brother that he managed to console himself with an attractive 'Eastern princess' who answered 'all the purposes of a wife without giving any of the bother'; he had no wish to be caught in European marriage by 'some bitch', unless an heiress. From the 1860s, however, it became increasingly shameful for an officer, civil or military, to live in a state which was normal in the previous generation, with part of his bungalow set aside for the Indian woman. Greater ease of communication with 'home' and the presence of more white women, leading to a slackening identification with the local community, explain the change.[16]

Nor can it be said that among those servants of empire who did marry was the incidence of marital happiness notably high. There were obvious exceptions, such as Bentinck, but of a more general condition a classic example is provided by Richard Marquis of Wellesley, who, as governor-general in India 1798–1805, made the most crucial conquests for the raj. He met Hyacinthe Roland (daughter of a French actress and a Parisian Irishman) in 1786. She became his mistress and bore him five children before he married her. In 1797 he went to India as governor of Madras. She refused to go with him. He made meticulous provision for his family, and then, 'torn with sorrow', lived alone for seven years. For the first two he was faithful, and hoped she would join him. He never forgave her for her failure to do so. Fundamentally, however, he appears to have been relieved to be free of domestic responsibility, and eventually abandoned himself to the brothels. Bitter hatred developed between his wife and himself. In 1801 she complained furiously that for 18 months he had written her not 'one affectionate or comforting letter', not one that had not been full of selfishness, vanity and ambition. She mocked the lack of philosophic courage which might have enabled him to be indifferent to decorations and titles: he, 'before whom all the rulers of Asia tremble' was 'devoured by fury' over them. He replied by commenting on the 'unbearable silliness' of her letters. The rift grew, and in 1810 they were legally separated. He then had other mistresses, among them Sally Douglas and Miss Leslie. His youngest son was threatened by the cut-throat associate of one of his whores at Covent Garden; the young man was reputed to be living the life of an effeminate 'Asiatic debauchee' in Ramsgate. 'I wish', said the Duke of Wellington (Wellesley's younger brother) 'that Wellesley was castrated'. The conqueror of India was not, in short, a stable family man, but lived a life of sexual tempestuousness and frustration.[17]

Sir George Grey (governor of New Zealand 1845–53, 1861–68, and of South Africa 1854–61) was completely estranged from his wife for 37 years, and, in the words of Sinclair, in the latter part of his career, as a lonely party politician, 'compensated for the absence of wife and friends by seeking, through his skill as a popular orator, the approval of the masses'. Marriage did Edward Eyre no good. His wife was rather silly, superior and sickly; marriage seemed to make him nervous of West Indians as he had never been of Aborigines; he and his wife were separated for two and a half years, and she at no time gave him as governor the social help which might have counteracted his shyness.[18]

Service of the empire brought tragedy to many families. The climate of Java and Sumatra killed Raffles's first wife in 1814; he remarried in 1817, and then lost four of the children of this marriage in 1821–22. In 1824 on his return home he lost most of his possessions (at least £25,000-worth) in a fire at sea, quite apart from his official and anthropological documents and 2,000 drawings on natural history. Raffles was only 44 when he died himself.

Similar misfortunes struck distinguished families throughout the century. Curzon's first wife died prematurely, shortly after his viceroyalty was over: it had hastened her end. The eighth earl of Elgin lost his first wife in Jamaica after shipwreck; and his son lost *his* first wife after years of ill-health made irreparable by his Indian viceroyalty. Lord Charles Somerset (governor of the Cape 1814–26) lost his wife in 1815: she never really recovered from the voyage out. He re-married in 1821. Sir John Pope Hennessy's infant son died of dysentery in Freetown, Sierra Leone.[19] Examples could be multiplied. The annual death rate of soldiers quartered in Bengal in the mid-1850s was 64 per 1,000 and 44 per 1,000 of their wives – a mortality rate three times higher than for officers in London. The rate was 78.5 per 1,000 in the West Indies, and 483 in West Africa.[20] Those who wanted greater assurance of domestic bliss were best advised to stay at home. Not all did so. The sense of public duty was sometimes very strong – as in the Elgin family, or the Brookes of Sarawak.

The white rajas of Sarawak provide interesting illustration for many of the points raised in this discussion. The first raja, James Brooke (1803–68) devoted his entire life to the interests of Sarawak and its people. He never married, although an illegitimate son, Reuben George Brooke, was the result of his only known experiment with the fair sex. Brooke had been wounded in the Burma war in 1825. Opinions differ as to whether the wound was in the lung or in the testicles. In view of the acknowledgement in his will of a son born after this event, it would certainly seem to be the case that Brooke did not believe himself to be impotent. The existence of the son was kept secret, and it is possible that the story of James Brooke's emasculation may have been given currency to explain his embarrassingly total lack of physical interest in women. For it is indeed indisputable that James Brooke was not of the marrying kind.[21] He showed, however, great affection for his nephews, one of whom he took with him to Sarawak in 1840, and the younger one (who eventually succeeded him) he doted upon. A letter from 'this great pet' ('full of his boyish pranks and thoughts') was a major emotional joy for James Brooke. He acquired other boy protégés all over the place, and was compulsively drawn to 13-year-old midshipmen. In 1843 he befriended the 13-year-old great nephew of the Bishop of Calcutta, and wrote of this 'fine little fellow':

I have got quite fond of him since he has been here; and somehow there is something in the position of a young volunteer of 13 years of age, which rouses one's kind feelings; so young, yet forced into manhood, to share privations and fatigues, when yet a boy. Since my nephew, Charlie, has embarked in the same line, I feel doubly inclined to be friendly with all the mids; ... I was delighted with a letter I have just received from the youngster.

Later in life Brooke shared confidences of this sort with Angela Burdett-Coutts, with whom he formed a most unusual platonic friendship.[22] This will be discussed later, but for the moment we turn to his nephews. The eldest, Capt. James Brooke, lost a wife and son (and was then disinherited by his uncle – who made no allowances for his nephew's emotional state after this tragedy – for 'disobedience'). Charles Brooke (1829–1917), the second white raja, was potent enough with women, but remarkably cold and indifferent towards his wife Margaret. Their first three children died of cholera, but there were three surviving sons. Their marriage ended when he destroyed his wife's pet doves and served them in a pie for supper. He reckoned that marriage lost an officer 99 per cent of his efficiency; compliant local mistresses, not burdensome European wives, was his prescription. Only five women were present when the raja entertained the entire European community of Sarawak to a jubilee dinner in 1887. The third raja, Vyner Brooke (1874–1963) was a compulsive womaniser, and, significantly perhaps, much the least efficient of the three white rajas, thus giving point to his father's dictum. But the third raja also had his troubles. He lived apart from his wife for the second half of their marriage, although maintaining friendly discussions with her about his endless stream of mistresses. And we have his wife's testimony that he was 'not good in bed'; to quote her own words: 'he made love just as he played golf – in a nervous unimaginative flurry'.[23]

The masculine nature of the imperial enterprise has been emphasised. The few women who contributed something to it seemed also to have been equally incompetent in love or to have repudiated their emotional lives. Mrs Caroline Chisholm has an important place in the story of Australia in the first half of the 1840s on account of her efforts to promote the immigration of women. Her first venture was running a Female Immigrants Home. Her efforts right through to 1857 (when her health failed) made her one of the most famous women of her time, and an inspiration to Florence Nightingale. When she married Capt. Archibald Chisholm it had been on condition that she should be free to do any philanthropic work she wished. Her husband loyally and self-effacingly kept to that commitment, taking an active, if sometimes grumbling, part in the advancement of her schemes. She assisted the settlement of some 11,000 immigrants in New South Wales in the 1840s, and then spent some years in England founding the Family Colonisation Loan Society, the most important private agency of its kind in the 1850s. Meanwhile her own family of six children had to take a decidedly second place to her efforts to promote the domestic happiness of other families. In 1851 her husband went back to Australia three years ahead of her to act as colonial agent for her society, which sent out more than 3,000 immigrants by 1854. Caroline Chisholm was never a fanatical crusader for women's rights, and the sacrifice of her own family life was probably a sadness to her, but it underlines the point that constructive achievement for the empire inevitably meant real sacrifice.[24]

Miss Angela Burdett-Coutts (1814–1906) was a very different kind of woman. Certainly she did not arrive early at sexual adjustment. Famous as the richest heiress in England, she declined many proposals of marriage, even, it was rumoured, from Wellington and Louis Napoleon, preferring to devote herself to philanthropy – and to her inseparable friend Hannah, her former governess. This attachment* survived even Hannah's 11 years of married life. Hannah Brown, however, survived her husband by 23 years, and it was not until Hannah herself had been dead for three years that Baroness Burdett-Coutts (as she had become) eventually married at the age of 67. Meanwhile she endowed the bishoprics of Cape Town, Adelaide, and British Columbia, introduced cotton-gins into Abeokuta, tried to rescue the fishing industry of south-west Ireland, and organised help for the wounded in the Zulu war of 1879. She became the friend of men who were congenitally hard-hearted towards women: men like General Gordon (whom she gave a letter case), James Brooke, Livingstone, Stanley and Moffat. She gave vital support to the Sarawak enterprise, making a gunboat and a £5,000 loan available and taking interest in a model farm on her estate at Quop. Brooke was impressed with her and from 1863 to 1865 she was his heir. In their remarkable correspondence in the 1860s they exchanged pressed flowers and accounts of their patronage of boys and young men. The Baroness seems to have been a species of female pederast, and in the course of her life she placed hundreds of destitute boys in training ships for the navy and merchant service. James Booke often wrote jointly to her and Hannah, and, regarding them as his only friends, was ever anxious for the health and welfare of those 'in whose society I have only hope of peace and quiet in this world'. In 1863 he took one of Angela's young friends back to Sarawak with him; his name was Charles La Touche, and Brooke sent her fond reports of 'your Charlie'.[25]

It is possible that a similarly platonic friendship existed between Matthew Nathan and Mary Kingsley, Charles Kingsley's niece (1862–1900), a naturalist and anthropologist who travelled in remote parts of West Africa in the mid 1890s. But she denied ever having had any love affairs: 'I make the confession humbly', she wrote, 'quite as I would make the confession of being deaf or blind. I know nothing myself of love'. But she knew a lot about West Africa and did much to help its peoples; she has a secure place in history.[26]

There were many lesser figures in our empire story, mostly men, who suffered degrees of emotional retardation – those who never got over being head-prefect at school, or for whom everything in life after membership of 'Pop' at Eton was an anticlimax. St John Brodrick, one-time secretary of state for war, at the end of his life reflected that no responsibility could ever compare with that youthful one.[27] Alfred Lyttelton (colonial secretary 1903–05) agreed: 'No position in after life, however great, could be as

---

* I refrain from calling it 'lesbian', since as Baron Corvo once observed, 'labels are more lethal than libels' (Fr. Rolfe *The desire and pursuit of the whole* (1953 ed) 186).

complete as that of a swell at Eton'.[28] Baden-Powell never got his Charterhouse days out of his system. Here we could elaborate what Cyril Connolly once called 'the theory of permanent adolescence'; an intensity of school experience so deep as to cause arrested development. It is interesting, for example, that Lord Curzon (viceroy of India 1899–1905) always kept a room at Kedleston as a replica of his Eton room; and he also kept a photograph album of his Eton contemporaries, mostly with the names, details and dates of death meticulously recorded. He was devoted to his wife, yet Ampthill thought him 'as variable and neurotic as a woman'. Curzon's isolation as viceroy reduced him to tearful self-pity, all the more intense since it meant rupture with one of his closest school-friends, St John Brodrick, who, together with Edward and Alfred Lyttelton (all older than himself) had at school patronised him and formed a quartet with him. And yet Curzon has been described as 'less Eton-orientated than many of his generation'. Metcalfe left Eton at 15 and was passionately addicted to his school memories, which gave him a strong bond with Wellesley, whose favourite personal secretary he became.

Although by no means all the empire builders were public schoolmen, at the very least we have to agree with Thornton that the public school spirit, and the clannishness associated with it, became one of the most potent of imperial elixirs. In 1898 an Old Etonian dinner was held to celebrate the simultaneous appointment of Minto as governor-general of Canada, Curzon as viceroy of India and J. E. C. Welldon as bishop of Calcutta; the menu card listed all Victoria's viceroys and governors-general of Canada, and showed more than half of them to have been Old Etonians. Clan loyalties of Eton and Balliol were paralleled, and sometimes reinforced, by groups such as Howe's Boys (of whom Metcalfe was one), a gang-fraternity in Calcutta, Wolseley's staff Ring (a select band of favourite officers) and Milner's Kindergarten. The great gods were team, code, honour and playing the game.[29] In Kipling's *Stalky and Co.*, when somebody says of Stalky, fighting on the north-west frontier, 'There's nobody like Stalky', the narrator replies, ' "That's just where you make the mistake", I said, "India's full of Stalkies – Cheltenham and Haileybury and Marlborough chaps ..." '. The Indian Civil Service, remarked Nehru (who had been to Harrow), 'embodied essentially the British Public School spirit'.[30] Santayana called Englishmen the schoolboy masters of the world and as Hannah Arendt noted, the colonial services were filled with men who had 'never been able to outgrow their boyhood ideals'.[31] The imperial masters showed a decided tendency to flog the natives, and this can hardly have been unrelated to the traumas many of them endured at the hands of sadistic prep-school masters. R. E. Codrington, charged at the turn of the century with the task of organising a civil service for North-eastern Rhodesia, especially asked for young recruits, preferably university men with teaching experience – men who became known locally as 'bum-switchers'. Again, Milner's attitude to the flogging of Chinese labourers in Johannesburg was so casual that when enquiries were made by ministers into irregularities he seemed to remember nothing about it.[32]

THE PROCONSULAR PHENOMENON

Why did so many Britons seek service overseas? There were opportunities for the exercise of talents and the indulgence of eccentricities greater than Britain herself could or would provide. Edward Eyre, George Grey and James Brooke belonged to a generation which desired to create something more than personal fortune from 'new' countries. Eyre left for Australia at the age of 17 saying 'I should be my own master, free from all control and taking an independent position in life. This was the great charm'. Metcalfe served India for 36 years, becoming increasingly unwilling to exchange large responsibilities, which gratified 'pride and duty' at the same time, for 'trifling and unworthy ones', such as being a country magistrate. Such men wanted big responsibilities, and some, such as James Brooke and Alfred Milner, could never have adjusted themselves to the demands of party politics – empire was to that extent an escape route for those disillusioned with Britain. Milner enjoyed the freedom of being able to act without what he called the 'blighting influence' of a domestic political system he regarded as dangerous, petty, hopeless, effete and wrong. Freedom from conventional restraints of all kinds was a powerful attraction, even at an apparently quite trivial level. Rhodes, for example, admitting to having been singularly rude, said, significantly, 'People who live in London cannot do these things – I can'. The empire was also a useful field for the mediocre to get ahead in, or for the slightly unbalanced to fill positions they could never have obtained under the constraints and checks of metropolitan society. Samuel Marsden, the turbulent priest who held a senior chaplaincy in New South Wales, was considered quite unfitted for his position by a commissioner of inquiry into the convict system. Wielding the axe and the birch with equal efficiency, he became a successful sheep farmer, while 'rum-dealing built his churches and missionary ships did his trading'.[33]

There were plenty of men only too ready to take advantage of the opportunity to exercise the freedom of action which crisis and isolation provided. One of the most striking features of imperial administration and expansion was the power of the 'man on the spot'. Throughout the century governors ignored or exceeded their instructions, especially in India and Africa. Occasionally this was because their instructions were totally inapplicable: Denison, for example, arriving in Van Diemen's Land in 1847, discovered that, although drawn up from the latest information received in London, they 'contemplated a state of things exactly the reverse of what I found to prevail'. Sir Geroge Grey's desire for independence of action led him to behave with extraordinary tactlessness and intolerance towards the colonial office; for years he got away with it. Sir John Pope Hennessy also disobeyed explicit but unwelcome instructions; the colonial office might criticise and rebuke, but generally backed him up. His career also showed the power a governor had to make or break subordinates at will.[34]

Lord Ellenborough had always opposed advance in the Indus Valley, but within a few months of arriving in India he confirmed in 1842 the annexation of Sind, having given his trust and support to Sir Charles Napier. Ellenborough was recalled, but Sind remained. The entire cabinet was against the blatantly aggressive annexation. Peel summed up the problem: 'Time – distance – the course of events may have so fettered our discretion that we have no alternative but to maintain occupation of Scinde'. The personal views and ambitions of Ellenborough and Napier enabled them, in an era of slow communications, to carry the day against the whole weight of the British Government and the East India Company.[35]

Carnarvon in 1878 spoke of the universal 'difficulties of frontier'. 'The same provocations, real or supposed', he wrote, '. . . the same temptation of those on the spot to acquire territory' were observable throughout all empires. In the ten years before 1875 Lagos was incorporated into a new Crown Colony Gold Coast protectorate, and a new authority assumed in the British Residents were appointed in the Malay States, and Fiji was annexed. In 1878 the second Afghan war broke out. In each case the men on the spot showed the same tendency to pre-judge the issue and exceed instructions. Their technique was not simply to report, but to act first and report a fait accompli, which was then usually approved. Sir Andrew Clarke in Malaya was the outstanding case, negotiating Malay agreement to a Resident in Perak rather than reporting on the desirability; once the Residency was established, governor Sir Wm. Jervois gave it more control than Carnarvon envisaged – which led to an occupying expedition. General Wolseley's ambition distorted the whole nature of the Asante campaign, quickly bringing about the major expedition which he was supposed to avoid. Commodore Goodenough fulfilled his commission to investigate in Fiji requests for annexation by accepting the cession of the islands. An ambitious man, it is plain, could always make use of the loophole in official British policy, the needs of security, which were constantly at risk where indigenous governments were unable to provide a framework of good order sufficient to satisfy British interests. Whitehall's instruction in effect was 'non-intervention – unless the safety of the colonies was endangered'.[36] This was something which it was virtually impossible to judge from London. The grandiloquent, wilfully enthusiastic Lytton disobeyed orders as viceroy, so dragging Britain into an unwanted war in Afghanistan.[37] The colonial office on more than one occasion between 1903 and 1906 had doubts about Lugard's forceful advances in Nigeria, but it had in the last resort to rely on his analysis of how serious any given rising might be.[38]

Even in the twentieth century there was one district officer in India who, after reading carefully through a new act promulgated by the Government of

India, wrote boldly in the margin: 'This Act will not apply in this District'. He effectively maintained his point.[39]

Sir Harry Smith (governor of the Cape 1847–52) justified himself for exceeding orders in South Africa in 1848 by saying 'my position has been analogous to that of every governor-general who had proceeded to India'. Like D'Urban, Smith had his particular initiative reversed.[40] But these were exceptional cases. Generally, the British government reluctantly accepted the initiatives of its proconsuls, and it did so increasingly as the century wore on. Rhodes, Mackenzie, Warren and Baden-Powell, who brought expansion to the northern frontiers of the empire in South Africa in the 1880s and 1890s, all ignored instructions which conflicted with their conceptions, and from 1884 they defied the colonial office with impunity. The colonial office was extremely reluctant to overrule Sir Hercules Robinson, because they did not think that they could find anyone equally able and experienced to replace him; and he also had two tours of duty in South Africa as George Grey had done in New Zealand. Milner, with his contempt for party politics and cabinet government, was only too anxious to pursue his own line, and although this was not possible under Chamberlain, Lyttelton deferred to him completely.[41]

The last years of the Unionist rule were the heyday of proconsular authority. Cromer's position was unchallenged. Balfour complained that Curzon raised India to the status of an independent and not always friendly autocracy. But as he recognised all too well, it was difficult to overrule prestigious officers who had detailed local knowledge. The problem was that these proconsuls gave too little thought for the general situation.[42] The Liberal government from 1905 did much to reduce their pretensions.

PROPS OF EMPIRE-BUILDING: SPORT AND SECRET SOCIETIES

Refusing to broaden the base of dominion by conquistador-like assimilation, the British overseas were heavily dependent on their own imported inventions for keeping up morale. The club, the Anglican churches, railway refreshment rooms, mock-Tudor taverns, masonic lodges, the golf-course, the race-course – all these played their part. In remoter regions an officer might have to make do with a flagpole and a rosebush, but even these could be peculiarly heart-warming. As far as possible too, social conventions and tensions were transported. Snobbery, pretentiousness and self-conscious social gradations and class distinctions flourished everywhere.[43]

There was always the 'bottle, the bullet and the bible' for consolation. Most people drank excessively. In 1861 the Canterbury settlers of New Zealand, 15,000 in number, maintained half-a-dozen breweries, besides importing more than three gallons of spirits, seven of beer and nearly two of wine per person. Officers and gentlemen were fanatical about champagne and Eno's Fruit Salt. The latter was used regularly by Curzon and Gordon, Gordon being accredited with the dictum 'the stomach governs the world'; the hydrographer and the superintendent of telegraphs in Siam 'never went into the jungle without it' (1883).[44] The soldier had his barrackroom comradeship – singing ballads while 'bulling' boots and brass accoutrements. He was unlucky if he was out of the reach of a railway, regularly bringing, in Winston Churchill's words, 'the letters, newspapers, sausages, jam, whisky, soda-water, and cigarettes which enabled the Briton to conquer the world without discomfort'.[45] Moreover, conquered peoples everywhere have always seen the need to provide brothels. Strict regulations frequently hedged their use by the British army.[46]

Everywhere the preference for equestrian sports, horse-racing and the hunt, quickly asserted itself. Absence of foxes was no deterrent; the Salisbury Hunt Club rode magnificently to hounds – after jackals.[47] It used to be said that the first thing a Frenchman built overseas was a café, the first thing a German built was a road, but the Briton gave top priority to a race-course. Turf clubs were established in Sydney and Hobart in the 1820s. In many Australian towns an important race meeting was declared a public holiday; railways were built to country race-courses that had hill-billy races but twice a year. Mafeking began in 1885, and its 2,000 white inhabitants soon built a race-course and a masonic hall. The first race meeting in Kenya was at Nairobi in 1900. Yet even two years later there were less than a dozen settlers there. Even in the tiny barren island of Perim in the Red Sea there was a locality always known as the 'race-course', though it was never raced on by anything.[48] Lord Cromer gives ample testimony to this point, quoting Curzon:

'From my own experience, I would say that the first thing an Englishman does in the outlying portions of the Empire is to make a race-course; the second is to make a golf-course' ... When I arrived in Cairo, less than a year after the battle of Tel-el-Kebir had been fought [1882], every department of the Administration was in a state of the utmost confusion. Nevertheless a race-course had already been laid out and a grandstand erected. A golf-course followed after a short interval.[49]

Golf in Calcutta dates from 1829.

Sir Hercules Robinson had the usual passion for racing, but was also a great believer in the promotion of British sport of all kinds among the 'natives'. This was one of the political duties of a governor, since 'sentiment and sympathy' were, he believed, a major and efficacious factor 'in the maintenance of the integrity of our vast and scattered Empire', and 'a similarity of taste in amusements is a guarantee for common sympathy in more important matters'.[50] Sir Arthur Grimble ascribed to cricket a spiritual value because of 'the moral teaching-force of the game in malarial jungle, or sandy desolation, or the uttermost islands of the sea'. He believed cricket to have replaced faction-fighting among the Gilbertese, one of whom told him it added a unique good fellowship to all the fun and discipline of the former activity.[51] An earlier governor, Arthur Hamilton Gordon, learned in the 1880s that since cricket had been introduced into Tonga, petty pilfering had virtually ceased as a pastime. Another cricket-promoting governor was Sir William Denison, who secured a good ground for Sydney cricketers in the 1850s (their club was founded in 1826). Parsis founded the Oriental Cricket Club in Bombay in 1848. Nigerian emirs as well as Indian princes became good cricketers, several of the latter playing for the M.C.C.[52] Football was a rather late developer, but it was played in Australia from 1829, and even in the 1850s on the China coast there was an annual soccer match between British officials in Hong Kong and Shanghai. Today football is played well nigh universally – it was the game of the informal empire – while cricket has never spread far outside the old formal empire. Boxing too has its place: it has been said that the Marquis of Queensberry's rules (1867) were a firmer link between the American West and the old country 'than Shakespeare or the English Bible'.[53]

Individual Britons overseas naturally had a wide variety of curious hobbies, some of which they kept to themselves, some of which required the co-operation of others. Sir Robert Hart, Chinese customs administrator, keenly established a brass-band among his employees. Sir William Denison moved about the world with packing-cases housing his collection of shells and a library of 2,000 books; he was also interested in collecting ferns. Sir George Grey tried to preserve Maori literature, and when his Maori manuscripts were destroyed by fire in 1848 he started all over again. He also built up a priceless collection of European manuscripts and incunabula. Sir Ernest Satow spent four years as diplomatic minister at Montevideo (1889–93) writing out in his own hand a Japanese translation of the whole of St Thomas à Kempis's *Imitation of Christ*. Sir Samuel Baker, before his Sudanese exploits, during his seven years in Ceylon created an English village, complete with an English bailiff, groom, yeomen and pack of hounds.[54]

Cecil Rhodes's hobby was dreaming 'cosmic dreams' and his vision of building a railway from Cape to Cairo is well known. More central to his preoccupations, however, was the formation of a secret society. He made his first Will in 1877 when he was only 34, leaving his money for the formation of a 'Society of the Elect' (based on Jesuit principles of organisation) to extend British rule and peace across the earth; he envisaged the occupation by British settlers of the whole of Africa, the Holy Land, the Euphrates Valley, Cyprus, the entire South American continent, the Pacific islands, the Malay archipelago, the seaboard of China, and Japan. With Britain and the United States then reunited, eternal peace could be established by the Elect.[55]

Rhodes was a lapsed freemason, and this leads us on to the consideration of an imperial factor infinitely more important than Rhodes's secret Society of the Elect. The role of freemasonry in building up the empire, and of its doctrines of brotherhood in sustaining the world-wide activities of traders and empire builders, is not easy to document. Its role in spreading British cultural influences has thus been seriously underrated.* In its English and Scottish form it is not a secret society, but it is a society with secrets, and not one given either to proselytising or to self-advertisement. Thus it is much easier to plot its geographical spread than to list its important members or assess its influence.[56] However, notable freemasons certainly included many army officers, among them the Marquis of Wellesley (grand master of Ireland 1782, 1821–28), field marshals Wolseley and Kitchener, and general Sir F. R. Wingate of the Sudan. The 11th earl of Dalhousie (secretary of state for war, 1846–52, 1855–58) was grand master of Scotland 1867–69. At least six colonial secretaries were freemasons: Lord Newcastle (1859–64), Lord Carnarvon (1874–78), Sir Michael Hicks Beach (1878–80), Lord Hartington (1880–82) – three in succession, be it noted – the Marquis of Ripon (1892–95, grand master 1870–74) and L. S. Amery (1924–29). There was at least one secretary of state for India, Lord George Hamilton (1895–1903), and three viceroys (tenth earl of Dalhousie, the eighth Earl of Elgin, and Ripon). Among the high commissioners and governors may be numbered Lord Durham (Canada, 1838), the 13th earl of Elphinstone (governor of Madras 1837–42 and of Bombay 1853–59), Sir Hercules Robinson (West Indies, Hong Kong, Ceylon, New Zealand and the Cape – twice at the latter post, 1881–9 and 1895–97), Lord Northcote (Bombay 1899–1903, Australia 1903–08), Sir Henry Blake (Bahamas, Newfoundland, Jamaica, Hong Kong, Ceylon) and Lord Ampthill (Madras 1900–06 and acting viceroy 1904). Notable 'colonial' masons included Sir Allen McNab (prime minister of Canada 1854–56), Sir William Whiteway (prime minister of Newfoundland 1889–94, 1895–97), Richard Seddon (prime minister of New Zealand), and in South Africa, Lord Chief Justice de Villiers, President J. H. Brand of the Orange Free State, and J. H. Hofmeyr snr.[57] In Ireland, Henry Grattan and Isaac Butt were masons; so was Daniel O'Connell, though after years of enthusiasm he strongly renounced it in 1837. There were others too, including Wellington and Rhodes, who were admitted to masonic lodges, but apparently never took it up seriously. Freemasonry tended to run strongly in some families. The dukes of Devonshire and the earls of Elgin were invariably freemasons, with the apparent exception of the 9th earl of Elgin; and between 1737 and 1907 there were 16 princes of the royal blood involved in it. However, despite its social prestige, British freemasonry (except perhaps in Ireland) never seems to have been so tightly interwoven with the Establishment as it was in Russia, nor has it ever dogged politics as in Latin

---

* To make this assertion is not, of course, to subscribe to a 'conspiracy' theory of history (such as was rampant in the nineteenth century itself), whereby everything can be explained by the machinations of secret societies, and British policy ascribed to dictation by freemasons – some continental writers believed Palmerston to be Grand Master Mason of the Universe, and (with rather better reason) Irish Roman Catholics regarded freemasonry as a device for holding down Ireland.

America. Essentially apolitical and non-sectarian, its significance would seem to have been widely spread through the social structure. J. M. Roberts says that eighteenth-century freemasonry was socially important because of 'the relief it provided from the triviality, narrowness and rigidity' of life, an escape from the 'stupefying boredom' of the provinces, at a time when escapes were few. This applies with even stronger force to overseas society in the nineteenth century. It catered to many instincts: philanthropy, mutual aid, neo-chivalry, the appeal of the mystical and occult, but above all to the satisfaction of simple social and fraternal urges. As Roberts observes, the social functions of masonry were many and 'their significance not easily exhausted'. It acted as an international mechanism off-setting the problems of travel and distance, introducing people into society in countries other than their own. More than any other single British cultural influence, certainly more than football or cricket, it 'caught on' almost everywhere.[58] It promoted a set of enlightened, liberal-minded, tolerant, but authoritarian and disciplined, values among soldiers as well as traders, and acted as a central focus of social activity for Britons overseas, often bringing together groups with no other common interest. It was indeed, as the 11th earl of Elgin (past-grand master mason of Scotland) has authoritatively described it, 'perhaps the most profound feature, socially, of the nineteenth century era' overseas, not only in the empire, but literally everywhere the British went to trade and fight, and wherever there was the remotest opportunity of establishing it. The earl of Elgin also points out how in this field as in so many others, the role of Scotsmen was out of all proportion to the size of their country. (There were for example 46 Scottish lodges along the coasts of Chile and Peru). The Irish were especially important in spreading military lodges; and in the domestic Irish context freemasonary became closely associated with maintaining the influence of the Protestant Ascendancy, not merely in landholding, but in professional and commercial worlds too. Its identity with the Ascendancy was reinforced by strong papal condemnations, repeated in encyclicals until 1884.[59] Its devotees believed freemasonry also to be in a very real sense not only a handmaid to the Church, to education and social order but also, in the words of the Ven. A. T. Wirgman, archdeacon of Port Elizabeth, 'a real link of empire'.[60] The connection is best attested in the case of colonial secretary Lord Carnarvon, pro-grand master 1874–90, for whom it seems to have been part of the 'living spirit breathing from the inmost centre to the utmost extremity', without which the mere extent of dominion was no real test of prosperity or success. He gave considerable attention to bringing uniformity into the practice and organisation of freemasonry in Canada and Australia, and his federal policy in South Africa involved masonic links. It was Carnarvon who, in March 1857, declared: 'Following closely in the wake of colonisation, wherever the hut of the settler has been built, or the flag of conquest waved, there Masonry has soon equal dominion. In Canada . . . it has reflected – and I will not stop here to enquire how much it has consolidated – the British Empire'.[61]

The 'Star of the East' at Calcutta was the oldest masonic lodge outside Britain, with George Pomfret as district grand master in 1728, only 16 years after the completion of the fort. Roger Drake, governor of Calcutta at the age of 30, was an active member; so was at least one member of his council.[62]

Undoubtedly freemasonry was coterminous with the empire by 1815, lodges having been established, for example, in Gibraltar (1729), Madras (1752), Bombay (1764), West Indies (1739), West Africa (1735), Boston, Mass (1733), Cape Breton and Louisburg (1746), Newfoundland (1746), Nova Scotia (1750), Quebec (1759), Ontario (1792), South Africa (1801), New South Wales (1803), Ceylon (1810) and Malta (1815). In addition, it is interesting to note that lodges were established in South America as early as 1735, China in 1767 and Indonesia in 1793. Thereafter, freemasonry was ever in the vanguard of expansion. The arrival of a British regiment frequently brought with it an active lodge, and if it were willing to receive civilians, it could play a lively part in spreading freemasonry throughout the globe. During the nineteenth century lodges were started in the Punjab in 1837, Egypt in 1862, Japan in 1866, Lagos in 1867, Auckland in 1842, Fiji in 1881. When the United Grand Lodge of England was established in 1813, 648 lodges were registered; by the end of 1862 there were 941 active lodges, of which 271 were overseas; by 1885 the numbers had risen to 2,134 and 617 respectively, and by the end of 1914, 3,743 and 905. Overseas membership was estimated in 1909 as including 50,000 Australians and 64,000 Canadians. These figures considerably underestimate freemasonic activity because they do not include the Scottish and Irish lodges, each of which had several hundred branches overseas. During the period 1800 to 1914, 502 Scottish lodges were chartered in the empire, and 69 more outside it. By 1914 virtually half (48 per cent) of all Scottish lodges were overseas; they were especially strong in Queensland, India, New Zealand, New South Wales and South Africa – in that order. Additionally, nowhere outside Britain has freemasonry flourished so greatly as in the United States.[63] American lodges spread widely in Latin America and the Far East. There was no competition in the West Indies and Asia, with British, French and American lodges often existing side by side. In 1865 the masonic hall in Shanghai was begun for the joint use of English, Scottish and American lodges. In South Africa, relations between British and Dutch lodges were friendly, and this perhaps helps to explain why the Dutch Reformed Churches and Afrikaner governments retain deep suspicion of it. Masonry never recognised the partition of Ireland in 1921.[64]

Secret societies, by no means restricted to masonic ones, were a central and permanent force in Irish history. A great many Irish freemasons were Orangemen as well in the Order's early days. But the Orange Order was more specifically directed to the maintenance of the Protestant Ascendancy, and lacked the respectability and discretion of masonry. The Orange Order was founded in Ulster border counties in the 1790s. By the 1860s it was reactivated in reaction to the Fenians to provide an invaluable link between Protestants at all levels of society, between the Ascendancy and the farming and labouring classes, thus strengthening the forces favouring the Union. In the 1870s it identified with the landed interest in reaction to Parnell's Land League. In December 1885 the modern Unionist Party was formed by the Orange Order: membership was and remained almost identical, and Orangemen determined its character. The Orange Order has also helped to perpetuate a system in which power and patronage were dispensed on the basis of a Protestant and Unionist commitment. Like freemasonry it spread overseas: to New South Wales 1835, Montreal 1825, Nova Scotia 1847, Ontario 1830. By 1870, when the Canadian population was four million, 100,000 Canadians were members of the Orange Order, and by 1914 this had increased to 250,000: the express aim was to keep Canada British. Lodge halls were social centres for pioneer communities.[65]

WHITE SKINS, WHITE MASKS: TECHNIQUES OF CONTROL

An anonymous writer in the *Spectator* in 1898 correctly observed that there was no power whatever in the hands of those who governed India or Africa, or Latin America for that matter, to resist a general effort of the population to throw the white races out. In such a situation the only course was 'to rule, as completely and with as little repentance, as if we were angels appointed to that task'. Any doubt or hesitation produced nothing but fear, and with fear disappeared the serenity of which alone good government could be born. The writer went on to argue that they could no more prepare a 'transfer of power' than they would 'grant such authority to the boys in school', although local opinions should be consulted assiduously.[66]

How then did the British equip themselves to rule as 'angels appointed to the task'? In its final form the code of conduct was found in a combination of Moses' Decalogue and Kipling's 'If —' (written in honour of Cecil Rhodes). There were army churches where the Ten Commandments were written up on one side of the altar and the lines of Kipling's poem on the other. George Orwell defined the five chief beatitudes of the pukka sahib: 'keeping up our prestige', 'the firm hand (without the velvet glove)', 'we white men must hang together', 'give them an inch and they'll take an ell', and 'esprit de corps'. In his novel *Burmese Days* the anglophile Dr Veraswami was convinced that 'hanging together' was the secret of British 'superiority to we Orientals'.[67] The focal point at which the British community 'hung together' – or perhaps 'hung out' would be a better description – was of course 'the Club', a combined and insulated social centre, forum and recreation-ground. The chief function of the Club was to keep Britons from 'going native', which is one reason why there was such resistance to the admission of non-European members. 'Blessed are the Clubs', wrote Goldwin Smith; yet even with them, he felt, the life of a young man in a city where he had no home could never be free from 'moral danger'. The Turf Club in Cairo was the 'social and national fortress' of the British Cairo community, many of whom spent from one to five hours daily in it. Leonard Woolf (who was in the Ceylon civil service from 1904 to 1911) described the Kandy Club as rather poky, not luxurious like a London club, but 'a symbol and centre of British imperialism, although perhaps we might not be fully conscious of it'. The atmosphere was, as he described it, 'terribly masculine and public school. Even if we were not all gentlemen, we all had to behave, sober or drunk, as if we were'. The club was used for dining, playing bridge and billiards. Woolf's only training as a cadet, he claimed, was in club conversation or at the dinner table. The club was a place of refuge where the white mask could be lifted a little. Outside it, appearances must be fully kept up: the British officer must have a stiff upper lip, dress for dinner, show the flag, stick to routine, fell large beasts in a single shot, show no fear or relaxation: above all the white man must not 'go native' or be able to emphasise common humanity with the governed.[68]

Orwell is in fact an extremely good witness when we try to build up the evidence of how the empire was managed. His father was in the Indian Civil Service. He himself was born in Bengal in 1903, and for five years (1922 to 1927) he was in the Indian Imperial Police serving in Burma. Out of this experience came a novel and his fascinating short story 'Shooting an Elephant' (1936), which tells of the policeman who had to shoot an escaped elephant, and in so doing had revealed to him 'the hollowness, the futility of the white man's dominion in the East'. Orwell writes: 'Here was I, the white man with his gun, standing in front of the unarmed native crowd – seemingly the leading actor of the piece; but in reality I was only an absurd puppet pushed to and fro by the will of those yellow faces behind'. Since the condition of white man's rule was that he spent his life impressing the 'natives', so in every crisis he had to do what 'the natives' expected of him. 'He wears a mask, and his face grows to fit it . . . A sahib has got to act like a sahib; he has got to appear resolute, to know his own mind and do definite things'. Every white man's life in the East, he concluded, was one long struggle not to be laughed at. Orwell was greatly shocked to discover that the soldiers were of all parts of the British community the most brutal to the 'niggers'. And yet Orwell recognised that in practice this lance-corporal swagger was absolutely necessary – 'you could not hold down a subject empire with troops infected by notions of class-solidarity'.[69]

The British ruled – or rather held in thrall – millions of the world through an Anglo-Saxonist 'magic' sense of superiority, by projecting the idea of their own unquestionable omniscience and effortless superiority.[70] Endless emphasis on the differences between 'natives' and themselves was one of the necessary props of the empire. They could only have ruled subject peoples, especially when hopelessly outnumbered, by honestly believing themselves to be racially superior, and the subject race to be *biologically* different. An extremely interesting example of the outward and visible form of this emphasis on difference was the sun helmet. The British built up a superstition about their greater proneness to sunstroke because of their supposedly thinner skulls (and therefore larger brains). The most cherished superstition or misconception about bodily difference was the skull. Thus, as George Orwell wrote, 'The thin skull was the mark of racial superiority, and the pith topi was a sort of emblem' of empire.[71]

All colonial empires, wrote Orwell, were founded on the fact that it was too difficult to believe they were ruling human beings as opposed to 'a kind of undifferentiated brown stuff, about as individual as bees or coral insects'. If there were fears – and Orwell thought all white men had them – the crucial thing was to keep this a secret from the subject population. If the 'natives' rose in revolt, then they had to be suppressed, which could only be done by methods which made nonsense of any claims for the superiority of Western civilisation. 'In order to rule over barbarians, you have got to become a barbarian yourself'. It was precisely this end-product which Orwell was describing which had been the subject of Cobden's anxious predictions a century earlier.[72]

Lugard provides us with an important illustration of how much depended on keeping up the white man's prestige. In 1890 in east Africa, when a servant made as if to retaliate for a very heavy clout, Lugard smashed his eye in, believing that any lesser reaction from him would have been the prelude to disaster:

No-one who has not been in Africa or India can fully appreciate the full force of this. The native looks on it as a sacrilege to touch a Sahib, and also expects little short of death from the Sahib if he should be fool enough to try conclusions. To this prestige the white man owes his ascendancy, and it *must* at any price be maintained, just as one would with a brute beast. This may sound harsh, but it is true, that the black man must respect the white in every possible way – even including physical force.

The white man in order to command respect must, Lugard thought, never dress in a slipshod way, he must live in a decent, well-ordered house, even if it was only a rondavel. In a revealing passage he wrote at Kampala in 1892:

I am strongly of opinion that 'pigging it' is rank bad policy in Africa. Insist on respect, and the observance of little ceremonies, make your house clean, neat, and embellish it in a small way all you can and make it as imposing as possible, and as you show that you respect yourself, so will the natives respect you. For instance, I allow no crowds to hang round the doorway and sit in the verandah. An orderly stands at the door to enforce this ... No-one, not even the katikiro, is allowed to walk in and sit down without invitation. He sends a message first.

Lugard regarded it as especially important for whites to support one another and not allow natives to play Europeans off against each other, for this would destroy the prestige 'on which alone we hold our own in Africa' – once lost, the Europeans would have to get out fast or have their throats cut.[73]

The attempt to stress the special and superior nature of the white man naturally led to some eccentric modes of dress. Sir Harry Johnston in Central Africa usually travelled under a vast white umbrella, so that people should always know where he was, and he attired his Sikh constabulary in white, yellow and black to symbolise the mixture of races present in Central Africa. Consul Rutherford Alcock transacted business in China in high style, dressed in full uniform with a cocked hat and six Spanish orders of chivalry acquired at a previous post.[74] It is by no means clear that non-Europeans did not penetrate the secret of this hollow swagger. Governor Sir John Pope Hennessy in West Africa in 1872 decided that the Africans knew full well the whites were not 'Superior Beings' – an opinion which colonial secretary Kimberley, however, regarded as rubbish.[75] But whatever the subject peoples thought, the fact remains that they could be ruled only with a degree of acquiescence. As Sir Arthur Grimble discovered in the Gilbert islands, it was the 'natives' not the officials who 'were the truly intransigent imperialists in that part of the world'. If British officers managed to convey the will of Whitehall to the islanders it was because 'they truly were our friends. We did not stop to think then how much more the maintenance of the Pax Britannica owed to their marvellous patience and courtesy with us than to the inherent virtue of ourselves or our system'. Leonard Woolf reported similar experience from Ceylon. Nothing could have been more dangerously precarious than the temporary pearl fishery camp of 1905, where 30–40,000 men, many of them habitual criminals, and some of them Arabs, were crowded together at Maduchchukaddai harvesting nearly 80 million oysters, from which the government made a profit of £150,000 – yet four civil servants, together with a few Tamil officials and constables and one interpreter, kept order and never even thought of the possibility of not being able to do so. Again, in 1910, as assistant government agent in Hambantota district, Woolf superintended the famous Kataragama pilgrimage at which 4,000 people gathered for a fortnight from all over Ceylon and South India; he was responsible for the administrative organisation as well as law and order, assisted by one district officer and a village headman – he had no staff and no police. Indeed, there were very few police in Ceylon, and outside Colombo and Kandy not a single soldier.[76]

Not all bore their conscious acquiescence as deferentially as Orwell's admiring Dr Veraswami or Grimble's happy Gilbertese. Nehru was a leader notably infuriated by the British 'psychological triumph' in consigning Indians to this state of acquiescent dependence. For many generations, he writes in his *Autobiography,* the British treated India as a kind of old-fashioned enormous country-house. 'They were the gentry owning the house and occupying the desirable parts of it, while the Indians were confined to the servants' hall and pantry and kitchen'. The only surprising thing to Nehru was that most Indians accepted the hierarchical ordering of impassable barriers as natural and inevitable. 'We developed the mentality of a good country-house servant ... The height of our ambition was to become respectable'.[77] Viceroy Minto said the ruling race could not have racial equality; the prestige of the white man, simply as a white, he considered to be one of the greatest British assets in India; India was largely governed by the 'mere prestige of British authority'; 'we cannot', he wrote, 'afford even the shadow of an appearance of weakness here. The strong hand carries more respect in India than even the recognition of British justice'. The basis of British rule in India in the nineteenth century was certainly, both in theory and practice, the supremacy of the British race, 'perhaps the strongest supporting mechanism of the British empire'.[78] But as some Englishmen realised at the time, this was not an idea for which anybody but the British could feel any enthusiasm. 'You are the conquerors and we are the conquered' was a phrase often heard on Indian lips. Force was the acknowledged basis of British rule; but it was force tempered with an ideal of justice and mitigated by the propagation of the idea that all were enfolded in the beneficent arms of the Great White Queen, the Empress of India.[79] Even the Irish are supposed to have had a sneaking affection for Queen Victoria. Non-Europeans found the matriarchal monarchy an attractive idea. They tended to turn a blind eye to the bureaucracy and fix their faith upon the Great White Mother. Nothing was done to disillusion them, and the Empress of India conception positively pandered to the fiction. Successfully too, as loyalty to the Crown seemed to grow in proportion to discontent. But fiction it was, and – despite Queen Victoria's personal enlightenment, tact and sympathy – it was the greatest fiction of all. The 'mystical truth', that the Queen was ultimately mistress of all was, however, much more vital to colonial administration than the material facts of cabinet government and anonymous civil servants. A shrewd Mosuto once asked Lord Bryce if the Queen actually existed or was purely a figment of the British imagination.[80]

The empire held together, then, by exercise of 'master's magic and gunman's gun' (the phrase is D. A. Low's);[81] by psychological bluffing techniques,[82] and by what one Victorian governor, Denison, called unashamedly 'a wholesome dread of our power', cultivated by a vigorous policy and the maintenance of a really efficient army. Inspire natives with this dread, he added, and Britain would rule with ease. Success had of course to be constant in order to produce real moral effect. Thus 'go and grit', 'moral strength' and the 'straightforward, dogged perseverance of our English nature' was or had to be the primary characteristic of an imperial people.[83] As Smuts recognised, British dominion rested on prestige and 'moral intimidation'.[84]

A stiff upper lip was nearly as important as 'grit', the sheer obstinacy of the 'moral force'. Emotion was as destructive of the mystique as indecision. Although greatly excited, Stanley would not show it on meeting Livingstone in 1871 at Ujiji. Instead of venting his joy naturally 'in some mad freak, such as idiotically biting my hand, turning a somersault, or slashing at trees', he opted for a deliberate formality. The famous remark 'Dr Livingstone, I presume', was one of studied courtesy. Stanley determined not to 'let my face display my emotions, lest it shall detract from the dignity of a white man appearing under such extraordinary circumstances'. Again, unwilling to admit he was tired and ill, Stanley left Nyanyembe for Lake Tanganyika while still weak from fever. Knowing it to be 'injudicious' he felt compelled to carry on since he had boasted 'that a white man never breaks his word'.[85]

The Victorian idea was that good government depended on personal qualities, not on training. The empire held together through a sense of loyalty among the administrators to certain standards, not a centralised system of administration. The emphasis was on public spiritedness. The paternal care of the district officer was far more important than the activities of metropolitan organisations. Ideas about good government were widely communicated even while a knowledge of social anthropology was not. These ideas rested on a middle class upbringing rather than any systematic philosophy. Personal contacts made through family, school and college, and in freemasonry, parliament, the civil service, business and church, created bonds which provided the principal means of patronage and promotion without a centralised system of recruitment to a career structure controlled by metropolitan officers.[86] It was rather a hit-and-miss affair, relying on commonsense and intuition: the only real training was 'controlled mistake-making' watched by an experienced official and so kept within safe limits. Even when recruitment procedures were improved from 1907 the emphasis was on judging candidates' merit in interview largely by their physical characteristics.[87] There always was a leaven of inspired officers but the recruit might not have the good fortune to serve under one. If in a truculent, autocratic and jingoistic era the affections of preliterate peoples remained tied to the British flag it was by the devotion and benevolence of the unknown administrators plugging away at their jobs in the field. But as Sir Arthur Grimble rightly says, it was 'the greatness of the men, not of the system'.[88] Humanity and devotion to the immediate calls of duty without thought of brilliant ends or ideal results were, in the last resort, the reason why the empire held together so long.[89]

The moral ascendancy owed much to a studied remoteness, efficiency and demi-god aloofness. Officials of the Indian Civil Service retired at 55. India never saw the giant old and feeble. Nothing was so certain to bring a colony's files onto the colonial secretary's desk than the smallest suspicion that its governor was heading for a nervous breakdown.[90] Unlike the empire builders of Spain and Portugal in earlier centuries there was no intermarriage, no intermixture of races and no mental acclimatisation. There were many well-tried means of political consolidation which the British never used. As a result, British dominion was less rooted in the soil.[91] It relied entirely on agreed tenets of character, on superiority of arms, on skilful administration, on racial arrogance, and on a global communications network.

Staged demonstrations of superiority were never difficult to arrange. In 1848 Sir Harry Smith, governor of the Cape, told African chiefs what would happen if they broke the royal oath of allegiance he made them take at King William's Town:

> 'Look at that waggon', he said, pointing to one at a distance which had been prepared for an explosion, 'and hear me give the word "Fire!"'. The train was lit and the waggon was sent skyward in a thousand pieces. 'That is what I will do to you', he continued, 'if you do not behave yourselves'.

The Mpondo did not fight the British. They simply accepted the facts of life as presented to them by Rhodes. He mowed down a field of mealies with machine guns before the eyes of the paramount chief and his councillors, and told them that their fate would be similar if they did not submit. Lugard outside Kampala on 17 March 1891 fired thirty to forty rounds on a Maxim gun. He hated wasting ammunition, but thought it worthwhile because of the great 'moral effect' in 'striking fear into those who are disposed to think they are a match for us'.[92]

Ill-staffed and vulnerable as many of the local administrative regimes undoubtedly were, the British generally remained masters of the situation, if only because the ultimate superiority of European arms was an inescapable fact of life. After the Mutiny only British troops in India had field guns. Moreover, the deployment of exiguous manpower was often achieved with considerable skill – an art which Lugard perfected in Nigeria.

By and large the British felt the problem of running the world was not particularly difficult – it was something which any school prefect could manage. When Harry East went east from Rugby School, his chum Tom Brown had no doubt that he would do well in the Indian Army, since 'No fellow could handle boys better, and I suppose [native] soldiers are very like boys'.[93] Lugard cast the emirs of Northern Nigeria in a prefectorial role under his headmastership, actually hoping that they would be taught to acquire an English schoolboy's ideas of honour, loyalty, and above all responsibility.[94]

With psychological and organisational techniques such as these, it took for example only 25 British officials at any one time between 1889 and 1896 to establish their authority over three million people in southern Uganda.[95] If the post-independence regimes of today are ruled by black men with white masks, as Fanon suggests, then the empire was even more certainly a system in which white men wore white masks, the masks of an apparently incontrovertible omniscience and infallibility.

PART TWO

6 The American Challenge

BRITAIN AND THE GREAT EXPERIMENT[1]

The victory of the American revolutionaries was in truth constitutionally enriching in the realm of political thought, a permanent addition to the experience of the world. It was a trauma the British could never forget. The Great Experiment challenged, fascinated, dogged them. To some Tory English aristocrats the success of American democracy was seen as a threat. Such men did not conceal their glee when the American Civil War broke out, nor seek to hide their identification with the 'aristocratic' South, 'the descendants of our banished cavaliers', as Wolseley called them.[2] Yet this dislike of and hostility to the Union was probably not a general feeling even among the privileged classes. Opinion was sharply divided, and there was much ignorance about America.[3] Lord John Russell reflected a widespread liberal view when he said:

> The joy which I felt at the overthrow of some of the despotisms of Italy is counterbalanced by the pain which I experience at the events which have lately taken place in America ... The Republic has been [an] ... example of a people in the enjoyment of wealth, happiness, and freedom, and affording bright prospects of the progress and improvement of mankind.[4]

Attitudes to America were ever ambivalent. Throughout the nineteenth century British politicians found corruption in American politics. There was a tendency to contrast unfavourably 'reasoned British principles' and 'democratic Yankee notions'. Intellectuals found evidence of a general deficiency in arts and letters, sensing what Henry Adams defined better than anybody: that the great drawing powers and generating energies which for centuries had directed the Western world, devotion to the Virgin and to Venus, were unknown to the American mind: 'An American Virgin would never dare command, an American Venus would never dare to exist'. Neither had any value as a motive force, and neither was feared: the best they could inspire in so materialistically oriented a community was fluffy sentiment. The dynamo had in America become the only symbol of ultimate energy and moral force.[5]

The admiration was there too. Earl Grey read aloud Tocqueville's work *Democracy in America* (1835) to his ailing wife – in French. Herman Merivale's minutes on colonial office files contain references to American example. Gladstone in 1852 called the United States 'the great source of experimental instruction, so far as Colonial institutions are concerned'. Roebuck admired the American statehood system: 'The whole thing was like a well-made watch – it went from [the start] and never ceased to go'. Cobden was fascinated by the 'portentous truth' that the Americans were free and teeming with future change. Bright admired the United States as embodying the cause of freedom, equality and anti-aristocracy: 'privilege has shuddered at what might happen to old Europe if this grand experiment should succeed'.[6]

The United States and Britain in the early nineteenth century were more intimately connected than any two other sovereign states. Rather than two separate economies, there was a single Atlantic economy.[7] J. S. Mill, Wakefield and Marx considered this special connection to be outside the normal definition of international trade. An informal Anglo-American partnership continued to direct the growth of the Atlantic basin; the United States was a 'colonial' economy before she took an increasing hold on the great continental interior after the Civil War. Britain was the United States' chief market, and the United States was largely dependent on Britain for textiles, hardware, iron and most manufactures. In 1838 about half the bonds of the Cotton States were held in Britain. Several British landowners, such as the Marquis of Bath, invested in western cattle estates. Several railway companies obtained decisive capital in Britain. British investment (private and unco-ordinated) happened to be in just those sectors which accidentally helped to maintain the United States as a complementary partner to industrialised Britain; there was little British capital in infant American industries because of the poorer expectation of returns. More than 90 per cent of Britain's tobacco came from the United States. There were tightly knit British immigrant communities of potters and Cornish and Welsh miners. But by 1860 the textile industry of New England had captured from Lancashire the domestic market for coarse cottons; this was the first modern industry to migrate across the Atlantic. Thus began her emancipation from her 'colonial' economic status – a process which put an end to any semblance of complementarity between the two regions of an Atlantic economy.

There were also links in the field of humanitarian endeavour. The philanthropic reform with the broadest connections was anti-slavery. The anti-corn law campaign also developed in an Anglo-American context. British cotton manufacturers were seeking an alternative to dependence on the United States, whose Southern economy was anyway an unsatisfactory market for British manufactures. Raw cotton they wished to get from India; and the Atlantic economy was to be revamped by the export of wheat from the United States to Britain. But this needed freer trade, especially abolition of the corn laws, which appeared to prevent the free flow into Britain of the rich yields of the newly settled prairies of the Northwest. Repeal of the Corn Laws would re-direct the energies of the Atlantic economy away from slave states of the South to a more natural intercourse between the progressive elements in British and American life. Thistlethwaite writes: 'The abolition of the Corn Laws was a materialistic agitation for the abdication of King Cotton and the enthronement of King Wheat . . .' It was another 20 years before American wheat began to flood the British market on the scale envisaged by the anti-slavery free traders. It was the nonconformist Manchester businessmen who felt the closest affinities to the United States; and their prophet was Cobden.

The connection flourished mainly before the Civil War, which marked an important stage in the economic evolution of the United States from 'colonial' to 'metropolitan' status, and after it, the concept of an Atlantic economy, based on complementary exchange and large-scale flow westward of labour and capital, became less valid. Henceforward Americans turned inward. The power of American ideas in Britain waned as the competition of an industrialised America profoundly disturbed British businessmen; the republic lost moral force. Britain was reforming; the American model proved irrelevant; its appeal to radicals disappeared; and in the next generation it was the conservatives who looked to the United States as a potential ally.

In the early nineteenth century there was also a 'Pacific economy' which linked Canada, Australia and New Zealand within the American orbit. Americans in these colonies were often influential. The Melbourne chamber of commerce was dominated by Americans, and recommended the 'New England' form of land settlement to Victoria after responsible government was established there. Other Americans and American land practices continued to influence the framing of Australian land laws in the 1850s and 1860s. In this way American practice profoundly affected the development of imperial and colonial land policies in the nineteenth century.

LATIN AMERICA

In some ways the distinguishing feature of European expansion in the nineteenth century was the collision of the expansions of Britain, Russia, France and the United States. The American empire pursued a global pattern of expansion from the very beginning of the century. Alexander Hamilton in 1787 talked of the United States' becoming the 'arbiter of Europe in America'. Soon she was thrusting politically in all directions – only the thrust towards Canada was halted; and that not until the present century. As late as 1911 the American mind was reluctant to admit defeat in this direction. Recognition of the permanency of Canada came in fact only in consequence of the First World War. The question before British statesmen was whether the United States or Britain was to be the dominant power in the New World.

The Monroe Doctrine of 1823 was partly negative – it attempted to circumscribe the freedom of action of Europeans, but as Van Alstyne writes, what really counted was

> the hidden positives to the effect that the United States shall be the only colonising power in North America and that it shall be the directing power in both North and South America. This is imperialism preached in the grand manner, for the only restrictions placed upon the directing power are those which it imposes upon itself. The Monroe Doctrine would be better described as 'the Monroe manifesto'.[8]

Canning understood the implications very well and devised his Latin American policy as a counter-measure to the pretensions of the United States. By 1824 nearly a hundred British commercial houses were established in South American cities. The British community in Buenos Aires alone was 3,000. About a third of Lancashire cotton imports came from Brazil. The Spanish American markets were important to Lancashire cotton manufacturers: the Manchester chamber of commerce considered them to be 'of the first magnitude and involving the safety of capital to an immense amount'. The Chamber persuaded the government to appoint British consuls in all the chief commercial towns of Latin America. It petitioned in 1824 for recognition of the newly independent states: so did Birmingham.[9] British brokers and commercial agents, who had eagerly awaited the opening of Spanish American markets with or without the permission of Spain, established themselves in one liberated area after another, with the help of the protection of the royal navy. The continent was flooded with British goods. An orgy of mining speculation was afoot by 1824–25, in gold, silver and pearls. The gambling spirit generated sensible projects like a Panama canal, as well as silly ones, such as an association of Scottish milkmaids to supply Buenos Aires with butter. Most revolutionary governments successfully raised loans in London. By the end of 1825, when the bubble burst, more than £20 million of British capital had been invested in Latin America, which was more than three times the amount invested in the United States. And at this date there can be no question that British power counted for more than that of the United States.[10] The Monroe Doctrine indeed was so much windy rhetoric without the unseen hand of the royal navy. Canning's famous proposal for a joint declaration warning off European powers was based on a truer understanding of the potentialities of a non-territorial Anglo-American partnership which would have fitted the basic facts of economic strategy much better than the Monroe Doctrine.[11]

In Latin America the political objective was at least as important as the commercial. Recognition of newly independent states was in part a bid for commercial supremacy and political prestige in Latin America, an answer to the United States bid contained in the Monroe Doctrine. The Peruvian consul wrote that it was 'desirable that the existing shackles to confidence and security should be withdrawn'. Commercial treaties would 'be the means of guaranteeing the security and protection which the British capitalist requires for the employment of his funds in mining'; they were 'desirable for our mercantile interests'. The Colombia consul wrote to Canning that British recognition of independence would 'dispel every apprehension for the future' and make prosperity increase; only this could bring stability; without this step 'British commercial enterprise cannot with safety enter into a fixed permanent and direct trade with Colombia'.[12] Canning had only one concrete request – equality of opportunity in trade (knowing that Britain must thereby predominate). When Bolivar pressed for an alliance, and what amounted to a protectorate, Canning dithered. He preferred to rely on the pervasiveness of British trade, prestige and example to win general confidence. Following the line of policy set by Castlereagh, so far, he said, was

> Great Britain from looking to any more intimate connection with any of the late Spanish provinces than that of political and commercial intercourse, that His Majesty would not be induced by any consideration to enter into any engagement which might be considered as bringing them under *his* dominion.[13]

One contemporary policy-maker, the president of the Indian Board of Control, said, 'In truth the trade already carried on with South America is too important an object to be hazarded'.[14]

Canning's encouragement of British commercial operations fell within the wider context of his desire to reduce United States influence in Latin America. Having recognised Colombia and Mexico he declared:

> Spanish America is free; and if we do not mismanage our matters sadly, she is English. . . . This thing achieved indeed, it matters not whether I go out of town or out of office; for it was the one thing needful in the present state of the world. And I most assuredly would have gone out of office, if I had been thwarted in it.

In 1823 he observed portentously:

> Monarchy in Mexico, and monarchy in Brazil would cure the evils of universal democracy and prevent the drawing of the line of demarcation which I most dread – America versus Europe.

The demarcation would divide a republican, vigorous New World from a monarchical, worn-out Old World.[15] He advocated recognition of Colombia and Mexico, first because they had British capital sunk in mining and territorial concerns of a more permanent interest than 'mere commercial speculation', but secondly,

> The other and perhaps still more powerful motive is my apprehension of the ambition and ascendancy of the United States of America [whose purpose was to organise a] transatlantic league of which it would have the sole direction I need only say how inconvenient such an ascendancy may be in time of peace and how formidable in case of war.

He stepped in to oppose 'a powerful barrier to the influence of the United States', but 'I by no means think it at present necessary to go beyond the mere relations of amity and commercial intercourse'. By stepping in between North and South America at Mexico, Canning was able to say in 1824: 'It is the Yankees who lose most by our decision . . . The United States have gotten the start of us in vain; and we link once more America to Europe'.[16] This sort of argument was accurately calculated to make the maximum appeal to his aristocratic colleagues. It fitted their conceptions to regard the new states as mere pawns in the diplomatic game. But there can be no doubt that Canning saw the necessity to redress the balance of the old world economically as well as politically by calling the new world into being.[17] His noisy oratory may have owed something to his actress-mother, but it also foreshadowed Palmerstonian declarations. Canning vastly overrated the importance of what he had done; but that he should have felt able to talk in this manner indicates the strength of anti-American feeling available for stirring up.

Except as a prophet of what might happen in the twenty-first century, Canning seems to have overestimated the prospective importance and influence of Latin America in the world – as well as the extent to which Britain could influence her policies and politics. If he dreamed that economic ties and friendship would produce close political ties, he was wrong. Latin America was not, even economically, an automatic success story. The British 'informal empire' took a lot of careful working-out; there were several false starts. Only from the mid-1850s did the real efficacy of the connection start to get under way, and only from the 1860s did Britain at last begin to cash in. Not until 1875 could Latin America be said to have become firmly integrated into the transatlantic economy.

In the first half of the nineteenth century, four things (according to Platt) held back the development of trade: a sparse and dispersed population, the successful maintenance of local domestic industry (except in luxury goods), political instability (leading to insecurity of life and property, and to reduced purchasing power), and poor to non-existent communications. From the 1860s railways made a real difference.

Although Britons were to be found in most coastal places of any consequence, British efforts were concentrated in the three most important markets of Argentina, Brazil and Chile. Major British banks got one-third of the deposits in Brazil by 1914, and one-quarter in Argentina and Chile. Elsewhere the difficulties were formidable. There were many unstable governments, in which politicians often made capital out of anti-foreign feelings and passed hostile legislation; states were frequently plagued with fiscal troubles which they tried to meet at the expense of the foreigner. Peru never seems to have been a significant area of British interest. Development everywhere was late.[18]

In Chile from the 1880s British interest in its nitrates, its trade, banking and railways, was substantial. Between 1879 and 1883, in the 'Nitrate War', Chile had annexed from her neighbours Peru and Bolivia desert provinces containing the nitrates. Subsequently the control of these deposits passed into British hands, notably those of John T. North. Because of Chile's economic and political weakness and instability, British capital took command by the end of the 1880s. But there was never any question of imperial political intervention, even during the 1891 Chilean revolution.[19]

The connection with Argentina had earlier beginnings. The Anglo-Argentine treaty of 1825 was a reflection of the high optimism of its period. It envisaged only a simple free-market relationship between industrial Britain and a raw-material producing country; the role of the state was reduced to guaranteeing the operation of a supposed automatic market mechanism. There was a long period of disillusionment; Argentina was a turbulent community for 50 years after its revolution. By any test, Canning's optimistic hopes were unfulfilled before the middle of the century. But from the 1860s Britain directed nearly all the large enterprises which came into being; the first long railway was opened in 1863. At least from 1880 Argentina became more important to the British economy than Egypt or China, or even Canada. It was mutton, beef, wheat and maize which gave Argentina so disproportionate a share in Latin American exports to Britain from the mid-1880s, and even the most cautious of historians concedes that it is difficult to exaggerate the importance of British trade with Argentina. Capital, business and technicians flowed in rapidly now, and made Argentina one of the economic wonders of the world. The dream of the early South Sea adventurers seemed to come true. Argentina, however, was not a semi-colony: its government always had full power over its economic relations — unlike Egypt.[20]

Brazil until the 1860s was by far the largest market for British goods in Latin America, and during this period, British goods were supreme among Brazilian imports. From the 1880s, however, British interest tended to shift markedly to Argentina, and the Americans gradually moved in. Even so, by 1914 Britain still had four times as much money invested there as America had, and one and a half times all other foreign capital combined. British enterprise and shipping were also predominant: British ships carried 5/13ths of the coffee export even though most of it went to the United States. British banks held 30 per cent of the total assets of all banks in Brazil by 1913. For most of the nineteenth century Britain supplied more than half of all Brazil's imports. Nevertheless, it could be argued that the zenith of British pre-eminence, especially on the political side, was past after 1827. In 1845 there was a frank revolt by independent Brazil against the kind of pressures the British had originally put upon the old Portuguese regime. The Brazilian government revoked the special favours granted to Britain and declared commercial and slave trade treaties annulled. Brazil won its point. The protest was not against British economic enterprise, but against the vexatious restrictions imposed by a stronger power on a weaker – the extra-territorial privileges, the consular concessions, and so forth. The Brazilians wanted to stop the tradition whereby 'it was always with a threat on its lips that the English government spoke to Brazil'. British merchants happily enough accepted the decline of extra-territoriality, feeling confident that special courts were superfluous. In the 1850s the Brazilians voluntarily enacted a comprehensive commercial code and lowered their customs duties, and then abolished the slave trade. They welcomed the superior capital resources which Britain could provide, and in order to secure them, many members of the Brazilian élite became ardent Anglophiles. Notable among them was Viscount Mauá, who considered it one of his most signal achievements to have helped to make the Amazon truly accessible to world (i.e. British) trade. He tried in the 1860s (not always with success) to transfer his foundry, shipyard, gasworks, and nearly a million acres of land, to British companies; he also tried to amalgamate his bank with a British one. Other Anglophiles included Joaquim Nabuco ('I am entirely under the influence of English liberalism', he said in 1892, 'as if I were working under the orders of Gladstone . . . I am an English liberal . . . in the Brazilian parliament') and Rui Barbosa, who waxed eloquent about the 'benign preponderance' of Britain in promoting Christianity and liberty in the world. Brazilian concessions for railways fell almost exclusively into British hands in the early days, and even at the peak of the coffee export era. The superintendent of the São Paulo Railway was an honoured representative of the Manchester Cotton Supply Association. Railways made the coffee boom possible, and were the principal British contribution to the onset of modernisation. This modernisation was not 'caused' by the British, but they had an important if limited part in it, being involved closely in building transport facilities, providing machinery, supplies and technicians, risking capital in pioneering the early sugar factories and flour mills, and investing in shoe factories and textile plants. Many British engineers worked in Brazil; Charles Neate and Henry Law remained there a lifetime.

Powerful competition from the United States had emerged by 1900. Britain would not oppose this because the Americans could provide stability without inhibiting the free penetration of British goods.[21]

Meanwhile useful apolitical bargains had been struck by large-scale British private enterprise in several parts of Latin America. One side needed

European capital; the other needed the help of local knowledge. It is not the case that Latin American governments were so subservient to foreign economic interests that they were incapable of promoting worthwhile infant industries.

Victorian statesmen increasingly accepted the priority of North American interests, first in Central America, and then, more reluctantly, in Latin America. Palmerston was forced to give way step by step 'on almost every disputed matter', and withdrawal from the Mosquito Coast in 1860 represented the end of direct political interest in the continent and the beginning of an attempt to collaborate with the United States. Force continued to be used occasionally in the last resort to obtain justice for unsatisfied business claims, but this was different from supposed intervention in internal affairs for the extension of British financial and commercial interests. 'Much of the history of British diplomacy in Latin America', writes Platt, 'is merely an eddy off the main current of British relations with Washington'. Diplomacy was neither energetic nor adaptable in Latin America, but static and mainly negative, superintended by a foreign office which cared little for the region, and carried out by diplomats who felt exiled into postings which they thought of as tombstones and not stepping-stones in a career.[22] British economic expansion in Latin America was thus the work of private businessmen; and the proximity of the United States increasingly determined the limits within which they could operate. There seems to be no doubt that throughout the century one major inhibition to greater activity by the government, one reason for the restraint with which British 'expansion' operated in Latin America, was fear of upsetting the United States.

RELATIONS WITH THE UNITED STATES IN NORTH AMERICA

Only since 1871 has the so-called undefended land frontier between Canada and the United States been truly undefended. This was as a result of the Treaty of Washington (1871). By the withdrawal of British military presence, Canada ceased to be a military threat to the United States and an irritant in Anglo-American relations. The fundamental premise of the treaty was British recognition of the supremacy of the United States on the American continent. Canadian independence was at last assured because it could not be a rival of the United States.[23]

Earlier in the century, however, rivalry was intense. Britain paid considerable attention to land fortification. A new citadel was built at Quebec in the 1820s at a cost of £236,500. The imperial government contributed £12,000 to the construction of the Lachine canal and the army itself undertook canalisation of the Ottawa in 1819; both were major and expensive projects. Suspicion of American ambitions in Cuba led to a strengthening of British naval force in the West Indies at the end of 1822. In 1825 a major report made recommendations covering 900 miles of Canadian frontier.

Without works costing £1,646,218, said Wellington, it was not to be expected that the inhabitants would do 'otherwise than look for the security of their lives and properties to a seasonable submission to the United States'. Canning in 1824 drew attention to the growing naval power of the United States, which seemed mainly directed towards trying to supplant Britain in every quarter of the globe.[24]

An opportunity to curb the growing power of America occurred in the Texan rebellion of 1835-36. The chance of improving the southern barrier to the expansion of the United States was not pursued very actively, mainly because Palmerston did not think it easy to influence the future of Texas, and because optimistically he hoped that it would not make much difference commercially whether Texas went into the Union or not. By the end of 1843 Britain and the United States appeared to be moving into open conflict on the southern frontier of the United States. Even so pacific a minister as Aberdeen was anxious to maintain the independence of Texas, partly because it offered an important alternative source of cotton for Lancashire and more generally because it seemed important to maintain a buffer against the increasingly aggressive American designs in the West. He renewed an initiative which seemed positively Palmerstonian. The belief, widely entertained at the time, that Britain intended to establish a protectorate over Texas, is without foundation. The Texan and Oregon boundary questions reached a climax in 1845. As far as Maine was concerned, Palmerston said in 1842 that it was not a rich country, 'but the question between the two countries was essentially military and political, not agricultural and commercial'. The United States wanted it because it intervened between New Brunswick and Canada, affording them a strong military position for attack, which had to be expected since their fixed aim was 'the expulsion of British authority from the continent of America'. Palmerston denounced the Webster-Ashburton treaty as an act of weakness which helped the Americans 'both physically and morally' towards their aim; and it was certainly no triumph for Britain. Ashburton believed he had averted war, but his critics were violent and accused him of everything from imbecility downwards. The frontier in the north and north-east was stabilised but he made no progress elsewhere. Perhaps Ashburton's chief claim to usefulness was the speed with which he settled immediate issues. It was all done in six months. Both he and Webster were bankers and already known to each other through Ashburton's American wife. Peel's attitude was that minor arguments over the strategic value of barren lands in North America were unimportant compared with the possibility of war with the United States, Britain's best customer. In September 1845 Peel advised firmly against any response to overtures from Mexico for the assertion of British interests in California, and he was equally positive five months later in forbidding any unusual naval activities on the Great Lakes.[25]

The defeat of Mexico confirmed the American union with Texas and brought in California, with its strategic harbour of San Francisco; only the northern part of Oregon became 'British Columbia'. This was a colossal if not final blow against any British attempt to establish a balance of power in North America. Palmerston from 1846, however, showed little inclination to mount a counter-attack.[26]

The Clayton-Bulwer Treaty (1850), providing for the neutralisation of a Panama canal, marked the first stage of British retreat from the Caribbean area; it was 'merely a paper dam against the further deterioration of Anglo-American relations'. Britain was interested only in free and equal treatment for British trade and communications generally; as Cobden said, 'the sooner we get rid of all connection with that region of earthquakes and volcanoes the better'. Palmerston loathed the Americans: 'disagreeable . . . totally unscrupulous and dishonest'. He was ready by 1859–60 to withdraw from the Mosquito Coast and the Bay Islands, since 'such ingenious rogues' would always circumvent any barrier Britain tried to maintain. A rapprochement with the United States seemed close at hand, but the outbreak of the Civil War ruined any chance it may have had. As a close neighbour, and the greatest of the maritime and commercial neutrals, Britain was bound to become involved in difficult and dangerous incidents.[27]

The *Trent* crisis* was the most dangerous single crisis in Anglo-American relations since 1815. Britain stood very firmly on her prestige. Clarendon wrote:

> What a figure . . . we shall cut in the eyes of the world if we lamely submit to this outrage when all mankind will know that we should unhesitatingly have poured our indignation and our broadsides into any weak nation . . . and what an additional proof it will be of the universal . . . belief that we have two sets of weights and measures to be used according to the power or weakness of our adversary. I have a horror of war and of all wars one with the United States because none would be so prejudicial to our interests, but peace like other good things may be bought too dearly and it never can be worth the price of national honour.

At the time of crisis Palmerston said that to lose Canada in battle 'would be a heavy blow to the reputation of England both for sagacity and strength'. To Palmerston prestige was not a mere matter of self-respect but a factor of material value in the attitude of other powers. Not everyone agreed with him. The *Trent* affair was trivial in that neither party actually wanted war, but it was fundamental in demonstrating that war was possible between Britain and

---

* The *Trent* was a British mail steamer; two Confederate envoys aboard were forcibᵢ seized in European waters by a Union naval captain in November 1861. Palmerston, regarding this as a clear breach of international law, wanted to send reinforcements to Canada even before receiving a reply to his demand for apology. The American secretary of state disowned the captain's action.

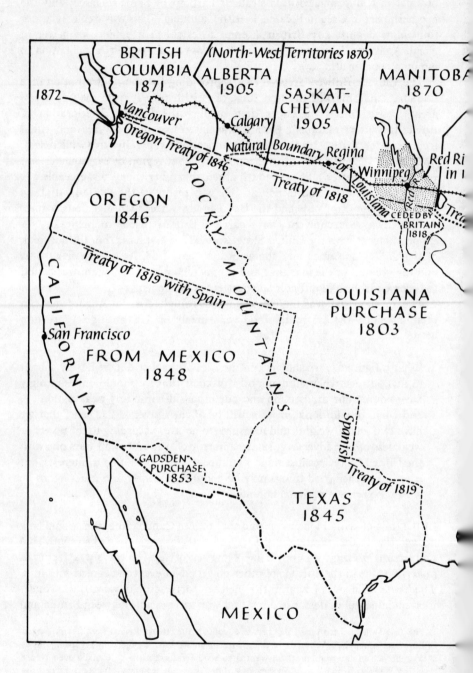

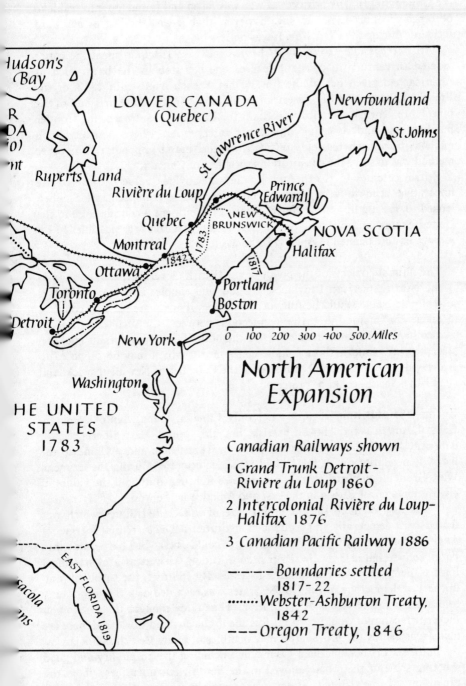

Hudson's Bay

LOWER CANADA
(Quebec)

Newfoundland

St Johns

St Lawrence River

Ruperts Land

Rivière du Loup

Prince
Edward I.

Quebec

NEW
BRUNSWICK

NOVA SCOTIA

Montreal

1783

Ottawa

1842

1817

Halifax

Toronto

Portland
Boston

Detroit

New York

0   100   200   300   400   500 Miles

Washington

**North American
Expansion**

HE UNITED
STATES
1783

EAST FLORIDA 1819

Pacola
ns

Canadian Railways shown

1 *Grand Trunk Detroit-
Rivière du Loup 1860*

2 *Intercolonial Rivière du Loup-
Halifax 1876*

3 *Canadian Pacific Railway 1886*

—·—·— *Boundaries settled
1817–22*

········· *Webster-Ashburton Treaty,
1842*

——— *Oregon Treaty, 1846*

the United States. The prospect of war was faced and found too intolerable to be repeated. This is not to say, however, that it was the last of awkward incidents during the Civil War. It was not.[28]

With the possible exception of the years 1871–95 Britain spent the entire nineteenth century in constant fear of another stab in the back, such as America had given her at the time of her French troubles in 1812, or the French at the time of her American troubles in 1778. For the first half of the nineteenth century she tried to contain the United States by erecting frontier fortifications and asserting diplomatic intervention where possible. Such methods became increasingly difficult, expensive and unpopular. The other method was to solve the constitutional problem of Canada.[29]

British colonies in North America had an obvious value because of the imperative need to keep a check on American aggrandisement. Stephen looked to 'raising up on the North American Continent a counterpoise to the United States' and was one of the first to see that this was possible. In an incisive minute penned in April 1836 he wrote:

> The ultimate objects of the policy of the British Government, in relation to the North American Provinces, are few and simple. Every end which is really desirable would be fully accomplished, if adequate security could be taken for maintaining the connection between the two countries as members of the same monarchy – if the outlet for poor emigrants could be kept open – and if those commercial interests which may be supposed to depend upon the colonial character of the Canadas, of New Brunswick, and of Nova Scotia, could be protected.[30]

By the 1850s Britain regarded not only Canada, Cuba, Santo Domingo, Central America and Hawaii at risk, but also Japan, East Siberia, South America, Monte Carlo and Ireland, and by 1868 Dilke added China to the list. When relations with the United States deteriorated during the Crimean War, Granville pictured Britain and France fighting to uphold the values of civilisation against Russia in the east and America in the west.[31]

It was not so much the increasing size of the United States which was feared as its democratic and republican institutions. The torrential energies of Anglo-Saxon peoples, it was thought, could best be harnessed into constructive channels by the British constitution, viewed as a monarchical form of democracy, restraining the excesses. By contrast, the turbulent and unchecked democracy of the United States was regarded as a threat not only to peace but to the values of civilisation. Thus Grey thought that the loss of the British colonies would be 'a misfortune to the civilised world'.[32] There are many reasons for the pro-Southern sympathies of many British politicians at the outbreak of the American Civil War (including the hospitality and good shooting some of them had enjoyed in the South), but uneasiness about the expansion of the United States was certainly one of them, and with

Palmerston the main one. British sympathy for the Southern States provoked widespread anger in the North.[33]

There is no doubt that the progress of the United States was found to be a frightening phenomenon. As J. R. Godley expressed it in 1854, contemplating the 'mammoth republic':

> *the* great peril which overshadows the future of the civilised world lies in the vast power and progress of the United States, coupled as their gigantic material resources are with unbounded energy and inordinate ambition. To raise up to this overweening power a rival on its own continent, would be a work far more valuable and important to England than the curbing of the power of Russia.[34]

The comparative threat of Russia and the United States was indeed pondered by many. It seemed as if the Mexican war had revealed one giant and the Crimean war had failed to shake another. But strong as Russophobia was in some quarters, it was from America that the threat was felt most acutely. As Grey wrote in 1848, the more he considered the state of affairs in the United States the more convinced he became that, as the effect of the ultra-democratic institutions of the Great Republic became more and more pronounced, they were dangerous to the peace of the world. He might not otherwise have attached much value to British possessions in America, but, as it was, he thought it 'of the utmost consequence that we should at least retain them long enough to raise them to a constitution in which they might maintain their own independence instead of being absorbed in the Union'. Thus Canada was extremely important to Britain, especially on account of its shipbuilding timber, the Halifax naval base and the British North American merchant marine, which was the third largest in the world.[35] Grey saw with perfect clarity that it was a vital national interest to prevent these naval resources falling into the hands of the United States. Roebuck was another who saw that possession of the St Lawrence by the United States would be fatal to the maritime supremacy of Britain. America would then have no frontier to defend and 'her offensive and defensive power would be increased by that acquisition to an extent that would render her influence dangerous to the general liberty of the world'. He too believed that a consolidated Canada would be an important 'counterpoise to the gigantic empire and influence of the United States'. The idea of a confederate union might be turned against its inventor to check her.[36] The attempt to link Canada to Britain in a permanent relationship by conceding self-government was an implicit and continuing ideological rejection of the American republican experiment, but it was also a strategic necessity. As Martin has observed, Canada was not given self-government on the parliamentary model to cast it off from Britain but to keep it out of the United States.

Thus it is only in a general context of an antagonistic struggle for hegemony between Britain and the United States that it is really possible to understand British policy towards Canada.[37] Canada was worth retaining as a check on the expansion of the democratic and republican United States. Responsible government was devised as the only means of retaining it. In Canada, the United States failed. The desire of the United States to have Canada was real and of long standing. The seventh article of the original United States Constitution provided for the admission of Canada without the normal requirement, applicable to any other state, that it must have eleven or more votes in favour of its joining. In 1775–76 there was an American attempt to conquer Quebec. The expedition, launched at a time when the American army was scarcely organised, when ammunition and heavy artillery were exceedingly scarce, was intended by Congress (with Washington's full support) to effect a permanent conquest, and it did in fact beseige both Montreal and Quebec – but it was repulsed.

There was another descent upon Canada in the war of 1812–14. Jefferson was disappointed at the failure in that war to 'liberate' Canada – he was to hold out even in 1814 for annexation, believing that the natural limits of the United States would include the Canadian provinces. In 1783 the United States asked for the whole of Canada to be ceded as a pledge of reconciliation, and Shelburne considered it quite seriously. Every subsequent decade showed some degree of American interest in continental dominion. From time to time in the 30 years after the 1840s the United States maintained special agents inquiring into the state of opinion in British North America.[38] The radical wing of the Republican Party showed much interest in annexation. Much later, in 1870 the United States secretary of state Fish suggested that Britain should withdraw from Canada in order to liquidate the *Alabama* claims.[39]

Both Lord Glenelg and Lord Durham thought entry to the Union would be acceptable to many Canadians. So, later, did Lord Elgin.[40] A legislative union of all the provinces, said Durham in his Report, would above all, 'form a great and powerful people . . . which, under the protection of the British Empire, might in some measure counter-balance the preponderant and increasing influence of the United States on the American continent'. The influence of the United States was all-pervasive, he noted:

> . . . it stamps, on all the habits and opinions of the surrounding countries, the common characteristics of the thoughts, feelings and customs of the American people . . . Its thoughts and manners subjugate them, even when nominally independent of its authority. If we wish to prevent the extension of this influence, it can only be done by raising up for the North American colonist some nationality of his own; by elevating these small and unimportant communities into a society having some objects of a national importance; and by thus giving their inhabitants a country which they will be unwilling to see absorbed even into one more powerful.[41]

The cultural pull of the United States on Canada was, and remains, very strong. Almost every Canadian household in the nineteenth century had personal connections with the United States, and read the same magazines. Societies such as freemasons crossed the border easily.[42] The presence of so many Irish in the United States provided an element anxious to obtain Canada. As Elgin noted, a 'reckless and powerful faction' in the United States advocated 'annexation of Canada as a species of retaliation for British misdeeds in Ireland'.[43] No British minister ever said anything separatist about Canada – every government was dedicated to maintaining the connection and preventing it going to the United States. Even Russell, who had said ambiguous things, declared in 1849 that to such an event he would never give his assent, because annexation would involve aggrandisement of American power, and the extension of an American trade barrier against British manufactured goods.[44] It was thoroughly understood that, if Britain could not retain the allegiance of Canada, it would pass into the Union. This would have a serious result upon the total position of Britain in the world. Elgin wrote dramatically: 'Let the Yankees get possession of British North America with the prestige of superior generalship – who can say how soon they may dispute with you the Empire of India and of the Seas?' The potentiality of America in the world was realised. After a visit to Niagara Falls, Elgin felt he had obtained 'an insight into the future of Nations'. Elgin quickly came to conclusions as governor-general; in 1848 he realised how powerful were the influences dragging Canada to the United States and how weak the hold of Britain and British institutions was on the affections of certain classes. 'Disaffection is not here as in other parts of the Empire a purely negative sentiment – It is the creature of positive preferences and hopes' – the prosperity and rapid advancement which might come with the 'great neighbouring and kindred nation', the United States. Alive to the necessity of treating Canadians tactfully, Elgin, with a homely analogy, warned those who said that remaining responsible for Canada was a nuisance:

If you say that your great lubberly boy is too big for the nursery, and that you have no other room for him in your house, how can you decline to allow him to lodge with his elder brethren over the way, when the attempt to keep up an establishment for himself would seriously embarrass him?

Hence: 'to render annexation by violence impossible, and by any other means as improbable as may be' was the pole star of his policy. Every issue of policy was indeed seen in the light of this general aim, from tariff policy to land settlement; and it led on to a consideration of federating the British North American provinces.[45]

How serious was the Canadian desire to be annexed by the United States? Elgin gradually came to a more optimistic view:

If half the talk on this subject were sincere I should consider an attempt to keep up the connection with Great Britain as Utopian in the extreme . . . annexation is invoked as the remedy for all ills, imaginary or real. A great deal of this talk is however bravado, and a great deal the mere product of thoughtlessness. Undoubtedly it is in some quarters the utterance of very sincere convictions; and if England will not make the sacrifices which are absolutely necessary to put the colonists here in as good a position commercially as the citizens of the States – in order to which *free navigation* and *reciprocal trade with the States are indispensable* – the end may be nearer at hand than we wot of.

There must be no talk of Canada as a burden endured of necessity. 'The English annexationists all take an £.s.d. view of the question . . . The more it is canvassed the more formidable will the difficulties appear, and the greater the sacrifices which Canada will have to make to enter the Union'. Elgin's analysis was that the grievances which led to the annexation manifesto of 1849 were essentially economic, not political, and therefore capable of being remedied.[46] 969 people signed the Annexation Manifesto. This document harped on the obstacles retarding material prosperity; it argued that there would be great benefits in economic integration with the United States (capital and wealthy settlers were kept out while there was a threat of war between Canada and the United States), and that it would remove the costs of attempting to defend themselves against such a war. But the memorialists did state quite categorically that without the consent of Britain 'we consider separation as neither practicable or desirable'.[47] In 1849 the United States was preoccupied in a bitter struggle to organise territories recently seized from Mexico, and so political circumstances towards meeting the annexationist demands were less favourable than they might have been.

By the 1860s it was only in British Columbia that there was anything which might be called a strong pro-American group, and even there the feeling was to a large extent a means of keeping Canadians suitably on edge. In general, the traditional dependence on Britain, and the traditional fear and dislike of the United States, together with a disinclination to change, especially to change a familiar culture, were strong. French Canada feared the omnivorous, all-embracing culture of the United States, but felt that a smaller federation would not be able to ignore the power and geographical centrality of the French-speaking province. Fear of the United States was bred upon boundary disputes, quarrels over the fisheries, and memories of the war of 1812.[48]

CANADA 1815–50

The Quebec Act of 1774 denied to Canadians the representative system announced in 1763, when Canada was conquered from the French, and instead set up a nominated legislature with limited power. Its effect was to encourage the French to maintain their distinctive legal system and their religion. After the American Revolution, Britain tried to create a strong Quebec as a counterpoise to the new republic. As a reward for their loyalty during the American Revolution, and as a gesture to the loyalists who moved into Canada, the Canada Act of 1791 conceded representative government of the time-honoured type. It also divided Canada into two provinces, one mainly French, the other almost exclusively British: Lower Canada (centred on French Quebec) and Upper Canada (later Ontario). The imperial intention was to assimilate Canada as far as possible both in constitutional form and social structure to the British model. Liberties and property rights had to be seen to be more secure than in the United States if Canada was not to be absorbed.[49] 60,000 Frenchmen counted for much as a counterpoise to the mutinous Americans, and the effect of the Canada Acts of 1774 and 1791 was to assist the preservation of the French nationality.[50]

In Lower Canada governors tended to choose their councillors from the English-speaking Château clique of Quebec, and in Upper Canada from the 'family compact' of the Anglican upper class. Governments were thus formed from a narrow oligarchy, and the assemblies, lacking real power, attracted grievance-mongers. There was, however, a real and deep-seated French resentment of the British settlers and their purposeful grip.[51]

In 1837 there were rebellions, if that is not too strong a word, small-scale but overt, in both Lower (led by L.-J. Papineau) and Upper Canada (led by W. L. Mackenzie). These did not represent any clear-cut ethnic conflict (many of Papineau's chief lieutenants were British Canadians), nor were they against the imperial connection, only against privilege and irresponsible oligarchies within the colonies – for example, although the French were three-quarters of the population of Lower Canada in 1834, they held less than one-quarter of the public places.[52]

Lord Durham was sent out to report. Prime minister Melbourne had no desire to see the Canadas separate themselves from Britain, if only because it would be fatal to his administration. Lord Durham had been ambassador to St Petersburg from 1835 to 1837. In January 1838 Durham agreed to go to Canada. He then delayed for four months while he prepared for a truly regal journey to take up his post as captain-general, high commissioner and governor-in-chief. His establishment was excessively opulent, as might have been expected of a man who once remarked that one could 'jog along' on a moderate means of £40,000 a year. Durham expected his assignment to take more than a year, and so he shipped out an army of grooms and servants, eight aides-de-camp, cases of silver, his sporting trophies, ornate furniture and horses. His own party consisted of 22 persons, including his children, and was accompanied by a band with a large number of musical instruments – which gave rise to the joke that Durham was going to make overtures to the Canadians. His immediate advisers looked rather disreputable, and may have damaged the impact of the mission.[53] They included Edward Gibbon Wakefield, whose penchant was for abducting heiresses by the most devious means (an addiction which led to imprisonment), and Thomas Turton as legal adviser, a man who had committed the unsavoury crime of adultery with his wife's sister. The size of the retinue indeed astounded the Canadians. His baggage alone took two days to unload. Then, clothed in brilliant uniform, on 29 May 1838 Durham rode up on a white horse from the banks of the St Lawrence. In retrospect this pomp and paraphernalia have looked ridiculous to some historians. But there can be no doubt that Durham correctly judged how to awe and impress Canadians, especially the French, and when he left unexpectedly early, on 1 November 1838, the streets were full with silently regretful crowds and a procession of 3,000 citizens. Whatever needs to be said in criticism of Durham and his *Report on the Affairs of British North America* (1839)[54] has to be qualified with the observation that he himself aroused hopes in a depressed and embittered community, and gave the appearance of being a well-disposed and clement man of charisma sufficient to solve the problem, if anyone could. His reputation as 'Radical Jack', part originator of the 1832 Reform Act, was important in this connection. He had unparalleled authority: to remodel a suspended constitution. If Durham needs defence against charges of high-handedness, reckless impulsiveness, ill-temper and arrogance, it has to be remembered that the health of 'the Dictator' (as even his friends called him) was exceedingly poor. He suffered frequent collapses, and lived from one physical crisis to another, so that his ability to hold public office at all was certainly a tribute to his tremendous will-power. He died in 1840, aged 48. If the report showed him to be massively anti-French, he was also totally impervious, unlike his predecessors, to the machinations of the oligarchical clique and accorded it no praise. And he got on well with Americans, another important achievement. Certain vital points in the situation he discerned with speed and accuracy. He won immediate popular confidence with his initial proclamation saying he desired to hasten the return of constitutional government. By the middle of July he wrote to Melbourne that the two provinces must be united in order to get rid of the mockery of British institutions which existed: 'The only remedy for all this [inefficiency and corruption] is the taking the great questions out of the hands of the local provincial assemblies and assigning them to a higher and less numerous body, composed of the better class, out of each province'. In the circumstances of 1838 that made good sense. He saw that the 'deadly animosity' between French and British must stop. He also exposed the fallacy of a policy based on the expectation 'that Englishmen renounce every political opinion and feeling when they enter a colony, or that the spirit of Anglo-Saxon freedom is utterly changed and weakened among those who are transplanted across the Atlantic'.[55] This was something that needed saying again, however obvious a truth it may seem. It is true that the solution Durham proposed was not original. He never claimed that it was. No new constitutional theory was needed, merely the following out consistently of the principles of the efficacious British constitution by introducing into Canada 'those wise provisions by which alone the working of the representative system can in any country be rendered harmonious and efficient'. Ministers must be *responsible,* that is to say, be able to command a majority of support in the legislature or resign if they could not. His critics rightly pointed out that it was not so simple a matter to do this in a colony because a governor would have two masters. But in the long run Durham's grand simplification showed a truer insight than the logical objections of his critics. The idea of responsible government for Canada was 'invented' by Robert Baldwin of Toronto, who may have begun to influence Russell directly in 1836 towards accepting the principle of self-government.[56] But it was Durham who gave it vital publicity and lent a famous name to the idea.

Where the Durham report ran off the rails is easy to see. It pleased no-one fully. It was riddled with traditional British official and mercantile contempt for the French Canadians. Durham could see no culture worth preserving and claimed he had not found a single French Canadian book. The French seemed unenterprising and fatally restricted by their church. As a diagnosis it may not have been wholly misplaced, but it allowed too little for the forces of cultural development. His belief that French culture must be swallowed up in the superior British one was something most contemporaries would have agreed about. But the fact remains that Durham wished to Anglicise the French and this in practice proved impossible. The report never had any good reputation in French Canada: indeed the bitterness aroused by its superficial and harshly expressed analysis of Lower Canada still survived in some measure well into the twentieth century. His condemnation of French culture was seen as a challenge, which became the impulse for a great intellectual awakening led by François-Xavier Garneau, who laid the foundations of a patriotic literature with his epic history of the French Canadian people.[57]

Even more damaging to the value of Durham's recommendations were his famous four reservations. The imperial government was to retain control of four things:

> The constitution of the form of government, – the regulation of foreign relations, and of trade with the mother country, the other British Colonies, and foreign nations, – and the disposal of the public lands, are the only points on which the mother country requires a control.

'A perfect subordination' on these points by the colony would, he wrote, be secured by the advantage it would find in continuing connection with the empire. Durham thus briefly disposed of the problem of dual authority, apparently unaware of how contentious the four points were. Whilst it is an exaggeration to say that the whole constitutional and political evolution of the empire into commonwealth can be summed up by tracing what happened to these four reservations,[58] it is nevertheless true that no commonwealth would have been possible until the imperial government had given them up. The division between internal and imperial affairs was incapable of determination and of enforcement. For example, as far as foreign relations were concerned, nobody knew exactly where the borders of Canada were vis-à-vis the United States – Aroostook was disputed between Maine and New Brunswick. The Americans had built a fort on the wrong side of the boundary by accident. The limitation of powers they imposed was also very serious. To reserve control of tariffs and land was a substantial invasion of fiscal independence. Two of the most important sources of revenue were land sales and tariff revenues. Since the line of division between imperial and local, between transferred and reserved subjects, was neither clearly marked nor enforced by statute, within a dozen years of 1848 the colonies had won the control they wanted over their own trade, tariffs and unalienated land. Foreign affairs was a more difficult matter.[59]

There seems to be little doubt that on the whole the Durham Report was for a variety of reasons badly received when it was published.[60] Durham had fallen out with Melbourne's government over the Bermuda Ordinance, which was disallowed on the grounds that he had exceeded his powers in sentencing eight rebels to banishment (instead of to death) and pardoning the other 150 or so prisoners. He resigned with a broken spirit. Men such as he do not like being overruled on technical quibbles. His report was not therefore issued with the authority of office. It came out at a time when there were so many publications about Canada that the public was perhaps bored by yet another, especially when it coincided with an interesting event, Glenelg's resignation. It was very readable, though not perhaps in the small type given it by the *Times*, but readability does not imply influence. There is no necessary connection between the report and the subsequent steps of British policy. The only immediate step was uniting the Canadas in 1840, but this proposal had been made long before, and in introducing the bill to bring it about, Russell went out of his way to say that Durham was not the source of the government's inspiration; and in fact a scheme worked out by Edward Ellice* seems to have been more influential. As to the possible influence of the report on the introduction of responsible government in Canada, suffice it to say that the Elgin-Grey conception differed considerably from Durham's, and in some crucial ways, such as treatment of the French, differed fundamentally. There is no evidence that Elgin ever met his father-in-law, (Durham died before Elgin married); and he wrote of 'my system' in 1853 without connecting it with inspiration received from Durham. The Durham Report was never debated in parliament, and even in the debate on the Rebellion Losses Bill only Brougham quoted it, on the 'conflict of races'. Responsible

* Edward Ellice (1791–1863): held cabinet office 1832–34; one of the best-informed politicians about British North America, on account of his long connection with the fur trade.

government was introduced in Nova Scotia and Canada (late 1840s), New South Wales, New Zealand and Victoria in 1856, Queensland in 1859, Cape Colony in 1872 and Western Australia in 1890. In no case was Durham invoked.

It is difficult to argue that the Durham Report bore full fruit in the achievement of Canadian federation in 1867, nearly thirty years later. The report contained inaccuracies, gross over-simplifications and palpable contradictions. To suggest a scheme of responsible government for small, rough colonies lacking really identifiable political parties required no small degree of imagination and possibly some wishful thinking.[61] Few people were in fact taken in by it. It was, however, exceptionally well expressed, and the ability to express commonplace thoughts in admirable form is not a gift to be belittled.

In many respects the report deserves deflation. It is entirely another question how far this debunking should involve Durham himself. He was in Canada for only five months, and that is a fact sometimes used to suggest that his importance must have been overrated. Yet consider what he achieved in those few months. He dealt with the rebel prisoners, and if this caused a break with Melbourne, it at least quietened popular discontent. He healed a growing breach between Britain and the United States. He provided Montreal with a rudimentary police force. He established a system for the registration of land titles. He recommended a British government loan for the construction of a canal from Lake Erie to the sea. He appointed sub-commissions to deal with the problems of the disposal of Crown lands and immigration, education and municipal government.[62] Durham was a man who got things moving. He may not have been the founder of the commonwealth, but he was certainly a proconsul of Caesarian dimensions. By his report he made it possible for British theorists to turn to and quote an articulate and respectable (in some senses at least) non-American authority, and this was not without significance.[63]

Of his successors, Metcalfe was respected but dying, Sydenham was hated by the French, Cathcart was a useless army officer, and, before Elgin, only Bagot wooed the French in society and in the street, but he was old and sick.[64]

Union was carried out in 1840. Meanwhile Russell had explicitly declined responsible government in 1839 as vague and potentially embarrassing. If a governor received instructions from the Queen, he argued, totally at variance with advice from his executive council, and he followed the latter, 'he is no longer a subordinate officer, but an independent sovereign'.[65] Nevertheless, abandoning the objections of strict logic, in 1846 Grey instructed Sir John Harvey, governor of Nova Scotia, to follow in practice principles of 'responsible government', by making it apparent that any transfer in political power from one party to another was the result not of an act of his, 'but of the wishes of the people themselves'; and by abstaining from changing his executive council until it was perfectly clear they were unable to carry on the government satisfactorily or command the confidence of the legislature. If there was a difference between him and his council, Grey advised that:

> concession to their views must, sooner or later, become inevitable, since it cannot be too distinctly acknowledged that it is neither possible nor desirable to carry on the government of any of the British provinces in North America in opposition to the opinion of the inhabitants.

The governor must mediate impartially and let it be seen that his conduct was guided not by personal favour to any particular men or party, but by a sincere desire to promote the public good.[66]

After an election in 1847 a Nova Scotia 'reform' government, led by James Boyle Uniacke, became on 2 February 1848 the first fully responsible ministry in the British empire. But as Mansergh has so well pointed out, its formation was the consequence, not of a British conversion to an abstract theory of colonial government, but of an appreciation of the relevance of the idea to situations in which they were faced with sustained and mounting pressure of colonial demand for such a government.[67] The great breakthrough had occurred only seven years after Russell's refusal to consider responsible government on the ground that a governor-general might be presented with two sets of conflicting advice, from the British Crown and from colonial ministers. His objection that a governor could not be bound by two possibly conflicting seats of authority, however valid in logic, had in practice to be ignored.[68]

If the Canadian problem reached some degree of stabilised solution for the remainder of the nineteenth century and even beyond, the credit for this must largely be given to Grey and the eighth earl of Elgin. Elgin had tact, a sophisticated sense of history, and a mind which was quick, vigorous and resilient. His firm convictions were tempered by a cool commonsense, a sense of humour and a keen awareness of the currents of popular opinion, so that he was well fitted to govern a turbulent colony evolving towards democracy. Alone among the men of his generation who wrestled with imperial problems, Elgin was without qualification a man with ability of the first rank. By tactful personal interviews and brilliant receptions he persuaded the French he was on their side.[69]

Like Stephen before him, he saw that, correctly handled, Canada could remain attached to Britain, 'though tied to her neither by the golden links of protection, nor by the meshes of old-fashioned Colonial Office jobbing and chicane'.[70] With responsible government fairly worked out, with free trade begetting contentment and material progress, there seemed to him no reason why the relationship should not be indefinitely maintained. It all depended on certain conditions, however. First, British institutions must be given unreservedly. 'I have been possessed', he wrote, '. . . with the idea that it is possible to maintain on this soil of North America, and in the face of

Republican America, British connection and British institutions, if you give the latter freely and trustingly. Faith when it is sincere, is always catching'. Secondly, Britain herself must stop thinking of the colonial relation as a provisional existence: this was he felt indispensable to the success of any colonial system. Thirdly, 'you must allow them to believe that, without severing the bonds which unite them to Great Britain, they may attain the degree of perfection, and of social and political development, to which organised communities of free men have a right to aspire'. It was a silly and dangerous idea, he thought, that colonies could only attain maturity through separation, and he repeated that there could be no peace, contentment, progress or credit in Canada if it was believed there that Britain took this view. Finally, he was deeply convinced that all attempts to de-nationalise the French Canadians was a wrong policy:

> Generally speaking they produce the opposite effect from that intended, causing the flame of national prejudice and animosity to burn more fiercely. But suppose them to be successful, what would be the result? You may perhaps *Americanise*, but, depend upon it, by methods of this description, you will never *Anglicise* the French inhabitants of the province. Let them feel, on the other hand, that their religion, their habits, their prepossessions, their prejudices if you will, are more considered and respected here than in other portions of this vast continent, which is being overrun by the most reckless, self-sufficient and dictatorial section of the Anglo-Saxon race, and who will venture to say that the last hand which waves the British flag on American ground may not be that of a French Canadian?[71]

His reasoning of course rested on the assumption that the maintenance of some connection was in the best interests of the colonists themselves. Colonial secretary Grey agreed with Elgin about that, indeed he felt it was even more important to the colonies to preserve the connection than it was for Britain herself: 'to them it seems to me difficult to overestimate its value'. Thus he was determined to make it plain that 'their material interests are prompted by the continuance of the connection'. Responsible government was seen as the only possible way in which the allegiance could be maintained and the interest made manifest. Grey wrote that their policy was 'the only one by which there is even a chance of maintaining the connection between Canada and this country. Our policy *may* fail in doing this; any other clearly *must* have done so'. Elgin's general aim was 'a liberal and straightforward application of constitutional principles to government'. In 1849 he arranged for the legislature of the united Canada to sit alternately in Toronto and Quebec, which helped to reduce the alienation of French and British. At the opening of parliament he grandly reinstated the use of French. Although on certain questions, the views of the Baldwin – La Fontaine ministry did not exactly square with his pre-conceived opinions, he acquiesced in them so long as they did not contravene the fundamental principles of morality, from a conviction that they were in accordance with the general sentiments of the community. He was determined to show the French he did not mistrust them and that he was not attempting to force them into a mould of his own making. The tendency towards bringing the imperial and local parliaments into dangerous antagonism could only be counteracted by the governor's acting with some assumption of responsibility, 'so that the shafts of the enemy which are intended for the imperial government may fall on him'. He summed up the policy of Grey and himself like this:

> In a word I contend that the essential distinction between our policy and that of our predecessors in office has consisted in the confidence which we have reposed in the good faith of the constitutional reformers and in the loyalty of the mass of the population of the province.[72]

The chief episode in implementing this policy was the passing of the 1849 Rebellion Losses Bill, a bill opposed by the British as being unduly partisan to the French, and of which Elgin disapproved in some respects, but to which he assented, notwithstanding riotous demonstrations by the Montreal British against him for so doing. Except as a symbol it attracted a wholly disproportionate importance. At first Elgin described it as a 'questionable measure', not wholly free from objection. To Grey he wrote of his regret that an addition should be made to the debt for such an object at such a time. Nevertheless he did not see how his present government could have taken any other course. Their predecessors had already gone more than halfway in the same direction. Compensation for rebellion losses had been a Canadian issue since 1837. The Rebellion Losses Bill proposed that only unnecessary and wanton destruction against property was to constitute an acceptable claim. It was shown, however, that even notorious rebels would be eligible for compensation for their out-of-pocket expenses arising out of the rebellions in 1837 in the former Lower Canada. Although the situation was complicated by the considerable damage which had been done, the bill probably did distinguish rather imperfectly between the losses of the loyalists and those of the rebels. The Tories at any rate argued that it gave rewards to the disloyal. A loophole enabling rebels to get compensation made it possible to say the bill invaded the imperial sphere. On the other hand, it was argued that this was a domestic matter and Canada was in effect self-governing – Bagot had, after all, already said, 'whether the doctrine of responsible government is openly acknowledged, or is only tacitly acquiesced in, virtually it exists' (1842). The bill passed the Assembly by 47 votes to 29. A majority thus wanted it, and it would meet a French grievance. Therefore, Elgin decided, that once it was settled satisfactorily, 'a formidable stumbling block' would be removed from the path of his policy. He refused to dissolve a parliament only a year old, or to 'pass the buck' to the British government by referring to them for a decision. As he explained to Grey:

> If I had dissolved parliament as the Tory wise-acres suggest, I might have produced a rebellion but most assuredly I should not have procured a change of ministry ... To reserve the bill would be an exhibition of weakness, and result only in throwing on you a responsibility which I ought to bear myself.

Refusal of assent might have produced a rebellion, thrown the whole population into Papineau's hands, and wounded 'the susceptibilities of some of the best subjects' Britain had in the province. The discussion of the bill threw into strong relief

> the passions and tendencies which render the endurance of the political system which we have established here and of the connection with the Mother Country uncertain and precarious. They elicit a manifestation of antipathy between races, and of jealousy between the recently united provinces ...

When the fury of the population of Montreal was at its height, a stone weighing 2 lb was hurled at him, and Elgin was twice pelted. The Montreal parliament was set on fire. Elgin wrote:

> It is my firm conviction that if their dictation be submitted to, the government of this province by constitutional means will be impossible and that the struggle between overbearing minorities, backed by force, and majorities resting on legality and established forms, which has so long proved the bane of Canada, driving capital from the province and producing a state of chronic discontent will be perpetuated.

Rioting and verbal rage went on for a week in Montreal. Elgin commented: 'We were for a time in great danger ... I did not before know how thin is the crust of order which covers the anarchical elements that boil and toss beneath our feet'. He came to the conclusion that the whole row was the work of the Orange Societies backed by commercial men who wanted annexation to the United States and political leaders who wanted places in government. [73]

Elgin was supported in the House of Commons by a decisive majority. Both houses of parliament, indeed, decided not to interfere. This was the only parliamentary test which responsible government ever underwent. As Martin suggests, perhaps the most important conclusion to be drawn from the events of 1849 was that any attempt to define responsible government would be attacked as an attempt to destroy it. [74]

It was the rebellion losses issue which induced Montreal merchants to circulate a manifesto advocating annexation to the United States; 'friendly and peaceful separation from the British connection, and a union upon equitable terms with the great North American confederacy of sovereign states'. The adoption of free trade by Britain seemed to have made the continuance of the British connection useless to Canada. The annexationists put first among the causes of the evils from which Canada suffered 'the reversal of the ancient policy of Great Britain whereby she withdrew from the colonies their wonted protection in her markets'. The Montreal Tories also resented Elgin's cordial relations with French Canadians. Those who opposed the Rebellion Losses Bill were nearly all bankrupts, desperate men looking to annexation as a last resort. The truth is that the commercial empire of the St Lawrence had collapsed; the Rebellion Losses Bill was merely the straw which broke the camel's back. The Montreal annexationists were not widely supported. As Creighton has shown, the old commercial system in the 1840s lost both its protected markets by the British 'declaration of economic independence' in 1846, and its last uncontested sources of supply by the American Drawback Acts of 1845-46, by which the United States laid claim to the trade of Canada west of Montreal. The most ambitious advance of the United States and the final withdrawal of Great Britain coincided disastrously. Canada turned first to reciprocity and then to annexation, which were the two expressions, economic and political, of her instinctive recoil on the United States. As Elgin recognised 'our commercial embarrassments are our real difficulty': of political discontent, properly so called, there was none. By 1850 the economic depression of the later 1840s had run its course, and with it, the annexation movement lost its power.[75]

Elgin was firmly convinced that the only thing which prevented an invasion of Canada by the United States to exploit British, and especially Montreal, discontent at the time of the Rebellion Losses Bill 'was the political contentment prevailing among the French Canadians and Irish Catholics'. In August 1850 he wrote to Grey:

The result of the policy which I have pursued with your concurrence and support has been briefly this. The French have been rescued from the false position into which they had been driven and in which they must perforce have remained so long as they believed that it was the object of the British government . . . to break them down, and to ensure to the British race, not by trusting to the natural course of events, but by dint of management and statecraft, predominance in the Province. To eradicate from the mind of a people naturally prone to suspicion a belief of this kind when deeply engrained was no easy task, but the startling events of last year and above all the furious assaults directed by the mob and press of the so-called British Party against the Queen's representative have accomplished the object. The French are restored to their normal condition and are therefore essentially a conservative element in the Canadian compound.

In the end, the sentiment of French Canadian nationality might 'furnish the best remaining security against annexation to the United States'. At all events, no reliance would be placed on Montreal collaboration:

> Montreal is rotten to the core, and if all Canada be like it, the sooner we have done with it the better.... A cure is not to be looked for – commercial distress, religious bigotry and national hatred, have driven a certain portion of the population here mad.[76]

CANADIAN CONFEDERATION

The idea of confederation was well known by the 1860s: 18 schemes had been adumbrated in the previous hundred years. But the real story does not need to be traced back so far.[77] The most prominent makers of Canadian confederation were George Brown, a newspaper proprietor, of demagogic and impulsive character; George Etienne Cartier, the French leader and extrovert corporation lawyer; Alexander T. Galt, a railway contractor and minister of finance, very intelligent, with the reputation of being a financial wizard; and John Alexander Macdonald, a lawyer who suffered from ill-health, which his critics said was worsened by drinking too much. Of these Cartier was conceivably the one to whom confederation owed the most: he was the dominant figure in Canadian public life before 1867 as Macdonald was after it. It was his conviction that a great 'Anglo-American' confederation would be to the benefit of all and the disadvantage of none which finally won a slim majority of French Canadian support for it: the voting was 27 to 21.[78]

In the history of the making of the confederation, much interest attaches to the way in which these four overcame a more limited and parochial scheme for a legislative union of the Maritime Provinces. For over a decade the Maritimes wanted an intercolonial railway to link Halifax and St John with Quebec and Montreal. The Maritimes (Nova Scotia, New Brunswick, Prince Edward Island) and Newfoundland to some extent wanted a union among themselves. They feared a larger Canadian federation, particularly because of the size of Canada's debts and supposedly high level of Canadian customs duties; under a federal system they feared that their own local revenues would not suffice to maintain the life-style to which they had been accustomed. Confederation seemed a ramshackle enterprise. The main problem for the confederation movement was that though it could get along without Newfoundland and Prince Edward Island, New Brunswick was essential as the link between Canada and Nova Scotia; when New Brunswick voted against it, the movement was temporarily at a complete stop. As a result of this set-back the big four went to London. Their last powerful card in an apparently losing game was British support.

The confederation movement arose out of the coalition of the big four, in 1864, made possible by Brown; it was remarkable since previously Brown and

Macdonald had been mortal enemies. The new coalition adopted a federal programme, and sought permission for a delegation to attend the approaching conference on Maritime Union. From that moment the two projects of British American federation and Maritime Union came into open competition. The Maritimers were quite ready to discuss the larger project at the Charlottetown conference.

In attempting to convince the Maritimers, Cartier tried to prove, in his rambling but hearty manner, how seaboard and inland provinces needed and complemented each other; Brown undertook to demonstrate how the combined resources would make a great nation; Galt investigated the financial side.

Britain was anxious for federation, putting a low estimate on Canadian loyalty and a high valuation on freedom from American entanglements. Yet her withdrawal was not abrupt or selfishly thoughtless. She delayed her departure until the British Americans had themselves decided on union; and during their difficult and dangerous period of nation-making, she repeatedly gave her military aid. Her retreat was unhurried, deliberate and dignified. Colonial secretary Cardwell had to exercise a fairly ruthless pressure on the unenthusiastic Maritime provinces to get them into the new Dominion. Without Cardwell the provincial jealousies of the Maritimes might well have been allowed to prevail – as they had done in the past. The curbing of lieutenant-governor Arthur Gordon of New Brunswick was particularly crucial. It was the British government too who forced on the Hudson's Bay Company and the Canadian delegates the deed of surrender by which the Company made the prairie provinces and the North-west Territories available to the new Dominion.[79] Brebner says:

> Fear of the United States and British pressure served to weigh down in favour of federation an almost even balance between inertia, indifference or even antipathy on the one side, and certain tendencies toward growth and collaboration on the other.[80]

There were three motives behind federation. It was a means to resolve political deadlock in the province of Canada and economic problems, as well as a method of dealing with the problem of the United States. The unworkability of the existing united system had become plain. The essence of confederation, wrote Keith, was the desire of Canadian statesmen to separate the two uncomfortable yoke-fellows.[81] The practice of self-government had become a farce. In the decade before 1864, there had been some ten changes or reshuffles of administration and by 1864 a deadlock which two general elections and four ministries in three years had failed to resolve. Goldwin Smith said 'the real father was deadlock'.[82] Population growth was accompanied by a growing demand for representation by population, a political problem which put impossible pressure on the existing system of government.

The economic pressures behind confederation are easy to state. Population growth was striking:

CANADIAN POPULATION GROWTH

	1841	1851	1861
(Upper) Canada West	c. 480,000	952,004	1,396,091
(Lower) Canada East	c. 670,000	890,261	1,111,586
Total	c. 1,150,000	1,842,265	2,507,677

This growth pressed hard upon existing land and food supplies. By the mid-1850s the line of settlement was coming up against the intractable rocks of the Laurentian Shield. All good agricultural land had been taken up. The limits of possible Canadian expansion had been reached. Interest in the region beyond Lake Superior revived. Eyes naturally began to be cast upon the Red River areas of the Hudson's Bay Company. This expansion of horizons marked an important psychological step from a 'colonial' to a 'national' mentality.[83] French Canadians hoped to create a new French-speaking province in the Red River settlement which would counterpoise the preponderance of the British in Upper Canada. Confederation ensured that the settlement would be put under the Union Jack. The rule of the Hudson's Bay Company in the north-west was becoming increasingly uncertain and precarious. Why should the north-west not be taken over from a moribund company, whose chartered claims were considered fraudulent, its rule bad, its authority to protect the north-west from encroachment feeble?[84]

A further element was the desirability of forestalling the United States in westward expansion. A few saw the need for action in Rupert's Land lest it fall into the hands of the United States, and argued that it could only be taken over by a large unit. There was anxiety lest adventurers from the United States should cut Canada off from the west coast. To support itself against the United States, Canada had to expand to the west. Because the United States was a continental dominion, Canada must be one as well. Confederation was the fulfilment of an old dream made possible by linking, with a railway, economically complementary areas. To make possible a stable economic structure, the wheat and grazing lands of the west, the lumber and gold of British Columbia, had to be brought in.[85]

Another economic consideration was the end of Elgin's Reciprocity Treaty with the United States in 1865. It is difficult to judge the real value of the treaty, but the Canadians *thought* it had produced the good times of the prosperous 1850s, and termination posed a threat to the underlying economic strength of British North America. This was especially true of the Maritime provinces. Only 2.85 per cent of Canadian exports went to the Maritimes, and only 1 per cent of her imports was drawn from them. There was no case for a federation including the Maritimes until the United States slammed the door. Thus only the action of the United States explains the adhesion of the Maritimes. The United States might indeed have prevented confederation by giving New Brunswick what it wanted: a compensating measure for the loss of Reciprocity, and a western railway. The United States refused such help because it felt that New Brunswick had been too sympathetic towards the South in the Civil War and did not therefore deserve help. Indeed the whole American attack on Reciprocity in Congress was on the ground that British North America had favoured the South unduly.

The Grand Trunk Railway (begun in 1854) was losing money at an alarming rate. It had been built parallel to the St Lawrence River, which had not helped it, and by 1860 it was the longest railway under single management in the world, 'a railway in search of a State'. Like the Hudson's Bay Company, the Grand Trunk Railway was in grave financial difficulties. In the latter case the solution, said Watkin of the International Finance Society of London, was expansion in two directions: from Canada to the western prairie lands of the Hudson's Bay Company at Red River (where a road and telegraph line were to anticipate a railway to the Pacific), and, in the east, a connection with a new inter-colonial railway from Rivière du Loup in Quebec to the Maritimes. The resources of the west would thus centre in Halifax. A scheme so vast needed a new political framework to implement it. (And in any case there had to be an extension of Canada in both directions, since Lower Canada would not finance a line to the prairies, and Upper Canada would not support the inter-colonial railway.) This scheme was blessed by British and provincial governments and by British bankers and railway builders. The proposed structure was in part an admitted abandonment of the old monopolistic Montreal dream of draining the middle continent, in favour of a new design of co-operative exploitation and complementary inter-colonial trade across the North. A primary condition of Watkin's decision to try to straighten out the affairs of the Grand Trunk was a confederation. Cartier was solicitor for the virtually bankrupt Grand Trunk; Watkin was its president from 1861. No group of men was more vitally concerned with the future of British North America than those who guided the destinies of the Grand Trunk. Cartier and Galt had invested in it. A railway became an integral part of the federating scheme. The idea of an inter-colonial railway was to the Maritimes of Nova Scotia and New Brunswick the only attractive feature of the federal scheme. Their attitude was – 'no railway, no federation', as their only interest was in a hinterland for their ports. By section 145 of the British North America Act (1867) the construction of a railway linking the St Lawrence and Halifax was to be begun within six months of the union's being formed. Railways gave people something to work for.[86]

When due allowance has been made for the political and economic reasons for confederation, it is probably true to say that the crucial factor was fear of the United States. The Civil War added enormously to traditional anxieties. The real significance of the war was that it embodied a military revolution. The American army expanded in size 20 or 30 times after 1861, creating a huge disparity in power with the British army. The Union casualties alone in any one of six battles were enough to have totally wiped out the entire British garrison in Canada. A voracious, unstoppable, self-generating war machine had been brought into existence. There was no precedent for any democracy's having so large an army. Joseph Howe complained that the United States' 'Northern dictatorship' had 'no parallel . . . among the despotisms of the Old World'. After Gettysburg and Vicksburg the Canadians viewed the American army with awe. It was new in spirit and arms as well as in sheer size. Memories of pre-war crises sharpened the sense of Canadian vulnerability. The *Trent* affair revealed the precarious state of communications everywhere in Canada, between New Brunswick and Canada especially, and it made evident the strategic need for an inter-colonial railway. [87]

Newcastle as colonial secretary toured Canada and the United States in 1860. He was not over-worried by Seward's talk, allowing for his 'hyper-American use of the policy of bully and bluster', but he did not at all relish the idea that a victorious post-Civil War army, 'composed of the scum of all nations', might possibly hold politicians to ransom – and to save themselves the politicians might direct 'this blood red stream on our possessions'. [88]

British encouragement of confederation was thus much stronger from 1864 than it had been before, partly because of Cardwell's decisive colonial secretaryship, and partly as a result of the Civil War, since it had led to a steady and rather frightening deterioration of relations between Britain and the United States. The United States alleged breaches of neutrality. [89]

Britain had long been worried by the costs of military defence. As the American Civil War dragged on these worries were seriously intensified. The growing estrangement between Britain and the United States brought home to imperial government the magnitude of British responsibilities in Canada. While the war lasted, British America was probably safe. But the end was sure to bring trouble. If the North won, it might, flushed with victory, power and unity, turn expansively upon British North America and exact a terrible revenge for its Southern sympathies. Canada's long immunity to external danger might be over. If the North lost, it might seek in Canada an indemnity and moral compensation for what it had lost in the South. In the autumn of 1863 the British government sent out lieutenant-colonel W. F. D. Jervois to examine and report upon present state and possible improvement of Canadian defences. The report frankly admitted that the western part of the province of Canada was indefensible. Gladstone now proclaimed the principle that his main aim was 'to shift the centre of responsibility' in defence from Britain to the colonies. Canadians must grow out of the 'sentiment and habits of mere dependencies'; Britain must help them to acquire a 'corporate and common feeling', assisting the formation of federation or union 'by every means in its power'. He was not interested in a union of the Maritimes; at the crucial moment the essential connection between Canadian defence and British American reorganisation had been heavily emphasised by him. Britain had supported the South, partly because if the South won its freedom, a new balance of power on the continent would ensure the permanent security of British North America. In such circumstances the North would be too exhausted and too intimidated to risk an attempt to gain northern compensation for southern losses.[90]

Politicians and newspapers in the American republic had been busily making a major grievance out of the exploits of the *Alabama* and the *Florida*, cruisers built in British shipyards and acquired by the South (Confederate) government, which had inflicted substantial losses on North (Union) shipping during the war. There was a notable accumulation of resentment against the British stored up in the republic. Pent-up feelings discovered an unofficial expression in the Fenian movement, aiming at fomenting rebellion in Ireland. Six months after the Civil War, the leaders of one militant branch of the American Fenian movement began to argue that the quickest way to Irish freedom was indirect – conquest of British North America. The small but real element of peril in this was its relation to Manifest Destiny. Most of the Fenian leaders were farcically incompetent. Demobilisation after the Civil War caused thousands of Irish veterans to turn their energies into the wild project of incursions into Canada. Although one-third of the population of British North America was of Irish descent, the Fenians miscalculated seriously if they supposed them to be disloyal. The Fenian Brotherhood was at work on the Canadian border from 1865 to 1871 to exploit anti-British feeling.[91]

The United States did indeed emerge from the Civil War powerful, truculent and expansionist. There were blunt annexationist pronouncements by leading American politicians, notably by secretary of state W. H. Seward. In January 1865 George Brown linked Canadian anxieties as having a background in 'the Civil War in the neighbouring Republic and the possibility of war between Great Britain and the United States'. Cartier focussed the issue more sharply in 1865: 'The matter resolved itself into this, either we must obtain British North American Confederation or be absorbed in an American Confederation ... The British provinces, separated as at present, could not defend themselves alone'. This was because the province of Canada lacked maritime resources, and the Maritime provinces lacked a large population and a hinterland. Canadians realised that henceforth they would have to accept responsibility for the costs of their own defence. They also saw that if war came in future to British North America it was unlikely to be for 'imperial' reasons, and that as a result they could hardly expect its costs to be borne by the imperial government.[92]

Thus, in view of the fear of the United States which had been heightened by the Civil War period, the unuttered truth was, as W. L. Morton has suggested, that in enacting confederation, Britain was recognising the supremacy of the United States – 'quietly, and in good order, with no word of surrender and no loss of dignity'.[93] The Civil War gave urgency to plans to achieve the local objectives of political and economic development as well as to the imperial desire for disengagement. It made it plain that tinkering with the constitution, or making budget cuts, was not enough. They had to make a nation in the shadow of a civil war which had convulsed a continent and threatened to embroil the English-speaking world.[94]

The goal of Anglo-American harmony was of overriding importance to the empire as a whole. The war demonstrated that sharply. In effect the Civil War helped to create not one but two nations on the American continent. British policy, arising out of the war experience, contributed much to Canada's preservation. Clarendon recognised quite clearly that unfriendly relations with the United States to a great extent paralysed British action in Europe. There was no doubt in his mind that if Britain were engaged in a continental quarrel she would immediately find herself at war with the United States. Withdrawal from Canada was a quick and effective escape from this problem.[95]

The British North America Act passed through the House of Commons without fuss in 1867. Canadian confederation was a remarkable achievement, and it began a state-building process which required further consolidation. It was not a mere piece of colonial politics, but one of the great national unions of the nineteenth century, and one central to the balance of power between Europe and America. Manitoba (prairie province) was rather hastily carved out of the Hudson's Bay territories in 1870; Louis Riel, the remarkable leader of the Red River rebel regime, was later executed. British Columbia entered the federation in 1871 – with the promise of a railway in ten years. It was so hard up for transport that it had been importing camels. Prince Edward Island joined in 1873 from financial stress. Saskatchewan and Alberta were formed in 1905 out of the North-West Territories, to deal with the inflow of settlers. Newfoundland finally joined in 1949, having rejected generous terms in 1869. By 1875, however, the new Dominion had nearly reached its natural limits. Britain pulled out of the North-West Territories partly to enable Canada to strengthen herself. The first detachment of the (Royal) North-West Mounted Police trekked west in 1874. Joseph Howe of Nova Scotia dropped his secessionist campaign and entered the federal cabinet in 1869. Industrialisation was assisted by a protective tariff in 1878. Times were hard for the rest of the century, but under Sir Wilfrid Laurier in the early twentieth century, Canada began to forge ahead economically.[96]

The transcontinental Canadian Pacific Railway was completed in 1885 and opened in the following year. Two more transcontinental lines were to follow.

Thus was created the cold kebab of Canada skewered on the steel spike of its railway lines.[97]

The most fascinating aspect of the study of constitutions is to observe the extent to which they draw upon analogy and precedent and upon the study of existing constitutions which it was thought might throw relevant light on the problems to be solved. For the Canadians there were two models: the British constitution and that of the United States. The 1867 Canadian constitution was strongly centralised, with all matters involving the development of the new country — territorial expansion, settlement, commercial exploitation and economic growth — all entrusted to the central government, along with all residual powers (that is, those not specifically allocated). One of the main reasons for this was admiration of the British constitution, especially among British Canadians. Walter Bagehot's *English Constitution* was first published in 1865 and was keenly read. Macdonald studied the Younger Pitt and Peel. As in so many subsequent transfers of power, the new authority largely stepped into the shoes of the old colonial one. Cartier felt that the Crown stabilised and dignified government and produced a decent gradation in provincial society which did not exist in the United States.[98] Macdonald had talked of 'founding a great British monarchy in connection with the British Empire'. The title 'Kingdom of Canada' was planned, but rejected out of deference to the susceptibilities of the United States. The word 'Dominion' was supported as the alternative by Carnarvon, who spoke of it as 'a tribute on their part to the monarchical principle and if somewhat in opposition to the institutions on the other side of the border, not in any offensive opposition'. It had long been hoped to anchor the independent constitution around the stable element which monarchy provided. From the late 1850s there had been suggestions that one of Victoria's younger sons might be King of Canada. Compared with the United States, monarchical Brazil was a model of political stability. The possibility of creating a colonial peerage was also discussed from time to time.[99]

If in many ways the chief characteristic of the federation was its tightness, this was partly based upon a supposed lesson from the United States. To Macdonald the Civil War was a lesson in constitution-making, and as he read Alexander Hamilton's contribution to the *Federalist Papers,* with their centralist bias, and studied the debates of the Philadelphia Convention (1787), he underscored those passages emphasising a strong central government. Macdonald concluded that there would be one body of criminal law —

I think this is one of the most marked instances in which we take advantage of the experience derived from our observations of the defects in the Constitution of the neighbouring Republic.

The *Federalist* also had a prominent place in Cartier's library. The power to legislate on all the important subjects, and on all residual matters of a general character not specially and exclusively reserved for local government, was vested in the federal government. Cartier said:

> This is precisely the provision which is wanting in the Constitution of the United States. It is here that we find the weakness of the American system – the point where the American Constitution breaks down . . .
>
> . . . I am strongly of the belief that we have, in a great measure, avoided in this system which we propose for the adoption of the people of Canada, the defects which time and events have shown to exist in the American Constitution.[100]

Federation was not based on European continental example but on actual experience of the United States and to some extent of the Anglo-Scottish union. The new technology seemed to exalt the principle of strong central control, for example, to stimulate railways and the flow of capital from abroad. Many Canadian statesmen would have preferred a unitary state, but opposition from the Maritimes and the French made this impossible.[101]

'The great political decision of Canadian politics in the Victorian age', it has been said, 'was not to confederate but to be British rather than American'. The fundamental purpose of confederation was separate survival in North America, and not emancipation from the empire. The American challenge was the great danger; the political connection with Britain provided the only ally whose support could redress the undue predominance of America. Britain continued to provide markets, capital, immigrants and diplomatic protection. And in the early years of the confederation at any rate, the commercial expansion of the mercantile community of British Montreal provided a base for the westward spread of banks and financial institutions.[102]

British policy in Canada in the nineteenth century seemed to be a striking success, and it became a blueprint for Ireland and South Africa. Carnarvon's draft confederation in the South Africa Act 1877 was based almost slavishly on the model of the British North America Act. The Gladstone papers on Ireland contain a complete copy of the British North America Act 1867, underlined and marked by Gladstone himself in many places. From the structure of the first 'Home Rule' memorandum on Irish government (20 March 1886) it seems that Gladstone mainly based himself on this Act.[103] During the second reading of the Home Rule Bill in 1886 Gladstone mentioned that he sat through and took an active part in the discussions on Canada in the 1860s:

> The case of Canada is not parallel to the case of Ireland. It does not agree in every particular, and the Bill which we offer to Ireland is different in many important particulars from the Acts which have disposed of the case of Canada. But although it is not parallel it is analogous. It is strictly and substantially analogous.[104]

Canada went down in the official annals of the British governing class as 'the greatest triumph of British statesmanship' – the phrase is Campbell-Bannerman's. The Canadian analogy gave encouragement to the Liberals who grappled with the South African problem in the early twentieth century. Dilke and Elgin agreed that after the Anglo-Boer war, the situation in South Africa was not any worse than it had been in Canada after the rebellions of 1837 and at the time of the annexation movement in 1849. But it was a dangerous delusion. As Hancock has said, it is easy in retrospect to forget 'the almost miraculous quality of the Canadian achievement', and to leap too easily to the conclusion that other peoples can easily copy it. [105]

THE MYTH OF A 'SPECIAL RELATIONSHIP' WITH THE UNITED STATES

The late nineteenth-century diplomatic *rapprochement* between Britain and the United States was extended on the British side to a whole myth of 'special relationship' supposed to exist between them. [106] It was a notion based on the misconception that the United States was simply 'forty Englands rolled into one' – a phrase taken up by Lord Derby in 1880. [107]

The genesis of the idea may be traced in nearly all the major writers on the empire: J. S. Mill, Seeley, Froude and Dilke. In his 1899 will, Cecil Rhodes provided for 35 American scholarships, compared with 60 empire ones. [108] This notion of special relationship, instead of remaining an intellectual flight of fancy, actually became a factor in British foreign policy, with sufficient toughness to survive to the 1960s. It was taken up by Chamberlain, Balfour, Grey, Selborne, Bryce, Hardinge and others. As a factor in British foreign policy the myth of a special relationship dates only from about 1890, as one of the desperate measures of self-deception, a hope that world leadership could be exercised by proxy. Claims to kinship with Americans were made by Britons much earlier, but they did not before the 1890s carry any suggestion that such kinship was naturally effective in international affairs. The myth was developed in Britain as a response to the growth of the United States to the rank of a great power. Its function was to enable Britain to withdraw gracefully from contests with the United States. Three important clashes occurred in the later 1890s – over the Venezuelan boundary, over the Hay-Pauncefote Panama Canal Treaty, and over the Alaska boundary. In every case it was Britain who made most of the concessions. She accepted herself as completely outclassed navally in the Caribbean, though earlier in the century she would have fought to prevent its becoming 'an American lake'. [109]

The Spanish-American War of 1898 in Cuba was viewed with some apprehension. But as Lord George Hamilton, secretary of state for India, wrote: 'the more the United States come out of their shell in one sense the better for us'. In North America Britain was the only power colliding with them; 'Outside they will find many causes of difference with the other

European powers'.[110] Cuba proved that the Anglo-Saxon race had the stuff of victory in it; this was the most important cause of Anglo-American rapprochement.

The contrast with Britain's reaction to the emergence of Germany to world power is striking indeed. Rising Germany worried her, whereas Britain chose to regard her own expulsion from the Caribbean as of no particular moment; she supported the American attack on 'outrageous' and inefficient Spanish rule in Cuba, and in general failed to see in the rise of the United States and in its pretensions to world power, any threat to her own position. If the expansion of Britain was a good thing with the force of a natural law, it was difficult not to admit the same for the United States. The different reaction to Germany was not so rational; the underlying assumption was that Britain and the United States had no real and important differences – if only Britain would ignore irrelevant irritations. Britain had no conflicting interests with the United States only because she chose to have none; the community of British and American interests in the Far East was largely illusory. Sympathy with the United States was 'a logical concomitant of the expansive impulses which brought the two countries into conflict'. In Latin America, Britain and America feared Germany more than they feared each other.

There had been no major disagreement for thirty years; Britain was surprised that they now arose and was ready to believe there must be some mistake. A concession to the United States was the least possible, the least revolutionary of concessions, one which involved the least analysis and the least re-organisation of the British world position; it involved no weakening of the British power position in Europe. The 'myth' did not prevent friction, but only moderated its effects; little regard was paid to the non-Anglo-Saxon strain in the United States, hence the phrases 'our American cousins' and the 'transatlantic branch of our race'.[111]

The belief in an essential unity with the United States gave declining Britain an emotional solace, but nothing more tangible. Changes in the rôle of the United States in the world were probably the most vital factors affecting the British international position in the decades before 1914. American population was increasing by leaps and bounds, while Britain was practically standing still. American exports to the empire alone were £160 million. All British businessmen were coming to agree about the desirability of some sort of collaboration with the American leviathan. As a result of these facts and new attitudes, the curious and persistent myth of special relationship was developed, and British policy towards the United States, hitherto antagonistic, underwent a 'decisive and far-reaching change'.[112]

Predictably enough, this myth was yet another of the political misconceptions taken up by Joseph Chamberlain.[113] In 1888 he declared that all parties in Britain had 'a cordial desire for a hearty and for a durable friendship' with the United States, a goodwill 'not untinged with envy'. At Philadelphia in 1888 he declined 'to be considered a foreigner in the United

States', partly perhaps because, like Kipling, Wm and L. Harcourt, the Duke of Manchester and Randolph Churchill, he had an American wife. In 1897 he spoke of his hopes that they could make war in future between the two countries absolutely impossible. While he believed that Britain desired to be on the best terms with all the powers, it was something more than a desire, 'it is almost a religion, with us to preserve constantly feelings and relations of the most friendly and cordial character with our kinsmen on the other side of the Atlantic'. Because of his Anglo-Saxon bias, Chamberlain's world view embraced the Americans among the chosen people, and impelled him to make room for them in any conception of closer imperial union. In December 1887 he spoke in Toronto:

> I refuse to think or to speak of the U.S.A. as a foreign nation. We are all of the same race and blood. I refuse to make any distinction between the interests of Englishmen in England, in Canada and in the United States. We can say with regard to all these peoples, the older and younger nations: Our past is theirs — their future is ours . . . I urge upon you our common origin, our relationship . . . We are branches of one family . . .

Chamberlain told the American ambassador that the 'two great co-heirs of Anglo-Saxon freedom and civilisation have a common mission'. This same anxiety to bring in the United States to redress the balance of a declining empire is equally evident in Kipling's invitation to the Americans to 'Take up the White Man's burden', a poem which was, it is not always remembered, addressed in 1899 to the United States on the occasion of her Cuba expedition.

Whilst it may be true that Chamberlain's advocacy of an alliance in 1898–99 was a temporary phase, the Anglo-Boer war increased the sense of identity. It was compared with the American Civil War, with the British (like the North) fighting for free institutions, political democracy and racial equality.[114]

Even when Chamberlain disappeared from the scene, the Liberal ministers of 1905–15 showed themselves to be exceptionally deferential to the United States, placing friendship with that power as a higher priority than good relations with Britain's own colonies. 'Undefended' Canada became a total reality from 1907, and in the same year, the governor of Jamaica was dismissed for showing insufficient deference to an American admiral who tried to help after the earthquake which shook the island.[115]

Although a good deal of ambivalence of attitude remained, the Anglo-American rapprochement was one of the major changes occurring in Britain's imperial century. Perhaps it was more apparent than real — there was no prospect of an alliance. Many businessmen continued to bewail the invasion of American companies and their British subsidiaries, and hostility remained in some commercial circles; some intellectuals (such as Lowes Dickinson, the

Webbs, and H. G. Wells) found much American materialism to criticise; but there was a widespread feeling that Britain must acquiesce in the 'Americanisation of the world', to use W. T. Stead's phrase. Britain determined to solve her problems by admitting the Americans as equal partners in the Pax Britannica, and the function of the special relationship myth was to soothe the doubts and to make this pill more palatable to swallow.[116]

7 The Indian Problem

In some ways the Indian empire was a nuisance. It involved many headaches, including the costs of defending it against Russia, and it embittered relations with other European powers, not only expanding Russia but also jealous France. By 1900 it had become an enormous military liability. Governing India was a task causing untold personal hardship and frustration. Two million Britons died in India. Everyone who went there suffered from the heat, the dust, persistent diarrhoea and recurrent dysentery, to say nothing of the risks of malaria and cholera; suffered too from the lack of privacy, yet acute loneliness, the long separation from wives and families, or, if wives joined them, the hazards of childbirth and infant health posed by a country lacking adequate medical resources. Not even the most highly placed escaped, and as Curzon wrote, 'over the Viceregal throne there hangs not only a canopy of broidered gold but a mist of human tears'. He had self-inflicted reasons for melancholy, but Dalhousie also testified that 'emoluments, honours and reputation are as a feather against what must be set in the other balance in India'.[1]

Obviously India brought its benefits. Even if (as Bryce suggested) India contributed more to Britain's fame than her strength, it was still true (as Curzon and Churchill said) that its possession made all the difference between being a first- and third-rate power. Mayo wrote: 'we are determined as long as the sun shines in heaven to hold India. Our national character, our commerce, demand it; and we have, one way or another, 250 millions of English capital fixed in the country'.[2] There was also a large army, and a potential reservoir of docile labour. And so India had its value, commercially, psychologically and militarily. The trade of India became especially important after the opening of the Suez Canal. State enterprise mobilised the supply of raw cotton, jute, wheat and tea. India's export values rose from only £23 million in 1855 to £137 million in 1910. Imports rose from £13.5 million to £86 million. By the 1880s India took nearly 19 per cent of British exports, and nearly one-fifth of overseas investment was in India. In the mid-nineteenth century *all* tea had come from China, but by 1900 most of it came from India.[3] Between the 1860s and 1890s the Irrawaddy delta in Burma became the largest rice-exporting area in the world. Once leave India, however, and it was assumed, often on Dilke's authority, that anarchy would ensue and trade would be extinguished.[4] It was a vital source of cotton supply for Lancashire. Far-Eastern trade was opened up as much by contact with Indian as European merchants. Calcutta grew in the latter part of the century into a vast trading centre, linking Europe and China via Singapore.[5] From the military point of view, it was the Indian army which made Britain a great power. Dilke described it as an 'army fit to cope with the most tremendous disasters' that could overtake the country.[6] But it was also a central strategic reserve and quite frequently used outside India, in which it was aided by the fact that India provided a training ground for service in every sort of climate, in mountain, jungle and desert. The ambit of Indian power is best indicated by the movement of her troops: to China in 1839, 1856 and 1859; to Persia in 1856; to Ethiopia and Singapore in 1867; to Hong Kong in 1868; to Afghanistan in 1878; to Egypt in 1882; to Burma in 1885; to Nyasaland in 1893; to the Sudan and Uganda in 1896. There was also talk of using them in 1863 in New Zealand in the Maori wars, in Cyprus and Alexandretta in 1878, in Hong Kong in 1884 and in the Persian Gulf in 1899, and South Africa too. Between 1838 and 1920 the Indian army was used outside India on 19 occasions. During the First World War Indian troops fought in Palestine and on the Western Front. Half of the British army was stationed in India, and often represented its only chance of seeing any action under fire. There was a regular army of a quarter of a million, a standing army out of the reach of the Bill of Rights, and a further reservoir, costing not a penny to the British taxpayer. Moreover Sikh police were introduced from India to Hong Kong in 1867, Singapore in 1881, Tientsin in 1896, and to Nyasaland.[7]

One of India's most important rôles in the empire was to furnish a supply of cheap and mobile labour after the abolition of slavery. Greedy planters turned from Africa to India. Glenelg saw the danger, and disallowed Mauritius and Demarara (Guiana) ordinances seeking Indian labour in 1836 and 1839. By 1838, however, more than 25,000 Indians had been shipped overseas, and by 1840 Mauritius had 18,000 Indian labourers. Russell saw that this could result in 'a new system of slavery', and the indentured system did indeed incorporate many of the repressive features of the old system. The basis of the nineteenth-century demand for Indian labour lay in the increased consumption of sugar and coffee. The consumption of sugar per head rose from 16.8 lb in 1820 to 34.8 in 1860, and the figures for coffee also doubled. Mauritius became the principal source of British sugar, exporting 134,048 tons by 1860, and a record 165,000 tons in 1865. The peak of this organised Indian emigration was reached in 1858–59, when 53,000 Indians went overseas, 44,397 of them to Mauritius, the remainder to Trinidad and Demarara. Mauritius became the most 'Indianised' of the colonies. Emigration to the sugar plantations of Natal began in 1860, and the pattern

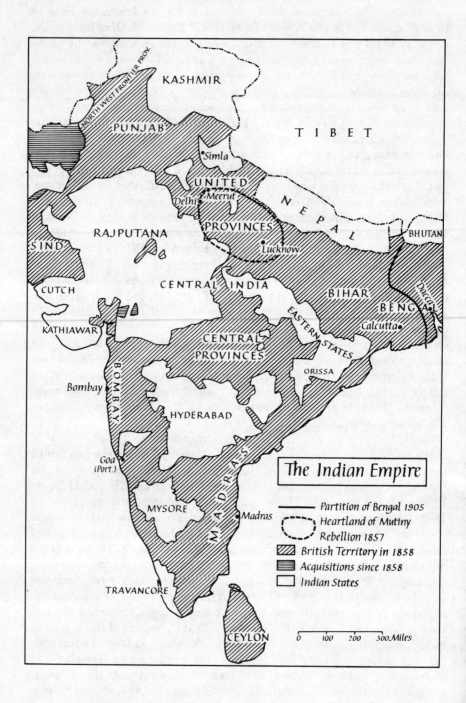

The Indian Empire

- ———— Partition of Bengal 1905
- ⌀ Heartland of Mutiny Rebellion 1857
- ▨ British Territory in 1858
- ▤ Acquisitions since 1858
- ☐ Indian States

0   100   200   300 Miles

of exported indentured labour was essentially complete by the 1870s, although Indians also found themselves in other places, including Fiji and Kenya – 19,000 of them were indentured to construct the Uganda railway, and 20 per cent of these were invalided back and 7 per cent died. Madras and Calcutta were the leading ports of embarkation; the Tamil districts of the south and the Gangetic plain (the North-west and United Provinces and Oudh) in the north were the chief sources of labour supply. In 1900 regulated emigration from Madras was 21,592, the non-regulated 324,600. It was, then, a system involving large transfers of manpower, quite on a par statistically with Atlantic slavery, and reproducing many of its features. Mortality on long voyages to the West Indies was appalling, and plantation conditions were frightful. The British, however, persisted in persuading themselves that wrongs were mere abuses, and irregularities were amenable to reform. Essentially it was thought to be an acceptable system – it was defended as necessary, and not 'uncivilised' like slavery. As a result, it was Indian labour which created much of the overseas wealth of the empire by exploiting the raw materials of the tropics.[8]

India also had its uses in character-training. W. E. H. Lecky wrote: 'India is proving a school of inestimable value for maintaining some of the best and most masculine qualities of our race'.[9] Dilke agreed: 'The possession of India offers to ourselves that element of vastness of dominion which in this age is needed to secure width of thought and nobility of purpose'. Britain could not let India go; one reason would be 'the hopeless insularity that would overtake the British people if deprived of the romantic interest that the possession of India lends to our national life'. If Britain were to quit India, she must leave her to Russia or herself. If to Russia, Britain would lose money and dignity 'by so plain a confession of our impotence'.[10]

British India was not a police state but a paternalist bureaucracy: the Indian government has been called a despotism of 'despatch boxes tempered by loss of keys'.[11] It was one of the most ponderous, ineffective and intensely conservative bureaucracies the world has ever known. Although it was reasonably uncorrupt, it is not necessary to see it as dedicated to Plato's ideal of a seeking to realise the good and the beautiful by a benevolent caste of 'guardians'.[12] Moreover, a despotism administered through two or three officers in a district numbering often over a million people was obviously a fairly light affair, and certainly produced nothing comparable to the detailed control exercised by European rule in South Africa.

THE SECURITY OF INDIA

For strategic purposes the frontiers of India were deemed to extend from Persia and the Red Sea to the Straits of Malacca. A sea-borne threat was not expected, but India was surrounded by relatively weak and unstable states, all vulnerable to European predators overland, especially Russia. One of the most important single facts about the possession of India was that it brought Britain into contact with another major and rapidly expanding power: Russia. The system of government in the Russian empire was not admired, and its expansion evoked a nervous response. Rutherford Alcock described Russia as 'this other Great Leviathan ... the largest boa-constrictor or predatory animal yet discovered', a 'modern colossus', which, 'stretching with giant arms across the whole breadth of northern Asia and Europe', threatened the wealthiest regions of two continents at once.[13] As Sir Robert Morier (ambassador to St Petersburg 1885–93) pointed out in 1888, 'a vague kind of Russophobia' was 'the natural inheritance of every living Englishman'.[14] From 1833 it was, as Palmerston defined it, an object of great importance to British interests to see how Russia could be prevented from pushing her advantage further. The essential problem of Indian defence from 1808 was on the north-west frontier; upon decisions taken there seemed to depend the maintenance of British rule in India, and therefore of Britain's existence as a first class power.[15]

'The Great Game' between the two empires was centred on Central Asia between the Iranian plateau and Chinese Turkestan, from the Pamirs in the north to the Hindu Kush mountains in the south.[16] Turkey and China could be viewed within the same context, though from the point of view of the defence of India, the nodal points of the contest were Persia and Afghanistan. The danger to the security of India was not acute so long as Persia, Afghanistan and great deserts separated the Russian empire and India. This safeguard was lost by 1884 when Russia finally succeeded in pushing her frontiers south until they were coterminous with Persia and Afghanistan. Between 1863 and 1876, a population of three million Muslims was added to the Russian empire. Between 1864 and 1869 Russia took control of the khanates of Chimkent, Tashkent, Khojend, and Bukhara. A new province of Russian Turkestan was ruled by a viceroy from Tashkent. She was at Merv by 1884 and Samarkand by 1867. The acquisitions of 1864–65 alone brought in 4,000 square miles and one million people. The momentum of the Russian thrust then switched to a south-eastward line of advance based on the Caspian Sea from 1878. All-in-all, between 1830 and 1880 Russia advanced 1,200 miles closer to India, and another 600 miles between 1880 and 1884 in the direction of Merv and Herat. In 1863 Russia was separated by nearly 1,700 miles of mountains and deserts from the most advanced outposts of British India. By 1883 this distance was almost halved, with Britain moving up only 200 miles from Jacobabad to Quetta. The acquisition of Merv by Russia in 1884 was crucial, and by March 1885 Russian troops had attacked Penjdeh in Afghanistan. Britain held herself ready for war. Well might Curzon take the view that these states (Turkestan, Afghanistan, Transcaspia and Persia) were 'pieces on a chessboard upon which is being played out a game for the dominion of the world'.[17]

Thereafter Russian pressure shifted to the Far East once again, where she

Russian expansion in Central Asia

had not moved since the acquisition of Vladivostock in 1860. In 1896 she acquired Port Arthur. Her expansion was made possible by the Trans-Siberian and Chinese Eastern railways built by Count Witte. From 1900 and especially after her defeat by Japan Russian expansion sharply swung back westwards, to Tibet, Afghanistan, and particularly to the penetration of Persia. There was a pronounced increase in Anglo-Russian hostility, and British policy in these regions had to be refurbished.[18]

A major problem for British policy in the face of this Russian expansion was the difficulty of interpreting Russian intentions. Did she or did she not aim at an invasion of India? Experts could not agree, and because they could not agree in assessing Russian aims, they were also divided in their opinions as to the proper response. Two schools of thought emerged: the 'forward' school and the 'masterly inactivity' school. The 'forward' school had strong Russophobia and believed that India should be secured from invasion by subjugating Afghanistan and Baluchistan, subsidising the Amir and occupying Herat, thus insulating India and planning to meet Russia well beyond the borders of India. This school was sometimes known as the Sind or Bombay school; its leading military proponent was Lord Roberts, and its chief political supporter was Lord Salisbury, who believed that India was singularly unsuited to a purely defensive strategy. The 'masterly inactivity' school was based on the Punjab and identified with John Lawrence. Its anti-expansionist view was that moving beyond the Indian frontier would only make a Russian invasion easier, with Britain having to meet it half-way, in difficult country, with possibly a hostile or exasperated population; the best defence of India was distance and natural barriers making invasion extremely difficult. This view seemed less plausible after 1884, when Persia might provide a route much less difficult. Thus, although there was fierce debate between these schools of thought between 1866 and 1877, as the century wore on, more and more people inclined to take a middle view, with perhaps a bias toward the more forward policy.[19] By the 1890s there was fairly wide agreement that a full-scale invasion of India was not likely for many years to come. In any case, the real danger – and of this there was the strongest possible evidence – was that Russia would use her position in Central Asia to bring pressure to bear elsewhere, or, in the event of a quarrel with Britain in any other quarter, distract Britain by a limited advance towards India. After the Mutiny the fear was not so much one of invasion but of subversion. Political intrigue and military demonstrations could prepare the way for a native uprising in India. Russia might present herself as the great alternative to British rule: every prince, warned Frere, might see in Russia 'a possible alternative claimant for Empire in India'.[20] Lord Cross (secretary of state for India 1886–92) said: 'It is an undoubted fact that the Russian Empire is looked upon in Central Asia as the growing and spreading power, and that the British Empire is not so regarded. So people worship the rising sun'. Salisbury emphasised the importance of prestige in governing India. However strong frontiers and fortresses were, he observed in 1884, 'if the *prestige* of the Power coming against you is greater than your own, it will penetrate through that barrier; it will undermine your sway; it will dissolve the loyalty and patriotism of those you rule.' The real danger, then, as Salisbury saw it, was of rebellion, 'the gradual weakening of respect for the English arms, disaffection towards the English Raj, and the gradual crumbling away of our resources before Russia has struck a blow against our frontier'.[21]

It was for this reason that it was the major object of policy to keep a chain of buffer states between India and Russia, and to ensure their freedom from Russian influence and intrigue. The anxiety caused by Afghanistan and Persia was seemingly endless, because the Amir and the Shah were both unreliable: the health of the one and the vacillations of the other contributed to many scares. The slaughter of the British mission at Kabul in 1879 at once jeopardised the equilibrium of the whole area. In 1881 Britain retired from Kandahar, the southern redoubt of Afghanistan, and so the Penjdeh incident in 1885 threw the issue of an Anglo-Russian war in Central Asia to the whim of the Amir.[22] The problem centred less on Russia's strength than on the weakness and instability of Persia and Afghanistan. Russia seemed bent on fostering internal decay in these states, and this was something Britain had to try to counteract.

In the 1890s attention focused on the northern frontier, in the area (500 miles across and centred on Gilgit) of Muslim states directly ruled by, or tributary to, Kashmir, but recognised as in the British sphere of influence. No-one supposed a full-blooded Russian invasion would come this way, since the nearest Russian military base of any size was at Osh, more than 900 miles across the Pamirs from Gilgit: the very lowest pass was $2\frac{1}{2}$ miles above sea level, and no grain was grown in the area. The northern frontier was of considerable importance, however, because it was the junction of spheres of interest, and the closest touching point between Russia and India.[23] It was here that the 'diversionary' and 'prestige' arguments were most potent. Viceroy Elgin calculated that it was perfectly possible for Russia to bring 3,000 or 4,000 men to Chitral and so lock up more than 20,000 troops in the garrisons from Peshawar to Kashmir. Such an operation could be checked by occupying Chitral with a small, but adequate detachment. After the assassination of the Mehtar of Chitral, the British agent at Gilgit was besieged in Chitral by the rebels. Plans to withdraw from Chitral were suspended, and Elgin recommended opening and guarding the Dir road, strengthening Chitral and greatly reducing the Gilgit garrison which could not effectively hold Chitral. Since Britain had acquired obligations to the tribes in this area, 'in any question with Russia our frontier is not the Indus, or the red line of the frontier . . . on a map'. If it were now to be laid down that Britain should 'await Russia on the Indus' not only would the whole frontier ignite in a blaze, 'but we might have dangers behind us that would paralyse our efforts'. Granted a spirit of intrigue among the tribes, an advance in force by Russia would be quite unnecessary to her purpose. A few hundred Russians in Chitral, and emissaries among the tribes, would cause an enormous number of men to be locked up along the Peshawar frontier. Nor did he believe the Russians would find the tribes as difficult to deal with as Britain had done. He thought it improbable that a Russian officer on the banks of the Oxus, only 60 miles from Chitral 'and other interesting places', absolutely unwatched, would content himself with sleeping in his tent. Sport, mountaineering, travel – there were many excuses to hand; and his chances of interference should be guarded against. Moreover, as the British agent at Gilgit 1889–94 pointed out, a thousand Cossacks in Kashmir would be a sensational opening move in any hostilities, turning the flank of the Peshawar defence line, and subverting the tribes of the Hindu Kush by promising them the loot of Kashmir; the northern passes afforded a difficult but not impracticable route for a force large enough to cause trouble in Kashmir. A major development in Russian military resources was noted, and it was certainly thought that the Russian army believed in the possibility of conquering India.

Elgin's argument was not accepted by the Liberal cabinet (now led by Rosebery) which had appointed him. However, the new Unionist government of 1895, guided by Curzon as under-secretary for India, reversed the decision of their predecessors to evacuate all positions beyond the frontier, and upheld Elgin's plan, at least to the extent of remaining at, and improving the road to, Chitral. This was decided in August 1895. Thereafter the Russians could never again hope to win an uncontested footing south of the Hindu Kush. This led to an immediate improvement and a really stable frontier in the north.[24]

Lord Wellesley took the initial step to bring Persia into the orbit of Indian foreign policy in 1798 by sending a mission to Teheran. In 1856–57 there was an Anglo-Persian war caused by Persia's fourth attempt to get Herat. The war was felt to be the beginning of a fight with Russia for India, because Persia in Herat would be the herald of Russia there. The Persians were forced to evacuate Herat and Britain got the right to appoint consuls wherever she wished in Persian dominions, the better to keep an eye on Russian activities. The preservation of Persian independence was greatly aided from 1825 by complete command of the Persian Gulf, where for the first three-quarters of the century Britain's ascendancy was indisputable – a *mare clausum*. In 1853 the Trucial States were induced to make a 'perfect maritime truce' between themselves, and in the 1880s and 1890s under the threat of challenges from Turkey, France, Russia and Germany, Britain further extended the treaty structure. The ultimate British interest in the Gulf was the security of the route to India. Salisbury wanted to utilise this strength in the Gulf by linking it by railways to the interior of Persia, at the same time connecting Persia and India, and Herat and India. Salisbury worked hard to establish the view that Persia was as significant to India as Afghanistan, but he never quite succeeded. His argument was that if Persia fell to Russia it would have a great 'moral value', making it impossible to secure the docility of Afghanistan without force, and diminishing British prestige in Indian eyes. [25]

'Were it not for our possessing India', Salisbury declared, 'we should trouble ourselves but little about Persia'. This is not to say that British commercial interests were non-existent. The maintenance of trade, particularly that based on India, was always a factor, and Britain was careful to detect and protest against any special treatment received by her trading rivals. But in the last resort, British policy was governed by political and strategic considerations. This was demonstrated clearly in the Anglo-Russian convention of 1907 which partitioned Persia into a northern sphere of Russian influence and a southern one of British with an intervening neutral zone. This arrangement was severely criticised because it appeared to surrender British commerce and finance in Persia to political convenience. Of course a good deal of the encouragement given to the economic interests had been in the hope that development would strengthen Persian resistance to Russia. [26]

Indian security was not only threatened from the north and north-west, but from Burma, the kingdom of Ava, as well. The creeping occupation of Burma was in three stages. The first Burma war of 1824–5 was fought defensively against the expansionist tendencies of Ava, and in 1826 Burma ceded all the gains she had made since 1782, including Assam. The second Burma war of 1852 was fought by Dalhousie largely in order to maintain British prestige in the face of an unco-operative Burmese regime whose control over its provincial governors had weakened. This led to the annexation of Lower Burma mainly to cut Ava off from the sea. The Rangoon traders now pressed for annexation to eliminate trade restrictions but the British government wished to maintain informal control. The accession of King Thibaw in 1878 made this impossible: the administration of Upper Burma gradually broke down and much of the king's authority passed into the hands of local war-lords; there was a serious rebellion in 1883. Coinciding with this weakness was the reappearance of France in Indo-China from 1881. Their control of the Red River would have given them access to the coveted Yunnan China trade, which Britain was trying to tap from Burma, and any development of French control in this region could pose an indirect threat to Indian security. A French company gained a concession for a railway from Mandalay to the frontier. There were rumours that France aimed to establish herself in Irrawaddy navigation; and improvements in the French commercial position might enable her to put pressure on British India. The region was becoming more important politically and economically, and no chances could be taken. By the time the third Burma war broke out in 1885, it may have been felt that the French threat was lessening; the government's aim (though not viceroy Dufferin's) has been described as trying, as in Egypt, to restore the working of informal influence. But Burma was no longer suitable for the maintenance of interests through informal control. Stable institutions had disappeared. Thibaw had massacred most alternative potential rulers. Dufferin described Burma as 'made of a soft molluscous consistence', and consequently far less adapted to serve the required purposes of a buffer state than Afghanistan. Annexation was made in 1886 of Upper Burma because Randolph Churchill thought it would finally and effectually protect India in the east. Dufferin did not want to reduplicate the disadvantages of the north-west frontier buffer state system, and argued from Egypt that indirect control was not enough.[27]

THE IMPERIAL IMPACT

So far as the conscious purposes of government were concerned, the great bulk of activity was directed simply to tax collection, and to the administration of justice, law and order. There was also, however, a notion of founding 'British greatness upon Indian happiness' (Bentinck), and both seemed by the 1820s to require the government to lead 'improvement', modernisation, on western lines. The new note introduced by Bentinck was that of placing India's total development more to the forefront and bringing in modern technology.[28] Three aspects of the work of the British in India call for comment – social and economic reforms including the abolition of customs they abhorred, the building of the railways and canals, and the introduction of English education.

In the so-called era of laissez-faire, India was 'being turned into a satellite of the industrial economy [of Great Britain] chiefly by State enterprise'.[29] The government came to manage a vast forest property, it had the monopoly of the manufacture of salt and opium; by the end of the century it owned the bulk of the railways and directly managed a considerable portion of them; it had constructed and maintained most of the important irrigation works; it owned and managed the postal and telegraph systems; it had the monopoly of note-issue; the State was directly responsible to a degree unknown in contemporary Britain for police, education, sanitation, medical relief, and ordinary public works; in times of drought it undertook 'famine relief' measures on the scale of a major campaign.[30] The first and continuing big task was land revenue settlement. Cornwallis in 1793 made a 'permanent settlement' with the *zamindars* or 'landed proprietors' of Bengal. The first British attempts to settle how much they should take as their share of the produce were confused by an exaggerated idea of the wealth of India and still more by their puzzled search for property in land. Cornwallis advised cutting controversy short by a simplification: he who paid the revenue was the owner. He might be a hereditary chief, a yearly contractor or tax-farmer, the descendant of a raja or a Mughal official; it was all the same, he was now the zamindar, the proprietor. These were made hereditary landlords at unchangeable rents. Thus it was hoped they would be encouraged to undertake improvements by the knowledge that any increases in productivity they were able to make would benefit them rather than attract heavier government demands on them. But in practice the system did not turn them into improving landlords; no Turnip Townshends or Cokes of Norfolk emerged in Bengal, and the rigidity of the settlement seemed to make them more ruthless with their tenants. There was a reaction against this method in the next generation of early nineteenth-century, increasingly utilitarian administrators. The Munro school at Madras, followed by Elphinstone at Bombay, Colebrooke in Ceylon, Raffles in Java, and supported by James Mill at East India House, distrusted the zamindars, the privileged classes, whom they felt acted oppressively, and instead idealised the simple virtues of a 'numerous free peasantry'. They all thought that they were turning custom-ridden serfs into industrious, free peasant cultivators or *ryots*, responsive to economic rather than 'feudal' stimuli. In fact the weight of indebtedness grew formidably. Gradually it dawned upon the British that at least in many areas, absolute property in land was vested in no-one, and that all classes connected with land possessed certain rights in it. Eventually 52 per cent of land in British India was held by *ryotwari* (without intermediaries) and 19 per cent by permanently settled zamindar proprietors, acting as agents between the government and the ryots. Meanwhile, Mill and Bentinck hoped to introduce land-holding British settlers who would speed up development and provide a model. From 1833 a small planter class, working tea and indigo, began to emerge.[31]

The government was extremely reluctant to sanction missionary work. It really got under way only from 1833, and then unofficially.

Considering the wide range of Indian customs and practices which the British found cruel or abhorrent – such as untouchability, murdering an unwanted daughter, sacrificing a first-born child, the burning of widows alive (*sati*), child marriage, agrestic serfdom in the south, and so forth – it is perhaps remarkable how slow and limited British intervention against these things was. The British moved with notable caution. In the first half of the nineteenth century only two customs came in for rigorous attack: sati and the gang-murder of travellers (*thagi*). As to the first: widow-burning was believed passionately by Hindus to be a road to heavenly bliss – a religious duty of high spiritual merit; but to western ways of thinking it implied a deeply dishonourable view of a woman's part in life; why should she die so painful a death? In 1813 they decided to insist that a widow must not be burned without a government certificate; she must not be pregnant or a minor, or drugged, or unwilling, and if she had infant children, there must be someone to look after them; but the result of this piece of red tape was to set a stamp of acquiescence on something done previously with a consciousness of official disapproval, and thus officially recorded burnings for Bengal rose from 378 in 1815 to 839 in 1818. Lord William Bentinck decided to abolish it, but only because he believed himself able to enforce it, on the assumption (shakily founded as it proved) that many enlightened Hindus felt as the British did. It was abolished in Bengal in 1829; Madras and Bombay followed in 1830. Of course sati went on in the numerous princely states, and because of their marital habits, 20 women often died, and sometimes more than 80, for every important man. Sati was part of the Hindu religion; though not enjoined directly in the oldest scriptures, it was extolled in the apocryphal writings. Then there was thagi, organised in 40 or 50 secret murder gangs or societies, undertaking mass murders of groups of travellers, including sepoys. Destruction not loot was the first object. The 'thugs' believed their booty to be merely the earthly part of their reward; the Thagi goddess willed murder as a means of maintaining a balance of population in the world. Once again it was Bentinck who gave the orders for the campaign to eliminate it. One of the thugs rounded up claimed to have killed personally 719 people, and felt miserable that by being caught he would not be able to notch up his thousand. Over 3,000 thugs were convicted after due process of law between 1831 and 1837. In 1837 a thousand more were awaiting trial; 2,000 were thought still to be at large. It is estimated that probably there were nearly 50 gangs and that they murdered between them 20,000 or 30,000 travellers every year. It was completely stamped out, after laborious effort, and there was nothing but praise for the British work here.[32]

The British were very slow in introducing railways, and only the military needs shown up by the Mutiny put real impetus behind their programme. Between 1845 and 1875 about £95 million was invested by British companies in Indian railways at a guaranteed interest rate of five per cent. Three motives may be distinguished. Railways could improve social conditions and spread civilisation. Sometimes there were genuine welfare motives; for example, a special famine line was built in the 1870s and others were subsidised to carry grain; investment cannot be explained entirely or even largely in terms of economic advantage. Sometimes, however, the government was anxious to encourage railways for commercial reasons. In a famous minute of 20 April 1853 (in a sense the fundamental charter of Indian railways) Dalhousie wrote:

> Great tracts are teeming with produce they cannot dispose of. England is calling aloud for the cotton which India does already produce in some degree, and would produce sufficient in quality and plentiful in quantity, if only there were provided the fitting means of conveyance for it.

But of course, he added, there were 'immeasurable political advantages' to be gained from a few railway lines radiating from Calcutta, Bombay and Madras, which would 'enable the government to bring the main bulk of its military strength to bear upon any given point in as many days as it would now require months'. But no purely military lines were built until the 1870s. There was pressure (frequently resisted by the government) from manufacturers to have railways built as the means of flooding India with their goods, and they also wanted to get more raw cotton out of India to reduce their dependence on the United States (80 per cent in the 1840s), especially as future slave emancipation was likely to disrupt the economy of the southern states. Sometimes there were military and administrative purposes in railway building, especially after the Mutiny: more miles were added in 1858 and 1859 than in the whole period (effectively only about eight years) up to that time. Fear of Russia was an influence. Lines were built with an eye to their strategic usefulness in mobilising and concentrating troops.[33]

The largest single unit of international investment in the nineteenth century was that of British capital in Indian railways. Government guarantee for the East Indian Railway (Calcutta–Delhi) and the Great Indian Peninsular Railway (Bombay–Coringa on the east coast) was negotiated in August 1849. Risk was borne by the government, but the profit accrued to the private railway companies; if profit failed to materialise, the investors would get their money back, and the railway entrepreneurs were at liberty to withdraw, leaving the state to run the unprofitable line. Such inducements were necessary to divert investment away from the United States and show how difficult it was to attract investment to a territory simply because it was in the empire. The first 20 miles of rail were opened in 1853. The government did not build these early lines, but in the period of railway construction in the 1870s direct government construction and management were adopted. The effect was of course to diminish village isolation in many areas, so reducing price fluctuation between districts. They hastened the demise of traditional industries, but indigenous industries probably suffered most in the first three-quarters of the century – *before* the effects of the railways were felt; and there was compensating employment to be found in the new plantation industries, the coal industry and the cotton and jute mills which developed *pari passu* with the construction of the railways. The railways, as in every other country in the world, widened local horizons, loosened some of the rigidities of the caste structure, and provided a basic physical unity in the sub-continent never before attained – all this contributed to making an Indian nation.[34] Eventually India had railways, roads, bridges and canals far ahead of anything to be seen elsewhere in Asia. The Grand Trunk Road linking Calcutta and Delhi is one of the most notable roads in the world and owed much to Bentinck. The Ganges canal became under Dalhousie longer than any European canal. By 1910 India had 3,000 miles of railway open and 1,500 under construction, and the canal system was the most extensive in the world. One important effect of improved communications was gradually to reduce the evils of famine; and famine relief was taken very seriously at least after 1868.[35]

The decision of 1835 to introduce English higher education was taken upon the advice of Bentinck and Macaulay, but also on account of Indian demand. It was a famous landmark rather than a policy with much in the way of immediate effect. The amount of government money involved was tiny. Bentinck's programme (which included vernacular elementary education) did not begin to operate until the 1850s, and then only in mutilated form. Universities at Calcutta, Madras and Bombay date only from the later 1850s. The pace of change was governed partly by the willingness of Indians to adopt English and to invest their money in schools and colleges. The advocates of the 1835 policy did not necessarily despise the classical languages of India, or wholly dismiss the value of its cultural achievements, as Macaulay did in his notorious minute. He blinded himself by his own rhetoric, misrepresenting the main 'Anglicist' position as well as the Orientalist position of men like H. T. Prinsep (who argued in favour of the Arabic, Persian or Sanskrit language as the medium of higher education). Its fame reflects nothing so much as the power of rhetorical fireworks over nineteenth-century minds. Macaulay spoke of discouraging 'the study of a literature' which 'inculcates the most serious errors on the most important subjects, a course hardly reconcilable with reason, or with morality'. Thus, all funds for education would be 'best employed on English education alone'. Quite what authority Macaulay had for his sarcastic description of Indian education is not clear. His leisure time in India was spent in prodigious reading of the Latin and Greek classics and not at all in studying the local culture.

Once English education had been introduced it was only a short step to confirm English as the language of administration. This was done in 1837. The educational decision, however, reinforced a theory about the direction of governmental development which had been a commonplace since Lord Hastings as governor-general enunciated it in 1818: that British dominion could not be permanent. Elphinstone (governor of Bombay 1819–27) agreed. Macaulay looked forward to the day when, having made India a wealthy, orderly society linked in the closest commercial connection with Britain, the political bond should become unimportant. When Indians demanded European institutions, said Macaulay,

> never will I attempt to avert or to retard it. Whenever it comes, it will be the proudest day in English history. To have found a great people sunk in the lowest depths of slavery and superstition, to have so ruled them as to have made them desirous and capable of all the privileges of citizens, would indeed be a title to glory all our own.

Twenty years later Charles Trevelyan hoped that European education would make Indians aim at improving the institutions of the country according to the British model, 'with the ultimate result of establishing constitutional self government'. This was, however, far enough off to be a safe talking-point. The Mutiny and the growth of the nationalist movement caused even a talking-point to be unacceptable, and such thoughts fell away. Meanwhile, the progress of English language administration was tardy. Up to 1860, Urdu and the derivative writer scripts remained the language of record for village land revenue records; after about that time there was a dual system. All the Mutiny criminal trials in the North-west provinces were in an Urdu writer's script. The numbers of English-speaking officers at the sub-district level were insignificant before 1860, and of course the number of Indian graduates was tiny.[36]

The slow pace of change was general. Stokes says: the first century of British rule to 1857 saw the gradual decline of warrior castes, the enhanced prosperity of thrifty agricultural castes, the expansion of cultivation, the extension of cash-cropping, the gradual fragmentation of landholdings and tighter dependence on the moneylender-grain-trader. But none of these changes went far. British conquest was felt most at the upper levels of society. Village life was not untouched by the pressure for change, but it was capable of absorbing it. Much of rural society was unaffected by the transfer of power at the top level into British hands. The imperial impact was uneven, and the village was the last level to feel it directly. The note of zeal and urgency associated with Bentinck, his ceaseless pursuit of 'improvement' in agriculture and communications and even manufacture, was not sustained by his successors. Most of the plans for law reform, educational development and scientific revenue systems were not translated into effective action until the 1860s, when the railway system was laid down and India's foreign trade began to leap forward. Least of all was there any real improvement in the standard of living for the masses. Some beneficial changes were made, internal peace and security were widely established, but beyond this there was little to show for the first century of British rule in India. Nor did it bring much benefit to Britain. Bright and the Manchester cotton interests repeatedly attacked the East India Company for its failure to build roads, railways and canals, since poor transport was the main obstacle to improving the quantity and quality of raw cotton.[37]

THE INDIAN MUTINY — REBELLION

The Mutiny was more than a purely military rising without political significance, but it was less than a national rebellion. Much had happened to shake the confidence of the civil population especially during Dalhousie's governor-generalship (1848–56). His annexations contributed to this. His victims included the Sikhs and the King of Oudh, respectively rulers of a large state and the most faithful ally of Britain. Education and science, the opening of railways and, from 1853, the introduction of telegraphs upset the traditional ways. Legislative interference had begun. The British had made it legal for Hindu widows to re-marry; a convert who had changed his religion was to be allowed to inherit property; convicts in gaols were made to feed in messes instead of each man separately. No-one knew what might come next. In part at least the Mutiny was the reaction of obscurantists against social change. These more general discontents may have included economic grievances. The zamindar was often broken by heavy assessments and the expense and delay of British courts; the merchant was often left only the 'trade in trifles' because the British monopolised all valuable merchandise; village craftsmen and artisans were thrown out of work by the introduction of British manufactures; the upper classes, denied their rightful status, found that 'in the Civil and Military Departments all the less lucrative and dignified positions are given to the natives and well-paid and honourable ones to Europeans'. The learned saw Muslim schools and colleges falling into decay, and to many it seemed that the British 'have promised no better employment for Hindoostanies than making roads and digging canals'. The Mutiny partly consisted of burning court-buildings, destruction of Government records, expulsion of the police and revenue establishments, and attacks on the new class rising under British laws and protection – the moneylender and the investor in land purchased at auction under the sale laws. The resumption of rent-free tenures in the 1830s, together with the decisions of the *Inam* Commission in the 1850s (resulting in the confiscation of 20,000 estates in the Bombay presidency) reawakened fears that the British wished to destroy the entire structure of land tenure in India.[38]

The British at the time distinguished three main causes. Ellenborough (governor-general 1842–44) believed the root cause was the British spirit of 'religious proselytism which is abroad', shown especially in the grants-in-aid to mission schools, exciting 'the apprehension that the government desires through education to convert the people': 'apprehension of interference with religion was the real cause of all these mutinies'. Disraeli described the Bengal sepoys as 'not so much the avengers of professional grievances as the exponents of general discontent' arising from a radical reforming system, attempting to change too much – a typical 'conservative' explanation. On the other hand plenty of British leaders defended the reform policy, claiming that the Mutiny was only a military affair: Vernon Smith (president of the Board of Control), Sir John Lawrence, the Duke of Argyll, and Sir Charles Wood. These men believed that the trouble arose from 'frantic fanaticism', superstition and unjustifiable fears.

Certainly among the sepoys there were special reasons for discontent. Added to the discontent which all men might feel, they found it difficult to adjust to modernisation of army structure and terms of service. They had a feeling that the army might soon be disbanded because Britain seemed nearly to have completed the work of 'pacification'. The General Service Enlistment Act 1856 meant that all new recruits in future must swear they would cross the sea for service (which would involve ritual pollution and no compensating extra pay). Cartridges for the new Lee-Enfield rifle had to be heavily greased, and they had to be bitten open to release the powder; if the grease contained tallow, from animals including pigs and cows, this would be an abomination both to Hindu and Muslim sepoys for which there is no parallel in western ways of thinking; it was not merely disgusting, it would damn them as well. No-one in Britain had thought of this; but the suspicious sepoy believed the British to be deliberately planning to break the sepoy's caste, thinking they would then find it easy to make a Christian of him as the only refuge. It was no use telling the sepoys that they could grease their own cartridges; they believed now that the paper of the original cartridges which they had bitten for years had been impregnated with the same offensive grease. The greasy cartridges merely provided the occasion for revolt, but there were deeper grounds of discontent. There was some justification for a general fear of religious interference; the feeling that it was a duty to convert to the Christian faith was growing among British officers. An act to prohibit polygamy had been debated.[39]

The Mutiny started at Meerut.[40] Three regiments shot their officers, broke open the gaol and set off armed for Delhi, 40 miles away. The titular king of Delhi was proclaimed emperor of Hindustan, Europeans were murdered, and within 24 hours Delhi was held by more than 5,000 armed men. The decision to make for Delhi suggests the existence of (unidentified) organisers and some collusion with the Delhi regiments. But it had not been thought out a long time ahead from on high: Meerut was in all India the station strongest in British troops. A centrally directed rebellion would have started anywhere but there. The Mutiny affected only Hindustan; key points there between Patna and Delhi were lost; Oudh, North-west provinces and central India were the main areas of trouble. Those who inspired it were not organised; they acted dispersedly, and as far as they could, on the one obvious source of power, the Bengal army. India could not fight a 'national war of independence' because there was no common cause. Most of the participants were pursuing their own private vendetta. The reaction of sepoy regiments in different places was highly erratic according to their local circumstances. Probably Spear's judgement upon its nature is sound: it was a military explosion which derived its force from social forces out of which it arose; the culmination of unrest produced by the clash of old and new. It was an extremely emotional expression of resentment; the cartridges blunder could have been retrieved if there had not been a pre-existing atmosphere of suspicion and ill-will; it was not the first war of national independence or a national revolt in the modern sense, but the 'final convulsión of the old order goaded to desperation by the incessant pricks of modernity'. The masses were widely quiescent. The Indian princes were not affected. Educated Indians remained aloof. Other organised bodies of Indians, such as the Madras and Bombay sepoy armies, were untouched. It would not even be true to regard it as a war which, like the European Thirty Years War, began for religion and ended for independence.[41] In the areas most affected, the Mutiny-Rebellion had the basic characteristics of a mass movement originating in peasant grievance. Among some Muslim communities there were plans for *jihad* (holy war against the infidel), but this fanatical religious dimension was limited. Some members of high caste but declining families had joined the army in order to retain social status: these peasant mercenaries of the north were inflamed by intolerable religious objections and threatened with slow displacement by lower castes and outsiders. They were recruits from regions undergoing recent political and economic dislocation. The two aspects, rural rebellion and military mutiny, were rarely concerted, although it is unlikely that there would have been a civil uprising without the prior mutiny of the Bengal army. Because of the close links with the civil community where large village brotherhoods existed, a rising of the army cannot be wholly separated from a rising of the people in the area. The revolt probably started in the army partly because of the solidarity of the sepoys with their families and villages, where religious and other suspicions and discontents were rife. Peasant grievances and disturbances were particularly marked in the Doab region between the Ganges and the Jumna. The Mutiny ended with a desperate last-ditch stand by die-hards.[42]

The Mutiny broke out on 10 May 1857, but its most notorious episode took place on 15 July at Cawnpore, where the rebel leader Nana Sahib had imprisoned in the *bibighar** the European women and children who had survived the attack on Cawnpore.[43] All 200 of them were murdered. The sepoys refused to obey orders to shoot them, and so butchers killed them with knives. A large number of bodies were thrown into the infamous well nearby. When British soldiers arrived on the scene they found the house still littered with underwear and female hair and running in blood. Wolseley described their reaction:

> A more maddening sight no Englishman has ever looked upon. Upon entering those bloodstained rooms, the heart seemed to stop. The horror of the scene was appalling and called up our worst angry passions ... a fiendish craving for the blood of the cowardly murderers ... The indignity which had been put upon a proud people by a race whom we regarded as inferior in every sense was maddening ... An all-absorbing craving for ruthless vengeance, that most un-christian of passions, was deep in all hearts.

Near-illiterate soldiers scrawled the walls with vows of vengeance, a cry heard 'wherever the English tongue was spoken'. There was no evidence of rape. Women had torn their clothes in an attempt to barricade the doors. But their bodies were stripped, hair and limbs cut off. The soldiers divided the tresses of one girl and swore that for every hair a sepoy should die. The Cawnpore massacre gave sanction to a retributive savagery which is one of the most shameful episodes in British history. General Neill determined that the punishment should be 'the heaviest, the most revolting to their feelings, and

---

* The name given to a house where Europeans kept Indian mistresses.

what they must ever remember'. He wished each offender to be forced to clean up a small portion of blood-stains, forced by the lash if necessary, before being hanged. This was a fearful punishment to those whose religion doomed them to perdition because of it. Those who objected were made to lick part of the blood with their own tongues. Neill admitted this was a strange requirement, but he believed it was one to meet the occasion and he held to it 'with the blessing and help of God'.[44] The *Annual Register* recorded a 'stern satisfaction' in reading of 'His righteous retribution'. It was not, however, confined to the actual murderers, but extended to any who had taken part in the Mutiny. The Indians may not have acted with premeditation. The British certainly did. Indian prisoners were blown from the mouths of cannon. The two sons of the emperor were murdered in cold blood. More serious was the indiscriminate slaughter in Delhi after its recapture – and even Palmerston wanted it razed to the ground. To the British it seemed that Satan had rebelled and the mark of a black skin was the mark of Cain. Later writers looking back on British retribution saw little to apologise for. Wolseley professed to be 'lost in amazement, mingled with a sort of national pride, at the smallness of the retribution we exacted, and how truthfully we can assert that mercy did season our justice'. J. W. Kaye in his *History of the Sepoy War* (1881) felt that the Word of God had been followed in allowing no mercy to murderers. Even so moderate a man as the *Times* correspondent, Russell, wrote that compared to Cawnpore, 'Sylla's [*sic*] proscriptions, the Sicilian vespers, the great *auto da fé* on Bartholomew's Eve, or the Ulster outbreak of 1641, were legitimate acts of judicial punishment'.[45]

The most important result of the Mutiny-Rebellion was the addition of hatred to indifference in the British attitude towards Indians. The 'mild Hindu' stereotype was replaced by a belief in his deceptiveness and cruelty. Conversely, the Mutiny was used as an exemplar of the virtues of the British race. Samuel Smiles in *Self-Help* found in British behaviour the highest standards of manliness and resource. Sir Charles Crosthwaite wrote: 'We are indebted to the Indians for the Great Mutiny which has well been called the Epic of the Race'. Here were deeds which every schoolboy should learn.[46] William Russell observed: 'What an earthquake to shake to pieces, what a volcano to smother with lava and ashes, has this mutiny been! Not alone cities, but confidence and trust have gone, never more to be restored!' – at best, many years must elapse before the evil passions excited by the disturbances would expire.[47] G. O. Trevelyan wrote in his book *The Competition Wallah* (1864):[48]

And now who can wonder that among a generation which has gone through such a crisis philanthropy is somewhat at a discount? ... The distrust and dislike engendered by such an experience are too deeply rooted to be plucked up by an act of volition.

In the 1860s Sir Charles Dilke noticed in all the hotels of India the appearance of the significant notice 'Gentlemen are earnestly requested not to strike the servants'. Canning wrote to Wood from Calcutta:

> You can have little idea how much India is altered ... We have changed from an aggressive and advancing power to a stationary one ... the sympathy which Englishmen ... felt for the natives has changed to a general feeling of repugnance ...

After the Mutiny there was less talk of independence – which Macaulay, Elphinstone and Charles Trevelyan had regarded as the goal – as desirable or inevitable. Very few hints were publicly given in the next 50 years that India might one day be governed by Indians.[49]

The actual effect on policy was complex, and at first intense. The British government took over from the East India Company and speeded up changes in every field.[50] Almost no more princely territory was acquired. In 1841 the East India Company had laid down the policy of 'just and honourable accession of [princely] territory', with a plan to control all India in 50 years. But Dalhousie was the last man ever to extend the British flag over an Indian state. Under Dalhousie, when a Hindu chief died without male issue, the general rule was to refuse to allow an adopted son to succeed. He acquired eight states by such 'lapse'. The important states of Satara, Nagpur and Jhansi lapsed on account of alleged misrule. After 1857, however, the natives states were no longer regarded as nuisances meriting removal. They were guaranteed security of existence, invited and assisted to undertake the task of self government. Royal warrants (sanads) were issued by Canning assuring them their governments would be perpetuated, accepting the succession of adopted sons in Hindu states, and accepting in Muslim states any succession regarded as legitimate in Muslim law. Two test cases, Baroda and Mysore, showed also that misrule would not be used as an occasion for annexation. In 1875 the chief of the Baroda state was deposed on account of notorious misconduct and gross misgovernment, but instead of annexation, the widow of the chief's predecessor was permitted to adopt as her son a boy selected by the British government from the Gaikwar family. Mysore had been directly ruled by British officials, without actually being annexed, from 1831; between 1861 and 1866 interference was intensified, but on the death of the raja in 1868 the British recognised his adopted son as his successor, and in 1881 (when the boy attained his majority) the country was formally restored to him after 50 years of British rule.[51] The proclamation of the Queen as Empress, if it has any significance, may be seen as part of a policy of conciliating the princes; making a personal tie for the princes with the Empress gave them something they were supposed to feel was valuable and dignified. As the nineteenth century wore on, so British statesmen came to feel increasingly and unanimously the virtue of princely rule.

Religious and social reform likewise came to an abrupt halt.[52] India was seen to be intensely conservative; total reformation was now understood to be at best a task of time and the utmost difficulty, at worst positively dangerous. Radical reform was no longer safe or fashionable. Fitzjames Stephen thought the masses were inherently ineducable. Observers analysed the causes of the Mutiny as a reaction to the attempt to change too much, and in particular drew attention to changes which conveyed the impression that the British were about to attack Indian religious feelings and prejudices. In 1854 for the first time religious neutrality had been breached by the government when it agreed to aid missionary schools as an inexpensive means of extending education, and in 1856 a grant had been sanctioned by the government of India to the Church Missionary Society to educate the backward Santal people. During the Mutiny a complete reversal of policy took place, and the British government vetoed the scheme in a despatch of 22 July 1857. This was followed by a general directive on 10 March 1858, that in consideration of what had happened

> no pains should be spared in enforcing on all public officers the most stringent rules of toleration ... abstaining from any covert designs on their religious feelings.

Bible classes were stopped in government schools, lest it should be said they were made an 'engine of proselytism'. Established reforms were not repudiated, but the hopes of fresh social reform were blighted, and almost all the initiative thereafter came from Indian social reformers.

In land policy the reaction was relatively short-lived, barely lasting into the 1870s. The apparent disaffection of the peasantry during the Mutiny meant the end of the ryotwari system of granting land settlements to peasants at the expense of the landlords, although no ryotwari settlement was undone. The peasantry had been used as the agency for social progress, but after the Mutiny the government immediately, if temporarily fell back on the *taluqdars,* the Oudh landowners, analogous to zamindars of Bengal, who had remained loyal during the troubles, and who seemed to be the only agency for the restoration of order. It had been planned to establish an egalitarian peasant society in newly annexed Oudh in 1856, but as the general populace joined in the sepoy revolt, with displaced taluqdars coming to the fore as leaders, and British authority was non-existent from May 1857 to the summer of 1858, the viceroy (Charles, Lord Canning) insisted on confiscating the land granted to peasants and restoring property to taluqdars if they submitted in full allegiance to the Crown. In November 1859 he authorised the grant of revenue jurisdiction and magisterial powers to the Oudh taluqdars. Yet only five years earlier the British had been making village settlements in the north-west provinces. Now they retraced their steps. Sir Charles Wood, secretary of state for India 1859–66, was convinced that they must deprive 'stirring elements' of any possible leaders by attaching the influential classes to British rule:

> the policy of suppressing or suffering to go to ruin, all the aristocracy and gentry of India is a mistake . . . We must be stronger with the natural chiefs and leaders of the people attached to us, than in leaving the people open to the persuasion and seduction of upstart leaders.[53]

John Stuart Mill writing in 1869 regretted the 'strong reaction in favour of setting up landlords everywhere' in India. The reaction in favour of landlords of the contemporary English type was occurring at the very time when British opinion was slowly beginning to turn in a contrary direction.[54] Thus it came about that developments in India and Ireland for a brief period ran in opposite directions. Policy in Ireland moved towards greater recognition and protection of the tenant, while in India the attempt to record and preserve the status of the tenant gave way to a policy more favourable to the rights and interests of superior landholders. The tendency by 1870 was towards the weakening of Indian tenants and the strengthening of Irish.[55] 'The need for such measures', said Wood in 1862, 'was the stern lesson taught by the Mutiny'. By a defining Act of 1869, 276 names were listed in Oudh as taluqdars: they and their heirs thus became a closed and exclusive society and no newcomers could gain admission. The British laboured after the 1858 re-conquest to make the taluqdars improving landlords and a socially responsible aristocracy, but such concepts were too artificial to take root. On the other hand, the government did not give itself over entirely to expediency; it did not lose a sense of responsibility for the welfare of the peasants. The Bengal government showed some sympathy with the humble peasant cultivators on the extensive indigo plantations of Lower Bengal when they defied their European masters in 1859 and shook off forced labour in 1862; this was the 'Blue Mutiny' episode.[56]

Historians do not at present agree about the extent to which the Mutiny-Rebellion changed British policies in India. In some respects – the main lines of railway projects, trunk roads and irrigation – schemes were approved before, and not as a consequence of, the Mutiny. In attitudes, the Mutiny crystallised and provided justification for broad shifts already under way. In other directions the effects may not have lasted much more than a decade: land policy was a case in point, and by the 1880s landlord interests were under assault again. Higher education continued unaffected; western education generally proceeded at a pace and intensity which was unprecedented, owing to Indian willingness to pay for it. And when urban, western-educated 'nationalist' leaders emerged, this pushed back the effects of the Mutiny. The half-hearted reliance, temporarily, on landlords may have been partly determined by a desire to check accelerating economic change, but not to reverse it. In any case, some experts (Wood and Henry Lawrence among them) were critical of the ryotwari settlements before the Mutiny, and questioned the wisdom of dispossessing the landlord classes. After the Mutiny the British wanted friends among the humble and meek without putting down all the proud. It would, moreover, be wrong to suggest that psychologically the Mutiny was something never entirely recovered from. Suppressed fear may have lingered on in Bengal and the area in which the Mutiny had occurred, but this is not to say that it was typical of the reaction of all British India.

Perhaps the main (and undisputed) lesson of the Mutiny was simply a military one. A strong European garrison was required, and the so-called 'native armies' were very tightly controlled in future. All field artillery was now transferred to Europeans, although before the Mutiny three-quarters of the gunners were Indian. Wood's military policy was confessedly one of divide and rule: he would not allow mixed regiments (in which as in the Mutiny 'the Oudh element' could, for example, leaven the whole army), but wanted them to be recruited on a district and community basis and then to operate in that area; but *within* a regiment he would mix religions and castes.[57]

ECONOMIC DEVELOPMENT AFTER 1850

To merchants and manufacturers of early Victorian Britain, India was an unsatisfactory place; businessmen could not reconcile themselves to the fact that Britain's greatest overseas possession took only one-tenth as much per head of British manufactures as Brazil; and Lancashire textile interests deplored India's deficiencies as a supplier of raw materials. And so to put this right, they campaigned for steamships and railways, and for government assistance in developing primary products, especially cotton. Distance was one basic impediment after the East India Company had lost its monopoly in 1833. Transport costs were high, and slow movement led to a deterioration in the quality of cotton. Businessmen, publicists and officials came to the conclusion that the chief reason for the low level of Britain's trade with India was directly connected with the lack of good *internal* transport. Hence R. M. Stephenson's plan in 1840 'to girdle the world with an iron chain, to connect Europe and Asia from their furthest extremities by one colossal railway', from London to Calcutta and on to China. Promoters of the Great Indian Peninsular Railway were able to capitalise on the great cotton shortage of 1846, resulting from the virtual failure of the cotton crop in the United States; having to pay nearly doubled prices for the greatly reduced supplies, Lancashire looked to India for relief. The Lancashire merchants regarded the railway from Bombay to the cotton districts 'as nothing more than an extension of their own line from Manchester to Liverpool'. One after another the outstanding chambers of commerce of the Midlands and Scotland, including Liverpool, Manchester and Glasgow, sent to the East India Company powerful letters of support for the Great Indian Peninsular Railway

(G.I.P.) in 1847, stressing the 'extremely precarious' dependence on American cotton. In 1861 the Manchester chamber of commerce called for an annual loan of £5 to £6 million to complete transport projects in India.[58]

The improvement in railways and steamships, and especially the opening of the Suez Canal, made fundamental changes in India's foreign trade in the latter part of the nineteenth century. Bombay benefited from the opening in 1869 of the Suez Canal more than any other part of the world (as Map 5 indicates). Capital was drawn into the production of new staples. The export of wheat on a big scale was made possible by the opening of the canal, and by the 1880s it frequently headed the list of exports. The export of raw cotton and jute replaced the former export of manufactured cotton goods. The Lancashire cotton famine of the 1860s gave a major fillip to the export of Indian cotton to Britain, and after 1866 there was a large-scale cotton improvement programme involving experimental cultivation, the establishment of model farms, and legislative regulation of production and marketing. The export of jute from Bengal began to expand notably after the Crimean War, which cut off Dundee's former supply of Russian flax and hemp; India filled the gap. Cultivation was improved, and by 1900 some 2.2 million acres were given over to jute. The first successful cotton mill was started in Bombay in 1853, but rapid expansion did not occur until the last quarter of the century. Cotton and jute mills could not become of importance until the improvement of transport and development of power resources made it possible to import and work the necessary machinery and plant. The tea and coffee industries of Ceylon were founded in the 1830s but did not become of importance until the second half of the century. The great value of Indian jute was first realised in 1838 when the regular export of raw jute to Dundee began. As quality improved, it permanently supplanted Russian materials. Its large-scale manufacture was started in 1855 at Rishra, near Serampore, when George Acland brought out a jute-spinning machine from Dundee; the first power loom was established in 1859; increase in exports was rapid from the 1870s, and by the end of the century Calcutta jute goods began seriously to compete with those of Dundee.

Although wild tea plants were found in Assam in the 1820s it was doubted whether they really were tea. Bentinck sent a special committee to China in 1834 to obtain seed and Chinese labour, with the idea of introducing the crop into the hilly districts of Northern India, and government plantations were started, but sold in 1839 to the Assam Tea Co. Ltd. In the 1850s the cultivation of the indigenous tea plant went ahead in Assam, Bengal, southern India and Ceylon, where a number of tea gardens were started with European capital. Whereas in the middle of the nineteenth century Britain obtained the whole of its tea from China and as late as 1869 obtained only 10 million lb from India compared with 101 million lb from China, at the end of the century it obtained only 24 million lb from China but 137 million lb from India.

The area under opium was greatly reduced from 1907 when the government made an agreement with China whereby the opium exports were to be annually diminished and eventually prohibited.[59]

Lancashire wanted a tariff policy which would provide free access for British manufacturers. Between 1859 and 1882 imported cotton piece goods paid 5 per cent import duty and yarn $3\frac{1}{2}$ per cent, but fear of competition from Indian mills led to a great agitation in Lancashire, which resulted in the removal of practically all India's import duties between 1882 and 1894, thus deferring to the interests of free trade and Lancashire; M.P.s were no doubt convinced that in filling Manchester's pockets they were following the laws of political economy and nature and increasing the world's wealth. But the measure was regarded by Lord Lytton's Council as contrary to India's interests, and they protested. The Council protested still more strongly in 1894 when, in order to raise revenues, the 5 per cent import duty on manufactured cotton was re-imposed, but, to rob it of any protective value a corresponding or 'countervailing' excise duty was clapped on Indian mill-made cotton, after more Lancashire pressure. Although it applied until 1917, it satisfied neither side. The moral loss of authority in India was enormous.[60]

The British are sometimes criticised for not planning a sufficiently ample development of Indian resources. The wisdom of the government's expenditure is questionable: one-third on army, half on civil administration in the 1880s. There was no improvement in agricultural prosperity on which the elevation of the masses depended, though by 1900 nearly £200 million of public debt (mostly for railways) and £300 million of investments in new industries, such as jute and tea, were held by Britons. The Indian merchant and moneyed castes failed to transform themselves into a modern entrepreneurial business class. Despite an enormous increase in economic activity, the mercantile classes remained confined to middle-men functions, as moneylenders, brokers, wholesalers, and distributive traders. Without a revolution in agricultural production, new wealth was ploughed back into moneylending, rack-renting and education for professional careers. Trading and moneyed groups like the Gujaratis or Marwartis extended the scale and geographical range of their economic activities without breaking through the confines of their separatist social system. India was kept within primary-producing limits. Control over factories and plantations in India was kept in a few powerful hands, who were 'upper' rather than 'middle' class. As the government was British there were none of the motives which the Japanese had to industrialise, and the British government looked with disfavour on government enterprise and on any policy which might thereafter threaten the growing sales of British manufactures. But more important than this as an explanation of India's lack of industrialisation in the nineteenth century was the fact that India's social traditions and institutions were uncongenial to native enterprise in modern large-scale industry. Despite good resources, and relatively easy access to foreign capital markets, Indians were diverted for the most part by cultural traditions and institutions from an active concern with applied science and technology. Those who had wealth were not disposed to apply it to the capitalisation of industry. At first, therefore, the provision of enterprise and technical knowledge and capital was left to foreigners, mainly British. The Indian-owned Tata Iron and Steel Co. Ltd. was not founded until 1907.[61] It was Dilke's opinion that Britain had crushed the princes without raising up the traders, and he pointed to the failure of 'a middle class' to emerge, which would have been the 'best buckler of British rule'.[62]

POLITICAL DEVELOPMENTS 1880–1905

After the Mutiny, Indian finances were in serious disarray, and British policy was governed largely by financial considerations. The British taxpayer would not pay a penny for India. The chief object of all British policy from 1870 was to keep the political temperature low, and to attempt by conciliation to contain pressure from any quarter, and to widen its range of collaborators. The British came to the conclusion that the only way to provide for the growing demand for various public utilities was to set up a system of local rating and allow local elected boards to fix the rates and spend the money. Modernisation increased governmental power, but also made it more dependent on the Indians who manned all but the topmost levels of administration, law and education. Viceroys Lawrence and Mayo were acutely aware that financial stringency made good sense of granting Indians a limited control of local affairs, because this devolution successfully put the costs of police and conservancy on the new municipalities. When municipal and local boards were founded in most provinces after 1882, economy was again the underlying motive, just as it was in Liberal policy towards Home Rule in Ireland. The widening of the representative system also brought more Indians into consultation about the management of their affairs without disturbing fundamental British interests. Many of these changes were associated with the viceroyalty of Ripon (1880–84). Ripon in 1882 aimed to foster 'the small beginnings of independent political life' and set up separate legislative councils in the three presidencies to provide a means of consultation and of discovering what Indians thought. He hoped to promote local municipal self-government. He was sharply aware of the need to use the educated Indian, but arrived at this conclusion from a defensive reasoning, stressing 'the hourly increasing . . . necessity of making the educated natives the friends, instead of the enemies of our rule', and preventing them from becoming 'through blind indifference or stupid repression a source of political danger'. Although he achieved no really significant advance, Ripon enjoyed great popularity among Indians.

A comparatively minor piece of legislation in Ripon's plans, the Ilbert Bill, drew enormous publicity. Its purpose was to give criminal jurisdiction over Europeans in the country districts to Indian magistrates and judges. This was opposed by the Bengal Europeans and the tea and indigo planters of Assam and Bihar, who saw it as threatening their authority over their employees, an end to beating them in fact. Gladstone backed Ripon, commenting on the 'saucy pride' of the British community in its dealings with non-Europeans. As enacted, the bill gave Europeans in the *mofussil* the right to claim trial by a jury with half European members; but qualified Indians were now allowed to try Europeans. Thus the first group actively to engage in political struggle with the raj was a European one, and their success was an inspiration to Indians themselves. Within two years the Indian National Congress was formed.[63]

The Indian nationalist movement is a complex phenomenon. Indian nationalists were not as in Europe the product of economic change and opportunity, but members of the traditionally literate castes who had enthusiastically sought the English education, the clerical and teaching Hindus. It was not the rich who went into the high schools and colleges of Bengal but people of high caste status but small incomes; less than 10 per cent were sons of traders. Universities in Calcutta, Bombay and Madras were fully operational by the 1860s. The really significant growth of the educated class occurred from the 1870s when the government began withdrawing its financial support for higher education. By the end of the 1880s educational expansion had become self-sustaining: Indian private enterprise was able to perpetuate it without government support. As Tilak said, English education was the 'milk of the tigress'; suckled on this, and unsterilised by government control, Indians would grow up in critical attitudes. Tilak and his friends made sacrifices to build up the Deccan Educational Society; Surendranath Banerjea (expelled from the covenanted civil service) became an instructor to Bengal students. Apart from Ripon, most of the British rulers failed to see the danger of frustrating the educated. Indian hearts were filled with high hopes by English education; but their rulers were not satisfying these hopes and aspirations. These men found civil service careers hard to obtain. S. Banerjea was thrown out (it was generally agreed he would not have been if he had been British); Tilak never took the examinations; the first Indian wrangler at Cambridge, A. M. Bose, failed because of the horse-riding test. By 1887 only a dozen Indians had entered the covenanted civil service by open examination, out of a service of nearly 1,000; the age limit was too low for most of them to prepare themselves. The nationalist movement was related to the thwarted would-be intellectuals and the frustration of the gifted. 55 to 60 per cent of undergraduates failed to obtain the B.A., and at Calcutta the failure rate was even higher. Its leaders were often lawyers.[64]

The Indian National Congress was found on 28 December 1885 with A. O. Hume, an Englishman and former district officer, as its *éminence grise*. Aiming at 'fuller development and consolidation of the sentiments of national unity', it was the first political attempt to approach the British government at an all-Indian level, and this remarkable organisation developed into the most important national party in twentieth-century India. Its foundation was therefore one of the most significant political events in India in the later nineteenth century. It was nurtured particularly in the Bombay presidency, and the dissension which nearly wrecked it, especially between 1904 and 1908, had a background in the faction struggles of Bombay Chitpavan Brahmin politicians, lead by the 'extremist' B. G. Tilak, and the 'moderate' G. K. Gokhale – struggles which went back to the personal quarrels of the 1880s. The function of Congress was to put demands to government at a high level on major all-Indian matters; unity was all-important, and leaders tended to evade any crucial issue which might threaten to divide them. Its existence was a necessary corollary and reaction to new forms of intensive government. Since its purpose was to present within the framework of the raj unanimous demands to government, and impose unity on the political society of India, it was virtually impossible to create a viable opposition group within the movement itself. It was always linked to a great variety of other political and social organisations in the localities, through which it built up a wide and heterogeneous support.[65]

Between 1886 and 1892 the British aim in respect of Congress was to forestall radical nationalist demands by offering timely concessions. The centres of political activity among Indians were to be moved from non-official reform associations and Congress to legally constituted municipal and district bodies and to provincial councils. In this context may be seen the Indian Councils Acts of 1861 and 1892 and the objectives of viceroys Ripon (1880–84), Dufferin (1884–88) and Lansdowne (1888–94). Lansdowne was conciliatory and recognised Congress. He rightly found it innocuous. Congress in its early years required no more than friendly and courteous treatment. The Indian Councils Act of 1892, passed under Lansdowne, though embodying the ideas of Dufferin, made tacit provision for the introduction of the elective principle where feasible. The representation of Indians on the central and provincial legislative councils was increased. It also extended the advice given by Indians to the governor-general and allowed a limited right of interpellation (that is to say, the right to interrupt to demand an explanation from a minister). But the councils still had a majority of officials, and the governor-general the right of veto. Nevertheless, the ideas of election and representation had been introduced. The Act was an extension to provincial and all-India councils of the elective principle which Ripon had introduced for municipal councils. Its immediate effect was tiny, but it did enable a small group of able new Indians to enter the national political arena.[66] Elgin (viceroy 1894–99) was inclined to move a little closer to Congress,[67] but this policy was sharply reversed under Curzon (1899–1905).

Curzon spoke of Indians in terms normally reserved for pet animals: at best they were 'less than schoolchildren'. 'Efficiency', he said, 'has been our gospel, the keynote of our administration'. He was not so much intolerant as insensitive. A man who was not really even aware of the existence of the lower orders in Britain could hardly be expected to register the full significance of the protest in India. His own domestic circumstances were so grand that napkin rings did not exist, since napkins were thrown away after they had been used once; soup was never served for luncheon. He enjoyed living up to the legend which was woven around such grandeur. He was unusually gifted, but his dictatorial temperament lost him many friends. It has to be remembered in assessing him that he was seldom free from racking pain in the back. His moods were infinitely variable and he often behaved harshly and tactlessly. A friend once said it was Curzon's misfortune to have the manners of minor royalty without its habitual incapacity. He was not unaware of the dangers of the 'damned nigger' attitude – 'it is painful', he wrote, 'to see the dominant race deliberately going over the abyss'. Yet on the whole he loved India more than Indians.[68] He believed they should be treated with justice. But this was simply a part of efficient administration, a job to be done rather than a duty to be fulfilled: 'my one object being to make our administration equitable, and our dominion permanent'. Congress he regarded as 'an unclean thing'.[69] Educated Indian opinion grew to dislike him intensely. Politically his viceroyalty was disastrous and represented no advance on the view he had advanced in a parliamentary speech on the Indian Councils Bill in 1892:

> no system of representation that would stand the test of 24 hours operation, would, in the most infinitesimal degree, represent the people of India. Who are the people of India? The people of India are the voiceless millions who can neither read nor write their own tongues, who have no knowledge whatever of English, who are not perhaps universally aware of the fact that the English are in their country as rulers. The people of India are the ryots and the peasants, whose life is not one of political aspiration, but of mute penury and toil. The plans and policy of the Congress Party in India leave this vast amorphous residuum absolutely untouched ... the constituency which the Congress Party represent cannot be described as otherwise than a minute and almost microscopic minority of the total population of India.

The feelings and aspirations of the people, he continued, could as little be judged from the plans of Congress,

> as you can judge of the physical configuration of a country which is wrapped up in the mists of early morning ... To propose an elaborate system of representation for a people in this stage of development would appear to me to be, in the highest degree, premature and unwise. To describe such a system as representation of the people of India would be little better than a farce ... The idea of representation is alien to the

Indian mind. We have only arrived at it by slow degrees ourselves, through centuries of conflict and storm ... it is only within the last 25 years that we have in this country entered into anything like its full fruition.

India, he concluded, amidst interjections of dissent, was sundered into 'irreconcilable camps by differences of caste, of religion, of custom'.[70]

Congress was a dignified debating society, passing moderate academic resolutions, wholly trusting and admiring Britain. The progress of self-government in white colonies gave cause for hope and confidence among Indians; Banerjea was confident in 1880 that Britain must see the anomaly of her grandest dependency's being governed upon wholly different principles. Elgin had been willing to hold the scales even between Congress and the government of India. Although Congress's effort slackened in the 1890s, Curzon underestimated the strength of Congress lamentably: 'The Congress is tottering to its fall and one of my great ambitions, while in India, is to assist it to a peaceful demise'. He profoundly disliked it. Seeing no need to conciliate any Indians, he ignored Congress and the moderate leader G. K. Gokhale. By love of India and paternalist administrative reform he was confident he could ignore the demands for political advance. Self-government was 'a fantastic and futile dream'; he objected to it 'in toto' because it was 'incompatible with the continuance of British rule in India'.[71]

In 1905 Bengal was partitioned, and a new province of East Bengal was created (with the capital at Dacca), and Assam was incorporated in it. The new province might be said to bear some resemblance to Ireland, in that Hindu large landed proprietors, often absentee landlords, found themselves in rent disputes with a mass body of Muslim cultivators. The administrative arguments for adjusting the boundary were strong: a province of 78 million was too big a unit, and parts of it, especially in the east, were notoriously, even deplorably, undergoverned and had always been so. The scheme began life as an administrative rationalisation and improvement which would redress the excessive preponderance of the Hindu *bhadralok* (the Calcutta-based upper-crust of Bengal society) in the predominantly Muslim eastern area, by encouraging the more backward Muslims and Assamese to take a larger share of posts in East Bengal. The scheme would also help Biharis and Orissans in Bengal to improve their position. Curzon gave the impression that the government had planned the partition simply for political reasons — to spite the bhadralok, diminish the status of the province and destroy the unity of the political aspirations of Bengalis. And he did in fact regard it as a desirable device to divide an unruly province, 'dethrone Calcutta from its place as a centre of intrigue', and weaken the influence of the lawyer class. He overstated the political advantages as much as he underestimated its political repercussions. These, for all his bravado about the agitation's being saved from being ridiculous by being childish, were in fact considerable. New tactics and organisations were created to facilitate popular political participation, including terrorist ones. Various grievances of Bengal's high-caste Hindus were caught up in the anti-partition agitation; new spokesmen for Bengal emerged, notably Aurobindo Ghose. In their hands the movement for the development of local industries, making the economy less dependent on the imperial power *(swadeshi)*, was protected by linking it to the call for a boycott of British goods. This developed into a more extreme programme leading to non-co-operation and passive resistance. The anti-partition agitation thus injected new vigour into the politics of Bengal and India.[72]

Curzon continued to believe the partition was 'merely the peg selected by the agitators . . . on which to hang their action'.[73] His successor, Minto, took a rather different view. Although feeling that some of the agitation had been unscrupulously fostered (particularly perhaps by lawyers who saw their business migrating from Calcutta to the large cities of the east), he believed that there was 'much more genuine feeling in the movement than the official mind is prepared to admit' in its unanimous belief in its administrative wisdom, and that local feeling had been treated too unsympathetically. Morley regarded it as a 'sad mistake', but did not think an immediate reversal would be expedient. Not all his colleagues agreed. Morley, however, seems to have accepted Minto's arguments that the quicker reconsideration was ruled out the quicker things would settle down: withdrawal would be taken as weakness.[74]

At the same time as the partition engendered excitement throughout India, far-reaching possibilities were also stirred in Asian minds by Japan's defeat of Russia. Curzon left a bitter legacy in India: discontent at his tyrannical ways had spread even to the princes. Although most of India was probably not greatly interested in whether or not Bengal was divided, there was widespread anger that Bengali wishes should have been flouted so openly. Such was the general situation when the Liberals came to power in Britain.

THE MORLEY-MINTO REFORMS[75]

The Morley-Minto reforms were in a precise sense what later generations would have called a package deal: order plus reform, and measures were taken to promote both simultaneously, with equal seriousness. To speak of the 'shadow of reform and the substance of repression' is, I think, to distort the whole ethos of the period. Nor is it true that Morley was reluctantly pressed into repressive acts by Minto. Morley genuinely believed that when murder and bombs followed newspaper incitement to murder, dynamite and rebellion, the freedom of the press was being abused, and a situation created which could mischievously imperil the progress of reform.

The reforms established the principle of representative government in the provinces and introduced a substantial measure of its practice.[76] In their day they were a definite concession to moderate nationalist demands, as they then stood defined by Gokhale. Morley saw a clear difference from Unionist policy, which was basically one of mere order without reform: 'Our Liberal experiment may fail. The Tory experiment of grudging and half-and-half concession is sure to fail'. His idea was to promote 'order plus progress' by getting away from two ideas he regarded as equally stupid: that they should merely keep the sword sharp or that they should merely concede 'one man one vote'. Hence there was a fairly rigorous Act against newspapers which might incite to sedition in June 1908, preceding the Indian Councils Act of 1909. Control of newspapers was given more comprehensive and permanent form in the Press Act of 1910. Minto's view was that 'a strong just hand' was needed; the press was the source of a poison gravely affecting the safety of India: inflammatory writings were widely read, and might lead to a panic among the Europeans followed by dangerous reprisals; but he also saw that 'we can no longer govern by repression alone with any hopes of ultimate success', and that opportunities must be offered 'of sharing our administration, to those Indians who are most capable of assisting us'. The government used an 1818 regulation empowering detention indefinitely without charge or trial. There was a Prevention of Seditious Meetings Act passed in 1907. Tilak was imprisoned for sedition between 1908 and 1914. Under the 1910 Press Act no newspaper could be registered without 'caution money' being paid. Certain societies were also proscribed, and discretionary disqualification of candidates presenting themselves for election to legislatures was also allowed. 'Our task', said Morley in September 1908, 'is double: to keep order on the one hand and to try to get at those roots of disorder on the other, whose vitality is due exactly to that system of government of which the Bureaucrat is the rather arrogant oracle'. The hope was that reforms would weaken 'extremists' and rally the 'moderates' against 'growing conspiracy'.

Both Morley and Minto were primarily concerned with agitation in India insofar as it seemed to threaten the security and stability of the British raj, but they did not entirely agree on the methods of meeting it. Morley described himself, perhaps not entirely seriously, 'as cautious a Whig as any Elliot, Russell or Grey, that was ever born', and as having 'no ambition to take part in any grand revolution' during his period of office. But he was determined to adjust the machinery of Indian government to meet the requirements of the changed circumstances in India. This took him some way beyond the reforms originally proposed by the government of India in March 1907. Particularly at his age he was inclined to lean to 'the homely doctrine of anything for a quiet life'.[77] Minto agreed with him that the government of India must remain autocratic. The ultimate control must remain vested in British hands and could not be delegated to any kind of representative assembly in India, since it was believed to be unsuited to India, whose safety and welfare depended on the permanence of the British administration. Any move in that direction was, wrote Minto, 'merely a sop to impossible ambitions'. The only representation for which the country seemed fitted was one by classes and communities, and that also only to a very limited extent. But both Morley and Minto recognised changing times and the need to share their tasks with the ever-growing ranks of educated Indians. Chiefly they aimed at a 'scheme of administrative improvement' which would enlist the support of moderate elements, forestall the growth of unprecedented opposition, and thereby strengthen British rule by placing it in a better position to do and defend its work. 'We must recognise individual ability and invite it to rule together with us', wrote Minto. Morley explained a serious disadvantage: 'We don't know the minds of the natives, and the natives don't know what is in our minds. How to find some sort of bridge? That's the question'. The reforms were intended to provide this bridge, to provide advisers who could 'give the key to many mysteries', not least Muslim ones. This latter consideration acquired special force after the formation of the Muslim League in December 1906.[78]

The main two features of the Morley-Minto reforms were: first, the admission of two Indians to the council of the secretary of state and one each to the executive councils of the governor-general and the provincial governors; and second, the expansion and liberalisation of the legislative councils. The first was a gesture intended to give concrete proof that race was no disqualification from high office. The appointment of an Indian to the executive council of the governor-general was the most important, as it was also the most controversial, issue. Minto thought the object was to achieve a 'counterpoise to extreme Congress doctrines'. Morley considered it to be 'the cheapest concession' which could be made, for it would leave the absolute control of British executive authority unimpaired. The Indian member would help to provide the information about how 'things strike that queer article the Native mind'. Morley and Minto easily agreed on the desirability of this, but their advisers were strongly hostile, and it took two years to get the proposal through. The choice of S. P. Sinha as this member was influenced by the fact that he was comparatively white and socially in touch with Europeans, whereas Dr A. Mukherjee, recognised as more able, was exceedingly dark-skinned: the line of least resistance as well as pure ability should, said Minto, be taken into account, and 'opposition in the official world would not be regardless of mere shades of colour'. Thus Sinha, a Bengali bhadralok, was appointed as Indian member.[79] The Indian Councils Act was mainly an extension of the Act of 1892. It increased the number of Indians in the provincial legislative councils and gave the councils non-official (nominated plus elected) majorities. The imperial legislative council also received an addition of Indian members, but here an official majority was retained. The principle of election, implicit in the Act of 1892, was now overtly recognised. The councils were allowed more time to discuss the budget, to move resolutions and to call for a division. The right of interpellation was extended and members could ask supplementary questions. Both Morley and Minto, however, vigorously denied the suggestions that these enlarged councils were intended to pave the way for the actual establishment of anything resembling parliamentary institutions. If that were the end product, Morley declared, he would 'have nothing at all to do with it': 'if my existence, either officially or corporeally, were prolonged twenty times longer than either of them is likely to be, a Parliamentary system in India is not at all the goal to which I would for one moment aspire'.[80] Minto likewise said that representative government in its western sense was 'totally inapplicable to the Indian Empire'.[81] The councils were already in existence, and what was now being attempted was making representation upon them more real and effective, so that they could function as better vehicles for expressing Indian opinions and afford the government additional opportunities both of becoming acquainted with the drift of public opinion and of explaining its own actions. Indians were not to control the administration but only to advise it. The spirit of parliamentary government in India was to proceed by making British government and parliament more aware of Indian opinion. Morley and Minto dismissed the ideal of self-government on the colonial model for India, which was the nationalist objective, as 'a mere dream' and an impossibility. They could not conceive of the government of India as anything but a benevolent, despotic but constitutional autocracy. They set themselves to 'hatch some plan and policy for half a generation', but were bent on 'doing nothing to loosen the bolts'.[82] Nevertheless, the nationalists welcomed the reforms, probably seeing that they could not possibly last half a generation. They interpreted them as an advance towards parliamentary government. So did Curzon, who realised that the councils must inevitably become 'parliamentary bodies in miniature'.

It has not always been clearly realised that the initiative for these Morley-Minto reforms was essentially Morley's rather than Minto's. Tactically, however, it was expedient to let it seem to be the case that initiative came from India. Morley recognised that Minto's desire for this was both 'natural and politic'. In this way it could be represented to the Indians that their government really was doing something for them. At home too, it helped Morley with Tory opposition, because he could always conveniently argue that he was compelled to act because the man on the spot – a Tory – demanded them. Even if Morley set the ball rolling, Minto could of course initially have come to similar conclusions independently, and he gave the impression of never being behind-hand in support.[83]

The one point upon which Minto exerted a decisive influence was not a happy one. Morley, while by no means disinclined to play off Muslims against Hindus, was suspicious of separate electorates, but the viceroy forced his hand. Morley reluctantly agreed to a communal rather than a territorial basis of representation. The day when Minto received the Muslim deputation – and assured it that the 'political rights and interests' of the community it claimed to represent would be 'safeguarded by any administrative reorganisation' with which he might be concerned – was a fateful day for India. While Morley wanted to satisfy the Hindu western-educated élite, Minto insisted that there were other equally important communities – the princes, the great landowners, the Muslims – and he seems to have conciliated Muslim separatist ideas in the hope of producing a counterpoise to Congress as well as of controlling a potentially dangerous community.[84]

How far were the reforms a new departure? Morley may not have seen the answer to this question at all clearly himself. He seems sincerely to have believed that self-government was not at all envisaged, but it is significant that his under-secretary, Buchanan, speaking in the House of Commons, claimed that they were a 'real step forward', intended partly to guide Indians into learning 'the work of administration and government in the only school worth anything, the school of experience'.[85] In effect, if not in intention, the reforms were the end of a phase in Indian politics and constitutional history. But whilst it is fair to describe them as a natural extension of the existing system, it may not be equally fair to follow the opinion of the Montagu-Chelmsford *Report on Indian Constitutional Reforms* (1918) that the 1909 reforms could not be 'justly described as embodying any new policy', since naturally the report wished to reserve to itself that historic role. As the report itself admitted, they constituted 'a decided step forward on a road leading at no distant period to a stage at which the question of responsible government was bound to present itself'.[86] The hope of reforms (rather than the reforms themselves) made it possible for moderates to control nationalist opinion in the critical years between 1905 and 1911, and thus it can be argued that these limited reforms helped India to make a more orderly advance than might have seemed possible in 1905.[87]

One of the most significant features of the reforms was the positive dislike of bureaucracy which underpinned them. The more one looks at them the more they seem to represent an attack on rigid bureaucracy, on the mindless official injustice which might lose Britain her Indian empire. They were more anti-Curzon than pro-Congress. Morley was constantly pillorying the 'tchinovniks', with the lesson of the Russian revolution of 1905 before him. To him, the reforms were designed to prevent Indian bureaucracy becoming a mechanical or military one, to make the government 'a trifle less encased in bureaucratic buckram'. The Indian civil service as a body was not half elastic enough, and Morley was sick of the silliness and 'wooden-headedness of the mere bureaucrat'. He set up a Royal Commission on Decentralisation in 1907, which reported in February 1909. Morley thought Gokhale would do well 'to insist on quietly making terms with the bureaucracy' on the basis of order plus reforms because 'we are no more in love with bureaucracy in its stiff routine, etc, than they are'.[88]

It is perhaps necessary to re-state the fact that the reforms represented a significant move beyond Curzon's régime. A decision to brush Indian political aspirations permanently aside in favour of immutable British administrative machinery might easily have come about. But Minto thought it a mistake to ignore Congress, and found official attitudes laughably conservative.

The last point to notice about the Morley-Minto reforms is the way in which they were symptomatic of the absence of constructive optimism in the Liberal government. The reforms were administrative rather than political, and this was because Morley thought 'political reforms alone will not carry us far and therefore we ought to encourage all manner of suggestions of a non-political range and to do our best to make something of them' – such as education. To Morley the memory of Home Rule was alone 'quite enough to quench any futile ambition to play the part of constitution-monger'. He described himself as 'cool and sceptical about *political* change either in India or other places'. Indeed, he even wondered if their reform policy and 'virtuous deeds' (such as trying to diminish ill manners towards Indians) would make 'a pin of difference' to Indian objections to British rule – politically he could not see that they were doing much more than 'drawing our hands through water'. The only chance was to try to make British rulers the friends of Indian leaders, and 'to do our best to train them in habits of political responsibility'. The raj was stupendous, but artificial, cumbrous and unnatural, and surely could not last even for many years to come.[89]

Minto's successor was Hardinge, who made two intelligent and important changes. He revoked the partition of Bengal in 1912 and he moved the capital from Calcutta to Delhi. In other words, he offered the bhadralok reunion in return for loss of their channel to the central government, and he conciliated the Muslims (who had not opposed the partition) by returning the capital to the seat of the Mughals. Hardinge was sympathetic to Indian aspirations, but obviously could make no further constitutional advance.[90]

8 Egypt and the Routes to India

The critical phase of western impact on the Ottoman Empire coincided with an advanced stage of political weakness and disintegration in Islamic society. Adaption to western ways was difficult not only for religious reasons, but for historical ones: European heritage was less highly regarded in the Middle East than elsewhere, partly because as late as 1683 military strength had carried the Turks to the gates of Vienna. Western innovations were stigmatised by fanatical Muslims as apostacy. Changes were often superficial and impermanent, but the destruction of old social bonds and obligations occurring in the nineteenth century was final. Powerful forces truculently opposed modernisation for much of the period, yet there were many Arab intellectuals, especially in Egypt, before 1870 who implicitly acknowledged the superiority of the West in all but religion. After 1870 there was a decidedly hostile reaction against the West as the involvement of Europe in the region grew.

Turkey proper never fell under European rule, but most of her peripheral provinces did; Egypt was occupied by Britain in 1882, and became a formal protectorate in 1914. During the nineteenth century the Ottoman rulers and the British had a common enemy: Russia. Both sides therefore looked to help from the other in containing the Russian menace.

The Victorian world picture, viewing things bifocally from Britain and India, 'tended to look on the Middle East not as a single region but as a desert with two edges, one belonging to the Mediterranean and the other to the Indian Ocean'. It was of interest not so much in its own right but as the area through which the short routes to India passed. Victorians had no admiration for Islamic society. Cobden regarded it as gripped in 'poverty, slavery, polygamy and the plague'.[1] But however unsatisfactory the dilapidated governments of Turkish Arabia, and, further afield, Persia and Afghanistan, Britain propped them up and maintained the integrity of the Ottoman empire, all in the interests of having a chain of buffer states through a whole wide zone. Partition was not thought to be the solution, particularly after the 1857 Mutiny-Rebellion in India discouraged further attempts at ruling 'orientals'.

It was hoped that Egypt and Turkey might be regenerated under friendly rulers, but this never really happened. It is quite clear that Palmerston's interest in the Ottoman Empire was not primarily commercial. He wanted to regenerate this 'rotten empire' in order to make it perform a strategic and political function; any trading advantages obtained for Britain were incidental.[2]

Before pursuing this theme, it is however worth noting that economic advantages were obtained, and that modernising programmes which did not fit British presuppositions were discouraged. The region was not regarded as a good potential market for British manufactures, but it could usefully export primary products, notably wheat and cotton. The attempt of Muhammad Ali's government of Egypt to diversify the economy was hampered. Even Cobden in 1836 despised Muhammad Ali's attempt to turn Cairo into a second Manchester in order to meet the needs of his huge army. He regarded him as a rapacious tyrant. He inspected the cotton factories and found them 'altogether presenting a waste of capital and industry unparalleled in any other part of the world'. The factories were dilapidated, and in one mill he found that because of engine failure power looms were turned into hand looms. He wrote bitterly:

> All this waste is going on with the best raw cotton, which ought to be sold with [sic] us . . . This is not all the mischief, for the very hands that are driven into these manufactures are torn from the cultivation of the soil, which is turned into desert for want of cultivation, whilst it might be the most fertile in the world.

Cobden was none too pleased by the pyramids either. He felt vexed at the enormous effort 'wasted' in piling six million tons of stone 'in a useless form', a quantity which was three times as much as in the Plymouth breakwater.[3] Muhammad Ali was probably using about 32 per cent of his cotton output in his own factories, 30 in number, and employing some 30,000 workers in the late 1820s. Perhaps 50 per cent of the raw cotton was wasted in the factories through ignorance or carelessness, and the spun article was of inferior quality. Cotton was not the only manufacture introduced. The British had no desire to see the success of this attempt to diversify the Egyptian economy. In 1838 Sir John Bowring was sent out to investigate the commercial possibilities of Egypt. His report (1840) strongly disapproved of the attempt to introduce a European-style factory system, an experiment as costly as it was unsuccessful. This was not, however, the view of a French investigator, A. Colin, but it confirmed Palmerston in his rejection of Jeremy Bentham's view of Muhammad Ali as the Peter the Great of the Muslim world. Palmerston agreed with Lord Ponsonby that Egypt had undergone only 'a spurious regeneration'. By 1849 Muhammad Ali's factories were mostly closed. There were no doubt good internal reasons for this collapse, but

British policy contributed to it.[4]

By the Convention of Balta Liman (1838) arranged between Britain and Turkey, Palmerston forced Muhammad Ali to abolish state monopolies which were basic to his economy; his right to additional duties on imports and exports (an important source of revenue) was restricted, by establishing a low external tariff of 8 per cent. It hastened his economic failure. The treaty of Balta Liman was widely recognised as a British triumph. The immediate gain in trade after it was considerable. Monopolies had to be abolished and duties restricted in Turkey also; the prohibition on the export of certain items was fully abolished; uniform and lower tariff rates were confirmed. All this helped to stimulate British trade. In 1842 only 250 British ships passed the Dardanelles; in 1852, 1,714. The grain exports of Turkey were negligible in 1838, but equal to Russia's by 1851. From total exports of about £3 million in 1838, a peak of £11 million was reached in 1848. In 1849 Palmerston said

If in a political point of view the independence of Turkey is of great importance, in a commercial sense it is of no less importance to this country. It is quite true that with no country is our trade so liberally permitted and carried on as with Turkey.[5]

This however was essentially a by-product of his original concern over Turkey, which was political: commercial considerations had only a marginal effect on British policy.

Palmerston wanted to make the Ottoman empire function as a barrier to Russian or French encroachment across British routes to India, hence his primary practical concern was to obtain reforms in the organisation of the army, navy and defence. Muhammad Ali was becoming too strong in Egypt with an army of 100,000 by the 1830s. He must not be allowed to begin the dismemberment of the Turkish empire by becoming independent, especially as he was considered to be a protégé of the French. Aden was acquired in 1839 to exclude Muhammad Ali from further penetration of the Red Sea. It was part of Palmun's attempt to check his expansionist tendencies. In the Turco-Egyptian war 1839-41 the Sultan was defeated. The French secretly backed Muhammad Ali. Palmerston determined to expel Muhammad Ali from Syria, and his policy triumphed in the Convention of London in 1841. Hopes of a French Arabian protectorate were smashed. Palmerston observed that Turkey was as good an occupier of the road to India as an active Arab sovereign would be. If Muhammad Ali had been allowed to hold Syria he would have dominated both possible Middle East routes to India, the overland Suez route as well as the Euphrates-Persian Gulf route. Muhammad Ali's army was reduced by Ottoman government order to 18,000.[6]

The British decision to uphold Turkey seems to have been largely dictated by general considerations of European peace and 'balance of power' and partly by security for the routes to India. Turkey thus became a pivot for the advance defences of India. France had to be kept out at all costs. 'The mistress of India', declared Palmerston, 'cannot permit France to be mistress directly or indirectly of the road to her Indian dominions'. Palmerston was worried also by growing Russian interest in Turkey after 1833.[7]

How did Palmerston propose to prop up Turkey? It had to be done by developing its internal resources. Palmerston laid down his programme for 'the regeneration of a rotten empire' in 1833:

> Our great aim should be to try to place the Porte in a state of internal organisation compatible with independence, and to urge the government to recruit their army and their finances and to put their navy into some order . . . If instead of granting out monopolies which ruin commerce, they would allow people to trade freely and levy moderate duties on commerce, they would find their revenue greatly improved . . .

If the Sultan could organise his army, navy and finances and get them into good order, 'he may still hold his ground'.[8] In 1837 he said the only way to strengthen Turkey was 'to spare no pains to improve the internal organisation of the provinces, to encourage productive industry and to protect commerce'. The increased revenues would be used for 'paying and organising an efficient army and navy', and for repairing and extending defensive fortifications by sea and land. Economic improvements were directed to this political end rather than to opening up a market for British manufacturers.[9] Lord Aberdeen in 1842 instructed Stratford Canning as ambassador to 'impart stability to the Sultan's government by promoting judicious and well-considered reforms', especially in the army. Britain would also have liked to see administration and the police improved, public officers chosen with more care, Christians treated with humanity, communications improved to develop trade and resources, and the chief cause of provincial discontent removed by a better system of collecting taxes.[10] The encouragement of commercial and financial reform as a basis for political stability remained one of the most important objectives of British policy from 1832. As in India, the British diagnosticians saw religion as the chief obstacle. Stratford Canning considered that 'the great mischief of this country is the dominant religion. This is the real "Leviathan" which "floating many a rood" overlaps the prostrate energies of this country'. It was up to the British, he thought, 'from without to keep up a steady animating pressure on the government'.[11]

The crucial phase of attempted internal reorganisation and westernisation in the mid-nineteenth century, from 1839 to 1876, is known as the Tanzimat, a word derived from a root meaning 'order' and implying reform. The 1876 Turkish constitution was the culmination of this period of reform, and it proclaimed self-preservation in its first article. Military strength was essential to meet the challenge of European powers, but attention was also given to reducing administrative abuses, and adapting western ideas of economic and political reform. The Turks did not shirk the tasks of preparing for the ultimate secularisation of government and the gradual development of administrative institutions reflecting the concepts of equality of all Ottoman subjects and the representative principle. Forced labour, usury, tax-farming were abolished as part of the 1839 Tanzimat reforms; a council for legislative activities was established with a guarantee of freedom of debate. Special secular schools for civil servants were provided. The changes made cannot be accounted for solely in terms of European pressure – indeed, some of that interference actually hampered reform. By 1876 there was a real improvement in administration and justice was more efficient. The tone of public life had changed perceptibly. Given the obstacles, the achievement was considerable; but the reforms failed to satisfy Britain. They also produced xenophobic reactions promoted by cosmopolitan Turks, mostly army officers, and a revulsion on a pan-Islamic scale.[12]

THE ROUTES TO INDIA AND THE SUEZ CANAL

Before the opening of the Suez Canal in 1869 there were alternative overland routes to India: one via the north Syrian desert, the Euphrates Valley and Persian Gulf, and the other via Alexandria, the town of Suez and the Red Sea.

The first British aim in the Middle East was to prevent Russian influence entering the Mediterranean, and if possible to avoid Russian control over the Black Sea Straits. The second was to keep French influence out of Egypt and away from the more southern of the two overland routes to India. Dundas in 1799 as minister of war wrote: 'The possession of Egypt by any independent power would be a fatal circumstance to the interests of this country'. The Persian Gulf eventually succumbed to an expansion of British influence from India dictated in part by the need to protect British trade against the piracy to which the sailors of the Gulf had gradually turned when Arab naval supremacy in the Indian Ocean was broken. Britain entered into treaty obligations to protect the shaikhs of the Aden protectorate and of Kuwait (1899, 1914), Bahrein (1861, 1892), Qatar (1916), and the Trucial coast (1916). Special treaty relations were made with the Sultan of Muscat and Oman (1891). The common aim behind them was to try to prevent the Arabs ceding their territory to anyone but Britain without British permission, partly in order to preserve the internal peace and safety of land communications in the Aden hinterland.[13]

The strategy for the defence of India was rather to guard the approaches than to fortify the country itself. The French very well understood Britain's desire to keep them out from Egypt. Muhammad Ali had always studiously upheld this British interest: 'this is your highway to India and I shall always promote it'.[14] However in 1854, the Frenchman Ferdinand de Lesseps obtained a concession for cutting the Suez Canal. Lord Clarendon in 1855

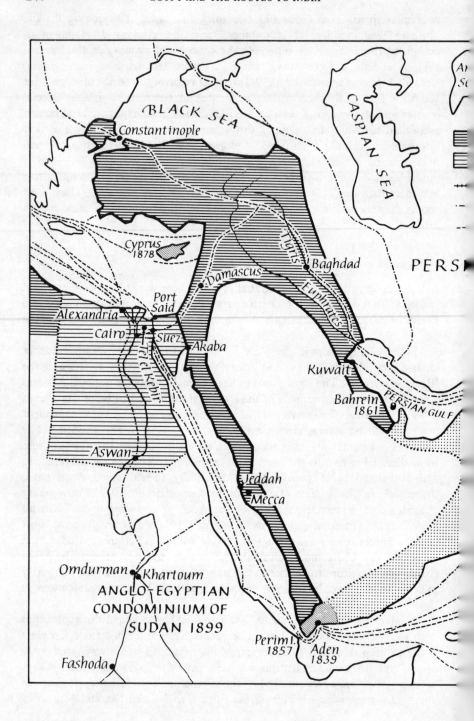

BLACK SEA

Constantinople

CASPIAN SEA

Cyprus
1878

Damascus

Baghdad

PERSI

Tigris

Euphrates

Port
Said

Alexandria

Cairo

Suez

Akaba

Tel el Kebir

Kuwait

Bahrein
1861

PERSIAN GULF

Aswan

Jeddah

Mecca

Omdurman   Khartoum

ANGLO-EGYPTIAN
CONDOMINIUM OF
SUDAN 1899

Perim I.
1857

Aden
1839

Fashoda

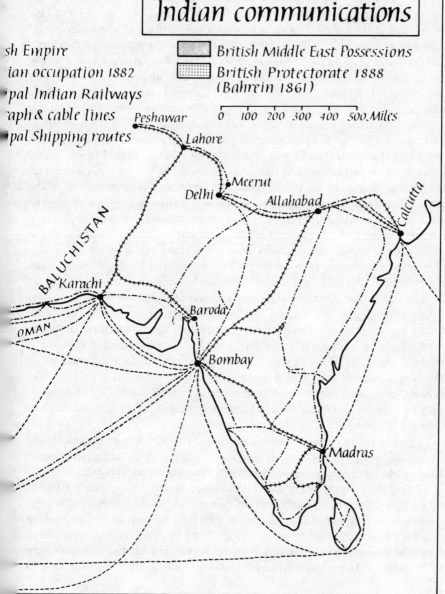

The Middle East and Indian communications

sh Empire
ian occupation 1882
pal Indian Railways
aph & cable lines
pal Shipping routes

British Middle East Possessions

British Protectorate 1888
(Bahrein 1861)

0   100 200 300 400 500 Miles

Peshawar
Lahore
Meerut
Delhi
Allahabad
Calcutta
BALUCHISTAN
Karachi
Baroda
OMAN
Bombay
Madras

said the British government was convinced that a canal would not facilitate intercourse between Britain and Asia, or give advantage to Egypt. Britain had command of the Cape route, her position in India was secure, and other powers could offer no serious competition in eastern trade. With a Suez canal she feared all this would end. The Clarendon despatch of 1855 laid stress on the way in which a canal would interfere with, and perhaps prevent, the completion of the Cairo-Suez railway, which gave Britain all she wanted from Egypt as a thoroughfare. Palmerston spoke vehemently against the canal at a cabinet meeting in August 1855. He feared that while 'giving passage to the navigation of all countries', a canal would 'take away the advantage we possess at the present time'. He tried to dismiss it as a visionary 'bubble scheme'. His objection was based on long-term political and strategic interests. As things stood, with the isthmus closed, there was an excellent natural bulwark for the protection of India and the containment of French influence. In a Franco-British war, it was feared that France would immediately seize both ends of the canal. 'It would in fact be a suicidal act on the part of England', said Clarendon, 'to assent to the construction of the canal'. British opposition checked de Lesseps's first attempt to obtain the sanction of the Sultan. The real objection to the canal was to its being a French scheme menacing British communications to India. Palmerston saw it as a French naval, rather than as an international commercial, route. Clarendon described it as 'essentially a French idea and a political rather than a commercial idea'. Russell said it made de Lesseps 'the veritable pasha of Egypt'. But British commercial men had always favoured the canal.[15]

Upon completion of the canal in 1869* the Cape route to India was by no means discarded. Very much more commerce in the 1870s used the Cape route than the Suez canal. The latter at first was exceedingly narrow, of doubtful depth and costly to use; it did not commend itself instantly to all shipping concerns; and it was unsuited to sailing ships as well as to the heaviest ironclads. But the overland route *did* vanish; it could not compete with the canal as a commercial artery, because bulky articles could not endure the necessity of two trans-shipments en route.[16]

The main factors bringing a closer concern with Egypt were the opening of the Suez canal, the decline of Turkish effectiveness as a barrier against Russia, and increasing misgovernment and financial chaos in Egypt.

The policy of regenerating Turkey had failed by 1876. Owing to the decline of Turkish power, a strengthening of routes was planned, involving a large scheme for military consuls in Armenia, who were to keep an eye on Russian military movements in frontier regions, and if necessary to organise a Christian militia if Russia came any nearer to the Mediterranean. Forces were to be supplied from Cyprus, which was accordingly obtained as a base in

---

* Verdi twice refused to compose an opera for the inaugural ceremonies. *Rigoletto* was performed, not *Aïda*, which received its première at Cairo only in 1871.

1878. Although the Ottoman empire seemed much less reasonable and secure as a bastion than hitherto, it was still thought not to be entirely hopeless. To make sure of Mesopotamia was still the main line of defence, as it had been in the days of Palmerston. Disraeli in 1876 called it 'moonshine' to think in terms of occupying Egypt; the canal must be defended against Russia in Armenia and Syria, and not on the line of the canal itself. Britain could, he supposed, occupy the canal whenever she wished in wartime because of her naval power. By 1877 Salisbury concluded that it was no longer practicable to defend British interests by sustaining the Ottoman empire. A bankrupt Turkey was incapable of insulating Anglo-Russian hostility. The time had come for a more direct defence 'by some territorial rearrangement'.[17]

Cyprus was taken as part of the revised strategy for defence of the routes to India. A base was required partly from which to watch the mouth of the Dardanelles, and to re-invigorate Asia Minor against a possible Russian advance. Only Cyprus seemed to combine the requisite characteristics of suitable location, size, population, defensibility, commercial prospects, with inoffensiveness (as a British possession) to other European powers. In order not to alienate France, Cyprus was annexed instead of Egypt, and in so far as there was any bargain, France got a much better position – in Tunis.[18]

Disraeli's acquisition of 17.7/40ths of the Suez canal shares in 1875 was made largely to prevent France establishing an exclusive control. The most perceptive comment was not Disraeli's to Queen Victoria ('You have it, ma'am') but the *Times's:* 'We have now an abiding stake in the security and welfare of Egypt'.[19]

Britain had been content with Egypt as it was, while a substantial land barrier existed between the Mediterranean and the eastern seas, but once that physical barrier was pierced by the canal (at the same time as Turkey was being subjected to increasing Russian pressure), British policy was forced to come to terms with the new importance of Egypt in her calculations.

European interests became deeply entrenched. Between 1838 and 1881 the number of resident Europeans increased from under 10,000 to more than 90,000. They organised cotton exports, banking, irrigation, acquired land and improved communications. Long-staple cotton was introduced as a cash crop only in 1820. The American Civil War provided a major stimulus to the export of Egyptian cotton. The value of the cotton export rose from £E1,430,880 in 1861 to £E11,424,000 in 1866. In the mid-1860s the area under cotton cultivation increased five times. Those who grew and sold cotton wanted to keep its profits to themselves, and so no other sectors of the economy developed. Levantine and European merchants directed this growth, but through the capitulations system they were extraneous to society, and their success did not lead on to reforming or remoulding the political régime. The capitulations enabled foreigners and their local collaborators or protégés to carry on their business outside the country's territorial jurisdiction; they thus established foreign enclaves diverting the loyalty of Ottoman subjects most active in economic activities. The system was not abolished until 1914. Unlike Meiji Japan, Ismail's Egypt could not interpose a barrier between its own economy and Europe. European money was drawn in by supposedly fabulous rates of interest (12 to 20 per cent on best security). The great contract and concession hunt of the mid-century, the 'rape of the Egyptian treasury', led by businessmen like Dervieu, depended of course on khedival acquiescence, whether this was given from gullibility, greed, improvidence or inordinate ambition. The National Debt increased from £3,300,000 in 1863 to £91,000,000 in 1876. By this time it could only mean one thing: bankruptcy. The loss of economic independence preceded the loss of political independence. 'The origin of the Egyptian question in its present phase was financial': thus wrote Lord Cromer in a famous sentence.[20] It was change and crisis in the local situation which brought about the British occupation.

An Anglo-French Dual Control was set up with the intention of making Egypt solvent again and strengthening the khedivate. Not wishing either to seize Egypt territorially for themselves in 1876, or to let the French place themselves across the road to India, the British, as Salisbury put it, 'resolved to share' the problem with France.[21] They hoped to regulate the situation from outside without an occupation. These plans were upset by a revolt in Egypt and a new government in France more interested in European than Egyptian problems.

In 1881 an Egyptian army officer, Urabi Pasha, led an army revolt, or at least asserted his freedom of action agianst the Khedive and the Dual Control, hoping to redress army grievances. The Khedive then also stood out himself against the Dual Control. Urabi's movement is best seen as a strong but vague coalition of different groups, all in some way affected by the financial régime imposed on Egypt by her European creditors after the declaration of bankruptcy in 1876. It included landowners fearing taxation, bureaucrats displaced by Europeans, army officers threatened with economies, and the *ulema* (the 'ecclesiastical institution', the learned 'men of the pen'). The revolt stemmed from the fact that a new Egyptian bureaucracy, new landowners, and new army officers wished to replace in power and influence an older Turco-Egyptian élite. The educated Egyptians in general resented the outsiders, and the peasants had grievances (as peasants always do); they rebelled against oppression and injustice and not consciously for abstractions such as liberty, freedom or 'national emancipation' – any sympathy with the masses was purely incidental. The revolt originated with personal disaffection and ambition among certain army officers. However, despite their solidarity, these men lacked the necessary qualities of leadership to succeed. It was an undisciplined movement with no specific programme, or at least one unequal to the forces the movement aroused. Urabi, it has been said, was chief of a military junta and a peasant leader, 'but neither of them thoroughly', and when things became difficult, he retreated into the traditional solaces of the old religious fraternities; he was ill-acquainted with western thought.[22]

Kimberley declared in 1885: 'Does anyone really suppose that if we did not possess our Indian Empire we should have interfered in Egypt?' In positively Palmerstonian language, Gladstone told parliament that 'for India the Suez Canal is the connecting link between herself and the centre of power – the centre of the moral, social and political power of the world'.[23] He defined the canal as 'the great question of British interest'. About 80 per cent of shipping passing through the canal was British in 1882, and 13 per cent of Britain's entire foreign trade went through it. Gladstone at first recognised the nationalist element in the Urabi movement:

I am not by any means pained, but I am much surprised at the rapid development of a national sentiment and party in Egypt . . . it seems to claim the respect due to it as a fact and due also to the capabilities that may be latent in it for the future. 'Egypt for the Egyptians' is the sentiment to which I would wish to give scope; and could it prevail, it would I think be the best, the only good solution of the 'Egyptian question' . . .

But the Foreign Office could see in Urabi a mere military dictator, while France wished to break the national movement and restore the Control. Egyptian national aspirations were not to be reconciled with continuing the full international financial control which the French demanded. As a result Gladstone's ideal solution of conciliating the Urabists became impracticable because of the priority given to concord with France and the Concert of Europe. Hence the Liberals joined with the French in an attempt to break the Urabi movement by external pressure and especially by a naval demonstration.[24]

Alexandria was bombarded after 50 Europeans there had been massacred. Gladstone's justification was that every legitimate authority had disappeared in Egypt, and 'a situation of force had been created which could only be met by force'. A thousand people died in the bombardment, and the admiral in charge was made a peer. Egyptian resentment was so deep that it was still alive in the 1950s. It created that very danger to the canal which it had been designed to prevent. Urabi's readiness to comtemplate interfering with its operation was regarded as wicked. Gladstone admitted that the insecurity of the canal was merely a symptom of Egyptian anarchy.[25] The confusion of his policy was complicated by his troubles in Ireland and South Africa; and also by a change of government in France, which brought to power a ministry preferring to concentrate its energies on revanche against Germany.

The Egyptian army was finally defeated by the British expeditionary force under Sir Garnet Wolseley on 13 September 1882 at Tel el Kebir. Urabi was imprisoned. The British drew up a timetable for withdrawal, scarcely realising that in fact they were now 'an Egyptian power'. Between 1882 and 1922 the British government repeated on no less than 66 occasions its intention soon to withdraw from Egypt.[26]

The khedivate was discredited, the Dual Control had collapsed, Urabi had been defeated. Lord Cromer was sent out as British government agent and consul-general in 1883. After the collapse of Egyptian military power in the Sudan, when Col. W. Hicks's 10,000-strong expeditionary force was annihiliated by the Mahdist forces, Cromer concluded that British presence in Egypt was essential to rescue it from chaos. Gordon was sent to rationalise the position in the Sudan, but he behaved irrationally and was cut off in Khartoum by the Mahdi and lost his life there. Only in 1896 was it decided to re-conquer the northern Sudan and re-establish law and order in the face of the rising strength of the Mahdist state. The British aim was to stiffen the resistance of the anti-Mahdist groups; the timing was determined by Italian difficulties in Ethiopia and Eritrea after their defeat at Aduwa, since it was felt that the complete withdrawal of the Italians from the area would only enhance British difficulties. A diversion in favour of Italy would be created by the advance south from Wadi Halfa, drawing the dervishes away from Kassala on the Ethiopian border. After the successful reconquest of the Sudan, Kitchener and Wingate from 1898 allied the administration with the anti-Mahdist groups. In 1899 an Anglo-Egyptian condominium was set up, under which, in effect, Egypt supplied the money while Britain determined policy and ran the administration with an élite corps of specially recruited officials.[27]

EGYPT UNDER CROMER 1883-1907

Because of Egypt's strategic position, British rule was a vast holding operation, with at first many branches of government unregulated. Attention was concentrated initially on finance and public works; dominant influence over justice and the interior was not acquired until 1892. Britain wanted above all to keep the Egyptian population quiet, and saw the need to cultivate some mass popularity by raising living standards through a controlled and limited modernisation.

The Egyptian army was disbanded after 1882; the new one was officered by the British. Partly as a result of the British occupation a new group – the urban rich – rapidly became the chief class of landowners from the 1880s. During the last three decades of the century the production of long-staple cotton became the dominant Egyptian economic activity, so that by 1914 it was responsible for 93 per cent of all Egypt's export earnings. Cotton acted as the spur to related agricultural improvements and public works. It was the reason why Egypt attracted heavy investment and acquired a higher ratio of length of railway track to inhabited area than any country in the world. But unlike the Meiji government in Japan, the British government did not create an atmosphere in which economic advance was accepted as natural and desirable. By 1914 there was little development in any part of the economy outside the cotton sector. The traditional sectors remained unresponsive to change. Cotton raised income, attracted foreign capital and greatly expanded trade, but it did not lead to the development of a genuinely modern economy. There was no attempt to diversify the economy. The British impact was really only to strengthen the trend towards developing irrigation, cash-cropping and a rationalised bureaucracy.

Reform and reconstruction of the administration and the cotton economy was enough to produce a rapid ferment of ideas. The Egyptians undertook a severe reappraisal of their society, their thinking being characterised by an Islamic preoccupation with religious and educational reform, and only gradually becoming more secular in outlook. The religious reform movement which gathered momentum between 1882 and 1906 was not really concerned with the creation of an Egyptian national state; the original impulses came from a wider Muslim reaction to European world expansion. The main impetus to secular political movements was not so much the political changes after 1906 but the material prosperity and progress. Three parties were formed in 1907: Hizb al-Umma (a moderate People's Party), Al-hizb al-watani (an extreme National Party led by Mustafa Kamil) and Hizb al-islah al dusturi (a khedival Constitutional Reform Party led by Shaikh Ali Yusuf). As in India the leadership often came from frustrated civil servants – Mustafa Kamil never got in, Muhammad Farid found his promotion delayed and got out. The system had little place for the newly emerging classes, especially at the administrative apex.

The British occupation brought real benefits to the fallahin, though these were probably not as great as Cromer imagined, nor as Milner stated in his book *England and Egypt* (1892), one of the most successful pieces of propaganda for British claims of beneficence ever produced.[28]

Cromer ('Over-Baring') was a prominent member of the Baring family famous for its financial and banking undertakings. Of all the major proconsular figures of the late nineteenth century, he was probably the cleverest. He was perhaps representative alike of all that was best and worst in these proconsuls, a symbol of their virtues and defects. The patrician pose and pompous oratory were accompanied by commercial obsession and counting-house meanness, the professed magnanimity by practised pettiness, the Olympian project by trivial errors, the attention to detail by neglect of basic trends, a sense of the broad sweep of world history by adherence to the narrow Victorian codes of an officer and a gentleman.

Cromer felt little sympathy for Egypt, but had a rigid belief in his duty to ensure the moral and material elevation of his subjects. However, his zeal for this tapered off with the years, and he became less accessible. It seems that Cromer was a classic case of a man's being corrupted by power, and the change has even been dated precisely to 1893. Thereafter he used all his ability to discredit the national movement. Cromer's policies and standards of conduct in his last years certainly deteriorated.[29] Overall, his 24 years were a time of impressive *administrative* achievement. His methods provided just the required financial antidote to the khedival spending sprees. Cromer, assisted by Milner in the finance ministry (1890-92), made Egypt solvent by 1891 and then prosperous. There were important scientific improvements in irrigation, leading to an increased population, increases in the cultivated areas, and a trebling of the cotton yield and sugar production in ten years. The incidence of taxation was lowered. *Kurbaj* for flogging and the corvée system of forced labour (twin instruments of oppression) were abolished. British administration started off by confining its activities to giving advice but ended by appointing British executives too. The foreign superstructure was strengthened. In 1885 about a hundred senior civil officials in the Egyptian government service were British. By 1906 they numbered more than a thousand. The resentment created more than offset the additional efficiency. Although he unduly neglected industry and higher education, Cromer made fewer mistakes and achieved more solid results than any other British administrator of his generation.

Cromer's views on the Egyptian national movement, and how to deal with it, became immensely influential in determining the approach of British statesmen in the twentieth century to other national protests. Cromer enjoyed unusual prestige. His responsibility for Egyptian affairs was more than 20 years long, and in the ten years between his retirement and his death in 1917 his advice as an elder statesman was sometimes directly called upon. His own view of the Egyptian case was largely coloured by his previous experience in India, as private secretary to the viceroy (1872–76) and finance member of the viceroy's council (1880–83). Thus it would appear that Cromer's Egypt was the medium of transmission to Africa of Indian experience and disillusionment. Indian experience was deeply ingrained in Cromer as in many of his subordinates. In the first decade, almost the entire staff of the irrigation department, led by Colin Scott-Moncrieff, were Indian trained. A large proportion of the financial experts also came from India. But more than this – the very principles of government were 'Indian' ones: the attempt to preserve and protect the cultivators as a conservative and stable influence, the belief in low taxation, the importance of public works in giving an impression of government power and beneficence. In 1900 Cromer instituted a system of post office savings banks on lines of the Indian system he had started in 1882. His failure to establish an agricultural department was in the unfortunate Indian government tradition of trying to match enormous needs with totally inadequate resources. He understood the essentially different position and purpose of Britain in Egypt, but was not sufficiently flexible to break out of his Indian mould.[30]

Basically Cromer denied the validity of the Egyptian national movement. An Egyptian 'nationalist' he contemptuously defined as 'a demoslemised Moslem and an invertebrate European'. 'The fact is', he wrote, 'that the Egyptians are not a nation, and never can be a nation. They are a fortuitous concourse of international atoms'. There were Muslims, Copts, Syrians,

Levantines and Europeans, who had more or less become Egyptianised. He was prepared to try to fuse these groups together and 'to move somewhat in the direction of making a nation of them'. But it was he thought absurd to suppose that this ideal could be realised in the lifetime of one man. Change could only be slow. A country which had for centuries been exposed to what he described as 'the worst forms of misgovernment at the hands of its rulers, from Pharoahs to Pashas', and in which at the end of the nineteenth century not even ten per cent of the men could write, could not be capable of 'suddenly springing into a position which will enable it to exercise full rights of autonomy'.[31] In any case, it was difficult for Cromer to see why there ought to be any change, since the masses were apparently content with paternalistic British rule. He experienced friendliness from all quarters except the 'small clique of ultra-nationalists headed by the Khedive'. He believed that the Khedive was personally 'the head and fount' of all the trouble.[32] Cromer in fact seems to have consistently over-estimated the power of the Khedive. Refusing to believe that the movement had any real support, Cromer attributed all opposition to the Khedive and thought the Khedive could have stopped it if he chose. (This seems to be the reason why Cromer's successor Sir J. Eldon Gorst set out to kill the movement partly by kindness to the Khedive. It did not succeed).[33] Believing then that the nationalist movement was the work of an unrepresentative minority of self-seeking agitators, Cromer urged that 'this wholly spurious and manufactured movement in favour of a rapid development of parliamentary institutions should be treated for what it is worth; and let me add that it is worth very little'. It did not in his belief really represent the voice of 'the intelligent dwellers in Egypt, whether European or Egyptian'. In such circumstances, the British duty was mainly to act as umpire or arbiter between contending groups, so as 'to benefit the voiceless masses'. Claiming to be the 'true friend' of the fallahin, he warned them against allowing themselves to be duped and misled 'by their pseudo-representatives, who, without a shadow of real authority, credit them with ideas which they neither entertain nor fully comprehend'.[34] Cromer believed that the only link between the governors and the governed was material interest. To ensure material prosperity and contentment was the only real good that could be done. An aggressive reforming policy would only result in undermining further the foundations on which the whole fabric of society rested. To do too much might lose the trust of the conservative masses. Thus, he concluded, 'there may be even worse evils than the continuance for a while of insanitary conditions and ignorance or illiteracy'. His unwillingness to support a more active reform policy was determined to a considerable extent by his belief that the East *could* not be reformed: 'it will probably never be possible to make a Western purse out of an Eastern sow's ear'; ignorance was too widespread, despotism too ingrained, Muslim religious influence too crushing and reactionary for reform ever to have any chance of success. Why then disrupt society futilely?[35]

This paternalistic approach inescapably led to the conclusion that Egyptians were hopelessly incompetent. He could not see that they were much better than the peoples of Afghanistan. To give power to the nationalists was, he wrote, 'only a little less absurd than the nomination of some savage Red Indian chief to be Governor-general of Canada'.[36] At any rate, so long as the British occupation lasted, to suppose that they could 'leave these extremely incompetent Egyptians to do what they like about local affairs' was in Cromer's opinion completely impossible and 'little short of madness'. Personal rule seemed the only possible method: the materials for any alternative he regarded as so unpromising that no rapid change could be made. In his considered opinion:

> To suppose that the characters and intellects of even a small number of Egyptians can in a few years be trained to such an extent as to admit of their undertaking the sole direction of one of the most complicated political and administrative machines which the world has ever known, and of guiding such a machine along the path of even fairly good government, is a sheer absurdity.[37]

One difficulty about Egyptians was their supposed untruthfulness, but Cromer generously admitted that when it came to good solid lying the untruthful Oriental was not in the same class as the Irishman: 'the latter beats him hollow'. Another obstacle was the sheer extensiveness of Egyptian demands.[38]

Cromer justified his denial of parliamentary institutions to the Egyptians by using the convenient, but to him no doubt real, argument that Britain had formerly been over-inclined to think that what suited Britain must necessarily be good for others too. This he decided was a 'very mistaken theory'. They should work with facts as they found them. And in Egypt the facts were distinctly un-British. He believed that it would take not years, but probably generations, to change the character of the Egyptian people.[39]

Much in Cromer's analysis was one-sided and distorted, but some of it had a kind of awful plausibility, and it cannot be dismissed out of hand. He was right about the pan-Islamic orientation, but wrong in underestimating the potential for change within it. He saw the real barriers which existed between social groups, but refused to recognise that a political movement could be a unifying force between them.

When he retired in 1907 his message to the imperial rulers was this: they should be sympathetic towards those who asked for 'moderate and reasonable and gradual extension of self-government'. But as to the 'extremists who exist in Cairo, as also in Calcutta and in Dublin':

> With these gentlemen I do not think it is possible to deal. They will not be conciliated save on terms which in India and Ireland spell political suicide

and in Egypt would involve a relapse into all the misgovernment and disorder of the past. .... I see but one method of dealing with this unrest and disturbance in Egypt and in India. It is to continue steadily to do our duty towards the people of those two countries, and to come down with a heavy hand upon extremists should they overstep the limits of the law. [40]

CHANGES IN EGYPTIAN ADMINISTRATION 1906–14 [41]

In striking contrast to their disapproval of Milner in South Africa and of Curzon in India, the incoming Liberal government of 1905 approved of Cromer and, broadly, his Egyptian policy. The prime minister, Campbell-Bannerman, praised him highly in 1907, in particular for his realisation that the 'regeneration of Egypt could only be effected through the Egyptians themselves' and that 'capitalists ready to develop Egypt on the lines of European finance' were undesirables to be kept out. [42] Liberal ministers had no higher opinion of Egyptian capacity than Cromer himself had. Lord Bryce had travelled in Egypt in 1888 and formed a poor opinion of the Egyptian: he seemed 'an exceptionally dull, plodding, uninventive person'. Winston Churchill did not think they could 'treat "Egypt" as a separate responsible power, whose view about her own interests may for good or ill be accepted as final'. Sir Edward Grey accepted Cromer's advice that it was important to dissociate the government from the opinion of some of their radical followers that a rapid advance towards Egyptian autonomy could safely be effected. In parliamentary declarations on 1 August 1907 and 31 January 1908 Grey denied that Britain could teach any nation in the world within a generation 'those acts of self-government which it has taken us several centuries to learn'. Premature establishment of self-government would not benefit the ordinary people, but only put back in power the 'arbitrary classes' with their régime of corruption, oppression and injustice. They must not forget that the old government of Egypt had crushed every quality in a people which was most essential to the exercise of self-government. The art of government was one of the things which took longest to teach, if indeed it could be taught at all. [43]

Towards the end of his administration, Cromer was prepared to make a small new departure by appointing Saad Zaghlul as minister of public instruction. Cromer was at this stage fully aware of the desirability of making Egyptians a real working factor in the higher administration, though the number of those who could 'with safety to the true public interest, be invited to occupy positions of this nature is very limited'. There were, however, a few men whom he accepted as suitable for such promotion, those whose nationalist objectives were not fixed upon the impossible ideal of regeneration on retrograde pan-Islamic rather than western lines. [44]

Sir J. Eldon Gorst succeeded Cromer in May 1907. Gorst was brilliant and strong, 'fiercely capable and achingly ambitious', and endowed with daunting energy. Officially at any rate, no general instructions on policy were ever announced, but it was widely believed that he had been selected in order to introduce a new spirit and practice into Egypt, and that he had a strong if vague brief.[45] The archives reveal that a deliberate policy was indeed arranged with Gorst when he went out; he was to make further steps in the direction of governing through Egyptians, building up from below on the basis of the existing governmental institutions.[46] Grey took 'entire responsibility' for steps taken in the next three years, 'though the policy itself is the original policy of Lord Cromer'. Grey was most concerned to establish continuity of policy between Cromer's regime and Gorst's, although the truth of the matter is that, gauging the strength of the national movement better than Cromer, he insisted on a change. He declared in parliament that Gorst went out to continue Lord Cromer's policy. Britain occupied Egypt, he added,

> in trust for the future of the country, and a part of the trust is to develop the aptitude, abilities and character of the people so as to fit them . . . to take in the course of years, their share in the government of their own country . . . But I warn the House that . . . progress must be slow.[47]

Gorst advocated working with the Egyptians gradually to improve and develop the existing Constitution laid down in 1883, 'as fast as the intellectual standard of the population merits'. But the premature introduction of representative institutions 'would inevitably result in a reaction fatal to the hopes of those who, like myself, are anxious for the day when Egyptian autonomy will be possible'.[48] The proof of fitness for further advance would be the ability to co-operate in working existing institutions.

In practice Gorst introduced five main measures preparing the Egyptians for self-government at various levels: (i) enlarged scope and powers for provincial councils (which Cromer had recommended), (ii) the appointment of a new ministry, (iii) the improvement of the conditions under which the legislative council and general assembly exercised their consultative functions, (iv) an increase in the number of Egyptians in posts of responsibility previously held by Europeans, and (v) the continued development of the educational system on national lines (i.e. increasing the amount of teaching done in Arabic by Egyptians).[49]

Gorst believed that the national movement had substance, legitimate grievances and could not be suppressed. He was not specially sympathetic to Egyptian nationalists: 'we shall only give them what is good for them'; the 'suaviter in modo' was not, he wrote, incompatible with the 'fortiter in re'.[50] In November 1908 Gorst reconstructed the ministry to obtain 'men who can be of use to us, and who can help us to keep in touch with the people of the country'. He hoped that if they could find ministers who were 'not quite such dummies as the present set', they might exercise a wholesome influence over the legislative council and the more moderate Egyptian critics. The new ministers were encouraged to attend business more frequently and to explain and defend the government measures which came before the council. This would, Gorst hoped, heighten their prestige and help to remove the impression that they existed merely in order to carry out British behests. In parliament, Grey stressed provincial councils as the first practical step and he adopted Gorst's general declaration as the expression of Liberal views.[51]

The parallels between this policy and the Morley-Minto reforms in India are obvious. Like the Indian changes, the Egyptian ones were part of a package deal of 'order plus reforms'. For Gorst, it should be recalled, introduced into Egypt the most coercive acts yet: the Press Law (1909) and the Criminals Deportation Act (1909).

Gorst encountered formidable difficulties, including the hostility of British officials. The new policy was a difficult one for his subordinates to administer: they did not all have his will-power and adaptability. The sceptical manoeuvered for a minimum of change; the earnest were over-enthusiastic. Among the Egyptians themselves, moderate nationalists were alienated. The result of trying to encourage the legislative council to exercise more responsible functions could not be shown to be very successful. Then the assassination by a Muslim fanatic in May 1910 of the new prime minister, a Coptic Christian, Butrus Pasha Ghali, precipitated a review of the whole policy being pursued. Ghali had been associated with various unpopular policies: the Dinshawai trials, the Sudan condominium, the Press Law and the Suez canal concession negotiations, and his murder came only a few weeks after the general assembly rejected the government's proposals for the renewal of the Suez canal concession in April 1910. Gorst commented, in sad and utter disillusionment at the failure of his experiment:

> From first to last the attitude of the members has been nothing more or less than an acute manifestation of Anglo-phobia, and the real hostility to the project is due to the fact that it was negotiated and prepared by the English advisers to the Egyptian government. It would be impossible to adduce a clearer proof of the present incapacity of the Egyptians for any sort of autonomy, and of the futility of expecting from them reasonable discussion or argument on important matters of public interest.
>
> I do not see that we could well have avoided trying the experiment of allowing these people to have rather more say in the conduct of their own affairs, but I am gradually coming to the conclusion that it has been a failure . . .

People still seemed to think they could achieve what they wanted by clamour. It would be a great advantage (he continued) if they could get rid of this idea once and for all, as it tended 'to unsettle the minds of the general public, and also does great harm in European financial and commercial circles'. Grey was also coming to the conclusion that they would have to do something to assert authority in Egypt. 'The action of the General Assembly, not its decision, but its manner of taking it, raises the whole question of whether we are on the wrong tack in advancing towards self-government from the top'. Grey thought the Egyptians had taken advantage of British attempts to increase their participation in the government, using them not to further good government but to agitate against the occupation. This could not be tolerated.[52]

At Grey's request, Gorst had a memorandum for the Cabinet ready by 22 May 1910. It posed the question: could the wish for self-government be met without seriously impairing the standard of administration attained under British control? It was too early to say with respect to the provincial councils, though the outlook seemed favourable. Results in the legislative council and general assembly were, however, extremely disappointing. Ministers had not been able to guide the council or build up a government party within it; the 'nationalists' violently attacked co-operation with the British. 'The conclusion is that the policy of ruling this country in co-operation with intelligent native ministers, is at the present time, incompatible with that of encouraging the development of so-called representative institutions'. In a choice between the two, Gorst recommended that the ministerial system should be preferred. There seemed to be no recognition that Britain had been actuated by a 'sincere and disinterested desire' to pave the way for the introduction of a more liberal constitution in due course. With the possible exception of the Khedive and his ministers, everybody seemed firmly convinced that this policy was a concession to clamour, and represented a diminution of British authority:

> Until therefore the lesson has been learnt that the rate of progress towards autonomy must depend upon the decision of the British and not the Egyptian people, the inevitable result of further concession could only be to provoke further agitation.
>
> In view of these considerations, I am decidedly of opinion that the time has come to cry a halt, and that to confer any real power upon the Legislative Council, so long as that body continues to maintain its present hostile attitude, would be a suicidal policy.[53]

Copies of this memorandum were sent by Grey to Cromer and to all Cabinet ministers. Grey himself agreed with the memorandum. Crewe thought it seemed 'so far as I can judge, to convey the commonsense of the situation'. Cromer commented that he had never intended the policy of gradually increasing the Egyptian share in the executive management of their own affairs to go 'at such railroad speed as has been apparently the case since my departure ... There is not the least use blinking the fact, however disagreeable it may be, that for the time being, personal rule is the only possible rule in Egypt'. The Liberal government now came to a similar conclusion. Grey admitted that they had moved too fast – a reaction was inevitable.[54]

Grey made an important announcement to the Commons on 13 June 1910, basing himself generally on Gorst's memorandum. The nationalists, he said, were a limited and not the most representative class in Egypt; they were not those who knew most about the fallahin, or who were most in touch with the Egyptians outside the towns. They incited to disorder whenever there was an opportunity.

> We are trustees in Egypt, [he continued] in the first place for the natives of Egypt themselves . . . We are also trustees – because we have no other title to remain in Egypt – of good order and public security there. We are trustees for the interests of Europe as well . . .

Then followed the declaration: 'The maintenance of good government and order in Egypt is the first object of the British government'. Authority must be asserted, and Egyptians who followed British advice must be protected from terrorisation and denunciation. There should be no misunderstanding about this. 'The British occupation must continue in Egypt, more so now than ever', because consolidation of the good work done depended on the British staying there. Finally: 'There will be no further progress in Egypt until they put an end to the agitation against the British occupation'.[55]

The attempt to extend the principles of self-government to the Egyptians, and so to redeem past promises, seemed premature, unless the British government were prepared to tolerate misgovernment, which they could not be. The blame for failure was squarely placed on the 'stupidity of the Egyptians themselves'. 'We therefore continue as before', said Gorst.[56]

Gorst died suddenly. His successor, Kitchener, was required to restore a deteriorating situation, channelling Egyptian energies into constructive non-political areas, while continuing a policy of cautious advance. He hardly fulfilled the second part of his brief. Some trifling but highly publicised concessions towards self-government were made in 1913 (when an enlarged legislative assembly was established), but did no more than induce an uncertain calm. Kitchener did not follow Gorst in demonstrating sympathy with Egyptian political aspirations, but concentrated on public works and agricultural improvement. His economic reforms, notably land drainage and reclamation, were grandiose and useful; he sought to improve agriculture and the conditions of the fallahin. Peasant loans were limited to nine per cent interest. He also tackled the neglected area of urban health.[57]

9 In Tropical Africa

With the exception of Zanzibar, the only part of tropical Africa to attract much attention from business interests before the last quarter of the nineteenth century was the western coast. Here, on account of relative accessibility and the Atlantic slave trade feeding the West Indian sugar islands, British trading interests were not only old-established but of fundamental importance to the operation of the whole Atlantic economy of the eighteenth century.[1] Sierra Leone was founded in 1787 as a humanitarian experiment, and became a home for liberated slaves after the abolition of the slave trade in 1807. After that signal event, Britain had three West African objectives: to suppress slave trading by other European powers, to promote alternative trades, and to make it play its part in ensuring the success of the new system in the West Indies. West Indian needs remained the dominant consideration, and sugar plantations were maintained. In 1843 the government assumed direct responsibility for sending recaptured Africans back from Sierra Leone, a re-emigration that West Indian governors had asked for since 1835. Between 1841 and 1867 no less than 36,000 Africans liberated at St Helena and Sierra Leone were shipped back to shore up the West Indian economy, while 100,000 Asians were drafted in. Nearly one-third of the Sierra Leone re-emigration took place in the 1840s.[2] In West Africa itself the increasing demand for slaves for Brazil and Cuba was met by the increasing strength of centralised states, notably Dahomey and Fouta Djallon, capable of supplying it.

T. F. Buxton of the Aborigines Protection Society led the campaign against the African slave trade. Palmerston supported him; the slave trade was the one subject he never joked about. Buxton was convinced that slave trade and legitimate commerce were incompatible – 'our great argument surely is: that the slave trade kills all other trade' – which was far from being self-evidently true. The idea that legitimate trade would in some mysterious way be an effectual way of stopping the slave trade was eventually seen to be clearly wrong in the 1840s and 1850s when the sale of slaves revived, but the palm-oil trade did not stop. The two were not mutually exclusive. The contention of Buxton and Palmerston failed to convince Africans because it was marked by a lack of demonstrable proof. And so there was no prolonged transition crisis because many areas were able to export slaves and legitimate products side by side for many decades.[3]

Attempts to establish legitimate trade laboured under difficulties beyond the obvious one of the unhealthiness of the west coast. The search for the right alternative staple export was not simple. In the Gold Coast region, palm oil, gold, and rubber were each in turn thought to be the effective substitute for slaves, but it was not until the 1890s that cocoa was found to be the right answer. During most of the nineteenth century there was also a considerable effort to develop raw cotton in West Africa. In 1850 the Manchester chamber of commerce induced Palmerston to send a mission to the king of Dahomey asking him to encourage the cultivation of cotton; similar attempts were also made in Liberia, Sierra Leone and Mozambique. In 1862 Palmerston said:

> I have long been of the opinion that Western Africa will provide a better and a readier source of supply for cotton than India, provided only that the slave trade can be abolished. Western Africa is much nearer than India; labour there is cheaper than in India, and cotton grows there in far more abundance than in India and European goods are much more wanted there than in India.[4]

As far as Nigeria was concerned, for most of the nineteenth century palm oil predominated. The demand for this grew in Britain because of the new fads of cleanliness and nocturnal illumination. But besides soap (in which it produced the lather) and candles, palm oil was needed for machine lubrication and in the tinplate industry. Railways needed 13,000 tons of truck grease every year by 1865. From the 1890s palm oil was also needed for margarine.[5] By 1850 Liverpool was producing 30,000 tons of soap a year – one-third of the total British output.

IMPORTS OF WEST AFRICAN PALM OIL

Year	Amount in tons
1810	1,000
1830	10,000
1842	20,000
1853	30,000
1855	40,000
1860–1900	50,000 yearly average

From a negligible quantity in 1800, British imports of palm oil were worth £1.5 million a year by the 1860s. Rather more than half came from the Oil Rivers of the Niger Delta. Palm-oil prices rose to their peak during the Crimean War; thereafter they fell steadily until the end of the century; the period of growth was at an end from the 1860s.[6] In the early decades of the nineteenth century, palm-oil exports grew very slowly; the growth in value was rapid in the 1830s; there was stagnation and disappointment in the mid 1840s and early 1850s; and a marked improvement in the mid-1850s. The position was steady at a lower level for the rest of the century – expansion was inhibited from the 1860s by competition from American petroleum, Indian ground-nuts, and Australian tallow – followed by a rapid advance in the twentieth century. Liverpool prices were £20 per ton in 1816, £42 in the late 1840s, £48 in 1854, and about £45 between 1854 and 1861; the figure was £37 between 1861 and 1865, and £20 between 1886 and 1890. Hopes of the legitimate trade were thus broadly speaking unfulfilled during the nineteenth century. West Africa was never again so important to the British economy as in the last few decades of the slave trade before 1807.[7]

The palm-oil trade had peculiar problems of its own. Transport problems prevented much of the hinterland oil from reaching the delta. Europeans had to stay much longer on the coast, because it took much longer ($5\frac{1}{4}$ months instead of 3) to collect a cargo of palm oil than of slaves. By 1850 a permanent establishment living on a hulk (or dismasted sailing vessel) was needed. Only sources of oil accessible by navigable waterways could be tapped – a considerable limitation. This was because it was difficult to transport, being heavy, semi-fluid or solid; the containers also were heavy, and only suitable for transport in bulk. Oil not only took longer to collect, but needed more stable political conditions on land.[8] Another problem was the tenacity of Europeans, but more especially Africans, to the slave trade. Some British captains continued in slave-trading with new names and nationalities: Capt. Philip Drake became Don Felipe Drax of Brazil. For the Africans, slave exporting was a much easier way of making money. It was a serious business, but also, as Burton recognised, like gambling, 'a form of intense excitement which becomes a passion'.[9] Palm oil was cheap, and brought less good returns than slaves. The king of Dahomey was said to be making £300,000 a year from export duty on slaves in the 1840s. The most important fact of the first half of nineteenth-century history in Africa was that the slave trade was not being suppressed.[10]

Added to this problem were the chronic local disturbances of the period. The transition to palm oil was accompanied by intense political and economic rivalry between African groups with a stake in the material wealth and firearms that accrued from European contact. Moreover, the Fulani invasion of the Oyo Empire in the 1820s threw the Yoruba paramountcies into an era of anarchy and disruption. After 1830 as the Egba consolidated their position at Abeokuta (harried by the Yoruba of Ibadan and the south-east) they fought for their share of the arms traffic to the interior and for a safe route of their own to the coast. In the 1860s the Yoruba wars restricted the commercial growth of Lagos.[11]

Finally, probably the fatal handicap was the unwillingness of the government to annex territory and place it under formal control. It seems that only establishing effective political authority on the troubled coast could have broken the slave trade and given honest merchants a fair chance to expand their business. The traders agreed that legitimate trade could best enter under the cover of military or political intervention. These men had little faith in the civilising nature of legitimate trade operating by itself. Because of the supposed indolence of Africans, Europeans were needed to give orders and set an example. This is why there were merchant demands for annexation: the Africans, it was thought, would not respond without direct coercion. Merchants certainly would not support territorial expansion for its own sake, but some felt it would help, though they may have exaggerated the assistance which commerce could expect from political authorities. Where there was a real basis for commercial expansion it could probably have taken place with or without territorial control. But in 1865, whgmvil war in Mellacourie region caused serious commercial setbacks, British and Creole merchants were persuaded to join their French rivals in inviting French protection. The need for government cojtrol was felt so desperately that at times any European flag was regarded as better than none.[12]

The British government hoped that legitimate commerce could be esished by a policy of minimum intervention: a patrolling naval squadron on the coast, the conclusion of treaties with African rulers, and some organising aid from consuls. The naval squadron was inefficient because the admiralty sent its worst ships and its most drunken captains. Treaties and consuls suffered from the absence of real coercive power behind them. A consul could try to enforce his will by an economic embargo on trade, but as one consul observed, 'a consul's moral force without a ship of war was a moral farce in these regions'.[13] The government placed most of its hopes in finding a 'strong native government' willing to collaborate in the forwarding of British interests. Asante, the Egba, Dahomey, Liberia, Nupé – all these and others besides were considered, the usual method being to send an envoy to report on their possibilities.[14] Best known of these was probably Sir Richard Burton who, as consul to the Bight of Benin (1861–65), was in 1863 charged by the foreign office with a mission to the king of Dahomey to enjoin upon him the joys of legitimate trade and cotton cultivation.[15]

This search for collaborators on the west coast was part of a Palmerstonian pattern which ranged all over Africa, including Ethiopia and Zanzibar. Palmerston appointed Walter Plowden in 1847 as consul at Massowa in Ethiopia with the primary object of fostering and protecting trade, reforming internal customs and treating for an alliance with the Lion of Judah, King of Kings.[16]

One possible solution was thought to lie in the importation of men of African birth 'trained to civilisation' in the West Indies, who could return to Africa and be the best teachers of 'the knowledge of true religion and arts of social life'. Resettled Sierra Leone Creoles were in fact the pace-makers in the nineteenth century for much of West Africa. The C. M. S. Fourah Bay (university) College was started in 1827, and its graduates formed the original educated African élite. There was a boys' secondary school in 1845, a girls' secondary school in 1849. In 1855 there appeared the first newspaper published by an African. J. Thorpe was called to the English Bar in 1850. Sierra Leone's Samuel Lewis was an outstanding example of successful response to Western culture, making a career in law and politics. Between 2,000 and 3,000 Sierra Leoneans, mostly of Egba descent, had emigrated to Abeokuta in Nigeria by 1851, which thus became the showpiece and spearhead of British trade, philanthropy and civilisation in Nigeria. [17]

Buxton in *The African slave trade and its remedy* (1840) argued that diplomacy and naval patrols had not worked. The only effective remedy was to attack the slave trade at source in Africa: 'Let missionaries and schoolmasters, the plough and the spade go together', and make free and legitimate trade and agriculture flourish under a liberated peasantry. Africans from Sierra Leone and America should be used as agents; these, protected by Britain, guided by missionaries, and working with capital from European merchants, would move inland (unlike Europeans) and act as cells of civilisation, encouraging the building of houses and roads and the cultivating of cotton and indigo. Buxton persuaded the government to sponsor the carefully prepared Niger expedition in 1841. It was intended to symbolise the whole civilised force of Great Britain. It comprised government-supplied steamboats, four government commissioners authorised to make treaties and explore the chances for establishing a consul somewhere on the Niger; scientists of all types, equipped with the latest instruments to make observations on climate, plants, animals, soil, people; commercial agents to report about trade, currency, traffic on the river; a chaplain and two C.M.S. missionaries to report on the possibilities of missionary work; agents of the Agricultural Society aiming to acquire land at a suitable point near the confluence of the Niger and Benué and to establish a model farm there. It was planned to settle on the farm 24 Africans recruited after wide publicity from Sierra Leone, and to manage it by two British agriculturists and an African catechist. The entire expedition was a large-scale public effort to convert Africans to western ways. The expedition was to conclude treaties which would condemn slaving and stimulate lawful trade.

The expedition was a disastrous failure. A model farm was established at Lokoja, but wound up because 45 of the 150 European members of the expedition died. Anti-slave trade treaties were not ratified. There was little positive result. Buxton died broken-hearted in 1845. But the Niger region had received publicity, and the expedition marked the beginning of new missionary enterprise in Nigeria. Thereafter, however, the government contemplated further advance with little enthusiasm.[18]

There was another expedition up the Niger in 1854 under Dr William Baikie, with the African Samuel Crowther as C.M.S. representative. Another in 1857, with 25 schoolmaster and evangelist emigrants from Sierra Leone, opened mission stations at Onitsha and Igbele. These were the first really successful steamboat entries up the Niger, because, thanks to newly employed quinine, they returned to the coast without a single loss of life.[19]

In 1850 Palmerston risked office in order to keep the preventive squadron in West Africa to fight the slave trade and bolster up the expansion of British interests in Nigeria. His instructions to John Beecroft, the first consul there, in 1850, required the consul to tell rulers that the principal object of his appointment was to encourage and promote legitimate and peaceful commerce. In 1851 the admiralty (at Palmerston's request) instructed a blockade of the port of Dahomey and sent a small force into Lagos, from which Portuguese slave-traders were ejected.

For the next ten years the British attempted to maintain a dominant influence through a resident consul, with the navy in the background. The attempt met with imperfect success. By the end of the 1850s, Lagos island was attracting attention as the possible centre for off-shore domination: a strategic fulcrum to open trade with a much wider area, in the same way as Hong Kong did for China, Singapore for the Malay archipelago and Aden for the Middle East. Lagos was in a chaotic condition. And so Lagos was occupied in 1861–62 with the hope that it would both support existing trade posts, assist the suppression of the slave trade, check the expansion of Dahomey, open and secure the hinterland for British commerce and establish British influence in the African interior. In the occupation of Lagos the main motive was fear of the French. Palmerston said 'if we do not take this step the French will be before-hand with us and to our great detriment'. According to Russell, the government was determined 'to establish and develop permanent commercial intercourse by this route with the interior of Africa'.

In launching a vigorous policy of commercial expansion in Nigeria, Palmerston hoped to use the Lagos base to check Dahomey's aggressive influence, sustain the Egba against it, and encourage neighbouring peoples to grow cotton for export. All this was to be done at the apparently simple cost of formalising Britain's position on a small island where she already held ultimate responsibility. As was not unusual, Palmerston was too optimistic. Merely holding Lagos could not achieve the objective of preventing the destructive wars of Dahomey and other states for the capture of slaves. Expansion of formal rule beyond the island was not contemplated, but indigenous paramountcy was weak. It was impossible for the Lagos administrators in the 1860s and 1870 to devise a trade agreement which would be accepted or respected by the Egba because of their latent hostility and suspicion of European territorial encroachment. The occupation of Lagos created more problems than it solved, and merely intensified rivalry with the French, who retaliated by installing themselves in Dahomey at Porto Novo.[20]

In 1865 the Select Committee on West African Settlements issued a report which recommended that the object of British policy should be to transfer to the Africans the administration of all the governments, 'with a view to an ultimate withdrawal from all, except, probably, Sierra Leone'. This meant only a withdrawal of formal territorial control in the interests of economy and not withdrawal of expanding informal and commercial enterprise. Sierra Leone was exempted because the navy appreciated the value of Freetown harbour, and because the colony had temporarily achieved a balanced budget and an expanding trade. But no-one took the idea of early self-government seriously, and as withdrawal was envisaged as something following self-government, this was even more remote. The resolutions for eventual withdrawal were never carried out, even in the Gambia, despite repeated negotiations. They did not fit the facts, which centred on a fresh and rapid expansion of trade and enterprise. Everything pointed to advance, not withdrawal, and European traders throughout West Africa demanded *more* and not less protection. The recommendations were also in themselves much guarded and qualified; withdrawal into informal influence was not thought possible 'wholly or immediately'.[21]

THE PARTITION OF AFRICA

You may roughly divide the nations of the world as the living and the dying . . . In these [dying] states, disorganisation and decay are advancing almost as fast as concentration and increasing power are advancing in the living nations that stand beside them . . . the weak states are becoming weaker and the strong states are becoming stronger . . . For one reason or another – from the necessities of politics or under the pretence of philanthropy, the living nations will gradually encroach on the territory of the dying, and the seeds and causes of conflict among civilised nations will speedily appear . . . These things may introduce causes of fatal difference between the great nations whose mighty armies stand opposed threatening each other.

No historian has ever succeeded in improving on this description, made by Lord Salisbury, of the atmosphere in which the partition of Africa took place. As an analysis of its cause, it directs attention unerringly to the disequilibrium of power which made the acquisition of territory possible in Africa; it is rooted in the European considerations which conditioned ministerial thinking; it warns us not to pay too much attention to the rhetoric of philanthropy.

One of the first events to focus public attention on Africa was Baker's expedition to the Sudan, 1869 to 1873.[22] In 1876 King Leopold of the Belgians began his Congo enterprise. France made forward moves in Senegal in 1879. In 1881 France occupied Tunisia, and in 1882 Britain occupied

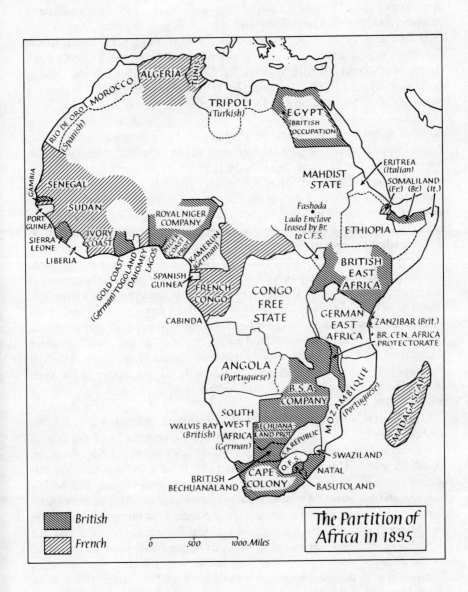

The Partition of Africa in 1895

British
French

0   500   1000 Miles

Egypt. In April 1884 Bismarck annexed Angra Pequena (German South-West Africa), German East Africa, the Cameroons and Togoland. Britain declared a Somaliland protectorate. In December 1884 the Berlin Conference apportioned the Congo and Lower Niger regions. In 1885 Britain declared protectorates over Bechuanaland and the Oil Rivers (Nigeria), and a year later chartered Goldie's Niger Company. In 1889 the British South Africa Company was chartered to secure Rhodesia. In 1890 by the Anglo-German 'Heligoland' Treaty British interests in Uganda, Zanzibar, Pemba Island, Witu and Nyasaland were secured. In 1894 Rosebery's cabinet declared a protectorate of Uganda, and in 1895 took over the Kenya area as well from the Imperial British East Africa Company. In 1896 Asante was likewise declared a British protectorate. In 1898 the Sudan was reconquered and an Anglo-Egyptian condominium set up over it in the following year. Two large Nigerian protectorates were organised in 1899.

Explanations of the partition are legion. There is no agreement among historians as to when it began, or who began it. The view taken here is that it was not Britain who initiated it, but that when other countries decided to embark on territorial acquisition, it was impossible for Britain to stand aside if she wished to protect her interests.[23] The question of why France and Germany should have embarked on this path is a complicated one and cannot be entered into here.[24] Suffice it to say that when these powers, for reasons of their own, took territory, Britain was reluctantly forced to follow suit. The opportunity – as well as the necessity – for taking territory arose out of the widespread breakdown or stagnation of indigenous political and economic systems. It is easy to condemn extension of Western rule as sheer acquisitiveness. But the brutal alternative would have been rule by irresponsible western adventurers, armed with all the resources of their civilisation to work their selfish will as they wished, without any superior control at all.[25]

Africa in the last thirty years of the nineteenth century was a notable example of what Sir Edward Grey described as an area 'in a position of minimum stability', or, as a modern political scientist might describe it, of 'power vacuum'. The collapse of the Turkish Empire in North Africa was accompanied by a variety of movements further south. Islam was widely reviving and pursuing its own expansionist policy. Some African authorities were seriously weakening, but there were also some expanding African powers on the up-grade, notably the Ethiopians, the Baganda, the Lozi and the Ndebele. In Buganda, for example, 60 raids by land and water are recorded for the 27 years of Mutesa's reign down to 1884. And in the next four years, Buganda was in almost continuous war with Nyoro.[26] In short Africa was a much-disturbed continent.

There is no doubt that in Cromer's view it was quite simply the anarchical condition of Egypt which led to its occupation: the necessity of a foreign occupation was a 'bald fact'. Misgovernment might have led to a renewed

French attempt to get a permanent footing. Gladstone recognised the call of duty to 'convert the present interior state of Egypt from anarchy and conflict to peace and order'. Salisbury saw the necessity of arresting misgovernment before it resulted in 'the material ruin and almost incalculable disorder to which it . . . will necessarily lead'.[27]

Merchants had always contended that, as Goldie put it, 'in uncivilised countries there can be no permanence of commerce without political power'.[28] The peculiarity of the partition period was the extent to which governments came to see matters in the same way.

The breakdown of control in Africa made it difficult to obtain economic advantages from Africa. Chamberlain defended the expedition against King Prempe of Asante in 1895 as necessary, because since 1873–74 this area, which was

> certainly rich in natural resources . . . has been devastated, destroyed and ruined by inter-tribal disputes, and especially by the evil government of the authorities of Ashanti . . . I think the duty of this country in regard to all these savage countries over which we are called upon to exercise some sort of dominion is to establish, at the earliest possible date, Pax Britannica, and force these people to keep the peace amongst themselves . . . The people are not a bad people. The natives are, on the whole, perfectly willing to work . . . but in such cases as that we are considering, the government is so atrociously bad that they are not allowed to do so. No man is safe in the enjoyment of his own property, and as long as that is the case, no one has any inducement to work.[29]

Warfare between Africans imposed severe handicaps on European trading. For example, early in 1879 many roads in Sierra Leone were closed by internal wars, and the number of caravans visiting Freetown dropped by 80 per cent. 'Rivalries among African rulers were complicated by [European] traders who sought to draw business to their own establishments, and to avoid customs duties'.[30] The condition of Africa was potentially dangerous. The local claims which were being staked out became increasingly entangled and confused. British statesmen were worried lest the Africans, being divided among themselves, and indulging frequently in petty wars, should tend to support one of the adjacent or overlapping incipient European spheres of influence (emerging for economic reasons mainly, but sometimes as a result of missionary activity) against the other, and that the Africans, by fighting each other partly on the basis of allegiance to rival European interests, might lead Europeans on the spot to fight each other as well, and so ultimately perhaps embroil the European powers themselves in war. This was the constant fear at the back of the minds of politicians, nourished by the large number of small incidents occurring between Europeans, and by risings and disturbances against Europeans, at the end of the nineteenth century, as well as by the classic example of missionary entanglement with local politics in Buganda. But chiefly it was economic rivalry. Salisbury's analysis quoted above provides the vital clue to the British motive in the partition. To prevent European conflict was a major reason for the partition. Only by imposing a strict control on the power vacuum could European powers feel safe from future disaster.[31] Despite acute – but in fact peaceful – economic rivalry, European powers generally acted in political co-operation. There is support for this thesis in a book by a distinguished Victorian historian, W. E. H. Lecky, *Democracy and Liberty* (1899):

> Experience has already shown how easily these vague and ill-defined boundaries may become a new cause of European quarrels, and how often, in remote African jungles or forests, negroes armed with European guns may inflict defeats on European soldiers which will become the cause of costly and difficult wars.[32]

At first the widespread absence of formal European governmental control enabled European adventurers and concession-hunters to pursue their rivalries without much restraint. Lugard and others pointed out the dire results of leaving vast areas of Africa in a state of indefinite and dangerous suspense, with firearms flooding in, with traditional rule violated, and no new system of control to take its place.[33] The unrestricted arms trade was one of the most serious problems. As European weapons improved in the 1860s and 1870s, especially with the introduction of repeating rifles, so vast quantities of obsolete guns were thrown on to the African market. The volume of this arms traffic must have been immense.[34] In addition, by 1907 Birmingham may have made 20 million guns for the African market. It has been estimated for the German and British areas of East Africa *alone* that between 1885 and 1902 something like a million firearms and more than four million pounds (weight) of gunpowder entered the region. Even by 1880 firearms seem to have been more than one-third of the total imports of Zanzibar. Estimates have been made which suggest that the Lozi of Barotseland had about 2,300 guns by 1875, the king of the Nyoro 2,000 by 1888, the kabaka of Buganda somewhere between 6,000 and 9,000 by 1890. Menelik of Ethiopia had about 100,000 guns with which to defeat the Italians at Aduwa in 1896. By 1896 the Shona and Ndebele probably had 10,000 guns of considerable variety. In 1904 the Herero were said to have 5,000 modern breech-loaders. The Pedi had 4,000 guns by 1860, and held Boer commandos at bay until 1876; the Zulu had at least 8,000 by 1879. Guns penetrated some South African societies deeply. The Venda traded guns to the Shona, teaching them how to manufacture ammunition and to repair guns. In Basutoland a virtual mania to possess them developed; attempted disarmament was a dominant issue in the Sotho rebellion of 1880. In the last nine months of 1873 more than 18,000 guns were imported into Griqualand West. The diamond- and gold-fields were

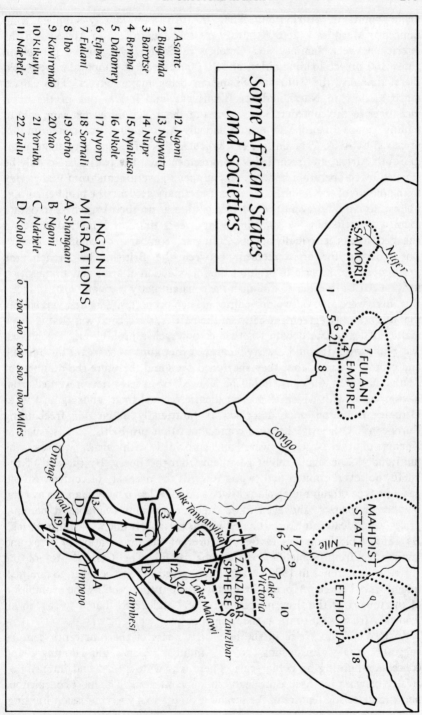

Some African States
and societies

1 Asante
2 Buganda
3 Barotse
4 Bemba
5 Dahomey
6 Egba
7 Fulani
8 Ibo
9 Kavirondo
10 Kikuyu
11 Ndebele

12 Ngoni
13 Ngwato
14 Nupe
15 Nyakusa
16 Nkole
17 Nyoro
18 Somali
19 Sotho
20 Yao
21 Yoruba
22 Zulu

NGUNI
MIGRATIONS

A Shangaan
B Ngoni
C Ndebele
D Kololo

major points of distribution. They in turn were largely supplied from
Lourenço Marques – 15,000 guns were sold from there to Africans in the
interior between January and October 1875; by 1879, 20,000 percussion
guns, 300 breech-loading rifles, and 10,000 barrels of gunpowder were sold
there annually, the Zulu and Shangaan being major buyers. This caused
much anxiety in Natal and the Transvaal, and it was one of the main
incentives to the confederation schemes of the 1870s. Firearms were sold in
mining camps in order to attract labour. A colonial office memorandum
prepared by A. A. Pearson in 1879 indicated this official anxiety about arms
in South Africa, and recorded wide agreement that the traffic could only be
stopped by co-operation between all European governments from Walvis Bay
to the mouth of the Zambesi. With extraordinary accuracy he prophesied that
unless they could prevent the Ndebele getting arms, their eagerness to obtain
them was such that 'we may in twenty years time, or less, find ourselves
engaged in another equally serious Zulu war'. Kimberley as colonial secretary
was working for an agreement between the British, the French, the
Portuguese and Liberia to prohibit the introduction of arms and ammunition
in West Africa in order to diminish the constant petty wars and disturbances.
But there were always two difficulties in such proposals. The first was simply
that of obtaining agreement between the parties, the second was that it was a
matter of legitimate debate whether or not such a prohibition, if achieved,
was really wise. It could always be argued that guns were useful for hunting
and crop protection, that they shortened wars and therefore the numbers of
deaths, and that Africans should be allowed, or at least not prevented from
having, arms with which to protect themselves and their lands against what
Hercules Robinson once described as 'unfriendly natives or freebooting
Europeans'. Otherwise it could come about that pro-British chiefs, such as
Kgama of the Ngwato, were underprovided with arms, whereas the
'unfriendly' Lobengula might get them from the Boers. By the end of the
1880s, however, opinion had swung towards the necessity of control. An old
gas-pipe type of gun might plausibly be said to be less bloody than the assegai,
but breech-loaders, and even more superior weapons available at nominal
prices would 'call into fresh life and vigour the gun-runners of South Africa'.
By 1889 a blockade was in force to prevent the importation of arms and
gunpowder from Somaliland to Pemba Island. The General Act of the
Brussels Conference in 1890 arranged for agreed steps to be taken to diminish
inland wars between Africans by means of arbitration and by the prohibition
of the import of the firearms between 20°N and 22°S, that is to say, in all
tropical Africa as far south as the Limpopo.[35]

A close look at Africa in the last thirty years of the nineteenth century
suggests that Europeans were indulging in gun-running and
concession-hunting on a big scale. There was wide-spread and intensifying
rivalry between localised European economic interests. The most conspicuous
and characteristic feature of the scramble on the spot was concession-hunting,

as it had been in Egypt and was to be in China. The Congo was an outstanding example, though there it followed Leopold's annexation rather than preceding it. Europeans committed atrocities in the Congo at an early stage: 32 Africans were tortured and executed for alleged incendiarism in 1879 – which shows how fragile was the basis of law and order on the Zaïre River.[36] In Swaziland the tangle of overlapping concessions was so serious as eventually to compel compulsory expropriation and land apportionment by a British government. King Mbandzeni conceded in land alone more than the total area of his kingdom, and sold all his private revenues to John Harington in 1889 for £12,000 a year. He even conceded the right to concede concessions – the culmination of concessions for mining, minting, tanning, for collecting customs and importing machinery, for oil and tobacco, for the right to establish everything from glassworks to pawnbrokers', from soda-water factories to orphanages, the right to hold auctions and sweepstakes, to take photographs and set up billiard tables and law courts. John Thorburn got a concession to build a hotel for the concession-hunters. Not unnaturally Swazi folklore came to speak of the 'documents that killed us'.[37] In such circumstances British officials were inclined to think that it would be better for the Swazi and other peoples to be taken over even by a formal Transvaal administration than by a set of wild or seedy adventurers. In backing Rhodes, Hercules Robinson argued that he could 'check the inroad of adventurers', since the rush of concessionaires to Matabeleland had 'produced a condition of affairs dangerous to the peace of that country'. The first concession from Lobengula was the grant of mining rights to Sir John Swinburne in 1869 in the Tati area to the extreme south-west of Matabeleland. Rhodes secured his own foothold by the concession negotiated by C. D. Rudd in 1888 by which Lobengula granted away his mining rights in return for a thousand Martini-Henry rifles and a 100,000 rounds of ammunition. This covered a wider area than the Tati concession, but unlike it, did not involve sovereign rights. The charter of the British South Africa Company could not in fact have been granted if there had not been concessions obtained from African chiefs. The Charter gave permission to certain British subjects to exercise any rights that African chiefs had conceded or might concede. Because Matabeleland and Mashonaland were reputedly rich in gold, speculators rushed in – German, Portuguese, Transvaalers and Cape Colonists bartered gin and rifles with Lobengula for mineral rights. Lobengula was seriously alarmed by the influx of concession-seekers by 1888.[38]

Petty adventurers without political aspirations helped to upset the balance and produced friction on frontiers, men like Carl Weise, a German-Jewish elephant hunter who became a political power in Ngoniland in Zambia.[39] In Nyasaland, taking advantage of African trustfulness, ingenuousness and inexperience, individuals and companies obtained ownership of land on which large numbers of Africans lived and tilled the soil. John Buchanan, a coffee planter, bought 3,065 acres in the future city of Blantyre for a gun, 32 yards

of calico, two red caps and several other tiny items. Sir Harry Johnston had to
make a report in 1892 after a survey of land claims. He noted that some
claimants had got 30, 40 or 50 square miles of territory with exclusive rights
of mining and road-making. He sorted this out, but left the Africans in
control of no more than two-fifths of the total land area.[40] It has been
concluded on the basis of a study of Ruanda-Urundi that by 1890 the
scramble for East Africa threatened to become uncontrollable. Concession
claims became increasingly entangled, and any solution might rapidly have
become impossible. Stanley in particular aggravated the situation. Britain
used Stanley's treaties for all they were worth, and perhaps much more than
they were worth. Regardless of economic value, competition for scraps of
territory increased. Ruanda-Urundi was the object of much European
bickering down to the 1910 Kivu-Mfumbiro Conference.[41]

Sometimes local administrations were in private hands, and it was this fact
which generated intense Anglo-German friction in East Africa after 1887.
Granville in 1885 explained to the German government how 'unnecessary
complications' must unavoidably result from imposing no check over the
action of individuals, and even officials, in such distant places. Harcourt in
the same year complained that British agents were getting Britain into
difficulties in every quarter of the globe.[42] Lord Salisbury plainly feared the
growing chaos in Africa. He suspected British officials with proconsular
pretensions, but he suspected European adventurers even more, doubting the
possibility of effectively restraining them: 'It is impossible to prevent the
danger of collisions, which might be murderous and bloody'. In South Africa
for this reason he was anxious to obtain agreement with Portugal, whose
agents were especially active in seeking concessions. Anarchy was
undoubtedly endemic in many areas of southern Africa. Hercules Robinson
advocated the extension of British rule to the Zambesi, since if Germany or
Portugal took 'possession of this waste country, fiscal and other restrictions
might be placed on the Cape trade with the interior which would prove very
injurious to British commercial interests in South Africa'.[43]

Even if it were possible to demonstrate that Africa did not in fact prove
economically interesting to British manufacturers, merchants and investors
until the twentieth century, this in no way disposes of the fact that among the
original motives of the partitioners was the thought or hope of possession
leading to economic benefits, even to the extent of providing areas for white
settler colonisation. Lugard is on record as having said that in 1870 the
colonisation of Africa was believed desirable and possible. It is a most striking
fact that contemporary commentators and the men who actually took part in
the processes of partitioning on the spot – men such as Lugard,[44] George
Goldie[45] and Harry Johnston[46] – were unanimous in ascribing primacy to the
economic motive. Lugard wrote in 1895 that foreign competition in
manufactures and the hostile tariffs imposed by other nations, together with
the depression of trade, had 'driven us to seek new markets and new fields for

our surplus energy'.[47] It is interesting, incidentally, that Lugard spoke of surplus *energy* and not surplus capital.

Early in 1879 Sir Robert Morier, British minister at Lisbon, wrote a letter to Salisbury trying to define a new African policy which would replace anti-slavery but avoid extension of territory and colonisation. His proposal was to 'make Africa available for the purposes which an all-wise "Natural Selection" intended, i.e. that of the nearest and largest storehouse of tropical produce, and of the only kind of labour available for the purposes of tropical production'. If Britain could 'make Africa available for commerce throughout its length and breadth', and get labour to produce goods for export, 'we shall have done all we need do and be our own benefactors and those of the rest of mankind'. Hence, he concluded, they should insist 'on the absolute get-at-ableness of every portion of Africa' and on the removal of all artificial commercial restrictions.[48]

French and British firms behaved more aggressively towards one another after 1875, when France deliberately tried to break into the richer and British-predominated markets of West Africa, especially on the Niger and Oil Rivers between 1880 and 1883. There were fears too that de Brazza would move north and seize the Ibo palm-oil producing lands of the hinterland. More European traders had been brought in by the steamship, while African merchants had also begun to compete. The more difficult economic situation of the 1870s led to strains, misunderstandings and conflicts between all the participants; Europeans found little scope for improving their efficiency without the political removal of constraints holding back the development of exports. There was a sharp drop in prices for palm oil in the mid-1880s. In this crisis a trade war was fought out in Lagos among Europeans and with African traders and producers in an attempt to pass on as much of their losses as possible. As Hopkins has established, of 12 European firms in Lagos in 1880, only five remained in 1892, and two of these were present in name only. Merchants pressed for political action, which was taken in Lagos to resolve economic conflicts. This was not a simple question of government's being 'manipulated' by traders – it made its own decisions in the light of what it assessed were the national interests of British commerce, and it made them from a fundamental belief in the hopelessness of achieving improvement by relying any more on African agency. Hence the establishment of the Oil Rivers protectorate of 1884 and the chartering of the Royal Niger Company in 1886.

Newbury has drawn attention to the intense commercial rivalry on the west coast in the 1870s and 1880s. Local disputes arising from differential customs zones, sometimes operating in a protective manner (against German or French spirits in British areas, and against British cloth and arms in French and German areas), created, he believes, a situation only to be remedied by the 'rationalisation' of partition: the impulse to extend European rule over the interior came mainly from local traders, supported by commercial and

shipping interests in Europe.[49] Both Britain and France wanted to extend the
area of their customs collection, either to raise more revenue or to assert
sovereignty or title, and every sign of an advance by one power was usually
counterbalanced by a move from its rival; so that, for example, Gouldsbury's
expedition up the Gambia River (1881), prompted by Rowe's desire for
counter-demonstration against French policy, had the effect of accelerating
the French penetration of Fouta Djallon. Salisbury suggested to the French
ambassador, Waddington, that the cause of many territorial disputes in West
Africa might be removed by an agreement to assimilate French and British
tariffs along the coast. The French were very aware that Salisbury's main
preoccupation was conflict between French protectionist policy and British
commercial interests. This fear of potential foreign tariffs was deep-rooted.
With so many eager competitors in the field, the *Times* felt, Britain could not
afford to neglect any country likely to yield new fields for commercial
enterprise.[50] Ministers and officials might not have gone so far as this, but
even Derby drew a distinction between keeping what was threatened and
wanting new acquisitions. As the Francophobe head of the African
department of the foreign office (1883–96), Percy Anderson, put it in 1883,
British trade in West Africa must not be placed at the mercy of French
officials; partly because this would increase her political and military power:

> Protectorates are unwelcome burdens, but in this case, it is . . . a question
> between British protectorates, which would be unwelcome, and French
> protectorates, which would be fatal. Protectorates, of one sort or another,
> are the inevitable outcome of the situation.[51]

At the end of a long career in the colonial office, Sir George Fiddes
(permanent under-secretary 1916–21) said it would be hypocrisy to pretend
that Britain went to West Africa, or remained there, other than in the
interests of British commerce.[52] This admission is fully borne out by
contemporary documents. In 1883 a colonial office memorandum complained
of the inconvenience caused for many years by the persistence of the French
in annexing or protecting isolated points alongside British territory, from
Lagos to Sierra Leone. The French did not attempt any real government or
administration, but the rights they claimed were sufficient to prevent Britain
from dealing direct with kings and chiefs when they ill-treated British
subjects. There was extensive smuggling, especially in spirits, at several
points. Nor could Britain exercise any effective control over the importation
of arms and gunpowder. It was useless to forbid it on the Gold Coast while the
Asante could draw abundant supplies from Assinie, and the French had no
means of enforcing any rules they might agree with Britain in thinking
desirable in principle. An extension of French interest to the Niger Delta
would be a matter 'of vital importance to British commerce', since it was at
the time almost exclusively in control of the Niger trade. But: 'if the French

are allowed to go on unchecked we shall find our trade excluded, and the Niger will become a French river from source to mouth'. It had to be remembered that the French colonial tariff in Africa was 'strongly differential in favour of home goods and home shipping, and wherever it is worth the while of the French to enforce it, foreign trade must ere long succumb and disappear'. The memorandum concluded that, in the interests of trade, the French might be bought out on the Niger by the cession of the commercially unpromising Gambia, while a fuller development on the Niger coast could become self-financing, especially with a proper control of arms importation and the checking of African wars in the interior 'which paralyse trade and cause wide-spread troubles and misery'.[53]

British economic interest in the partition is apt to be distorted by considering only the successful acquisitions. It is often forgotten that Britain was fitfully interested in Katanga. Harry Johnston pressed its claims on Salisbury in 1890. It was, he argued, 'an important piece of territory which we need' to complete Nyasaland; it was well known to have copper and believed to have gold – thus it was the richest country in minerals in all Central Africa; 'it is fairly healthy and has a fertile soil,' and its peoples were 'peaceful and industrious'. Moreover, he added, King Leopold 'had no right to it'.[54] By this he meant that although the sovereign rights of the Congo Free State probably covered Katanga there had been no explicit concession and no effective occupation. It was still an independent African state. Rhodes decided to make a bid for it. The British South Africa Company sent two expeditions. The first failed. The second never even crossed the borders of Katanga. The foreign office had no intention of pushing these claims, and encouraged British investment in the Katanga company in the hope of ending agitation for a British annexation. When the Union Minière was formed in 1906 to exploit copper, half the capital was British. As late as 1908 there were widespread suspicions that Britain looked to the reversion of Katanga. This was not the case, but it is an indication of the suspicions aroused by an earlier, more overt interest.[55]

That British interest in West Africa was basically a trading interest is unlikely to be contested. More controversial is the nature of British interest in East Africa. Analysis of Clement Hill's foreign office memoranda reveals a strong economic interest here too. Since the slave trade had been checked, commerce had made great strides. Hill contended that the region was rich in minerals, that cereals could be grown and cattle raised with success. He pointed to an excellent climate in the mountain ranges of Kilimanjaro and Kenya. He posed the question whether, in view of French trading rivalry on the west coast, it might not be better to exploit the commercial possibilities of the east coast instead. Johnston and consul Holmwood also urged the commercial possibilities. Colonists might grow rice, coffee, sugar, wheat, and fruit and supplement a trade tapping ivory, wax, iron and hides. The imports of Zanzibar increased from £500,000 in 1875 to £850,000 in 1884, and exports from £600,000 to £1,000,000 in the same period. The hinterland might fall to the sultan of Zanzibar; 'the healthiest, and perhaps, the most valuable portion of East Africa' was Kilimanjaro. Outside pressure came from men, many of them powerful, such as Lord Aberdare, Mackinnon, Baron Rothschild, Jacob Bright (brother of John), who regarded East Africa as a new Australia as well as a new India, and a place of potential for Manchester goods. Lugard regarded Uganda as an El Dorado, 'to be secured at all costs' (1891). The Germans also saw it as an El Dorado, and although the British got a large field for enterprise they had to sacrifice Kilimanjaro. Kirk stressed the importance of retaining Mombasa, not only for its strategic value, but as 'the natural outlet of the most promising commercial field in East Africa'. There were of course other considerations. As Clement Hill defined them these were: the importance of the Cape route to India, and the existing trading connection between India and the east coast, especially at Zanzibar – the intrusion of a foreign power could damage both. There was also the fact of a Muslim population on the coast with a connection with co-religionists in Sudan, the Red Sea area and the Persian Gulf, which, 'if not close, is none the less real'. He emphasised the desirability of Britain's exercising 'a preponderating influence' over these Islamic and Indian elements.[56] But there was also the commercial potentiality, though this was not pressed by Zanzibar merchants. East Africa had been made much more accessible after the opening of the Suez canal in 1869. British desire for cloves, tea, coffee and ivory was strong. By 1870 Africa, and especially East Africa, supplied 85 per cent of the world's total ivory consumption – then much in demand for knife handles, combs, billiard balls, piano keys and ornaments. The average annual import of ivory into London more than doubled between the 1840s and the 1870s.[57]

In Rosebery's decision to keep Uganda, the strategic argument for controlling the Nile headwaters was kept in view, and the Uganda railway (whose purpose was troop movement) was built on the same gauge as Egyptian railways, in case a link were ever to be made. But two other considerations outweighed the strategic one. Uganda was 'the paradise of slave-dealers', and if they were given back their 'happy hunting-ground', Britain would be 'guilty of a grave and perhaps criminal dereliction of duty'. Moreover, withdrawal would also involve the massacre of Christians, with an effect on the public mind comparable to that produced by the fall of Khartoum. Acting for the Imperial British East Africa Company, Lugard entered Buganda in 1890, and two years later, in alliance with the Protestants, defeated the kabaka Mwanga and the Roman Catholics. This dominant and victorious Protestant Christian élite secured its own position by alliance with Britain, an alliance valuable to both, especially against their mutual enemy, the Baganda Muslims. Uganda was retained in 1894 with British public opinion clearly pronouncing in favour on account of the Christian stake there. Mackinnon and the company directors were not acting primarily as businessmen looking for personal profit, but had the patriotic satisfaction of securing territories which could be valuable economically and strategically, holding the area for an ill-defined British influence. The leading shareholders were officials and philanthropists, including T. F. Buxton and Mr Burdett-Coutts.[58]

Chamberlain's general argument was that if Britain had remained passive, the greater part of the African continent would have been occupied by her commercial rivals 'who would have proceeded, as the first act of their policy, to close this great potential market to British trade'. Not to be forestalled in these markets of the future was 'a matter of life and death'.[59]

One must be careful not to give the impression that 'British prestige' did not matter in the partition of Africa. Sir Percy Anderson, éminence grise of the British part in the partition, saw the scramble mainly as a problem of maintaining British power and prestige in an increasingly hostile world, though to this end he seems to have thought that Manchester should be stirred to look after its interests. He countermoved against every French and German advance.[60] Sanderson's monumental investigation of activities in the Upper Nile leads convincingly to the conclusion that at the turn of the year 1898–99 considerations of national prestige and territorial possession were more decisive than any supposed imperial defence strategy on the headwaters of the Nile. The condominium of the Sudan went far beyond anything required by the latter consideration, but was necessary because the British public wanted a tangible reward for its exertions and regarded Gordon and Kitchener as heroes to be honoured.[61] Moreover, it would seem that, ultimately, the quarrel between Britain and France which culminated in 1898 at Fashoda was not about the security of Egypt and the Nile, but the relative status of the two powers. Fashoda has to be seen in the context of the British plan to assert control over the whole of the Sudan. 'The natural or acquisitional feeling has been aroused', lamented Salisbury in 1887.

Perhaps the clearest example of running up the flag purely from an unalloyed desire to keep the foreigner out comes from South Africa. The fear of Germany in this region was very strong. The Victorians were unnerved by German seizure of the Cameroons – 'predatory proceedings', Derby called them. It was suspected that Bismarck would then try for St Lucia Bay, which might lead him formally into the Transvaal if appealed to as protector. In the colonial office it was feared that 'a hostile cordon drawn round the Cape from Angra Pequena to Zululand would effectually cripple us'. One official, returning from the Berlin Conference, got the impression that the Germans were almost certain to annex any place on the coast of southern Africa which was left open for them. British difficulties would, it was thought, then increase tenfold because Germany might try to use her position to interfere between the British government and the Boers. A German presence was regarded as 'a dangerous complication' which would increase the difficulty of dealing with Africans and Afrikaners. German traders would almost certainly try to prevent British control of arms supply to both.[62]

Britain became interested in Bechuanaland only after Germany had annexed South-West Africa: the annexation of British Bechuanaland then became of urgent importance as the territorial wedge between the German hinterland and the Transvaal.[63] The same fear of a junction between Germany and the Transvaal led to the annexation of St Lucia Bay and the hitherto unoccupied coastal region between the Cape and Natal. Gladstone saw that apprehension of German rivalry was a factor in the South African aspect of the partition. He said on 9 December 1884: 'It seems that wherever there is a dark corner in South African politics there is a German spectre to be the tenant of it.' Gladstone thought that Derby was quite right in wishing to have 'a continuous line of coast in South Africa'. The reason for this was the necessity of safeguarding the Cape route to India, which was threatened by French interest in Madagascar (acquired by France in 1893). The Suez canal could not possibly be used in time of war, and so Britain had to secure the 'only alternative and only feasible route' in wartime, the Cape route – as Lugard argued forcefully. £90 million-worth of commerce ordinarily went by the Cape. It would have been £200 million if the Suez canal were not used. In 1898 the Cape still carried 37 per cent of the total value of British trade with the east.[64]

Roland Oliver has suggested that if the partition had been delayed even 30 years, most of Africa to the north of the Zambesi might have passed into the world of Islam. Much earlier Burton predicted a Muslim conquest of the continent.[65] Rivalries in Africa were not simply between Europeans. In one sense the partition of Africa was a device to contain or counteract the expansion of militant Islam, which the British as well as the French feared greatly; and it could be described as a struggle for control of north and central Africa between Christian European and Muslim Arab-Africans. By 1880 politicians in Paris and London had begun to talk of a dangerous pan-Islamic conspiracy, a fanatical Muslim resurgence, giving the slave trade a new lease of life. The most famous events in the Islamic revival were Urabi's rising in Egypt, the revolt of the Mahdi in the Sudan, and the persecution of Christian missionaries and their followers in Buganda in 1884–86. It was thought that the Mahdist *jihad* was precursor of a general and formidable offensive movement through the Islamic world. There was certainly a later parallel in Somaliland, where the so-called Mad Mullah was in rebellion 1899–1904 and 1908–20. As far as the West African situation is concerned, Kanya-Forstner has shown how fear of Muslim resistance and determination to crush it had dominated French military thinking for almost half a century by 1890.[66] Lugard was vitally interested in controlling and limiting Islam. This fear of Islam provided one reason for keeping Uganda. Uganda was important to British interests throughout north and south-central Africa as a Christian state – for it seemed definitely to have thrown in its lot with Christiantity as the new 'established' religion. Buganda was one of the few states to experience a 'Christian revolution', and already had 32 martyrs by 1886. It was therefore not likely to originate any fanatical Muslim movement, but instead to form a barrier against the spread of any such movement as might arise, and perhaps be a means of spreading Christianity to the surrounding areas. Likewise Nyasaland, in the opinion of Anderson of the foreign office, could not be abandoned, because the Arabs would make it their stronghold and the consequences would be disastrous.[67] Retention of these two states seemed to produce the desired result. In 1905 Sir Charles Eliot, sometime governor of Kenya, wrote of Uganda: 'In view of the power which Islam has shown of spreading among African races, and the damage done on the Upper Nile by the Khalifa and the Dervishes, the existence of this Christian state must be regarded as a great guarantee for the preservation of peace'.[68]

Raymond Aron once wrote of the partition as 'the consequence – indeed the inverse picture – of the general state of peace'.[69] All European powers were anxious that Africa should not threaten that peace. In the last resort all agreed that their friendship was more important than their African interests. It was one of the aims of the Berlin Conference of 1884 to limit the effect of future African disputes on international relations in Europe and to reduce the danger of friction which lay in general ignorance of Central Africa. According to Malet, who attended it, Britain's aim was to help prevent 'the anarchy and lawlessness which must have resulted from the influx of traders of all nations into countries under no recognised form of government'. There was quite a strong move, supported by Britain, to neutralise the whole African continent.[70] It was generally understood at the time that the African activities of different powers had to be adjusted within the context of their European relationships and their mutual concern about Africa. Somaliland was declared a British protectorate in 1884 in order to contain the anarchy consequent upon the dissolution of the indigenous government, and to prevent the danger of foreign encroachment on the line of communication to India; it was also a major source of food supply for the Aden garrison.[71] But in 1896 the administration of Somaliland was transferred from the government of India (acting through Aden) to the foreign office: although Aden was geographically a convenient centre from which to administer the Somali coast, the viceroy could not know enough of the political considerations which would decide the action to be taken there as in other parts of Africa, 'because they are inseparably bound up with European politics'.[72]

THE BASES OF GOVERNMENT POLICY 1895–1914

African adjustments to European intrusion were of great variety, though a general distinction may be made between those states and societies who came to an accommodation with alien rule and those who resisted it with force.[73] Some of the most successful and peaceful adjustments were made by states with well-developed trading systems, such as the palm-oil producing states on the west coast, Nupé (the 'Black Byzantium' of Northern Nigeria), or the Lozi of the Zambesi flood-plain in Barotseland (Zambia). States which depended on raiding or slave-dealing for their economic survival, such as the predatory Ndebele of Rhodesia, or the slave-trading Yao of Malawi, tended to resist.[74] The leaders of some states welcomed the British as allies in local power struggles. In Nkole (Uganda) the British were welcomed as the arch-disposers of power.[75] The Tswana and Sotho hoped for British protectorates which would prevent them from falling into the hands of the Boers. The Pax Britannica was no figment of the imagination and its benefits were welcomed by states previously victimised in traditional politics. There were some states with a degree of sophistication and expansive power which led the British to handle them with wary circumspection. Foremost in this category were the Fulani emirates of Northern Nigeria, and Buganda, states which the British did not want to fight, and which therefore they had to accommodate to. This is why 'Indirect Rule' evolved in Northern Nigeria, and why a specially privileged position was negotiated for the Ganda in the Buganda Agreement of 1900. The corollary of this quasi-alliance arrangement was that Britain almost automatically adopted the stance of traditional Buganda hostility towards the Nyoro and underwrote the expansion of the Ganda state. The Buganda Agreement put 40 per cent of Nyoro under the Ganda.[76]

Resistance took many forms. The Nandi in Kenya showed their disapproval of British intrusion by chopping up telegraph wire into ear-rings, refusing to pay hut tax and removing the bolts from the Uganda railway. A punitive expedition put a stop to this in 1905.[77] In Sierra Leone, Bai Bureh led a rebellion against hut tax in 1898, because his people believed that payment of tax deprived them of ownership of their homes, and (by logical extension) would mean that they had no right to their own country.[78] The most formidable protest was launched by the Ndebele and Shona peoples in 1896. It was their misfortune to be right in the direct path of the powerful expansive thrust launched northwards under the direction of Rhodes. The Ndebele had been conquered in 1893; their post-pacification grievances included the breaking of promises, resentment over the treatment of their women, confiscation of land, two seizures of cattle, labour conscription, and taxes. Their troubles were compounded by a series of natural disasters (locusts, drought and rinderpest) which seemed to coincide with the British intrusion.[79]

The subjection of African states thus took many forms. Sometimes existing states were taken over, like Zanzibar, where government in the name of the Sultan was in fact entirely undertaken by British officials; the British Resident was the first minister of the Sultan. By contrast, in Buganda no British official served the Kabaka; two parallel structures of government co-existed. In the 20 kingdoms of Southern Uganda there was no case between 1890 and 1900 in which a previously dominant authority made a successful rapprochement with the British. Rulers and chiefs became dominant as a result of alliance with the British. The use of force was widespread among these 'stateless' societies. Between 1909 and 1918 only in one year was there no punitive expedition to the Langi peoples of Northern Uganda. Most areas of Kenya were at some time subject to British military or police operations well into the twentieth century.[80]

Taxation was introduced ubiquitously and it was hated universally. Sometimes it seemed as if the motive for taxing was as much to force the Africans to work as to raise revenue. In South and Central Africa one of the major changes resulting from the British intrusion was labour migration to the mines of the Witwatersrand. Labour was drawn from Mozambique on a large scale, but it is estimated that in 1907, for instance, 18,000 men left Nyasaland for the Rand mines. By 1913 an average of some 185,000 Africans a year worked in the Rand mines, often for only six or eight months at a time. This was short-term migration: rural labourers and peasants 'raiding the industrial economy for cash' in order to pay taxes, buy bicycles or clothes, and to save enough money to make a marriage. The absence of men-folk from African communities for such long stretches of time had disturbing effects on social life.[81]

It was part of Africa's misfortune to be brought under European control at a time when racial attitudes were harsher than they had ever been before. Optimistic theories of regeneration had been discredited but no effective alternative was devised. Thus, just at the very time when it was urgently necessary to decide how to govern new African territories, there was pessimism, confusion of thought, and a conditioning undercurrent of apprehension about possible uprisings. The only points clear to British rulers were that they must keep law and order, and that if beyond this basic task they, with all their wisdom and experience, were uncertain what to do, how much less able would Africans themselves be to solve the problem. They were still regarded by the British as children.[82]

Disillusionment with African progress in the areas of older-established influence, especially when it was seen as paralleled by disillusionment about Indians, put the whole of imperial policy towards non-Europeans into reverse gear. By the end of the nineteenth century Africans were trusted much less than they had been earlier. This had marked practical results in Church and State, especially in West Africa. Henry Venn, secretary of the Church Missionary Society 1841–73, had seen the necessity of establishing an indigenous ministry. He appointed the first African bishop, Samuel Crowther, together with another African, James Johnson, as superintendent of interior missions. From 1870 the younger generation of missionaries rejected Venn's policy. Crowther was tormented and insulted until he was forced to resign. After Crowther there was no full diocesan African bishop again until 1953.* Exactly the same retrogression occurred in business and government

---

* It is pleasant to record that the C.M.S. College for Training at Selly Oak has been known as Crowther Hall since 1969.

administration. Africans holding positions of responsibility in the West
African Company were dismissed in the amalgamation of 1879, and
systematic pressure was exerted by Goldie to drive them out of the Niger
River as independent traders.[83] There was a deliberate reduction in the
number of Africans holding positions in the Gold Coast civil service. In 1883,
nine out of 43 higher posts were filled by Africans; by 1908 only five out of
274 senior civil servants were African, and by 1919 only two. Yet offices at
every level from the highest downwards had at some time or other since 1843
been held by Africans. Incipient distrust is observable from the later 1850s,
but as late as 1872 governor Pope Hennessy had recommended dispensing
with the service of Europeans. Similarly in Sierra Leone, in 1892 Creoles held
18 out of 40 senior posts, but by 1912 only 15 out of 92, of which five were
abolished in the next five years as their holders retired. (By 1908 unrestricted
competition to the Ceylon cadet service was abolished; it had brought in a
number of West Indians and Africans; the experiment was pronounced a
'ghastly failure'.) The key policy decision was made in 1873 with colonial
secretary Kimberley's directive that, 'except in quite subordinate posts we
cannot safely employ natives'. As far as the west coast was concerned, he
wrote, 'I would have nothing to do with the "educated" natives as a body. I
would treat with the hereditary chiefs only, and endeavour as far as possible
to govern through them'. De-tribalised, educated Africans were spoken of in
1886 by a colonial office official as 'the curse of the West coast'.[84]

Revulsion – the word is scarcely too strong – against the educated classes
was something which took place throughout the empire in the late nineteenth
century. Macaulay's policy was wholly out of favour. It seemed in India to
have bred nothing but discontented 'agitators'. As early as 1876 Salisbury
condemned the 'deadly legacy' from Metcalfe and Macaulay': the newly
educated class which could not be 'anything else than an opposition in quiet
times, rebels in time of trouble'.[85] The British were determined not to make
the same mistake in Africa. In Egypt, arguing directly from Indian
experience, Cromer emphasised the necessity for industrial training: 'it is at
least conceivable that every carpenter or bricklayer or mason you turn out
will be one unit detached from the ranks of the dissatisfied classes'. (Cromer
described himself as proceeding steadily on the principle of Burke's maxim
that the main thing for a reformer was to decide what not to reform.) [86] As far
as South Africa was concerned, Selborne believed (in the classic
eighteenth-century manner) that 'a wisely graded education will make the
domestic servants and employees better and more useful as domestic servants
and employees'. Elgin laid some stress on the encouragement of industrial
education in Nyasaland. Indian experience had led him to conclude that
western literary education, even at Eton and Sandhurst, did not make a man
happier or more loyal to Britain. In Northern Nigeria, Sir Percy Girouard
was most anxious that education should be less westernised. Sir John Rodger
on the Gold Coast agreed.[87] The government notice announcing the opening

of Bo School in Sierra Leone in 1906 defined its aim as one of enabling the
boys

> to acquire a good education without loss of their *natural* attachment to
> their respective tribes. Tribal patriotism is to be strengthened; Mende
> pupils, for instance, are to be taught in such a way that they will prefer
> Mendiland to any other country; so with Timinis, and all the other various
> tribes represented in the school.

Pupils at Bo lived in compounds similar to those in their home villages, ate
their own foods and had their group relations with one another ordered along
traditional lines.[88] The early twentieth century was a period when the right
general policy was honestly believed to be the 'development of native
institutions on native lines'.

The basic assumptions upon which all discussion and planning of African
policy took place were four in number.[89] The primary one was that nothing
could be done for Africans if it involved regular spending of the British
taxpayers' money. Any development must be self-financing within each
territory. The second assumption was that the first duty was to law and order
and efficient administration. The third guide-line was that change must be
slow and not such as to provoke violent reaction: there was an indefinite time
ahead, and *festina lente* was a good motto. Finally, and quite fundamentally,
it was assumed that Africans were irremediably inferior, even to Asians. The
idea that Indians could be equal was now regarded as an unqualified mistake.
American experience reinforced this scepticism, shared equally by politicians
as different as George Hamilton, Churchill, Balfour and Selborne.[90]

The concept of 'Indirect Rule' arose naturally out of these four
assumptions, the prevailing pessimism and the dictates of expediency. Sir
Arthur Gordon as governor of Fiji (1875–82) had worked fairly
systematically through Fijian chiefs.[91] Sir William MacGregor, first
administrator of British New Guinea, had followed his example. But 'Indirect
Rule' was a method most closely associated with Lugard, and he indeed gave
it a more precise meaning, feeling his way first in Uganda (rule 'through and
by the chief'), and finally in Northern Nigeria, which he made the classic seat
of a pilot scheme. It seemed to be the cheapest course. It was the answer to
exiguous resources – though Lugard had more resources at his command than
many governors. It had roots in the Indian experience of Lugard and Elgin.
The Fulani seemed unavoidable collaborators. The Fulani emirs Lugard
regarded as 'an invaluable medium between the British staff and the native
peasantry'. It would be difficult to find anyone capable of taking their place,
and the danger they would constitute to the state if ousted from their
positions could not be ignored. His successor Girouard agreed: 'If the Fulanis
were ousted from power today, they, as the best educated in the land, would
become the focus of intrigue and rebellion, and unless banishment of some
30,000 to 50,000 was part of the same policy, anarchy would ensue'. Those

African institutions which had survived in the struggle for existence were regarded as having in some sense proved their worth and should therefore be preserved.[92] Indirect Rule presupposed the availability of a conservative, benevolent squirearchy of independent English gentlemen with an unerring instinct for paying due outward respect to traditional African authority. But essentially Indirect Rule began as a reflection of political pessimism, and in many significant ways it was a baulking of real issues. Devising a genuine and fresh governmental policy for Northern Nigeria would have been a demanding task. The old nineteenth-century reluctance to make large commitments was still apparent in the adoption of Indirect Rule. Huge and forbidding problems existed in the densely populated Muslim areas of Northern Nigeria. The possibility of *jihad* enjoined peculiar caution, though Lugard was determined to found the British title to rule on right of conquest. By amalgamating the administrations of Southern and Northern Nigeria in 1914, in effect he rejected for all Nigeria the older ideals of Afro-British partnership. It was a final decision not to create a new Nigerian nation, a repudiation of Venn's dream of a 'kingdom which shall render incalculable benefits to Africa and hold a position among the states of Europe'. The status quo in the North was not only preserved, but the principles attuned to it were spread to Southern Nigeria.[93] Indirect Rule was a policy, or an evasion, which would never have been originally adopted if the British had felt sufficiently confident to devise something more assertive. Although flexible enough to allow Lugard to act positively, its chief beauty was that it made as few changes as possible and by-passed the western-educated. It was really a conservation scheme, a means of keeping law and order rather than a constructive framework within which modernising developments could take place, a means of controlling people rather than facilitating change.[94] Its main weakness was its embodiment of a disastrous miscalculation as to with whom the future was to lie. The British backed the wrong horse by preferring the strong traditional authorities to the newly educated urban élite. This preference for the hereditary chief and the unsophisticated peasant ('the salt of the earth') arose directly out of Indian experience, transmitted and refined through Cromer's Egyptian administration, and backed by Chamberlain.

After 1914 Indirect Rule was to be increasingly extended in a doctrinaire way, with a nearly pathological obsession, to more and more parts of Africa. The political pattern of British regimes in Africa in 1914 was, however, much more varied than it later became. And it was not a pattern which wholly inhibited economic change.

It is not always realised how much economic development was achieved in Africa in the twenty years before 1914. It simply is not true that, once having parcelled Africa out among themselves, European governments forgot about it.[95] Nor was public interest dead. Lever made persistent efforts to secure facilities for his soap industry in the palm-oil belt in Sierra Leone, Southern Nigeria, and the Belgian Congo between 1907 and 1913. In May 1906 a great deputation from Lancashire met the prime minister and other senior cabinet ministers to press for the development of Nigeria by a railway which would open up cotton-growing districts. Between 1909 and 1912 no less than 82 tin mining companies entered Nigeria with a total capital of £3.8 million.[96] The Gezira cotton growing experiment in the Sudan began in 1900, and by 1905 nearly 24,000 acres were under cotton, of which 16,000 acres were irrigated. A loan of £3 million was raised for this scheme in 1913 and subsequently augmented to £6 million in 1919. In retrospect this can be seen as one of the most constructive developments ever undertaken in any country under European control.[97] Railway building was pressed ahead with some speed. The railway map of Africa today is virtually the same as it was in 1914. In Nigeria $6\frac{1}{3}$ miles of track were laid in one day.[98] After the Uganda railway, linking Lake Victoria to the coast, was completed at a cost of over £8 million, top priority was given by Britain to a rail link between Kano in Northern Nigeria and the coast. Between 1906 and 1911 alone, a thousand miles of rail was laid (or was in process of being laid) in British African territories. £200,000 was being spent on a scheme to link up Lakes Victoria and Albert in order to tap the Congo trade. Cotton was successfully established in Uganda as a commercial crop by 1909 and sisal in Kenya by 1907. In the Gold Coast and Nigeria together, cocoa exports increased from 110,000 cwt to 882,000 cwt in the seven years before 1913, and West African palm-oil production more than doubled, giving a figure of £5,300,000 by 1913.[99] By 1910 the Gold Coast, with 40,000 tons of cocoa a year, was the world's largest producer. From 1910 the rising world price of rubber led many British businessmen to interest themselves in Africa.

Whatever doubts there might have been during the partition about the economic value of some of the new acquisitions, these doubts were fully removed everywhere, except for Somaliland, by 1906. There was deep interest in developing cotton, palm oil, ground-nuts, cocoa, rubber, and coffee; the Royal Niger Company started several experimental plantations. Because of this the colonial office recognised that it could no longer confine itself to questions of politics and administration, but must promote material development. It began to equip itself with various expert advisory committees dealing with agricultural and medical research, and improved its ties with existing agencies, such as the Royal Botanic Gardens at Kew and the Imperial Institute. Botanic stations were opened at Lagos in 1887 on the Gold Coast in 1889. Priority was given to efforts to prevent and treat the diseases which affected men, beasts and crops; solutions to this problem had to be found before any commercial progress could be made. Strict control of land and water assets had also to be maintained, and in this connection the Northern Nigeria Land and Native Rights Proclamation of 1910 marked a vital new departure: official recognition that the first duty of government was to give priority to Africans in undisturbed use of land rights, prevent alienation, prefer leasehold to freehold, and preserve existing custom rather than introduce European concepts of land tenure. Peasant production had proved itself; the key innovations were made by Africans themselves, so that by 1910 African ground-nut production was more important even than British cotton in Nigeria.[100]

10 The South African Question

BANTU DEVELOPMENTS: THE MFECANE

Of all the regions of the world where Britain sought to exert influence none exhibited such complications, and therefore presented such intractable dilemmas, as South Africa. Cape Colony was conquered from the Dutch in 1806 and retained in 1815 because of its strategic importance on the route to India.[1] The Boers became increasingly disaffected towards British rule, and, as a pastoral people, showed a disconcerting tendency to sprawl further in the interior in search of 6,000-acre farms.[2] Conditions were not attractive to British emigrants. Until the discovery of diamonds in 1869 and the Witwatersrand gold in 1886 its economic future looked bleak. The settlers were constantly in trouble with the large Coloured and Bantu populations, who displayed great energy. There were many wars. Britain felt herself to be caught between conflicting duties: between her liberal concern for the whites and her humanitarian concern for the blacks. Was South Africa going to be another Canada? Or had it, on account of the large non-European population, to be treated as another India?

After many hesitations and after-thoughts and changes of approach, it was easy to conclude by the 1880s that South Africa was perhaps an insoluble problem. So at least Gladstone thought, and Sir Charles Dilke agreed that the task of ruling it was all but impossible. To withdraw, however, could lead to anarchy, endangering British interests, whether strategic, economic or humanitarian.[3]

South Africa's history as an area of white settlement was largely shaped by the size and wide dispersion of the Bantu majority.[4] Shaka Zulu was a remarkable man who in a little over ten years before 1828 rose from the leadership of a small tribe of some 1,500 people in an area of about 100 square miles, to the rulership of a toughly-structured kingdom of two million people of diverse origins inhabiting 80,000 square miles. This feat involved securing a transfer of popular loyalty from clan, family and traditional chiefs to a compound state under a military commoner administration. It was made possible by a much more ruthless warfare pattern than had hitherto prevailed. The Zulu state he set up was so strong that it survived the mismanagement of two incompetent successors to pose a considerable threat to the European community in 1878, and under Cetshwayo to inflict a grievous defeat upon it. This state-building process and its repercussions disturbed a large section of the African continent. Shaka was a much feared and ultimately a much resented leader. Shaka's tyranny caused refugee movements and stimulated several breakaway imitators. This dispersion is known as the *mfecane*. Its origin, clearly, was related to a population increase and land shortage, but a possible desire to expand trading opportunities through fresh state-building cannot be ruled out.[5]

The dispersion of the Nguni took place over enormous distances during a period of some 35 years. These moving societies spread out in four main thrusts. Soshangane moved north-east into what later became south-eastern Rhodesia and Mozambique, and founded the Shangaan empire of Gasa. Zwangendaba moved north-east as far as Lake Nyasa to form a fragile Ngoni state which split further after his death. Mzilikazi, unlike the two afore-mentioned leaders, was not connected with groups of Shaka's rivals but was a rebellious general of Shaka himself. Mzilikazi moved northwards into the Transvaal, and after defeat there by the Boers in 1837, moved off again into what is now Rhodesia to form the centralised Ndebele kingdom. All these three movements initiated from the Zulu storm-centre round about 1821–22. The fourth movement started from Lesotho, moving north-west under Sebetwane, and, evading the Boers and the Ndebele, found resting place in Barotseland, where their Kololo state conquered and absorbed the Lozi inhabitants. Mzilikazi has the distinction of being the only African who offered any effective resistance to the Great Trek. Zwangendaba, starting with only a few hundred followers, marched 2,000 miles and then built a large nation many thousands strong. Not all the notable state-building was done at such a remove. Nearer the Zulu heartland, the Dlamini clans established a tough Ngwane or Swazi state, Moshweshwe forged the Sotho state out of many disparate elements, and Faku, chief of the Mpondo, brilliantly held his people together in the face of wave after wave of invasion. Meanwhile the Thembu were forced south, and a group of refugees in Xhosaland took on the name Mfengu and adopted western ways more readily than their settled Xhosa neighbours.[6]

The broad significance of the nineteenth century for the Bantu was that they became a labour force without independence or initiative. This was not, however, an inevitable or continuous process. Many African peasants eventually became wage-earners in the white man's economy as a result of pressures, complex, intense and various. 'By precept and persuasion, aggression and annexation', the elements of European civilisation were remorselessly introduced among them.[7] First and foremost they found themselves labouring on European farms. The remnants of societies broken by the impact of Shaka, such as the Mfengu, entered the Cape Colony as soldiers and farm labourers, and the results of the 1857 cattle killing initiated

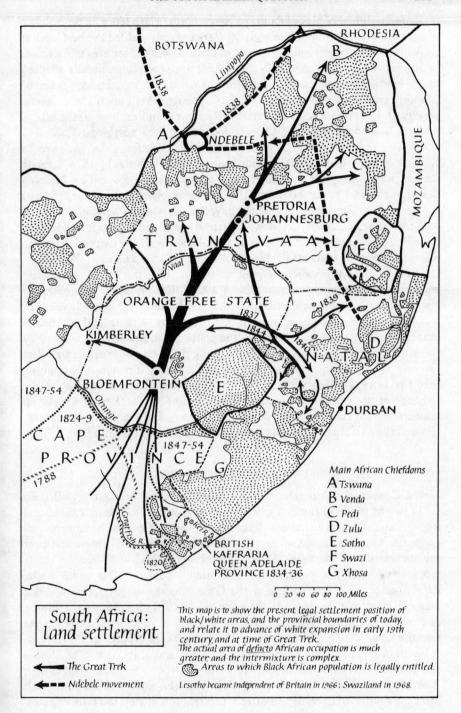

BOTSWANA

RHODESIA

Limpopo

1838

1838

B

A

1838

NDEBELE

1838

C

MOZAMBIQUE

PRETORIA

JOHANNESBURG

T R A N S V A A L

F

Vaal

ORANGE FREE STATE

1839

KIMBERLEY

1837

1844

1840

D

N A T A L

BLOEMFONTEIN

1847-54

Orange

E

1824-9

DURBAN

C A P E

1847-54

P R O V I N C E

G

1788

Main African Chiefdoms

A Tswana

B Venda

Great Fish R.

C Pedi

D Zulu

Koke R.

E Sotho

BRITISH

F Swazi

KAFFRARIA

1820

QUEEN ADELAIDE

G Xhosa

PROVINCE 1834-36

0 20 40 60 80 100 Miles

South Africa: land settlement

This map is to show the present legal settlement position of
black/white areas, and the provincial boundaries of today,
and relate it to advance of white expansion in early 19th
century, and at time of Great Trek.
The actual area of <u>defacto</u> African occupation is much
greater, and the intermixture is complex.
   Areas to which Black African population is legally entitled.

⬅━━━ The Great Trek

⬅┅┅ Ndebele movement

Lesotho became independent of Britain in 1966; Swaziland in 1968.

major resettlement of black labourers. Every border clash left a larger number of Africans embedded in white society. Wars not only yielded the best land to the whites, but a considerable measure of control over the services of Africans.

And yet down to the mid-1880s many African peasants successfully adapted to upheavals. Not all became labourers, without an intermediate stage of adapting traditional subsistence farming to new market opportunities. Some smallholding peasants competed effectively against whites, both in the sale of produce and in purchase of Crown lands at sales in north-east Cape and Natal. In the 1860s the Cape possessed neither the means nor the need to clear all white-owned land of African occupiers, and in Natal by 1874, Labour was so short owing to five million acres of land being occupied by Africans that Indians had to be brought into the sugar plantations on indentured contracts. Even in the Transvaal the government was too weak and tenuous to keep African occupation down. African agriculture began to decline, however, under the impact of mineral discoveries, with the determined white effort to coerce peasants off the land in order to get cheap mining labour. [8]

Africans also put up a strong political fight against the subjection of their chiefdoms. This was only accomplished with difficulty, and by methods not always scrupulous. Some were beaten violently by guns (for example the Pedi and the Zulu), some by being tricked into concession of their land (the Swazi 'documents that killed us'), some by 'the politics of intimidation' (suffered by the Mpondo and East Griqua), some by outright annexation (such as the West Griquas sitting on the diamond fields), and some by diplomatic bargaining (like the Tswana). [9] For years the Orange Free State hammered away at the territory of the Sotho and annexed large areas of it. The British stepped in temporarily in 1868 to help Basutoland; when Cape administration was restored the result was a not unsuccessful Sotho protest: the Gun War. [10]

ECONOMIC PROBLEMS AND THE ROOTS OF SEGREGATION

Unlike Canada and Australia, staple crops suitable for marketing in Britain could not be made to flourish in South Africa, and so to attract capital and immigrants. The white labour force in the early nineteenth century was exiguous. The climate was afflicted by droughts. Unreliable climate and poor soil meant that wool, coffee, sugar and tobacco all failed to become staple crops; wine was not good, and wheat was expensive. The cattle trade, supplying meat to ships calling at the Cape, was the most important single factor in economic expansion in the years before the 1830s. Before the mining discoveries of the 1870s and 1880s wool came nearest to being a staple, and was the chief source of wealth at mid-century. Wool exports mounted from 5.5 million lbs in 1851 to 25 million lbs by 1862, and at its peak in 1872 wool was the basis of the economy, but this was far from being comparable with Australian development. Transvaal wool was the lowest grade in British markets. South Africa failed to attract capital, and, owing to cattle diseases, locusts, wars with the Bantu and drought, domestic capital was very slow to accumulate. Until 1860 Cape Town could not afford the necessary breakwater and docking facilities. Very few opportunities for employment or land existed to attract the immigrant. In 1835 there were only 90,000 whites in South Africa. The yearly average addition between 1820 and 1860 was a mere 750 immigrants; and even in the years of high British emigration from 1847 to 1850 only a few thousand chose to enter South Africa. Yet between 1837 and 1846, 100,750 British people emigrated to Australia.

Thus it was only the great mineral discoveries which belatedly galvanised the economy and provided it at long last with a major export staple and a bigger domestic market. After diamond production began, the total receipts of the Cape treasury doubled between 1869 and 1872, and in the 12-year period from 1870 the value of diamond exports exceeded the value of the agricultural and pastoral exports of the previous 36 years. Capital was readily invested at 4 per cent. Diamonds gave railways the initial, vital push, and after gold discoveries, investment flooded in. As with gold rushes elsewhere, local markets with high purchasing power for agricultural products developed rapidly. Thereafter the economic structure of South Africa continued to rest on gold.

The first big impetus to African industrial employment came with the opening of the diamond diggings at Kimberley in 1869–70. Mining was from the beginning virtually dependent on African labour. By 1874 there were 10,000 Africans at Kimberley, some of them coming from as far away as Barotseland. After 1886, there were the Rand gold-mines, which required an even larger labour force. Recruitment was often by bargaining with chiefs, none too solicitous for the welfare of their subjects, though direct recruitment using brandy and fraudulent misrepresentation was also practised. By 1899 there were about 160,000 African mineworkers on the Witwatersrand. Railway building now forged ahead, and this brought yet more Africans into the European economy, for example in the western Cape. It was not an attractive job and recruitment was difficult. Resort was sometimes had to kidnapping.[11]

It is now absolutely clear that the mining revolution determined the entire future of Africans in South Africa. The pattern of discrimination and coercion was profoundly shaped by the needs of the mines, and the new phenomenon of migrant labour made great changes in African life-styles and organisation, turning states into rural reservoirs of labour. It not only divorced men from their families but hindered the acquisition by Africans of urban political skills. The restructuring of the labour market, which took place after the discovery of diamond- and gold-mines, provided the pattern for much of the twentieth-century economy, a pattern dominated from the first by black unskilled labour, subject to a colour bar, and in a weak bargaining position in industrial relations because the magnates had the support of the law to ensure adequate labour supplies – taxation pushed Africans into white

employment, and land regulations pushed them off the land; and the
magnates developed their own monopolist recruiting system. The labourers,
often migrant labourers, were organised in a compound system which had its
prototype in the traditional form of farm labouring community. But there
were special reasons why this form of organisation commended itself to the
ex-farmer prospectors: diamond workers were put into compounds in order to
check illicit diamond buying, and the Rand migrant gold workers were treated
similarly because of the need to house them cheaply. The differential line
between skilled and unskilled was drawn rigidly; the first legal colour bar was
enacted in the Transvaal in 1893. White miners saw themselves as a labour
aristocracy. The later architects of apartheid in all sectors of the economy
took the goldmining industry as their model. Rhodes, as the leading mining
magnate of his day, played an especially dominant role in the evolution of a
harsh racially-determined labour system. He imposed a poll tax which forced
all families to some extent out of subsistence and into the cash economy; he
pioneered the break up of communal landholding systems with his Glen Grey
enactment, ensuring individual tenure in certain areas, and did so with the
full intention of creating a supply of landless labourers. The result, it is said,
was a degree of exploitation never achieved by a plantation system of
slavery.[12]

There can be no doubt that the roots of segregation in modern South Africa
were really put down at about the time the word is believed first to have been
used there – in the first decade of the twentieth century. Nor is there any
doubt that its ideological and future legislative shape was first modelled by
the British rather than the Afrikaners, who were not a significant political
force at the time. The key document is the Lagden Report of the South
African Native Affairs Commission 1903–05. Lagden's own personal premise
was that 'there is and must be a dividing line between semi-barbarism and
civilisation'; he saw white supremacy as axiomatic, and race and colour as
legitimate differentials in granting political rights; he saw the African as a
wage labourer rather than as a peasant farmer. He envisaged an economic
colour bar and pass laws to regulate an adequate cheap black labour force.
Two features were clearly set forth in the report. First, the principle of
territorial segregation, with reserves set apart for Africans, and the racially
exclusive and final delimitation of land areas. Secondly, there was to be
political separation too – the introduction of separate voters rolls, African
communal representation, and (though the Report was not unanimous about
this) the abolition of individual Cape African franchise. Not only was the
Commission made up entirely of British members, the Report was received
with scarcely a murmur of protest either in Britain or South Africa. It has
also been demonstrated that the notorious Union Land Act of 1913 (which
first enacted a policy of territorial segregation) was based upon Lagden's
principles; the British government admitted as much in 1913, and no
responsible historian will now deny that the guiding principles of the Union's

policy specifically and precisely emanated from this Report and this Act — produced in a decade which saw a sustained attack on an independent African peasantry and ever-increasing labour coercion in every part of South Africa.[13]

There is, however, room for argument as to *why* this occurred. There is a strong tendency in some quarters to see these policies (and logically, even Union itself) as a capitalist plot to produce for South Africa cheap labour, and a specific attempt to formulate a native policy appropriate to the conditions of capitalist economic growth. Apart from the fact that the British government disliked 'capitalists', and certainly was never manipulated by them, such a view is too narrow. It sees South Africa in far too isolated a context, and it underestimates the extent to which racial discrimination for its own (or at least non-economic) sake was a motive political force at the turn of the century.

The British government arrived at conclusions which suited the mining magnates, but they did so by a wholly different route. They stressed in South Africa black representation through native councils rather than extension of the franchise: but principles of segregation and restraint were concurrently advocated and applied in areas where no 'capitalist' involvement had penetrated significantly — such as Northern Nigeria, and Kenya (where Indians were feared for their supposed insanitary state), and Western Australia (where the aborigines were treated as insignificant from the economic point of view as from every other). In every case the health reasons for segregation were frequently stressed, and South Africa was no exception. In the formulation of the thoughts about native policy by British and South African segregationists (such as Milner, Selborne, Seely and Lionel Curtis), the influence of the Southern states of the United States of America was far more important than 'capitalist' influence. Moreover, it is wrong to consider the early twentieth century as one in which segregation was *created*: Bryce was nearer the truth when he saw the need as not to *start* segregation but to *maintain* it.[14]

It is true that the safeguards for African interests in the High Commission Territories which were appended to the Act of Union were not such as to inhibit migrant labour, but this was not because the government wished to help capitalists, but because they were so imbued with the strength of the moral proposition which Churchill formulated: 'no man has a right to be idle and I do not exempt the African'. And if there was a fear of African voting dominance under an 'open' system, this was based on moral and political grounds rather than economic ones. It is hard to believe that there would not have been segregation in South Africa even if the mines had never opened. The commitment of the Dutch Reformed Churches to 'separation' began in the 1860s, and has ever thereafter been an enormous (and non-economic) influence in underpinning an ideology which eventually culminated in the 1930s, under its guidance, as 'apartheid'.[15]

ANGLO-BOER RELATIONS: FROM TREK TO WAR, 1835–99

The Cape was a Dutch colony founded in 1652, conquered and retained against the will of most, though not all, of its inhabitants, in 1806. The first British leader of any stature to descend upon the colony was Dr John Philip who was superintendent of all the London Missionary stations in South Africa from 1819 to 1851.[16] In 1820 some 5,000 British settlers were sent out to the eastern Cape with government assistance, a notable addition to the colony's scanty white population. It was the first attempt to make a British colony in South Africa in spirit as well as in law, and indeed the first European planned emigration of the nineteenth century.

The Great Trek of Boers out of the Cape Colony occupied almost a decade after about 1835.[17] The explanation is not easy to be certain about. The original motives are shrouded in secret planning. Followers may not have agreed with the inner impulses of their leaders. The view taken here is that fundamentally it was a Boer national rebellion against British government, an attempt to replace a London government, believed to be wrongly motivated, by a more local, effective and suitable one. By 1845 some 14,000 Boers had crossed the Orange River. The rebellious character of the movement was masked by the existence of ample frontier lands into which they could move. The leaders did not fight the British government because they were able to place themselves beyond its effective reach, even though in theory they remained British subjects until the 1850s, and the practical effects of their supposed flight into principled emancipation was hardly exhilarating: life in the exposed frontierlands was hard. This was not a random spreading out caused by uncontrolled land-hunger (though such a pastoral imperative could explain its size), but the deliberate re-settlement of a disaffected community. Long preliminary investigations and surveys were made by 1834 in Natal and as far north as the Zoutpansberg mountains in the northern Transvaal. The immediate timing of the decision to move may have been the closing of the frontier. Sir Benjamin D'Urban had annexed Queen Adelaide Province and thus raised hopes of obtaining free land in new areas. Colonial secretary Lord Glenelg abandoned the province by a despatch dated 26 December 1835. He felt its retention would only aggravate frontier problems. D'Urban had upset the colonial office by referring to the Xhosa inhabitants as 'irreclaimable savages'. (It seems that the first word worried them more than the second, since it implied pessimistic aspersion cast upon mission work.) But behind this final disgust at the attempt to maintain a fixed, restricted boundary, there were two broad causes of complaint which had been gradually building up in the Boer mind, and which had already led to plans for the Trek.

One of these causes was the growing insistence on Anglicising the Boers, but except in the schools, the policy was only softly applied. This timidity annoyed people without changing their old habits. English was made the official language from 1827. The Dutch monetary system was scrapped, and in 1827 the British judicial system was adopted. Settler participation in government was kept down. The Boers not unnaturally felt that Britain wanted to reduce them to political, economic and cultural vassalage. At the same time they felt that the British government was insufficiently able to keep and impose order on Africans, though they perversely opposed most violently an attempt to enrol them in a militia. The other cause of difference was over native policy. An early manifestation of discontent (it was no more than that) came with the minor Slagtersnek rebellion of 1815. This resulted from the attempt by a circuit judge to arrest with a Hottentot levy a Boer called F. C. Bezuidenhout for alleged maltreatment of a Hottentot herdsman in his employ. Bezuidenhout was killed resisting arrest; his brother swore vengeance and led a rising of 60 armed men. The original proceedings were thought by him and the Boers in general to be unjust. Six rebels were hanged in 1816, and the episode bit deep into folk memory because in four out of six cases the rope broke.[18] Two pieces of legislation were found especially infuriating. By Ordinance No.50 of 1828 the Cape government cancelled various restrictive laws (1787–1819) hitherto applying to Hottentots, Coloured and Africans. It seemed to give whites and Coloureds equality before the law. Henceforth all free persons, regardless of colour, were to have equal access to the courts and the same rights, including those of land-holding, although many legal and civil differentials remained. Passes for Hottentots were abolished. Then came the emancipation of slaves in the British empire in 1833. While there were only 35,742 slaves in the Cape, and few of the Boer frontiersmen had slaves, all of them had servants, and the anti-slavery movement's nagging fight to improve the status of all black people gravely affected Boer authority over their own servants. Livingstone noted that the Emancipation Act had made the Boers 'exceedingly vexed with the British government'. Piet Retief, one of the chief leaders of the Voortrekkers, commented in his Manifesto of 2 February 1837: 'we can see as the result of this prejudice, nothing but the total ruin of the country ... it is our determination ... to preserve proper relations between master and servant'. His sister, Anna Steenkamp, was even more explicit. She said they trekked because they objected to:

> the shameful and unjust proceedings with reference to the freedom of our slaves – and yet it is not their freedom that drove us to such lengths, as their being placed on an equal footing with Christians, contrary to the laws of God, and the natural distinction of race and religion, so that it was intolerable for any decent Christian to bow down beneath such a yoke; wherefore we rather withdrew in order to preserve our doctrines in purity.

Anna Steenkamp also mentioned the turbulence and arrogance of the blacks and the absence of compensation for property despoiled in their raids. The essential Trekboer doctrine was eventually enshrined in clause nine of the *Grondwet* (or fundamental constitution) of the South African Republic in

1858: 'The people will admit no equalising between the whites and the coloured inhabitants, either in Church or State'.[19]

The effect of the Great Trek on the Bantu was immeasurably disastrous. The Boers moved into the desirable fertile area with 15 to 50 inches of rainfall a year. The area of contact and conflict between black and white was immensely widened, and relations came to depend, not on humanitarian principles laid down in London, but on a handful of ignorant and scattered farmers whose technology was scarcely superior to that of the Bantu and who relied on their guns to get their way, being as much deficient in financial resources as in political or administrative experience. The movement into the high veld intensified the religious sanction the Boers believed they had for their feeling of separateness. It also intensified their intellectual retreat into a defensive *laager*. They had no books except the bible, and the bible seemed to provide a mirror image of the Great Trek. Captivity, Exodus, the Promised Land, God's Chosen People: the Old Testament seemed to speak directly to the Boers. The Trekboer was an extremely interesting creature, the most important example of a European group which cut itself off from the mainstream of European life (though partly because the climate compelled trek in order to achieve all-the-year round grazing), and set out on a line of evolution on its own. By the 1850s there was not much trace of any external influence on the Transvaal constitution except the bible. The Orange Free State constitution was more open to American influence and European advice. But many Boers had not the faintest glimmerings of any theory of mankind except that provided by the Old Testament; the Africans were to some of the Boers heathen to be rooted out before the Lord. This was something the British of the time, in a short-lived humanitarian phase, had been unable to accept. Obviously it was the most unstable and restless Boers who trekked. Piet Retief changed his home at least four times before he ever thought of trekking.[20] Not all the Boers trekked,[21] but the Great Trek remains an important event in South African history, and the central event in the evolution of the Afrikaner mystique. Politically the fragmentation of the area was greatly increased. The British annexed Natal in 1843 to keep the Boers off the coast, and continued to hem them in during the 1860s. The main two Boer republics were recognised in the 1850s: the South African Republic (Transvaal) informally and vaguely by the Sand River Convention of 1852, and the Orange Free State by the Bloemfontein Convention of 1854. These were not recognitions of equal states by Britain, but represented rather the line of least resistance, the sequel to military defeats by the Bantu, and contemptuous abandonment of a handful of isolated, land-locked, obdurate pastoralists in chronically bankrupt states, with the belief that Africans, wild beasts and insects would polish them off in no time at all. There was much faction-fighting within these small-scale communities: the political division into several republics was paralleled by the co-existence of three (and at one time four) Dutch Reformed Churches. By 1857 territorial fragmentation was at its maximum. There were five republics and three colonies, together with a number of thoroughly viable African chiefdoms, such as the Zulu, Gasa, Ndebele and Shona.[22]

The abdication of British responsibility for African interests implied in the recognition of the South African Republic and Orange Free State contrasts strangely with her concern in the 1830s. From the mid-1850s, however, there was a general hardening of racial attitudes towards non-European peoples,' and the fire had long since gone out of the humanitarian movement. As a result, for the remainder of the century, and indeed at least down to the enactment of the Natives Land Act (1913), the British government did not find disagreement about native policy a serious point of issue between them and the settlers in South Africa, whether British or Boer.[23] At the same time, the vital force of the Bantu was gradually diminishing. After a series of so-called Kaffir wars lasting almost a century after 1778 (when the Great Fish River had been fixed as the boundary of the Cape), the natural reaction to so much storm and stress was total neglect of the Bantu. The Xhosa broke themselves in the millenarian cattle-killing episode of 1857. The Sotho were pre-occupied in holding themselves together against external attack and internal divisions. The Zulu under their last great leader Cetshwayo were smashed after their defeat at Ulundi in 1879. There was severe conflict around the whole horseshoe-shaped frontier area of black and white contact in the later 1870s. The issue was in doubt, but finally the whites gained the upper hand, fundamentally aided by the mineral discoveries which at last made it possible to run European-style states in the bush. Thus from the 1880s it was possible for the first time for the Bantu to be disregarded, though they had previously played a central part in South African history. For the remainder of the century it was not relations between black and white which held the centre of the political stage, but the duel between the British and the Boers.

Why was it that the Boers became ever more discontented with British rule? Imperial assistance in removing the Zulu and Pedi threats in 1879 paradoxically diminished any further advantage to be seen in British imperial presence. Troubles renewed themselves when the British annexed the Transvaal in 1877 as a preliminary to the setting up of a projected South African confederation. This was Carnarvon's scheme, though he was by no means the first to advocate it. Governor Sir George Grey had planned a federation in 1856.

In the 1870s there were four attempts to bring about a confederation of the South African colonies: by Kimberley in 1873, by Carnarvon between 1875 and 1877, by Hicks Beach in 1878–79 and by Kimberley in 1880. All failed, principally because they were attempts to impose unity in advance of any local demand. The most forceful effort was that made by Carnarvon, but not even he was able to overcome local objection. He failed to convince the Cape Dutch that co-operation with Britain in an internally self-governing dominion could mean anything more than the old 'yoke of England'. The Cape did not like the idea that she would have to bear the financial burdens of the native policies of her impoverished neighbours. Carnarvon pushed ahead with a ruthless and doctrinaire enthusiasm, and sent out Froude, whose academic cocksure confidence and rash oratory nettled the British and, despite his good intentions, provoked the Boers.[24] Carnarvon had bold conceptions, but when it came to putting them into practice he was hesitant and indecisive; 'Twitters', Disraeli called him. And so he failed to fulfil his aims of disengagement accompanied by the setting up of a new imperial bastion which would secure strategic interests and protect the Africans.

After annexation, an Afrikaner national movement developed,[25] and the Transvaal Boers hit back and defeated the British at Majuba Hill. Gladstone's government then signed the Pretoria Convention in 1881. This restored self-government to the Transvaal, subject to something called British 'suzerainty', an unexplained word, though the historian may be tempted to equate it with 'informal empire'. Gladstone probably meant it to include the powers of sovereignty without its obligations, to imply overlordship without direct rule, and control without administration. It was, even for devious Gladstone, a highly ambivalent conjuring trick. Britain retained control over external policy, native affairs and troop movements. So was the Transvaal independent or was it not? The Boers at any rate hated all the 33 clauses of the Pretoria Convention, which they described as 'a glass of milk with 33 dead flies in it'. Gladstone now became worried by the belief that it was vital to hold the loyalty of the Cape Afrikaners. Reaction to the 1877 annexation extended to the Cape where the *Bond* party was founded in 1879 to work for a 'united and self-dependent South Africa'.[26] Links between President Kruger and the Cape Afrikaner Bond were close between 1881 and 1883 and a common sympathy united them. In all probability this was a transient link. But the British needed to create a loyal colonial Afrikaner community in the Cape as a counterpoise to Kruger's republic. Gladstone accordingly embarked on a conciliatory policy towards Kruger, but it was really the Cape he was giving way to rather than Kruger. The London Convention of 1884 created the framework of policies and politics which ultimately resulted in the Anglo-Boer war, since Kruger saw no finality in it. The most contentious of all matters was that the vital point was unsettled. The convention tacitly withdrew all control except approval of treaties, but omitted mention of the word 'suzerainty' which was nowhere expressly abolished. The convention gave back to the Transvaal its old title of South African Republic. The convention was a major concession to the Boers, and a recent historian has seen it as clear evidence that Britain was already being hustled out and Gladstone was in effect 'abdicating to Kruger'.[27] By the time gold was discovered on the Witwatersrand, Britain had already lost the initiative, and could do no more than try to limit Kruger's expansionist policy. It was axiomatic that he must at all costs be prevented from getting independent access to the sea. Britain managed to achieve this, but in all other directions the Boers broke out of all the boundaries set for them in 1884. They were largely alienated from Britain by 1881. The British defeat at Majuba left a bitter legacy. The Boers were thereafter contemptuous of the British army and everything British. For years afterwards, in any personal quarrel, Boers would taunt the British by reminding them of their humiliation at Majuba.[28] By 1884 Kruger was already relatively so powerful, backed by the moral force of the rising tide of the Afrikaner nationalist movement, that the fulcrum of power had already moved from Cape Town to Pretoria.

This shift was merely confirmed by the 1886 discoveries of gold on the Witwatersrand in the largest quantities the world had ever known. The Transvaal became the key to South African prosperity and 'the richest spot on earth'. The definitive confirmation in 1895 of the fact that the Transvaal was sitting on the world's largest supply of gold meant that a Boer-dominated future for South Africa was probable. British miners settling on the Witwatersrand had no political rights: they were 'Uitlanders'. Like African leaders, Kruger tried to turn concessions (brandy, dynamite, etc) to good account.[29]

After the failure of all attempts to federate South Africa as the preliminary for disengagement from an increasingly intractable situation between 1856 and 1880, both Liberal and Conservative ministers (who had equally followed this policy) recognised for the future that unity could not be imposed in advance of any local demand. But the search for a 'federate and quit' solution still went on, though in a quieter and less provocative way. It was revived when Cecil John Rhodes as prime minister of the Cape (1890) attracted the support of Hofmeyr's Bond party on a basis of expansion to the north by colonial (as opposed to imperial) agency. Their alliance made it possible to plan a British-sponsored closer political union. If Kruger had been prepared to enter a South African commercial union as the prelude to the political one he could probably have obtained his desired independent access to the sea. But Kruger was not prepared to sacrifice his own Transvaal-sponsored federal movement to that aggressive federal movement based on the Cape which had been acquiring imperial support from the end of the 1880s. Ripon as colonial secretary wrote in 1894 that he was looking to 'a sort of Federal Union of South Africa . . . in which we of course should have the hegemony and no more'. If this could have been achieved he would not have minded leaving the Transvaal under a republican form of government.[30] In a very definite sense the whole crisis decade of the 1890s can be interpreted as one of local conflict between two alternative federal schemes: a Transvaal, Boer-dominated one and a Cape, British-dominated one. Responsible government was granted to Natal in 1892 partly to promote the British federal movement.[31] When the British government threw its weight decisively behind the English-speaking colonists, the Anglo-Boer war broke out.

Bad relations between the Transvaal and the British government were seriously deepened by the Jameson Raid. Old wounds had begun to heal, and relations had steadily improved in the decade before this event, which took place at the end of 1895. But as a result of it, all possibility of reconciliation was thrown back for many years, perhaps forever.[32] The Jameson Raid took its name from Dr Leander Starr Jameson, administrator of Mashonaland, Rhodesia. He led a well-liquored British posse from British Bechuanaland into the Transvaal (then in effect a foreign state) on 29 December 1895 and ignominiously surrendered to Boer commandos four days later. The raid was a fiasco. Rhodes had intended to foment Uitlander discontent in Johannesburg and to support a projected internal revolt there by sending in Chartered Company police waiting on the Transvaal border. But this was action he wished to defer. Jameson jumped the gun. The whole idea of *a* raid and British official reaction to *the* raid was shocking; 'inexcusable in its folly and unforgivable in its consequences' is not too severe a judgement.[33] An unproven hypothesis by Blainey suggests that the idea of a raid was plotted by deep-level mining magnates, who might not have had political objectives, but certainly had economic grievances against Kruger's régime, such as its dynamite monopoly. Or, if Trapido is right, a need to rationalise control of the labour force (as a major part of an overall need to cut costs) in the face of inadequate state power to achieve such ends, could point in a similar direction. The financial backing came largely from Beit, to the tune of £200,000. Rhodes's stake was a mere £60,000.[34] Although *a* raid was planned before Chamberlain took office, he liked the sound of it, became an accessory before the fact, and hoped to get political advantage from it. Chamberlain and Rhodes could be cleared of charges of complicity in *the* raid and a probable uprising in Johannesburg.[35] In the subsequent Committee of Inquiry Chamberlain was shielded and exonerated. Even the Liberal Opposition was anxious to protect the good name of Britain and had no love for Kruger's republic. The Committee condemned Rhodes, but Chamberlain then condoned Rhodes's part. These processes of exonerating and condoning did, if possible, even more harm than the event itself. The Jameson Raid and its aftermath gave birth to a new form of self-conscious Afrikaner national feeling, which laid stress on the exclusiveness of the wronged group and its need to close the ranks. The Raid renewed suspicion of all aliens, whatever their origin. It was the effective beginning of all subsequent permanently-rooted Afrikaner resentment of the British. Its seriousness was recognised in Britain where it produced one of those rare occasions when imperial events became a major issue in domestic discussions.[36]

The Anglo-Boer war broke out on 11 October 1899, some two years after Sir Alfred Milner had become governor of the Cape and high commissioner for South Africa. The war has sometimes been called 'Milner's War', sometimes 'Joe's War'. Such labels are wide of the mark.[37] The Anglo-Boer war, like any other, was not a matter of personalities (although there is no denying the incompatibility of Milner and Kruger), but a conflict of inter-state interests.[38] The question was: who was to run South Africa? Was the future of South Africa to be found in a British-dominated federal dominion or in a Boer-dominated federal republic? Neither side was really prepared to make significant concessions, although Kruger, when it was too late, was prepared to make ones denied earlier. After the Bloemfontein Conference of June 1899 Kruger saw the truth sadly: 'It is our country that you want'.[39] It was not a question of getting votes for Uitlanders (treated, declared Milner, like 'helots'), though that cause was pressed into service at a late stage as a *casus belli*. Captain March Phillipps, who had several months' experience living and working among the Uitlanders before the war, knew perfectly well what he was fighting for. In 1900 he wrote: 'my own reason for fighting is plain and strong. I am fighting for a united South Africa'. As for the mass of Uitlanders, he added, they had no grievances: 'We used to read the London papers to find out *what our grievances were;* and very frequently they would be due to causes of which we had never even heard'.[40] Campbell-Bannerman rightly described it as 'the silly franchise question'. Nor, on the other hand, was the war merely a matter of the Transvaal's fighting for its independence. Kipling on a visit in 1900 saw quite clearly that the Boers made no secret of their intentions: 'they want to sweep the English into the sea, to lick their own nigger and govern South Africa with a gun instead of a ballot box'.[41] Perhaps his view was expressed too emotionally, but the main burden of it is to the point. There was in the Transvaal positive aggression; Kruger nearly lost power to Joubert for giving it inadequate expression. And if Milner played brinkmanship, so did Kruger. The difference was that Kruger was subject to conflicting advice and prone to clumsiness in diplomacy. As a result his obstinacy was out-manoeuvred.[42]

For an accurate statement of what the war was about we can do no better than turn to the statements made by Milner and Chamberlain. Milner said it was 'the great game between ourselves and the Transvaal for the mastery of South Africa', the game of 'uniting South Africa as a British State'. This British state was to be large and just, but it was not to be one in which the Africans would have anything but a subordinate place: 'the *ultimate* end is a self-governing white Community, supported by a *well treated* and *justly governed* black labour force from Cape Town to Zambesia'. Wide horizons, expanding horizons, were involved. And furthermore, Milner expressed the hope that South Africa was going 'not only to federate itself as a free nation like Canada and Australia, but to be one of the means of federating the Empire'.[43] As for Chamberlain, he thoroughly agreed that they must strengthen 'the weakest link in the imperial chain'. 'Our supremacy in South Africa', he said, 'and our existence as a great power in the world are involved'. Or again: 'What is now at stake is the position of Great Britain in South Africa – and with it the estimate formed of our power and influence in our Colonies and throughout the world ...'[44] In innumerable ways Kruger's régime seemed to treat Britain as inferior and to defy her. This could not be allowed. Kruger had in fact touched the British on a most sensitive spot: their fear of becoming one of the dying empires of the world, the pessimistic realisation that Britain as a world power was in relative decline, especially compared with Germany. The Anglo-Boer war has to be seen in its international setting. The Cape route to the east remained vitally important: and political supremacy in South Africa was threatened by the new wealth of the Transvaal. In 1898 German naval expansion had begun and this contributed to the sense of urgency felt by Chamberlain and Milner. The intervention of Germany in South African affairs from 1890 enhanced the tendency to see the question in 'great power' terms and to make the strengthening of the weak link in the imperial chain all the more necessary. The Boers were not only blocking the creation of a British-dominated consolidation but seemed bent on introducing Germany into southern Africa. It was universally believed that the search for British supremacy in the Transvaal was being undermined from outside as well as from within. The Germans seemed to be stiffening Boer resistance to British designs. There was close public co-operation between Germany and the Transvaal between 1894 and 1896. Germany took a keen interest and gave diplomatic support. By this time the Transvaal had a population of 5,000 German immigrants and an investment of 300 million marks, a substantial stake. After 1896 a large and wealthy German community developed rapidly, giving Kruger's government considerable assistance in those business activities from which it hoped to shut out British capital.[45]

It is a measure of Chamberlain's general anxiety that he made three fatal mistakes. He greatly exaggerated the threat to British interests in South Africa, believing in a non-existent pan-Afrikaner conspiracy, perhaps backed by Germany. He believed that the Transvaal would yield to firm diplomatic pressure, and he seriously under-estimated the confidence and aggressiveness of the Boers. Worst of all, he chose Milner for the office of high commissioner, a man who only confirmed him in his other errors of judgement.[46]

Other people found it hard to believe that so much was at stake, particularly when it seemed as if the war was being fought to redress Uitlander grievances. Thus Merriman wrote:

> People in England seem mad. One would think the Empire was engaged in a death grapple with a Napoleon instead of being on a piratical mission to stamp the freedom out of two little states whose united population would not make that of a second-rate English town! What a spectacle for those who hate us and sneer at our hypocrisy.[47]

To Smuts and F. W. Reitz the war was the culmination of *A century of wrong,* the title they gave to propaganda pamphlets written on the very eve of war. Smuts complained of British lies, insults and injustices: the claim to 'humanity, civilisation and equal rights, upon which the British Government bases its actions, is nothing but a cloak for that hypocritical spirit of annexation and piracy which has always characterised her actions in all her relations with our people'.[48] A partisan statement, certainly, but Britain had unquestionably been guilty of foolish aggression, in 1877 and 1895 as well as 1899, and throughout the imperial century her policy had vacillated. Issues had been shirked, hesitations had abounded, and retrocessions had been made. The Boers had not been conciliated. The Bantu had lost all the best land. The British taxpayer had paid out millions simply for the privilege of being execrated as the perpetrators of an unspeakable tyranny.[49] During the course of the war the liberal historian G. P. Gooch wrote in his contribution to a book about the empire: 'Till the advent of Krugerism, the balance of evil-doing lay with us'. This was, perhaps, in the circumstances, about as far as he could go without being accused of treason; it would be interesting to know if in other circumstances he would have included the qualification.[50]

There is no truth in the notion that Milner and Chamberlain became prisoners of the magnates and allowed Rhodes to drag them into war. Milner and Chamberlain successfully influenced them and used them for their own purposes. Nor were they subject to public pressure: rather the reverse. Milner was an adroit propagandist, deeply involved with the press, and controlling successfully at this time the flow of information to the public.[51]

If it was not an unpopular war, there was nevertheless an uneasy feeling in Britain that all was not well. 'Pro-Boers' protested. Emily Hobhouse became famous for her denunciations. One participant regarded it as the last of the 'gentlemen's wars', another founded the boy scout movement on some of its practices. But Campbell-Bannerman, and in private Milner also, spoke of 'methods of barbarism'. Harcourt, Morley and Lloyd George were also openly critical. Opinion upon the war divided families. At all events it was a chastening experience, bringing international unpopularity as well as evidence of military muddle.[52] It was concluded by the peace of Vereeniging in 1902. Kruger died in exile, a martyr. The war gave the Boers victims to mourn, including 20,000 women and children who died in ineptly administered communal concentration camps* designed, in part at least, to protect them, but probably set up chiefly as part of the strategy to end the resistance which the women could stiffen in their menfolk. There was a common cause to work for, the restoration of republican government. The conquered and war-torn republics became Crown Colonies for which Milner was responsible.[53]

THE POST-WAR PERIOD OF RECONSTRUCTION, 1902–07

Troubles did not come singly to the Boers. In 1896 rinderpest killed more

---

* While 'concentration camp' did not immediately acquire the stigma associated with it after the Nazi era, it will not suffice to regard the British ones as humanitarian devices – the intention was to precipitate the surrender of the commandos.

than one-third of the cattle in the Transvaal and Orange Free State. War accentuated the resultant rural dislocation. Kitchener's scorched-earth policy meant the destruction of 30,000 farm buildings, together with agricultural implements. The countryside was devastated, while the British towns were unscathed. The urbanisation of the Afrikaners began after the war, with six per cent of them in towns in 1904 and 20 per cent by 1910.[54]

Milner's reconstruction policy had two aspects, Anglicisation and land settlement.[55] As far as Anglicisation was concerned, English was the only official language of Milner's colonies. The Boers were displeased by the suppression of their language in government and by the dismissal of their officials. Milner's director of education, Sargant, proposed to build schools on the Winchester model, where youths would be taught 'to ride, to shoot from the saddle ... to command Natives as a midshipman at home learns to command a boat's crew' (1904). Candidates for teaching posts had to testify that they were 'in sympathy with the intention of the government to make the Orange River and Transvaal colonies permanently part of the British dominion'. But Milner never really attempted to win the allegiance of Boers to the imperial cause: Anglicising them was merely a minor gambit which could not affect South Africa's political destiny. Milner's main faith was pinned on land settlement. As he saw it, the essential imperial interest was simply to keep the Boers quiet until a demographic revolution, based on a big influx of British settlers, had overtaken them. In 1901 Milner wrote: 'I never lose sight of the fact that the "conciliation" of our former enemies ought never to be our *first* object', which he said ought to be one of making sure of the position by strengthening the British element, whether the Boers liked it or not.[56] Thus, is it any wonder that Milner produced a big growth in Afrikaner national consciousness?

Milner needed a large and rapid expansion of the mining industry to enable the economy to support a vastly increased population of British settlers. Thus his whole policy was in the direction of considerable state interference and control of financial and economic activities – but he retained the initiative. The political destiny of South Africa seemed to depend on the development of mining. Milner's plan was to produce more revenue by expanding a growth-industry. The revolution would hinge on immigration. His view, and it was widely shared, was that nothing could keep the Boers in check except a numerically superior British population. A Women's Immigration Department was set up, ostensibly to bring out nurses, nannies, governesses, and maids, but actually to bring out potential wives, in order to prevent settlers marrying Boers.

Milner's plans failed. First of all, land settlement was a flop. By 1906 only just over a thousand settlers had been placed in the Transvaal at a cost of about £2½ million. This gave rise to a Churchillian quip: Churchill disapproved of spending 'so much money upon the settlement of so few'. It was neither remunerative nor wise, he added, 'to try to change the character of a country by planting out farmers as if they were orchids'.[57] The rents were fixed too high. Regulations for settlers were based on Australian and New Zealand precedents which imposed conditions tougher than were common in South Africa. The government seemed unable to implement the scheme properly – and so the settlers were dissatisfied. The Boers naturally hated it. They could not rid themselves of the fear that the scheme was one of expropriation. Thus everybody was put out. The demographic revolution failed to occur. The census of 1911 indicated that the Boers made up 54 per cent of the total white population.

Then Milner failed to get the mines working again fast enough. By 1902 the number of Africans in mines had dropped to 30,000 owing to the alternative work temporarily available. Numbers were slow to pick up because of post-war reduction of wages and revolt against Portuguese recruiting companies. After a desperate search for alternative African labour, Milner came to the conclusion that needs could only be met by introducing the Chinese. By 1906 47,639 Chinese had arrived and the total labour force of 161,327 was at last back to about its pre-war level. At its peak in 1907, Chinese labour accounted for 27 per cent of the total.[58] The price paid was a heavy one. The cry of 'Chinese slavery' on the Rand damaged Milner's reputation and contributed greatly to the Unionist defeat in the 1906 election. In South Africa, British opinion about Chinese labour was divided, but the Afrikaners were strongly opposed to it.

Milner's bureaucratic Kindergarten was unpopular. His young men seemed tactless, aloof, haughty, inexperienced. They administered old laws much more vigorously. This was all the more intolerable because they were youngsters. It is not, however, entirely true that Milner deliberately preferred or unduly promoted the clean-limbed blue-eyed boys from Balliol. In fact he cast his net widely, and (it is said) included a brown-eyed American with athlete's foot as well as a green-eyed Cypriot with a squint. Be that as it may, the bureaucracy they generated was, as Churchill described it, 'costly and none too efficient'. Their language was just like that of the schoolboy comic papers of the day. Opponents were 'beasts' and 'rotters'; they also had a kind of perverse schoolboy code which made it perfectly legitimate to practise deceit and manipulation in achieving their ends. The unpopularity of the bureaucracy was accelerated by continual and severe criticism of it by the whole range of the white press. Milner conspicuously neglected to explain what he was doing. The disintegration of his Transvaal administration is incomprehensible unless it is seen against the background of its humiliation at the hands of the local English-speaking press as well as the Afrikaner newspapers. Discontent stirred up by journalists and Church leaders was not countered by adequate development schemes. Milner himself exaggerated what had been done in this respect, perhaps confusing rehabilitation with development. Only mining magnates seemed any better off as a result of his endeavours.[59]

The first act of the Liberal government on coming into power in December 1905 was to announce that Chinese labour importation would be stopped forthwith. There were, however, 47,000 Chinese on the Rand and they could not all be sent home at once. Moreover, several thousand more had already been indentured. Thus the Liberal government remained for the time being responsible for the working of the system their followers had denounced as slavery. It was this consideration above all others which led them to try to introduce responsible government into the Transvaal with all possible speed. This they did in December 1906, framing a constitution which they hoped would maintain British preponderance and produce an electoral victory for tʰe British. They did not wish the first ministry of a newly self-governing Transvaal to be a Boer ministry, and they looked to Sir Richard Solomon as prime minister designate. But *Het Volk* won a majority of the seats in the election of February 1907 and Botha had to be sent for as prime minister. Despite careful if hurried investigation on the spot by the West Ridgeway Committee, Liberal electoral arithmetic went astray. Policy thus looked more magnanimous than it was ever intended to be.[60]

In 1907 the Orange Free State also obtained responsible government. And once all four states in South Africa enjoyed the same form of government, federation between them became a matter of immediately practical politics. It was a conclusion wanted both by the Boers and by the British government. The British were happy because the initiative seemed to come from themselves, in the shape of the Kindergarten's so-called 'Selborne Memorandum'.[61] The Boers were happy because they felt that time and demography were on their side and would ensure them dominance.

THE MAKING OF THE UNION[62]

The Afrikaners wanted closer union partly because they conceived it to be an anti-capitalist, anti-magnate device. As early as 1899 Smuts had openly expressed his fears of the 'soulless gold-kings'. In 1906 he wrote, privately, of the mortal war South Africa was waging 'with organised money power which is corrupting politics'. 'As long as we stand divided and separated . . . the money power will beat us . . .' Smuts, then, viewed the closer union campaign as a means to checkmate and break the power of the magnates in the Transvaal, to prevent them from 'capturing supreme power here and so over the rest of South Africa'. Botha too said federation would 'lift South Africa out of the rut of selfish commercialism in which it is now stagnating'.[63] The anti-capitalist feelings of rank-and-file Afrikaners in this period were based on memories of the Jameson Raid as well as on the beginnings of their movement as landless wage-labourers into the cities, which gave them their first view of capitalists as a class ranged against themselves.[64]

The Afrikaners also saw closer union as a means of fulfilling their old desire to be rid of British interference. In April 1908 Botha said he looked forward to Union because British M.P.s would no longer be able to stick their fingers in the pie with impunity. Smuts regarded unification as 'the only alternative to Downing Street which is a most baneful factor', on account of 'the malevolence of Conservative Government and the stupidity of the Liberals'.[65]

The halfway house of a customs union buttressed by railway agreements between the independent administrations had been tried and found wanting.[66] Goals also existed which could not be achieved within the existing political framework: in particular there was a desire to create a firm base for national expansion. Ironically, Smuts, who so fiercely denounced the British empire in A century of wrong, would himself dearly have loved to found an empire. Indeed it was in this very pamphlet that he propounded his idea: 'From the Zambesi to Simon's Bay' let it become 'Africa for the Afrikaner'. A 'Greater South Africa' would fill up and dominate a sub-continent. His vision was of Cape Town to the Equator, building bridges of control right up to Kenya and Ethiopia. He and Botha also had their eyes on German South-West Africa and Mozambique.[67]

Fulfilment of long-term objectives was also a reason for British government support for closer union. At least from the 1860s the overriding consideration of South African policy was to get out of South Africa just so soon as strategic security and African interests could be reasonably safeguarded. It was obvious that in fact, in Robinson and Gallagher's apt phrase, South Africa was 'a colonial society receding beyond imperial control'.[68] By 1909 the right moment for withdrawal seemed to have arrived. Botha and Smuts in power quickly commended themselves. They got rid of Chinese labour and handled the problem of the Indian community sympathetically. Their new Transvaal government seemed frank, friendly, reasonable, helpful and trustworthy; their government compared more than favourably with Deakin's Australia, to say nothing of Delamere's Kenya. Anti-British feeling seemed to be diminishing all round, and there was frequent testimony to improvement in treatment of Africans. The two desiderata, strategic security and African interests, then, it seemed would be safe. It was hoped that closer union would promote the interests of the Africans. How, it was argued, could Africans hope to be better off while the whites were at loggerheads? The first thing necessary to improve matters for Africans was to resolve the inter-white quarrel and suppress panicky small states like Natal. The more liberal attitude of the Cape might percolate through the whole of South Africa. The idea was hopelessly misguided, but held in good faith.[69]

There was one new consideration which made the British regard closer union as a matter of urgency. Lyttelton, Selborne, and Seely all believed that in an Anglo-German war (regarded by 1906 as inevitable) the Germans would use South-West Africa to launch an attack on South Africa and provoke a general rising of the Boers. Thus there was still a strategic need to strengthen the weak link in the imperial chain.[70]

A National Convention of South African governments began its deliberations at Durban in October 1908. A draft bill was ready by February 1909; it passed through the Westminster parliament on 16 August 1909, (at depleted sessions because the grouse-shooting season had begun on the 12th) and the Union was established on 31 May 1910 with Botha as first prime minister.[71]

Within ten years of each other, two dominions in the empire adopted different kinds of constitutions, so different in fact, as to be polar opposites. Why in contrast to Australia did South Africa adopt a union? The unitary constitution rested partly on an appraisal of the peculiar necessities of South Africa and partly on a gloomy interpretation of the working of federal régimes in other countries.

The apparent economic and administrative necessities of South Africa, railway and native administration especially, seemed to predicate strong central control. Moreover, the regional inter-mixture of British and Boers seemed also to indicate the wisdom of legislative union – no province could pretend to solely one nationality, and thus the impulse to protect cultural claims by a rigid federal regime was greatly weakened. Federation would present a whole set of economic problems resulting from the fact that, unlike Australia, two of the units would be land-locked. Clearly South Africa was a single economic unit. And federations were expensive.[72]

Smuts presented the Union case, and presented it forcibly, logically and persistently, against opponents of much weaker intellectual drive. His campaign was skilful, even cunning. Smuts made certain that federation should scarcely be mentioned by suppressing strong Canadian and Australian advice in favour of that traditional solution within the British empire.[73] Merriman, the Cape prime minister, supported him. And so did Curtis of the Kindergarten.[74]

On the opposite side there were two groups of federalists, one in the Cape, the other in Natal. Of the Cape federalists, F. S. Malan changed his mind and became a convert to union ('No man . . . will deny that it is necessary to place the Native policy in the hands of a central government'.) J. H. Hofmeyr elected to oppose union outside the convention, while W. P. Schreiner could not attend it because he was defending the Zulu chief Dinuzulu against charges of treason. Thus it came about that the federal cause at the convention was left in the hands of the Natal delegates. Unlike Hofmeyr and Schreiner, the attachment of Natalians to federation was not based on a hope that it would be in the better interests of the Africans: their concern was the purely selfish and parochial one of protecting their own interests.[75] But Natal was the weakest of the colonies and so much despised that the federal cause was doomed in its hands.

The choice of a unitary constitution was made partly on the basis of a fairly systematic study of existing federal models. At first federation seemed to be the only solution, but gradually union was seen to be better. The British government arranged for materials on the working of federal institutions to be supplied by Canada and Australia, Germany, Switzerland and the United States.[76] These countries commended their federal institutions, but it seemed to the South Africans that they were expensive forms of government and difficult to change. As Merriman said, the South Africans were as a white community small and not likely to receive many more immigrants, so that 'concentration of power seems to be almost a necessity for us'.[77] The looseness of the Australian federation seemed undesirable. President M. T. Steyn thought it provided an object lesson not to rush into a federal solution.[78] The early years of Australian federation were indeed full of tensions. Collapse seemed probable, and the Australian Labour party advocated a change to union.[79] The United States system led Smuts and Merriman to wonder whether under a federation the non-elective judiciary might appropriate political functions. Moreover they chose (in a harsh assessment) to see the American Civil War as caused by the federal constitution. Smuts also decided that in the United States 'the sovereign power was so dispersed as to be ineffective for the essential purpose of civilised government'.[80] The idea that F. S. Oliver's book *Alexander Hamilton: an essay on American Union* (1906) exercised any significant influence on the choice of constitution may, I think, be discounted.*

Finally there were arguments from Canadian analogy. One line of thought was urged by Chief Justice de Villiers, who wielded great influence at the convention, of which he was presidejt. He decided after a brief visit to Canada in the summer of 1908 (he had been before in 1894) that friction was inherent in federal systems. Another line of thought led to the conclusion of Smuts and Merriman that Canada was at least on the right track in having a strong central government. They both read Egerton's *British Colonial Policy* and H. E. Egerton and W. L. Grant's *Canadian Constitutional Development: Selected speeches and despatches* (1907). Smuts commented: 'The Canadian Constitution supplies some very useful ideas for us in South Africa'.[81] In the last resort, however, it has to be stressed that calculations about power in South Africa brought them to decide upon union, not reading about frictions in Australia and Canada. Britain had little choice but to accept a unitary constitution. Botha hinted that if it were refused he would have to build a

---

* L. S. Amery regarded union as 'largely due to the influence of Oliver's brilliant presentation of the case for a strong central government' *(My Political Life, I, 269)*. It is supposed to have become the bible of the Kindergarten in their promotion of union. There are two reasons for doubting this. The first is that *Alexander Hamilton* was published in May 1906 and was not read by a leading member of the Kindergarten, Geoffrey Robinson, until September, while the decision to 'go for union' was taken in June, or July at the latest (Nimocks *Milner's Young Men* 77–8). The second reason for doubt is that at no point did Oliver suggest, or imply, even in his long 44-page polemical conclusion, that there was a lesson for South Africa in American history. It is true that he praised strong central unifying institutions, but his message was solely directed towards the constitution of the British Empire as a whole. Oliver was an amateur historian writing about a then unfashionable subject. He was a draper – employed by Debenham & Peabody.

tariff wall around the Transvaal and leave the rest of South Africa to fend for itself. But in fact Britain herself believed a strong central government to be desirable.[82]

Thus the South Africans formed a legislative union in which all power was concentrated in parliament as fully as in the United Kingdom. Outdoing the United States, Canada and Australia with their compromise capitals, the Union created three capitals. Cape Town was the seat of parliament. Pretoria was the seat of the executive (and that was what really mattered), while Bloemfontein became the seat of the Appellate Division. Both Dutch and English were allowed as official languages.

One particularly important long-term effect of the Act of Union was that whilst it united South Africa it divided southern Africa. The Rhodesias, and the High Commission Territories (Basutoland, Bechuanaland and Swaziland) were provisionally left outside.[83]

After the Union, Bantu, Briton and Boer did not live happily ever after.[84]

In 1913 a Land Act was passed which shocked most of the officials in Whitehall. Although based on the Lagden report, it went far beyond it in the harshness of its restrictions on Africans. Its primary object was to lay down the principle of territorial segregation, and Hertzog (the major influence behind it) adumbrated a concept of autonomous African states under control of the white parliament: a concept which looks rather like that of today's 'homelands'.

The last flickers of a dying traditional order were seen in the Natal disturbances of 1906 to 1908 which combined millenarian undertones with modernist overtones. It was the last big violent African protest for a long time. Only four years later African modern politics began, unequivocally. In 1912 a meeting at Bloemfontein was called by Dr P. K. Seme. It was attended by mission-educated Africans, setting out to attain what they considered to be their constitutional rights in a non-racial way. The Rev J. L. Dube was elected president of the new organisation. He was thought to be the right man to weld the unity between the African peoples which Congress set itself to achieve. Of the 11-man executive, four were ministers of religion, three were lawyers, two were teachers, one (S. Plaatje) a newspaper editor, and one a building contractor; they were mainly Cape-educated, and five of them had received additional education overseas. Their motto, Dube suggested, should be *festina lente*. The African National Congress was thus launched in 1912 as the South African Native National Congress – a product of rising political consciousness which had nineteenth-century origins, stimulated by the white union and by the legislation which followed it. It was a reaction against the exclusive European version of union, and it was hoped to pursue cultural advance in the context of western impact while acting as a political pressure group designed to extend the area of liberty in South African life. There was a vision of common humanity and no sense of racial vendetta. The 1913 Land Act quickly gave Congress something to bite on, since it raised fundamental issues of political ideology. The ferment of protest against it enabled Congress to consolidate its support widely, and to organise a deputation to London in 1914. Its reception, by colonial secretary Harcourt, was extremely frosty.[85]

11 Empire in the Antipodes[1]

The founding of Botany Bay convict settlement was not primarily a statement of British interests in the east, either economic or strategic. The decision to send convicts there was a despairing but not random solution to a penal problem. It was not chosen in 1786 because of its potential in producing flax or timber, but mainly because the United States, Canada and the West Indies had all refused to take convicts, and alternative sites in Africa and Newfoundland were rejected as unsuitable. Only in Australia could a site be found large enough (a consideration which ruled out places such as Gibraltar or St Helena) where there was no population able to protest. The convict settlement was thus a by-product of the loss of the American colonies, where convicts had formerly been transported. Temporarily from 1776 they were housed on hulks moored in the Thames, but there were too many convicts for this to be a permanent solution.[2]

The early history of Australia is full of paradox and peculiarity, irony and sudden changes of circumstance. Round about 1860 a man was fined £10 for shooting a rabbit belonging to John Robertson – a few years later John Robertson was spending thousands to clear his lands of this 'pest'. The tiny colony of Victoria was represented at the 1851 Great Exhibition by a token bag of flour, but ten years later was supplying one-third of the world's gold production and one-sixth of Britain's wool import; it had 46 per cent of all the Australian population and 70,000 more settlers than had inhabited the whole of Australia and New Zealand in 1851. But the main paradox was the change in Australia's imperial role: how a convict settlement was transformed into 'John Bull's Greater Woolsack' – a development unlikely to have been foreseen by the first governor, Arthur Phillip, as he surveyed his 700 or so convicts. Eventually, in order to stimulate the supply of wool, there were clumsy essays in state-assisted migration, and, 'whether as a gesture of despair or as a daring venture of faith', the grant of self-government in the 1850s.[3]

In setting up the penal colony few paused to consider the effect on the aborigines. Although successive governors were not unmindful of their responsibilities in this direction, and one, Sir George Gipps, in 1838 risked odium for hanging white men for murdering aborigines, settler brutality and pastoral greed soured relations. Conveniently the aborigines went down like nine-pins under the assaults of European diseases. Tasmanians were extinct by 1876, though here the white man had a more direct responsibility in actual massacres; on the mainland aborigine numbers fell from perhaps 300,000 in 1788 to barely 80,000 a century later.[4]

Joseph Banks in 1798 held it to be inconceivable that such a country, 'situate in a most fruitful climate', should not produce some raw material of importance for British manufacture, but he did not expect sheep to be the answer. And indeed until the 1830s whaling led the field – proximity to the whaling grounds was for 50 years one of Australia's few assets. The whole of British interest in the early years was focused on the coasts and not the interior. There was some interest in acquiring strategic harbours near the oceanic trade routes; indeed, until the confirmation of Singapore in 1824 as a British possession, Australia had a prospect as a base for penetration of the Eastern Archipelago. It was wool which alone caused the interior to be opened up.[5]

Merino sheep were introduced after some preliminary experiments by John Macarthur in 1797,[6] and in the foundation of the industry Samuel Marsden, a senior chaplain of the colony who also took the gospel to New Zealand, had an important part, both practical and prophetic.[7]

Early Australia was a tough place even outside prison. There was no indigenous edible fruit or plant and no Australian animal gave milk. There were few women: only one to every three men in 1831. By and large the convicts did not provide good stock. After a few years transportation ceased to be used for trivial offences, and the criminals were real ones by any standard. Sydney in 1836 was described as the most immoral town of its size in the empire.[8] Gradually matters improved, not least, perhaps, as a result of the crusading work of Mrs Caroline Chisholm in providing greater outlets for paternal instincts by encouraging the emigration of women and by founding in 1846 in London the Family Colonisation Loan Society. She had been out in Australia herself for several years, and concluded that 'For all the clergy you can dispatch, all the schoolmasters you can appoint, all the churches you can build, and all the books you can export, will never do much good without "God's police" – wives and little children'.[9]

Wool production in Australia became significant from 1820. If from the very first some men on the spot had designated wool as the staple, it was Yorkshiremen who, from the 1830s, ensured that they were proved right. This was because the British need for raw wool increased remarkably. The United Kingdom imported 31 per cent more wool in 1862–65 than in 1858–61. By the nineteenth century the British industry had become wholly dependent upon foreign supplies, as an indirect result of the rising demand for mutton and the success of Bakewell and his pupils in breeding sheep to supply it, thus rendering British sheep useless for wool. Homegrown wool had by 1824

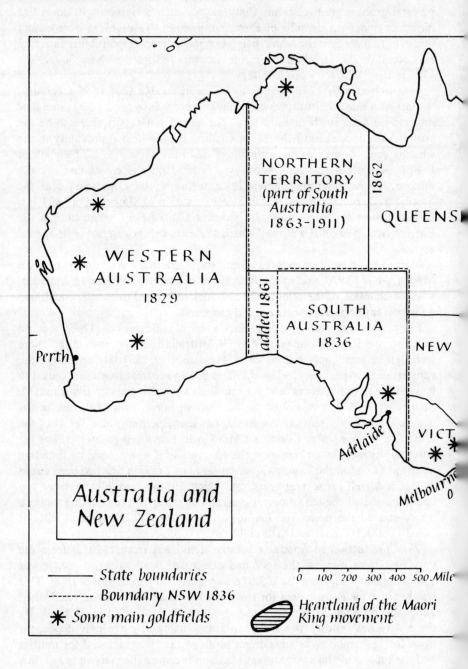

NORTHERN
TERRITORY
(part of South
Australia
1863-1911)

1862

QUEENS

added 1861

WESTERN
AUSTRALIA
1829

SOUTH
AUSTRALIA
1836

NEW

Perth

VICT

Adelaide

Melbourne   0

**Australia and
New Zealand**

——— State boundaries
--------- Boundary NSW 1836
✳ Some main goldfields

0   100 200 300 400 500 Mile

Heartland of the Maori
King movement

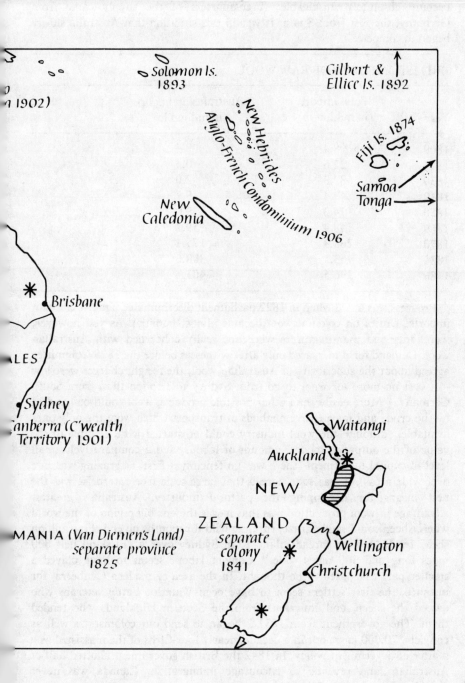

Solomon Is.
1893

Gilbert &
Ellice Is. 1892

New Hebrides
Anglo-French Condominium 1906

Fiji Is. 1874

Samoa
Tonga

New
Caledonia

1902)

Brisbane

LES

Sydney

Canberra (C'wealth
Territory 1901)

Waitangi

Auckland

NEW

ZEALAND
separate
colony
1841

Wellington

Christchurch

MANIA (Van Diemen's Land)
separate province
1825

become absolutely unsaleable; three-quarters of the supply came from
Germany, the rest from Spain. It was in this situation that Australia slowly
began to compete.[10]

BRITISH IMPORTS OF RAW WOOL

Year	Total import (in million lb)	Australasian import (in million lb)
1800	8.4	–
1824	22.6	0.4
1830	32.3	2.0
1840	49.4	9.7
1850	74.3	39.0
1860	148.4	59.2
1870	263.3	175.1
1880	463.5	300.6
1886	596.5	401.4

Progress was aided when in 1822 parliament discriminated against German
imports. Duties on colonial wool became almost nominal. As yet, however,
merchants and manufacturers were not really concerned with Australian
wool. Demand for it increased only after witnesses before the 1828 Committee
agreed about the superiority of Australian wool; the freight charges were low
– it cost no more for wool to go from Sydney to London than from South
Germany.[11] More easily than other possible products, wool could be handled
by the crude and inexpensive methods of transport which were the only ones
available. Although the wool industry could be started with, relative to the
value of the output, a modest amount of labour, and a comparatively small
level of capital investment (there was no fencing at first, as grazing was safe
over wide areas), it was soon agreed that large-scale free enterprise was the
best means for developing the pastoral industry. Australia's greatest
advantage in wool production was that it was the one big region of the world
where sheep could safely graze, running wild for months on end. Five million
sheep by 1841 were spread inland from Sydney over a grassland belt 800
miles long and 300 miles wide.[12] Convict labour seems to have played a
smaller part than used to be thought. In the area of modern Canberra, for
instance, the first settlers seem to have been Waterloo battle veterans who
owned the sheep, and emigrants from the Scottish Highlands who tended
them. The government from 1831/2 began to send out colonists as well as
convicts. 70,000 came out in a decade, nearly four-fifths of them assisted as a
matter of government policy. In 1842 the British government allotted half of
Australian land revenue to encourage immigration. Canada was never
considered as the beneficiary of a large government emigration programme.

Grey justified subsidising emigration to Australia, saying in 1848:

> Australian emigration is of the greatest possible advantage to the empire in general, as affording a field of enterprise to more ardent spirits of the mother country, who in the present peaceful times, cannot find a suitable career at home; and also as creating and increasing thriving communities in that part of the world with which our manufacturers carry on a large· and lucrative trade.

Between 1837 and 1846, 100,750 emigrated to Australia and New Zealand, of whom 80,500 were assisted from the Land Fund.[13] But Australia was never an attractive destination for migrants without government pressure or assistance. Before 1831 the cost of passage was prohibitive to the class usually desiring to emigrate. The hardship and distance were equally great. In the early days of transportation the voyage out was counted the worse half of the punishment.

As a result of immigration of men who had never been to prison, it became clear that Australian society was in danger of being organised on two contradictory principles.

Lord Liverpool in 1825 said these colonies must be regarded as 'integral parts of Great Britain, as much as London or Liverpool'. The principle of organising Australia as a gaol was under challenge. But despite the fact that wool was becoming the significant economic link with Britain, British policy did not deliberately foster the pastoral industry at first – at least not until the end of the 1820s. Until then the government continued to think mainly in terms of the convict system. John Bigge was sent out in 1819 to recommend means of ensuring the continuation of deterrent punishment while economising on its costs. He concluded that 'the idea of continuing punishment and profit is not an incompatible one'. Colonial secretary Bathurst accepted most of Bigge's recommendations. Ex-convicts would not be allowed any more free land. Convicts were divided into categories; those supposed capable of reformation were handed over to pastoral settlers for employment (and thereby removed from the contagion of the prison atmosphere), while the worst offenders were gathered together under stricter discipline. The assignment system, while it no doubt encouraged settlers with capital to emigrate, was begun as the solution to a problem of convict administration, and not as a means of promoting the production of wool. Two-thirds of all the convicts who peopled Australia arrived after 1820, and the peak year was 1840, when 56,000 convicts were undergoing punishment. Nevertheless by then the gaol principle was losing.[14] By 1850 there were more colonists than convicts. The transportation system was gradually contracted, being stopped in New South Wales in 1840 and Tasmania in 1852. This came about not so much because Britain wanted to bring benefit to the colonies or herself, but because it was decided in the short heyday of humanitarian influence that transportation was a cruel and wasteful system, wicked, expensive and decreasingly a real deterrent. It was first condemned in 1838 as too shameful to continue, but it was rapidly revived as convenience dictated. Little consideration if any was given to Australian wishes or needs.

Gold discoveries finally ruined the convict notion. It was generally conceded from 1852 that the proximity of Tasmania to the goldfields made a convict society even there an intolerable menace. Gold swamped almost completely the remnant of convict society.[15] The population trebled in ten years, and the discovery of gold gave British businessmen fresh confidence in the Australian colonies. The effects were most startling in Victoria, which was suddenly raised from obscurity to predominance both in terms of its size and economic contribution. Stirred by gold, Victorian immigrants were men of more diverse skills and talents, many of better background and perhaps more vigour, than Australia had yet received.[16]

The importance of gold can be exaggerated, however, in all-Australian development. Victoria was exceptional (though important, as one-third of the population lived in it even in the later nineteenth century). By 1851 the general direction of economic activity had been largely determined, and gold merely accelerated the trends; many of the goldfield communities were not deeply interested in politics, and it would be a grave mistake to acclaim the gold-diggers as the true founders of modern Australia.[17] The gold rush was over by 1854. There was temporary set-back in the progress of sheep-farming, but by 1861 the sheep stations were again employing as many men as 'before the gold'. Gold had brought in new labour (150,000 in two years alone), new capital, new opportunities and an enlarged domestic market for agricultural products, all of which in the long run helped the pastoral industry. In 1841 there were five million sheep. By 1851, with 438,000 inhabitants, Australia had become the chief exporter of wool to world markets; there were $17\frac{1}{2}$ million sheep. By 1860 there were 20 million, and by 1890, a hundred million sheep.[18]

The outward impulses of the British economy were applied on a comparatively large scale to the exploitation of Australia for profit. British investment was the 'motive power' of the transformation and development of Australia, and in the period of feverish expansion 1834–40 it was especially concentrated on the pastoral industry, and was only replaced by investment in mining after gold was discovered in 1851. Throughout the nineteenth century at least three-quarters of Australian total overseas trade was carried on with Britain. Even in 1937, nearly 52 per cent of exports went to Britain, and 41.5 per cent of imports came from Britain. In the 1930s wool was still the principal item of Australian export (only in the 1850s were minerals more important). The development of Australia was directly the result of increasing consumption of wool by British textile manufacturers; because the market for textiles was good, potential investors thought Australia was a sound investment, and thus the capital was provided which financed development. It was of course theoretically possible for Australia to have developed a different export staple, but she was forced to develop wool because the credit investment facilities were in London, and the Australians had to balance their borrowings by corresponding increases in exports for which there was a British demand. Australiá came to look like a classic case of the simple economic model of a satellite or dependent economy supplying food or raw material in return for capital and manufactures. Its capital and its immigrants were almost exclusively from Britain. British needs and markets were entirely preponderant. The wool, wheat and gold required by Britain tended to scatter the population and delay the growth of urban industry. But there are two important qualifications to this thesis. First, whilst it may be true that in general terms much of the development of Australia was dictated mainly by the British economy, this does not extend to colonisation. The connection of emigration with the needs of the British economy was not so close as the export of capital. The peopling of Australia cannot be understood as a reflex of needs of the British textile industry – because the pastoral industry did not require much labour; because the extent of migration exceeded the needs of the pastoral industry; and because the peopling of Australia was affected more by the lure of gold than of wool production. Secondly, it was not *merely* a dependent relationship (though it was that). Australian economic history was not just a footnote to the British Industrial Revolution, nor was Australia only a sheep-run for the benefit of British at the expense of Australian interests. Australia was not exploited. The enormous concentration of Australia's population in the eastern cities from the 1850s, was not determined by British fiat, although urban immigrants had no love for the bush. Australian living standards in the nineteenth century appear to have been considerably above those in Britain. The rate of economic growth was far higher in Australia, the economic fluctuations less violent. And Australia managed to control her economic decisions. [19]

In many ways the most interesting feature of Wakefield's long and tedious book *A view of the art of colonisation* (1849) was the lesson it purported to draw from the loss of the American colonies. The sole cause of their revolt, Wakefield argued, was infringement of colonial rights to municipal local self-government. Delegation of authority for limited purposes need not conflict with 'strong cohesion to the centre'; indeed there ought to have been more control of the American colonists: 'of real, effective, fruitful control, there has never been half enough'. The institutions of a colony should resemble those of the metropolitan country, and the national character of the settlers should be harmonised with that of the people of the mother country. Hereditary and monarchical institutions should be transported, since 'men do not forfeit their love of distinction by becoming colonists'. Wakefield wished to attract 'a very superior class of people' to emigrate. The ideal colony would be 'an extension, though distant, of Britain itself'. Adoption of his scheme, he had claimed as early as 1829, would 'tend more than anything to preserve an intimate connection between the colony and the mother country'. The structure of colonial society should reproduce the hierarchical British structure of rich, large, loyal landlords controlling a deferential labouring tenantry. Local self-government would help to bring out the better sort of colonist and thus remove not only the stultifying association between emigration and penal transportation but also the causes of colonial revolt.

Wakefield's other main theme was the necessity for a proper or 'sufficient' price to be paid for land. No public land ought to be sold to those whose object was to get land as cheaply as possible or to the labouring classes. Labourers must remain labourers at least for a considerable time, because no 'capitalist' would emigrate unless his labour supply was assured. With a sufficient price, capitalists would be attracted to emigrate in the hopes of higher profits. Or so his argument ran.[20] In fact the theory proved impossible to operate.

Wakefield was not an original thinker, but he was a successful populariser and he was adroit at publicity. More than anyone else he was responsible for removing the stigma from emigration that had turned well-to-do or aspiring people from it. It was a good idea for the government to sell land relatively dear in order to subsidise emigration. But he was a capricious, unscrupulous, unpredictable, insufferable, restless man, strident and sulky by turns. Wakefield was the son of a land agent and was definitely implicated in land speculation. In the founding of South Australia he provided an overall vision, but his few ventures in organisation provided the new colony with its most embarrassing problems. It was difficult to determine what a 'sufficient' price was (especially in areas surrounded by free land), and this difficulty was a constant source of contention among his followers.[21] His plans were doomed to fail since the degree of authority which the British government had in the colonies was strictly limited; it was an era of neglect, and administration was in its infancy. The government used his terminology but lacked the will and the means to produce a uniform system.

In fact most of those who went to South Australia did so in the hope of making a colony free from the political patronage and evils of the privileged established church. To many of the settlers, religious liberty simply meant the absence of any politically dominant church, and their hero was George Fife Angas, one of the members of the Colonisation Committee. He had the Company floated almost single-handed by January 1836: 'My great object', he declared, 'was in the first instance, to provide a place of refuge for pious Dissenters of Great Britain, who could in their new home discharge their consciences before God in civil and religious duties without any disabilities'. He spoke of his hope that South Australia would become the headquarters for the diffusion of Christianity in the southern hemisphere. It was the first British colony without an established church.[22]

Western Australia was founded by Capt. James Stirling at Swan River in 1829, in order, he claimed, to prevent the French or Americans taking the unclaimed half of the continent. But this huge area remained remote from the rest of Australian development.

The first step towards representative government was taken in 1849. But the report of the committee for trade and plantations of the privy council on the proposed Australian constitutions recommended legislatures for South Australia and Van Diemen's Land, but declared, significantly, that Western Australia was not yet ready to fulfil the vital condition of sustaining the expense of its own government by means of local revenue.[23] Before the discovery of gold in about 1850, however, progress to full self-government generally was slow because of British misgivings about the 'immaturity' of scanty colonial populations preoccupied with making money and constructing the rudiments of society. But the discovery of gold led to enlarged and altered communities, involving problems which the home government had no wish to tackle, such as the regulation of the gold-fields, the troubles with Chinese labour, and so forth.[24] In December 1852 the government announced its recognition of colonial grievances and significantly changed circumstances, referring to the way in which gold discoveries had 'imparted new and unforeseen features' to the political and social condition of the colonies. It was 'a state of affairs which has no parallel in history', and was expected to 'stimulate the advance of population, wealth, and material prosperity with a rapidity alike unparalleled'.[25] The government was impressed by the generally good behaviour of the mining communities and by the firmness and judgement usually displayed by the local authorities in circumstances so strange and difficult. Thus, while there was a more urgent necessity 'to place full powers of self-government in the hands of a people thus advanced in wealth and prosperity', the colonists had at the same time 'given signal evidence of their fitness to regulate their own affairs'.

After the discovery of gold the population of New South Wales rose from 187,000 in 1851 to 350,000 in 1861, and that of Victoria from 77,000 to 540,000; the total Australian population also rose, from 438,000 to 1,168,000.

An important despatch from colonial secretary Newcastle in August 1853 referred to opinions that 'its as yet slight connection with the soil, and its addiction for the engrossing pursuit of material progress' still made the Australian population unfit to exercise any increased powers of self-government. But even if that opinion was not well founded (as he hoped it was not):

all will agree as to the extreme difficulty of withholding political privileges from bodies of men to whom the maxims now prevailing in British domestic policy afford so strong a right to claim them, and of keeping our fellow-subjects in Australia on a different political footing from those to whom these rights have been fully conceded in America.

Hence, Britain planned to remove impediments to responsible government in

Australia.[26]

Victoria having been separated from her in 1851, New South Wales in 1853 gained a constitution with facultative provision for responsible government, which her conservative élite did not take up with any enthusiasm.[27] New South Wales and Victoria received responsible government in 1856, together with Tasmania and South Australia; it was granted to Queensland in 1859 after detachment from New South Wales. South Australia was enlarged by the incorporation of the Northern Territory in 1863 (which was not separated until 1911). Western Australia (Swan River) had to wait until 1890 for responsible governmenp. By the 1890s, therefore, Australia was subdivided into six self-governing colonies, with six different sets of tariffs, mainly directed at each other. Postal and telegraphic services were separate, defence arrangements unco-ordinated. The judicial processes in one colony could not be enforced in another. Railways were built to different gauges, and patents taken out in one state conferred no protection in any other.

AUSTRALIAN FEDERATION

It took sixty years of spasmodic official effort and fluctuating public interest to bring Australian federation into being, despite an extraordinary homogeneity of population when compared with Canadians or Americans. There was, however, no overriding motive for unity before the 1880s to counteract colonial provincial attitudes and rivalries. Arguments of convenience, about the advantages of a common tariff, standard railway gauges and more economical administration were regarded as academic. Rivalry between New South Wales and Victoria dogged all attempts at co-operation, Sydney pitting itself against Melbourne and Victoria's protectionist policy causing alarm to free-trading New South Wales. A distracting political instability had followed the introduction of responsible government. In the first forty years of responsible government New South Wales had 29 ministries, Victoria 28 and South Australia 41. Above all, in her relative isolation and with the royal navy to protect her, Australia was threatened by no external threat. In this respect there was a marked contrast with Canada.[28]

Some of these inhibiting factors were however weakened from the 1880s. As Mansergh has noted, the most obvious environmental change came with the intrusion of European powers other than Britain into the Pacific, a change much resented, even feared, by the colonists.[29] With the arrival of the French and Germans, dreams of undisputed British Australian or Anglo-Saxon hegemony in the south-west Pacific dissolved. A conference to discuss 'the annexation of neighbouring islands and the federation of Australia' was held at Sydney in 1883. Deakin said the chief stimulus to it was fear of German aggression in New Guinea and French annexation of the New Hebrides; Victoria had planned to send an occupying force.[30] The

Australians hoped at first to include in any federation New Zealand, Fiji, and possibly other Pacific islands. In 1883 Queensland hoisted the flag in New Guinea but this initiative was disowned by Gladstone's government. It was shown that Queensland could not act alone. All the colonies wanted eastern New Guinea and realised after their failure to secure it – the Germans annexed a large part of it not already occupied by the Dutch in 1884 and acquired a protectorate over all the north-east part in 1886 – that some sort of federal union would give them the power to speak with a united voice on such questions. There was fear of French criminals escaping from New Caledonia and descending on Australia. By 1890 Germany had also acquired islands of the Bismarck archipelago, and at a conference in Melbourne, Sir Henry Parkes (1815–96, five times prime minister of New South Wales) argued that if in 1883 there had been a central government in Australia, it could have annexed New Guinea. This was exceedingly unlikely, but had emotional force, especially when coupled with rhetoric about Australia's destiny, which he said ought to be as 'mistress of the southern seas'. French ambitions and German annexations were not perhaps external threats of a catastrophic kind, but colonial politicians were genuinely worried about them at the time, more so than the Australian public was aware, and even sober loyalists criticised British negligence in the face of foreign 'aggression', especially in 1899 when Germany annexed Samoa after New Zealand had proposed it three times. This, together with British hesitancy over the New Hebrides, finally convinced Australia of Britain's uselessness.[31]

If the external threat was relatively weak compared with that which threw Americans, Canadians or Swiss into federations, some politicians tried to make a boast that unlike previous federations they would come together not in fear but freely from a sense of national consciousness. Certainly there was a vague but definite élitist opinion that they could make an Australia to be proud of, a new Britain in the southern seas, purged of many of the faults which they saw in the old country.[32] Parkes called on the colonies to 'rise to a higher level of national life which would give them a larger space before the eyes of the world': a colossal united Australia ruling the south seas 'would be a power from the day of its birth'. His successor as leader of the New South Wales federal cause, Edmund Barton, talked of 'A continent for a nation, and a nation for a continent'. The Sydney *Bulletin* constantly boasted that the British race was better represented in Australia than in 'cosmopolitan and nigger-infested England'. Many years later, the country's most distinguished historian gave it as his opinion that if such a creature as the average Briton existed anywhere upon earth it was in Australia.[33] It could be the case, then, that Australian federation ought to be seen at least partly in terms of that general manifestation of Anglo-Saxon racial consciousness which had so many followers in the 1890s.

Racial solidarity in a more specific sense could have been important. It was probably no accident that the first thing which was demanded from its first parliament was a permanent guarantee that the country would remain forever white. An Immigration Restriction Act was passed within one year. The strongest testimony to the point came from Deakin:

> No motive power operated more universally . . . [or] more powerfully in dissolving the technical and arbitrary political divisions which previously separated us, [than] the desire that we are and should be one people, and remain one people, without admixture of other races.[34]

There had been conferences in 1880, 1888 and 1896 to unify the immigration laws. The numbers of Chinese were brought down from 38,000 in 1891 to 33,000 in 1901. A special conference on Chinese immigration in 1896 made it seem urgently necessary to have a federation. An M.P. from South Australia said that if federation was essential on any ground it was on this one. The Chinese were unpopular because they always remained alien, in distinct 'quarters' often of a notorious character, so that they were not so much settlers as powerful invaders, and they threatened the image of an egalitarian, casteless Utopia. Many Australian politicians and writers dwelt upon the Yellow Peril: a mass Chinese infiltration from the north.[35] Australia was torn between the desire for racial purity and economic progress. The benefits which the Chinese could bring economically had already been demonstrated all round the world: in Canada, Ceylon, Borneo, Singapore, New Zealand, the United States and Malaya. As was once observed of them, the Chinese had the push and resource of a Yankee, the financial and business ability of a Jew, the coolness and acquisitiveness of a Scot, the patience and temperance of a Turk, the strength and toughness of a mule, the digestive powers of an ostrich and the staying qualities of a steam engine – all rolled into one. But if this made coolies good railway builders, and willing to undertake unpopular tasks it also posed a threat to hard-won ideals. Thus the constitution gave the federal parliament powers to legislate on immigration and emigration, relations with the Pacific isles, naturalisation, aliens and racially discriminatory matters. A 'White Australia' policy was inherent in federation.[36]

As in all federal movements in all times and in all places the economic reasons for coming together were strongly argued. Not all the conducive factors were economic, but in one form or another most were associated with an economic motive, including fears of the Chinese. The colonies had quite deliberately developed their economic and fiscal policies independently. The extension of railways, built with different gauges, and the irritation of border customs duties across boundaries which bore no relation whatever to natural economic divisions, intensified awareness of estrangement. The difficulty of uniform inter-governmental action against labour disputes was vividly demonstrated in 1890–91, when individual governments took measures against trade unions organising industrial strikes across colonial boundaries.

Desire for common legislation for tariffs grew in the early 1890s when the spectacular financial and banking collapse of 1893 brought home to business circles the essential community of interest between them on an all-Australia basis, since they began to see how the misfortunes of one colony affected the rest. Thus it has been not unreasonably observed that the depression of the 1890s was in a sense the proximate cause of the federation.[37] The problems of the economic situation became matters of general public concern. Federation might alleviate some current economic problems, and although it was never suggested as a universal panacea, it could certainly be viewed as a convenient palliative. Economic influences contributed to the new sense of urgency which was felt in the 1890s as never before.[38]

Thus by the 1890s politicians had come to accept that certain important matters, such as defence, immigration, Pacific expansion, tariffs and economic crises, could not be tackled adequately by individual colonies. For some years they had tried to deal with common problems by special conferences, and this system was found wanting as an alternative to federation. It had proved difficult to arrange mutually convenient times and places for meetings. Delegates considered the furthering of their own colonial interests as their first concern. The conferences were powerless to take executive action, and there was no guarantee that individual governments would act upon their recommendations. By 1883, only three out of the 23 subjects discussed at conferences had been dealt with adequately, and of those agreements which required uniform legislation not one was carried out.[39] A Federal Council had been formally instituted by the British government in 1885. It was a very loose link, from which New South Wales stood aloof completely. South Australia sent representatives only spasmodically to the biennial meetings. After three visits to the United States and one to Canada in the years 1882–84, Parkes was more than ever convinced that this was not the answer to Australia's problems.

Parkes in 1889 called for a forward move towards a full-blooded federation. Ministers conferred in Melbourne in 1890 to discuss his proposals. The outcome was a National Constitutional Convention held in Sydney in 1891. A draft constitution was prepared, which New South Wales failed to approve, and the whole issue was substantially dropped for three years. Attendance at the 1894 Ottawa colonial conference may have stimulated matters again. Another conference of premiers was held in Hobart in 1895. The crucial task of hammering out a constitution was done in 1891 and 1897–98. Popular approval was sought in referenda between 1898 and 1900, and the Commonwealth of Australia came into being (with a constitution basically that drafted in 1891) on the first day of 1901.[40]

Even in the final stages of the federal movement from 1897 to 1900 popular support was never strong. Political leaders had convinced themselves of its desirability, but the electorates were swayed hither and thither by a mass of conflicting arguments as to whether or not federation would bring advantages to them.[41] In New South Wales there were lively free-trading fears of protection, which might be forced on her by Victoria, her industrially aggressive neighbour. Queensland was divided internally between the tropical north and the more temperate south, the latter fearing that federation would bring agricultural and industrial competition. Western Australia was divided between its old farming population in the rural areas and its new goldmining immigrants who had no deep allegiance to the colony and no inhibitions about federation. In the end, the rural community was so strongly against federation that Western Australia had to be coerced into federation by the imperial authorities. Western Australia was the only colony actually to vote against federation in its referendum, and was required to hold another to produce the necessary majority in favour, which it duly did. Chamberlain drew the attention of Western Australian dissidents to the fact that Australian federation would simplify relations with Britain, make them more frequent, unrestricted and cordial, and he hoped it would be 'a great and important step towards the organisation of the British Empire'.[42] Deakin also regarded it as a preliminary to imperial federation. This may not have had a wide appeal, but most people did want Australia to have a stronger voice in world affairs.

As was only to be expected in the circumstances, there were wide areas of disagreement as to the nature of the constitution which Australia should adopt. The strength of the 'State's rights' groups was so powerful that Australia emerged with one of the loosest federations in the world, with the central Commonwealth government having only limited and expressly enumerated powers. Both Parkes and Deakin had originally favoured a strong federation on the Canadian model, but by 1891 concluded that this simply was not a matter of practical politics.[43] The influence of the United States constitution was strong, but not followed slavishly. James Bryce's *American Commonwealth* (1888) was regarded with uncritical awe, widely read by the framers of the constitution, and much quoted. Deakin described it as a textbook 'of the very first rank for the philosophical study of constitutional questions'. In 1897, he paid Bryce a notable tribute: 'an authority to whom our indebtedness is almost incalculable'. The actual drafting was mainly done by S. W. Griffith and A. I. Clark, Parkes's influence being positive but very general. The founding fathers were mostly lawyers and businessmen, some relatively wealthy; less than half were born in Australia.[44]

Canberra was eventually founded as a compromise new capital to resolve the rivalry of Sydney and Melbourne. State loyalties remained extremely strong, and in its first decade especially, the future of the new Commonwealth of Australia under its prime minister, Deakin, looked bleak.[45]

NEW ZEALAND[46]

In 1914 the French observer André Siegfried noted that New Zealand was the most faithful of the British colonies. Its distrust of Australia coincided with 'unlimited confidence' in Britain.[47] This reflected exactly the view of Sir George Grey, prime minister of New Zealand 1877–79; New Zealand would not join an Australian federation because it might sink her into insignificance and it would lose her the direct tie with Britain; he would enter no federation except one with Britain.[48] By the end of the nineteenth century New Zealanders always regarded Britain as 'home', and loyalty to it was uncritical. The force of this loyalty was not necessarily traditional or historically continuous. New Zealand was, however, the only place where Wakefield took a hand in carrying his theories about 'harmonising with Britain' into effect, and only in Canterbury did his system come near to being carried out with some success. The New Zealand Company and other propagandists talked a great deal about establishing a model colony, and of New Zealand as 'the Britain of the South' – perhaps in reaction to the plain fact that New Zealand's early history was as an extension of the Australian and American frontier societies rather than of Britain; many of its permanent characteristics (not least its egalitarian atmosphere of good fellowship) linked it to the Europeanised Pacific and New World. Marsden regarded its evangelisation as part of his New South Wales mission; constitutionally New Zealand was technically part of New South Wales in 1840 and 1841; and by 1851 probably half the white population of Auckland came from Australia. A nineteenth-century American historian, Frank Parsons, called New Zealanders the 'Yankees of the South Pacific', and the country 'a little America, a sort of condensed United States'. After the withdrawal of the imperial troops in 1870 there were a few rumblings that annexation to the United States should be sought.[49]

To most of the settlers, and to the New Zealand Company, the imperial treaty of Waitangi (1840) with some of the Maori chiefs seemed an elaborate farce, because it guaranteed the latter full and undisputed possession of their lands and fisheries, and allowed them the rights and privileges of British subjects. It was in fact a political gesture without legal force. The consequent restrictions on alienation of Maori lands appeared to be a blow aimed directly at the settlers, in folly and malice. In the 1840s, and until after the end of the Maori wars, relations with Britain were bad. The Company's journal in 1841 said that the colonists were 'literally spurned as though they had been pursuing an unworthy object, instead of the heroic work of spreading the British name on a remote part of the globe'.[50] The directors of the Company wrote in 1847:

The aim of this Company is not confined to mere emigration but is . . . to transplant English society with its various gradations in due proportions, carrying out our laws, associations, habits, manners, feeling – everything of England, in short, but the soil.[51]

Contemptuous and distrustful treatment of the settlers was therefore bound to provoke alienation. The annexation of New Zealand in 1840 was brought about fundamentally by problems of law and order, an imperial humanitarian desire to curb the crime and rapacity of 2,000 British settlers and traders, many of them from Australia, and their conflicts with the missionaries. One reason was the desire to protect the Maoris, and this was why self-government for the colonists was not granted without limitations. The imperial government recognised its obligation to maintain troops in New Zealand as a safeguard for peace with the Maoris, and since Britain paid a large sum for defence it felt entitled to retain in its hands the administration of Maori affairs, 'which at any moment may involve the employment of those troops, and the consequences of an expensive conflict'. Pursuing Britain's special obligation to see that the rights of settlers were not used to the injury of the Maoris, colonial secretary Newcastle thus defined policy in 1863:

> The Home Government has therefore been anxious to preserve an effectual authority in the management of native affairs, either until the amalgamation of the races had proceeded so far as to break down the sharp division of colour which at present exists, or until a system of government had taken root in the Colony which, by assigning to the Maoris some recognised constitutional position, would furnish some guarantee against oppressive treatment of the less educated race, and would thus at once satisfy and protect them.

Control was reluctantly retained and it failed. Governor George Grey attempted to 'assimilate' Maoris to European civilisation, but the race problem eluded even his dexterity, and he could not solve the crucial land question. Thus by the mid-1850s a situation developed which had no parallel in Australia or North America. The colonists frustrated every imperial attempt to make the governor's control of native affairs effective (responsible government was introduced with reservation of Maori affairs to the governor). New Zealand rapidly acquired a mid-century reputation for being the most troublesome by far of all the colonies, and one more exposed to serious danger than any other. Every extension of European settlement entailed displacement of Maori owners, and colonial pressure on the Maoris to sell land was severe. In 1854 the first European parliament met, and a Maori proto-national movement began in the same year, anticipating by more than half a century a similar kind of reaction in South Africa. In 1858 a Maori king was elected, with the title Potatau I, in a conscious attempt to imitate and supersede European organisation. The kingdom was a loose federation of Maori groups, but united in its determination not to sell any more land. The 1858 census revealed (fatefully) that Europeans were now numerically preponderant over the 58,000 Maoris.

It is usually said that governor Browne started the first Maori war in 1860 by trying to stop it. At any rate he hoped a show of force over the disputed government land purchase in Taranaki would break the deadlock which threatened the peace of the colony, but he seriously underestimated the resistance led by Wiremu Kingi in Taranaki. The Maori wars of the 1860s (which the Maoris called *te riri pakeha*, the 'white man's anger' or 'quarrel') involved 10,000 British troops, as well as colonial forces and Maori collaborators. The able chief Wiremu Tamihana and his people made peace in 1865, but the king did not submit until 1881 – many Maoris stayed where they wished, and no European for twenty years dared enter this 'King Country'. The death roll was not specially large, about 3,000 all told. Some three million acres of Maori land were confiscated, though in practice the Maoris were able to keep half of it; nevertheless the confiscation intensified bitterness against Europeans. The wars broke the Maori will to resist, despite the late injection of a new messianic force, the *Hau hau* movement; and the peacetime land courts made sure that the colonists won the war as well as the battles. Another seven million acres of land were legally transferred between 1865 and 1892.

The wars convinced Britain that she must free herself of Maori responsibility, and the troops were withdrawn in 1870. The British had never been convinced of the necessity for war; Newcastle having been unable to see why the Maoris should not honour their king, even if his name was 'Potato'. Responsibility for Maori affairs was now handed over to men who were not trusted in Britain. By the mid-1870s, however, Granville's courtesy to New Zealand delegates, a guaranteed loan, and a new colonial office tone had quietened disloyalty, and economic recovery diverted attention towards exciting work.[52]

In the late nineteenth century New Zealand was gaining in political independence but becoming ever more dependent economically. The gold rushes increased her white population from 33,000 in 1853 to 412,000 in 1878. Bonds of sentiment and the ties of a dependent economy were fortified from 1882 with the coming of refrigeration. The most important change in the New Zealand economy between 1870 and 1895 was the striking improvement in communication. The effect of refrigeration in ships was such that the cattle herd expanded by 30 per cent between 1891 and 1896. In the years between 1895 and 1914 as much land was brought into use as in the whole of previous development.[53] Trade with Australia decreased and New Zealand's orientation was twisted strikingly towards Britain. In 1880 New Zealand's main export was wool: 50 per cent of the total, which was a little over £5 million. By the early years of the twentieth century exports of dairy produce were just as important as wool exports. In 1880 exports of meat, butter and cheese were negligible, and in 1881 more butter went to Australia than to Britain. In 1870, 46 per cent of exports were sent to Australia, but in the 1890s only 16 per cent. The long-term prospects of export trade with Australia were, plainly, nothing like as good as those with Britain. By 1895 the export of dairy produce was as follows:

NEW ZEALAND DAIRY EXPORTS 1895

	To Britain	To Australia
Cheese	£142,913	£6,264
Butter	£215,619	£7,975
Meat	£1,315,994	£8,732

By 1913 exports had soared to the £20 million level. The European population of New Zealand was then 1,085,000. [54]

There were thus good economic reasons why New Zealand stayed out of an Australian federation: it was irrelevant to her commercial prospects and economic problems. This induced public apathy. But there was another reason too. Unlike Australia, 1,200 miles away, New Zealanders were interested in the area of Pacific Ocean to the north-east of them. Her Pacific aspirations might not be served by federation. These aspirations had been present from the beginning. For example, John Crawford, agent for the New Zealand Company in the west of Scotland in 1840, held that New Zealand was fitted 'to become the Great Britain and the seat of Empire of the Southern Ocean', and Charles Buller declared in the House of Commons in 1845: 'A British Colony in New Zealand would be the natural master of this ocean, the irresistible arbiter of all its complicated relations and important interests'. Sir Julius Vogel, the prime minister, notified his willingness in 1873 to assist Britain 'in the great national work of extending the British dominion throughout the unappropriated islands of the South Pacific'. Thereafter every New Zealand premier for thirty years advocated New Zealand expansion, especially in Samoa. Sir George Grey added his view that nature had ordained New Zealand 'virtually to be the future Queen of the Pacific' (1883). Nevertheless he attended the federation meetings even in 1900; and Seddon, hoping to keep options open, tried in vain to get an amendment by which New Zealand might join later on the same terms as the original states. [55]

New Zealand colonists were almost exclusively British, with some fellow-feeling, perhaps, that they had, unlike Australians, gone out 'not in despair but hope'. Thus they closely identified themselves with their own government, which was felt to be benign. [56] This apparently led to a precocious development of the welfare state under a Liberal government, 1891–1912, led by prime minister Richard Seddon (1893–1906) and assisted until 1896 by William Pember Reeves. These men gave New Zealand a real place in the world. Her Pacific aspirations may not have come to much. But no longer was it an isolated community which could be ignored; rather it was becoming the pioneer of social legislation and racial harmony which became a model for other democracies. Reeves himself eventually became director of the London School of Economics.

It is not clear why New Zealand in the twentieth century has enjoyed remarkable success in race relations, but three points are perhaps especially relevant. One is demographic balance: in the nineteenth century disease and warfare reduced the Maori population from 200,000 to 42,000, that is to say to a level where it could not (unlike South Africa) overwhelm white predominance, and at which Maoris might even die out. Another important point was the nature of the economy: New Zealand had no plantations, and the settlers did not need to employ the Maoris as a source of cheap labour on their farms. Once separated from their lands (they had only eight million acres left by 1912), the Maoris could be tolerated and, from the economic point of view, ignored. And there was an ideological consideration too: unlike most other peoples in the non-European world, the Maoris seldom evoked hatred. Even during the 1860s four seats in parliament were reserved for Maoris to represent Maoris; this was followed by the introduction of government schools and a conciliatory policy towards 'King Country'. New Zealand had been founded during the heyday of humanitarian attitudes (it was unique in this timing), and hopes of racial assimilation never entirely died out. The spread of 'Social Darwinism' worked in favour of Maori reputation, since it allowed them top place on the scale of non-European civilisation. There was no significant demand for formal segregation in the late nineteenth century, partly because the Maori enthusiasm for European civilisation became so great. Perhaps in so small a country they had little choice.[57]

THE PACIFIC ISLANDS

In the southern seas, millions and millions of seals and whales were attacked from the end of the eighteenth century. Seal furs fetched excellent prices in China. Whales yielded oil for candles, whalebone for umbrellas and corsets.[58] By the 1830s fur seals had been made virtually extinct. By the 1840s, whales were dying out, and the southern fisheries collapsed for the remainder of the century.

The 'fatal impact' of the white man in the Pacific Ocean extended to human beings as well. By 1830, about 150 whaling and sealing ships called regularly at Tahiti. Sometimes it was three years before they put into a European port, and the sailors desperately needed girls. The crews were exceedingly disreputable because they led an unenviable life. Deserters, together with escaped convicts from the penal colony established at New South Wales in 1788, could, armed with a musket, behave exactly as they liked on small islands. There were at least a hundred of these degenerate outcasts living on Tahiti at the end of the 1830s. They introduced guns, alcohol, and venereal and other diseases. The population of Tahiti fell from 40,000 in 1770 to 9,000 by 1830. The non-convict settlers of Tasmania, numbering 13,000 by the 1830s, organised a manhunt against the indigenous inhabitants, reducing them from 5,000 to a couple of hundred in 1835, of whom only 50 survived another seven years.[59]

It is therefore not surprising that the Pacific was the first area to which Protestant missionaries felt called. Not until 1817 did an (unenforceable) act of parliament require murders committed in the islands to be dealt with in the courts of New South Wales. From the 1820s the royal navy visited the islands, intermittently meting out rough justice, trying to check the lawless Europeans in these incipient missionary theocracies.[60]

The South Pacific provides a notable illustration of the way in which missionaries were sometimes the advance spearhead of expansion. For several non-European peoples the first white man they saw was a missionary. Missionaries were in South Pacific islands at an early date: the London Missionary Society in Tahiti and Tonga from 1797; the Wesleyans in Tonga from 1826, Fiji from 1835, and New Zealand from 1823; the Church Missionary Society was in New Zealand from 1814. Not until the 1840s did European governments move in, the British annexing New Zealand in 1840, the French taking Tahiti in 1842. Until this happened, missionary theocracies constituted the only westernised forms of government. Tahiti was transformed into a Christianised polity. Missionaries acquired a deep-seated hold throughout Polynesia because of the moral power of their conciliatory teaching and their uniformly disinterested conduct.[61]

Bishop George Selwyn's episcopal commission in 1841 encouraged him to see New Zealand as the centre of a system, a 'fountain diffusing the streams of salvation' over the Pacific. The letters patent defining the diocese of New Zealand fixed the boundaries at 50°S to 34°N. This was a mistake, but Selwyn was delighted. It is 'God's providence', he declared, and made 12 voyages into this enormous area, going further and further into Melanesia. By 1854 he had visited about 50 islands. He was a true pioneer of European civilisation in the Pacific Ocean, because the Sydney traders had fought shy of these northern islands and visits by ships of war had as yet been few.[62]

Cook's voyages had won for the British a sort of primacy of influence in the Pacific Ocean, or so at least the Australians and New Zealanders believed. They regarded it as a British sphere; trade was based on Sydney and Auckland. The work of British missionaries confirmed this influence in many of the island groups of Polynesia and Melanesia. Between 1841 and 1874, however, the British government acquired no territory, although Lord Aberdeen in 1845 stressed that the government 'will not view with indifference the assumption by another Power of a Protectorate which they, with due regard for the interests of those islands, have refused'.[63]

In the 25 years after 1850 one of the main concerns of the missionaries was the migrant labour traffic and the abuses to which it gave rise. From the middle years of the century the main Pacific exports were whale oil and guano,* and neither required political control. But from the 1870s there was

* Accumulated bird-droppings, used for fertilisers.

a growth of plantations, under German, French, British and American control, in many islands; they produced copra and experimented with other crops such as cotton. These plantations needed large amounts of labour. Missionaries were quick to oppose the use of kidnapping ('blackbirding') as a means of getting labourers out of the New Hebrides and the Gilbert Islands, from whence they were sent to Peru (where the labourers collected guano in off-shore islands), Queensland and Fiji in the 1860s. Although their accounts were often exaggerated, their publicity prepared the way for the annexation of Fiji in 1874, which in turn inaugurated the period of partition in the Pacific.

The tendency to abuse in recruiting for labour the unsophisticated islanders is obvious. There were outrages and murders by the islanders in retaliation, culminating in the killing of the first bishop of Melanesia, Patteson, in 1871, an event which sharply focused British attention on the problem. Patteson had complained that unscrupulous labour recruiters had used his good name, and sure enough, when he next visited an island where this had happened (Nukapu in the Santa Cruz group) he was clubbed to death by a relative of a kidnapped islander. The cabinet discussed this, and re-activated a draft bill prepared in 1862. The Act of 1872 was intended only to root out abuse from a system regarded as essentially unobjectionable and useful – Patteson himself had advocated regulation and not suppression. Kidnapping was made an offence; vessels engaged in the traffic could be seized.

After 1868 a major destination for island labourers was Queensland, which by 1884, with 57,000 acres under sugar, had become, after Mauritius and British Guiana, the most important producer of sugar in the empire. The numbers of islanders employed in Queensland in any given year between 1883 and 1904 never fell below 7,500, with an average of about 8,500 and a peak of 11,443 in 1883. At about that time mortality was 147 per thousand. The Queensland enabling act made no provision for effective supervision at the places of recruitment, which were in the most backward areas of Melanesia, particularly the New Hebrides and the Solomon islands. It was falsely assumed that the islanders understood enough to make a fair contract.

Disorder thus grew in the islands as a result of European economic demands and activities. The tiny indigenous societies were unable under this pressure to sustain an adequate framework of law and order. Disorder lead to increasing rivalries and conflicts between Europeans, which, as in Africa, threatened to produce total collapse. By the 1880s officials concluded that only full European control, gradually extended, could rationalise and stabilise the situation. Exactly as in Africa, an interlocking of European economic rivalries with the decay of local systems of law and order produced a political problem which only partition could resolve. Pressure for this was strong from Australia and New Zealand: they wanted precautionary annexation in Fiji, Samoa, the New Hebrides, Rapa, New Guinea and so on. Where British governments could satisfy themselves that there were good reasons and suitable opportunities they reluctantly agreed; and among the possible good reasons was of course the desirability of sometimes not alienating Australian and New Zealand opinion at a period when Britain needed every friend in the world she could muster.[64]

In Fiji, the principal chief Thakombau (who was a Christian and not at all opposed to westernisation) offered cession. A commission sent out by Gladstone's first ministry reported that if the offer was refused they saw 'no prospect . . . but ruin to the English planters and confusion in the native government'. Serious matters, retorted Gladstone, but not in themselves sufficient reason for annexation, especially since, he added, trade did not need the flag, and Fiji might reproduce the troubles of New Zealand. In 1872 Kimberley hoped New South Wales might annex Fiji, but New South Wales refused. After further negotiations the Disraeli ministry concluded that annexation was unavoidable and accepted the offer in 1874. Carnarvon declared in July 1874: 'There are English settlers in such numbers, English capital is so largely embarked and English interests are so much involved in the peace of the islands, that it would not be safe to fold our arms and say we would not have anything to do with the islands'. He also stressed a moral obligation. There was no doubt that by 1873 Fiji was in a state bordering on anarchy, partly because of the strains which British settlers had put upon the Fijian polity, especially through the establishment of plantations with an insufficient local labour supply. The European settlers disliked taxes and the authority of the indigenous courts.

Government acquiescence seems to have been given mainly because possession of Fiji would cut away the root of abuses in the labour traffic of the Pacific by controlling the lawless European settlers in Fiji. There was also some small strategic interest in a possible base intermediate between Sydney and Vancouver. But on the whole, its acquisition was exceptionally altruistic.[65] Colonial office officials stressed the duties of the 'greatest maritime power in the world' to deal with the brutalities of its subjects. Fiji, said its first governor, Sir Arthur Gordon, must not be allowed to become 'a collection of migratory bands of hired labourers . . . disgraceful to our rule'.[66]

Disraeli tried to get the new colony called the Windsor Isles to flatter the Queen, but she stuck to Fiji as the proper name. Carnarvon tried to persuade the governments of New Zealand, Victoria, Queensland and New South Wales to contribute £4,000 a year each to the new government of Fiji, as they would benefit by regulation of the labour traffic. Queensland refused.[67]

Carnarvon's Western Pacific High Commisson (1877) was designed to avoid making further annexations. It should be seen as a rather weak experiment in providing order and jurisdiction without assuming sovereignty. Neither it nor the annexation of Fiji was inspired by economic motives. The cotton boom had burst; Fiji was bankrupt and required a treasury grant-in-aid; the claims of Europeans to land titles were frequently disallowed in whole or part.[68]

In 1888 and 1889 a number of small or uninhabited islands were annexed by Britain as possible relay stations on a Pacific cable, but Britain was slow to bring other islands, such as the Gilbert and Ellice Islands and the Solomons, under her control. When she did so, it was largely to placate the Australians. Southeast New Guinea was made a protectorate in 1884 to conciliate them. The admiralty thought the Gilbert and Ellice Islands useless and only in 1892 did Salisbury and his colonial secretary Knutsford agree that they would rather face the difficulties of a protectorate 'than the alternative of letting the Germans into our sphere of influence'. Britain tried to resist the growth of German political interest in Samoa, which alarmed New Zealand. But eventually by the Samoa Convention of 1899 Britain renounced her rights in Upolu and Savaii in favour of Germany and in Tutuila and Manua in favour of the United States. Germany renounced hers in Tonga and Niue, and ceded Ysabel and Choiseul in the Solomons.[69]

The status of the islands in the New Hebrides group had been indeterminate since 1888, when France and Britain warned off other powers. By the end of the nineteenth century the islands were in grave disorder. Under insistent pressure from Australians, worried by the fact that they were the last remaining territories in the South Pacific not legally administered and concerned about the future of Presbyterian missions if France had full control, Britain eventually arranged with France a condominium. The 1907 settlement did not wholly satisfy the Australians.[70]

The positive urges for British expansion in the Pacific were weak. Ward sees a 'policy of minimum intervention', but Morrell questions whether there was any British policy at all. There was no continuous thought about Pacific problems, which were regarded as a tiresome nuisance, especially when an acquisition was urged upon the British government by Australian and New Zealand settlers, who had genuine strategic, religious and economic interests in many of the islands. Most of the islands (Samoa was an exception) were not mere pawns in international bargaining at the end of the nineteenth century – there were local circumstances which explained which parts came under which flag. Pacific islands had some naval-strategic value. In some senses, it has been remarked, their seizure was a 'by-product of a certain state of technical development in navigation and telegraphy'. Warships carrying a limited quantity of fuel required coaling stations, and cables required landings. Considered merely as commercial markets and sources of raw material, most of the islands were far less worth striving for than Africa. The smaller islands were useless as markets and produced little save coconuts, exported in dried form as copra for the margarine and oil factories. Some also had valuable deposits of phosphate; but in general their economic resources (including those of the New Hebrides) were negligible in the world context.[71]

12 Expansion in East Asia

Sir Stamford Raffles (1781–1826)[1] was lieutenant-governor of Java from 1811 until 1816, during the wartime occupation of the Dutch colony. He became passionately interested in it and its peoples, whom he regarded in the classic 'noble savage' tradition. His next assignment was as governor of South-west Sumatra from 1818 to 1824, when this island too was handed back to the Dutch. Raffles then returned to Britain; he founded the London Zoo. He is perhaps best remembered for acquiring Singapore. The British object was not so much territory as trade, but he realised that no purely commercial establishment could succeed in the archipelago. Britain needed in the eastern seas 'a great commercial emporium and a fulcrum whence we may extend our influence politically as circumstances may hereafter require'. He was the first Englishman in the nineteenth century to pay serious attention to Japan. Ideologically, he saw that commerce could dispense blessings which would leave enduring monuments to British virtue, especially if education was made to keep pace with commerce: he was proud of the schools which he established in the east.[2]

Following an eighteenth-century tradition which had looked at the possibilities of Balambangan, Riau and Penang, for a long time Raffles searched for a suitable entrepôt, well adapted for communication with native authorities and giving a general knowledge of what was happening in Indonesia. Such an entrepôt would be the base from which British commerce was protected from pirates and European rivals, and the centre of a commercial system which, by its rivalry, would force the Dutch in Java to maintain a more liberal system than they had done before the British occupation. For him Singapore broke a spell: the Dutch were 'no longer the exclusive sovereigns of the eastern seas'.

Raffles acquired Singapore, destined to become a great bastion of empire, by rather inglorious means, to wit, by a dubious treaty with a seedy local chief Dato Temenggong (a hereditary high official of the sultanate of Johore), who had to be kept as an honoured resident on the island, where he was suspected of imparting useful information to the pirates who continued to prey boldly on Indonesian traders in the immediate vicinity of the port. Raffles then intervened in a succession dispute in Johore, proclaimed a displaced sultan as sultan again and obtained from him the concession he wanted. In 1819 Singapore had only 150 inhabitants, mostly fishermen and pirates. It required a good deal of imagination to see in this decayed place the desired emporium and imperial fulcrum. With reluctance the British government accepted Singapore. In 1822 and 1823 Raffles was busy organising it with superhuman speed. He had the harbour and adjacent coasts correctly surveyed, he allotted lands, laid out the town and roads, established a land registry, set up an institution for the study of Chinese and Malay literature, and started to raise sufficient revenue without taxing trade.[3]

Between 1814 and 1824 the achievement of Raffles and his friends was not to deprive the Dutch of any positive advantage, but to cut their pretensions down to realistic size, or to put it another way, to ensure that Dutch privileges were confined to opportunities they could really use, and that otherwise the field was open to British enterprise. The Anglo-Dutch Treaty of 1824 was based on new principles for dealing with British trade in the eastern seas: principles which owed much to Raffles's years of pondering upon the whole problem of the relationship between political control, commercial development and foreign competition. By the Anglo-Dutch Treaty of 1824 Britain got Malacca in return for surrendering Benkulen; Britain agreed not to form settlements or make treaties south of the Straits of Singapore; it confirmed the British acquisition of Singapore, although separating it from the rest of the archipelago was without precedent. The Dutch promised not to interfere in Malaya. The treaty also established that the archipelago would be substantially a sphere of influence for the Dutch, though it conceded freedom of navigation to British shipping in the eastern seas. The spirit of the treaty was to confirm a territorial dominion to the Dutch, while providing opportunities for British commerce, that is to say, it left the Dutch to do the work and the British to reap the advantages. This is a clear example of techniques of control which were later regarded as ideal. The basic principles of British policy in the region were thus strikingly set forth. The route to China through the Straits was safeguarded: this was a primary objective of the whole treaty. Castlereagh had long urged the Dutch to co-operate in allowing the British a 'fair and friendly' commercial competition; the alternative would be costly to both. Otherwise the day could not be far off when naval stations in those seas would involve unnecessary expense, and commerce would be sought through dominion, and 'dominion through the intrigues and disputed titles of endless sultans that abound in those seas'. Canning saw the Dutch and British as joint 'exclusive Lords of the East'.[4]

In 1826 Singapore, Penang and Malacca were amalgamated as the Straits Settlements, of which Singapore became the capital in 1832. It grew speedily. By 1823, nine firms of European merchants had moved in. By 1827 there were 14 substantial houses with business connections in London or Calcutta.

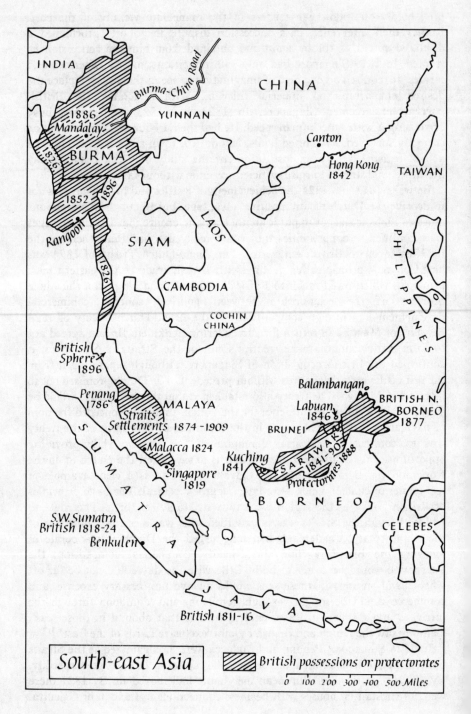

INDIA

Burma-China Road

CHINA

1886
Mandalay·
1826
BURMA

YUNNAN

Canton

Hong Kong
1842

TAIWAN

1852

1896

Rangoon

SIAM

LAOS

CAMBODIA

COCHIN
CHINA

PHILIPPINES

British
Sphere
1896

SUMATRA

Penang
1786

MALAYA

Straits
Settlements 1874–1909

Malacca 1824

Singapore
1819

Kuching
1841

Balambangan

Labuan
1846

BRUNEI

SARAWAK
1841–90

Protectorates 1888

BRITISH N.
BORNEO
1877

BORNEO

CELEBES

S.W. Sumatra
British 1818–24

Benkulen

JAVA

British 1811–16

South-east Asia

British possessions or protectorates

0   100   200   300   400   500 Miles

Its position as a pivotal distributing centre for British goods was assured by mid-century. The amount of shipping using Singapore increased by a third between 1869 and 1871 and this necessitated the expansion of its dockyard facilities. Singapore fully justified its early economic expectations. It was Alfred Holt & Company's base for the firm's East Indian and Australia trade. Holt entrusted his business to Walter Mansfield's agency, in which T. C. Bogaardt was increasingly prominent from 1872: he started a fleet of small steamships based on Singapore, which acted as feeders and distributors to Holt's main cargo lines calling at Singapore.[5]

Between 1786 and 1867 the small, weak Malay-Muslim states were 'busy committing political hara-kiri'. There was constant war between the different sultans, and frequent civil war between rival claimants to thrones; the power of the sultans declined, and even petty rajas were able to establish themselves as independent local rulers, free to plunder; piracy flourished and trade declined.[6]

By 1870 between £100,000 and £200,000 was invested in Selangor tin – most of it lent from Singapore not from Britain. The Straits Settlements colony suffered threats to trade, revenue and security as a result of rivalry between Malay rajas and between clans of Chinese labourers in the tin-mines: rivalry so bitter as to threaten the tin mining industry with collapse. The government was not interested. But when the Selangor Tin Company conjured up the strategic threat of another European power's obtaining a footing on the Malay peninsula, trading interests based on Singapore gained the immediate ear of the government. Governor Ord by reports and actions created conditions which forced the British government willy-nilly into intervention. The peninsula was undoubtedly in an anarchical state. The unprecedented disorders of 1872-73, however, merely provided the occasion; troubles had been endemic for years. The new factor in the situation was the threatening interest of other powers. Although exaggerated, the fear was real enough. France was pushing forward in Cochin China, and the Dutch in North Sumatra in the 1870s. Sir Harry Ord had wanted to intervene because of foreign rivalries from the Dutch and French and Germans, which had created a general feeling that any advantage neglected by one power would certainly be seized by another; this rivalry was intensified by the opening of the Suez canal which brought commercial advantages to the Straits. Although the British tinplate industry was the largest in the world in 1874, and increasingly dependent on Straits tin, the amount of British investment was insignificant, and the government certainly felt no concern to develop the tin trade. In all probability the government agreed to advance because of the sudden fear that Germany was about to forestall Britain. The mere hint of a foreign base in the peninsula was taken very seriously; there was no hard evidence to hand. Malaya was not thought to have any intrinsic importance, but its occupation by another power might strike a fatal blow to China trade and the route to China via Singapore. The result was the establishment of

Residencies in, and control over, Perak, Selangor, and Sungei Ujong in 1874.[7]

By 1883 after law and order was restored, Malaya was the largest tin-producing country in the world; by 1890 it produced 37 per cent of the world total, and 45 per cent by 1914. Tin production was virtually monopolised by the Chinese. Not until 1897 was a satisfactory system of tapping rubber discovered, which made plantation production in Malaya an economic proposition. These plantations were largely built up with the resources of external capital. The rubber industry was firmly established by 1910. Simultaneously there was a large-scale entry of British magnates and engineers into tin-mining.[8] The government was alarmed about the damage which could be done by rash concessions, and brought pressure to bear on the Sultan of Johore to exercise great care and to accept no railway financed other than by the Federated Malay States government; a Resident was placed in Johore in 1914. Concern for the role of Malaya in the routes to the east remained basic to British policy: economic development was never pursued at the cost of political stability.[9]

A similar concern also guided policy in Borneo: throughout the century the basis of Borneo policy was to prevent the northern part falling into foreign hands, because of its strategic importance on the flank of the vital sea routes to China. The British North Borneo Company was set up in 1881 under British government charter to rule the area under at least the nominal authority of the sultans of Sulu and Brunei. The advent of France in Vietnam and Cambodia provided a positive reason for strengthening the British position in Borneo; nor did Britain wish to see any extension of Dutch, German or Spanish power, although the real threat to commerce was a French one.[10]

BROOKE RULE IN SARAWAK

The white rajas of Sarawak constitute the only case in the history of the world where a European private dynasty ruled a large portion of the non-European world for a century. The three rajas were James Brooke (1803–68), his nephew Charles (1829–1917) and the latter's son Charles Vyner who ruled until 1946 when Sarawak was at last annexed to the British Crown. With only a handful of European helpers, the Brookes brought peace and eventually contentment to a fierce population inhabiting 50,000 square miles of territory. Unable to rely on London support, James Brooke's contest with the local powers was less unequal than elsewhere. He had to compete on local terms and this makes his achievement unique in nineteenth-century European rule in South-east Asia. Charles Brooke was a stern man and even without gunboats he maintained authority thanks to his prestige and organising ability. Why did they do it? Sarawak was not a place where Europeans could get rich. The mainspring of their rule, it has been suggested, was the 'soul-filling satisfaction' they derived from ruling and conscientiously ordering, with high integrity and an absence of self-seeking, the affairs of subject peoples. The very existence of Brooke rule in Sarawak is a reminder that there was an altruistic belief in civilising mission among men on the spot.[11]

James Brooke's youthful ambition was to find a useful 'sphere of action': he was more interested in making a name for himself than in making money. He wished he was rich, but the mere struggle for wealth and quietness seemed like 'betraying a higher and more sacred trust'. The desire for wealth or aggrandisement would hardly have tempted him into such isolation, inconvenience and anxiety as Sarawak involved; indeed, it was his opinion that style and luxury had to be sacrificed in 'a grand experiment' of introducing better customs, settled laws and protection for Iban rights, and generally conferring western blessings on 'an oppressed race'. To confer lasting benefit and moral influence could only, in his view, be achieved if he were not thought to be pursuing selfish advantage. In any case he considered himself ignorant of the business world, and privately he tended to look down on it.[12] In quite a poetic passage he explained his inner drive:

> Could I carry my vessel to places where the keel of European ship never before ploughed the waters – could I plant my foot where man's foot had never been before – could I gaze upon scenes which educated eyes had never looked on – see man in the rudest state of nature – I should be content without looking to further rewards. I can, indeed, say truly that I have no object of personal ambition, no craving for personal reward; these things sometimes flow attendant on worthy deeds, or bold enterprises, but they are at best consequences, not principal objectives.

It was a creed shared by many others of his generation.[13]

Under his successor Charles Brooke expansion was less inhibited. Starting from one river valley based on Kuching, by 1905 Brooke rule extended as far as the Lawas River opposite Labuan. The once-powerful sultanate of Brunei was reduced to a tiny enclave surrounded on the landward side by its former fief, Sarawak.[14]

James Brooke was born in India and joined the East India Company's army at the age of 16 as a cadet. He admired Raffles, and consequently disliked the Company for its refusal to support Raffles's plans for Borneo. By the end of 1813 Raffles had established British authority all round the coasts of Borneo except for the far north-east, but the government refused to recognise the need for territorial control which Raffles believed necessary for commercial settlement. Brooke agreed with Raffles. His ideas were rather more romantic, but essentially similar. Brooke resigned from the Company in 1830 and travelled in the Far East. With the legacy left him by his father he bought a schooner and arrived in Singapore in 1839, where he was commissioned by the governor to take a message to Raja Muda Hassim of Sarawak. He found the country corruptly governed, torn by insurrection and ravaged by pirates.

Brooke's help and advice to local administrators was such that he was implored to stay and became raja of Sarawak. He had gained the confidence of the sultan of Brunei, and in September 1841 Brooke was formally installed in return for making a small annual payment or tribute to the sultan. He now set about the tasks of suppressing piracy, head-hunting and slavery and reducing internal warfare.

By 1838 the British were forced to revise their 1824 idea of co-operation with the Dutch because the Dutch in Java from the late 1820s had not maintained the spirit of Raffles's system; commercial monopoly was re-imposed; they also imposed heavy duties on British textiles entering Java; and they asserted that the establishment of Dutch supremacy in Indonesian states, even without territorial possession, permitted the levying of duties (excluding British textiles in favour of Belgian) as in possessions. Hence the British government in order to limit Dutch expansion became anxious to establish the minimum conditions for the development of British commerce in North-west Borneo; it seemed impossible to attain these elsewhere because of Dutch competition and the Indonesian pirates. Brooke followed Raffles's romantic and optimistic concept of reanimating the decayed Malay Muslim states into their former glory, preserving them from the Dutch and extending British trade. He especially wanted to refurbish the old empire of Brunei with a measure of Europeanisation to ensure its modern existence, to guide rulers into reforms and help them to effect them. He was in favour of Palmerston's policy of 'regenerating rotten empires', aiming to 'reanimate a falling state, and at the same time extend our commerce'. Brooke believed the Dutch encouraged piracy in order to injure Singapore trade, and he described them as 'those thick-skinned, muddle-headed canallers'. Was 'the English lion for ever to crouch beneath the belly of the Dutch frog?', Brooke asked in 1841, pointing to the need for action in Borneo, because if the Dutch got hold of it, 'then farewell hope, for Dutch rule, with respect to natives, is a palsy, and death to British manufactures'. He knew that he had to avoid a 'second New Zealand' or a smaller India, but he still hoped to make Borneo a 'second Java' by gradually opening it up to commerce.[15]

In 1848 he obtained full instructions from the foreign office to 'afford to British commerce that support and protection . . . peculiarly required in the Indian seas, in consequence of the prevalence of piracy, and by reason of the encroachments of the Netherlands authorities in the Indian archipelago'. In 1844 the foreign office appointed Brooke as agent to the sultan of Brunei, 'to facilitate the suppression of piracy and the extension and protection of British trade'. In 1847 the British government, noting the strengthening of the Dutch position in Borneo and elsewhere, officially appointed him governor of Labuan and consul-general for Borneo, with a knighthood. The acquisition of Labuan commended itself not only because it was an excellent harbour and coal had been discovered, but because it was an island. The hope was that it would be a coal depot, a base for piracy suppression and a regional entrepôt.

It became neither. The British government did not wish to be drawn any deeper into Sarawak or Brunei; Brooke was a convenient instrument, and Labuan a limited liability.[16]

James Brooke launched a big expedition against the sea Dayaks, an unusually dangerous breed of pirates, whose depredations indiscriminately affected Malays, Chinese, Dayaks and anyone else who got in their way along hundreds of miles of coast. With the help of the royal navy the pirates were crushed at the battle of Batang Marau on 31 July 1849. The steamer *Nemesis* caught up 88 small boats in her paddle wheels and smashed them. Brooke's Malay and Dayak allies showed no mercy. Between 300 and 500 sea Dayaks were killed (out of 4,000), while 500 more died from wounds or exposure. Pirate villages were destroyed.[17]

This episode attracted considerable interest and furious controversy in Britain. Radicals fulminated about the massacre of 'innocent savages'. A commission of inquiry was held. In 1854 it established the piratical character of the sea Dayaks. The whole case against Brooke had rested on the assumption that they were not pirates. Brooke admitted that his policy had been 'high-handed against evil-doers'. In taking a commanding line against the pirates, he believed it was a means of protecting the lives of innocent people. He regarded Cobden's cry of humanity as merely, in the east, 'humanity to vicious governments, but not to the masses of the people'. Brooke was not the sort of man to misuse power by over-severity: ruthless, maybe, but not inhuman. The Radicals accused him of being an unscrupulous adventurer exploiting natives in order to amass a fortune. As L. A. Mills pointed out as long ago as 1924, to anyone who has studied Brooke's career, 'the charge is so grotesque as to seem unworthy of refutation'. Brooke's critics included Gladstone, Cobden, Bright, Sidney Herbert, Joseph Hume and the earl of Ellenborough. The background to these virulent attacks upon him (and the action of the royal navy) in press and parliament lay in the fact that Brooke incurred the hostility of a powerful section of the commercial world between 1847 and 1851 by trying to exclude European speculators from Sarawak. Moreover his reputation for impartiality had been damaged by his tendency to exalt the interests of the people of Sarawak over those of Britain: in other words, he seemed to have acted more as the raja than the consul-general.[18] Brooke thus had fervent admirers as well as enemies. He became the hero of schoolboys, authors, and young George Goldie. Palmerston, King Leopold of the Belgians, and Charles Kingsley were also admirers. Kingsley dedicated *Westward Ho!* to him, and defended him against criticism. In his best parsonical manner Kingsley wrote, privately:

> My spirit is stirred within me this morning by seeing that the press are keeping up the attack on him for the Borneo business. I say at once that I think he was utterly right and righteous ... 'Sacrifice of human life'?

Prove that it is *human* life. It is beast life. These Dyaks have put on the image of the beast, and they must take the consequence. . . . Do you believe in the Old Testament? Surely then, say, what does the destruction of the Canaanites mean? If *it* was right, Rajah Brooke was right. If he be wrong, then Moses, Joshua, David were wrong . . .

Kingsley himself now put on the image of the beast and launched into vivid denunciation:

You Malays and Dyaks of Sarawak, you also are enemies to peace . . . you who have been warned, reasoned with; who have seen, in the case of the surrounding nations, the strength and happiness which peace gives, and will not repent, but remain still murderers and beasts of prey. You are the enemies of Christ, the Prince of Peace; you are beasts, all the more dangerous, because you have a semi-human cunning. I will, like David, 'hate you with a perfect hatred, even as though you were *my* enemies'. I will blast you out with grape and rockets, 'I will beat you as small as the dust before the wind' . . . I think the preserving that great line of coast from horrible ouprage, by destroying the pirate fleet, *was* loving his neighbour as himself . . .

This pathological outburst was a foretaste of the harsher racial attitudes of the later nineteenth century based upon deductions from scripture. To God, claimed Kingsley, 'physical pain is not the worst of evils, nor animal life (too often called human life) the most precious of objects'.*[19]

James Brooke remained raja, assisted increasingly in the 1850s by his energetic nephew Charles. Charles was instrumental in ensuring Brooke triumph between 1854 and 1863 in the contest with a diverse Muslim ruling class for influence over a predominantly pagan Iban and Melanau population.[20] The Borneo Company was established in 1856 despite James's misgivings, and a bishop of Labuan installed to look after the 3,000 Christians. The régime survived a rebellion of Chinese workers in 1857. James Brooke basked in Palmerston's favour, and as a result was employed on missions to Siam and Vietnam.

It is worth pausing to consider his mature views on the government of Sarawak. He realised that it was no good to treat its peoples as, without qualification, inferior, or their religion as deserving of nought but denigration. He was one of the earliest servants of empire to reject India as a

---

* It is not particularly edifying to recall that Kingsley was Regius Professor of Modern History at Cambridge, 1860–69, and in a seminar declared that the North American Indian was a savage, 'not a natural man but a most unnatural beast, playing all manner of unnatural and unwholesome pranks upon himself'. (F. E. Kingsley (ed.) *Charles Kingsley: his letters and memories of his life* (1877) II 267).

model: 'Let Sarawak resemble India in no single respect', he ordered in 1860, 'more particularly in becoming a military government'. His idea was, as he wrote in 1861:

> That a native government guided by superior intelligence, and acting in accordance with native pride and feeling, with European support when needed to maintain order, would promote the welfare of the people and largely increase commerce generally. In time it would raise the native inhabitants, and repay a hundredfold the small effort and the small outlay made by the Protecting Power.

He dissociated himself from 'the vulgar class of rulers who take much and spend much'. 'Surely,' he wrote, 'there is a duty which civilisation, joined to power, owes to the people of every land, struggling to advance in the path of good government?' It irritated him that most of his contemporaries would not see 'that Eastern peoples may be governed and raised by appealing to the pride, and right feeling, which pulsates in their hearts, exactly as it does in those of the Western world'. If this were realised, Britain would spread civilisation and happiness more successfully. The important thing to Brooke was to act on the principle that 'the duty of government is to promote the well-being of the mass in their way and according to their ideas'. The 'civilised' government should give a helping hand, protection and encouragement:

> Upon the practical success of this principle depends trade, civilisation, and religion, and all the good things which flow out of them if *rightly conducted*. But dissension and anarchy, stirred up by superior knowledge, render trade a curse, civilisation a sham, and religion an hypocrisy! We can point to practical results in Sarawak, and they should not be despised because upon a small scale. Principles are applicable from the smallest to the greatest things.

In 1866 he publicly proclaimed that his principle was 'to rule for the people, and with the people, and to teach them the rights of free men under the restraints of government'. The majority in the 'council' secured a legal ascendancy for the native ideas of what was best for their happiness: 'The wisdom of the white man cannot become a *hindrance,* and their English ruler must be their friend and guide or nothing . . . '.[21]

James Brooke never supposed, however, that his ambiguous personal *tour-de-force* could last. If Britain would not underwrite the enterprise he would look to Belgium or France – 'one nation is the same as another for the purposes of Sarawak': he was prepared by 1861 to seek support from any European nation who would give it upon fair terms. Progress depended on security, which could not be provided from local resources. In desperation –

and in gratitude for her support – between 1863 and 1865 Baroness Burdett-Coutts was heir to the fief of Sarawak. Sarawak could not stand alone, and James feared that the new state would die with him. 'We must succeed in gaining protection or perish'.[22] Elgin as viceroy of India sent a commission of enquiry (1860) to see whether it should come under the foreign office, but despite admiralty nervousness that it might tempt the French, Dutch or Americans, it was not until 1888 that the British government (with some equivocation) recognised Sarawak as an independent state under the protection of Great Britain. James had been a poor administrator (being perhaps too idealistic) and handed on to his nephew a disorganised and impoverished state. By 1871, however, Charles had paid off the £5,000 loaned by Baroness Burdett-Coutts and greatly extended the boundaries of the state. Charles established a sound economy, agricultural improvement, an effective civil service, and he introduced many public works. While respecting local custom he prepared the way gradually for selective change. He kept out European planters: only three Europeans owned rubber estates by 1917.[23]

The triangle of relationships between Sarawak, the sultanate of Brunei and the British government was so complex that even Palmerston (who claimed to be one of the three persons who ever mastered the intricacies of the Schleswig-Holstein tangle) found it impossible to understand the precise nature of it. Though British control over Sarawak, Brunei and North Borneo was strengthened by the protectorates of 1888, total partition did not come about: and what was left was a private dynasty in Sarawak, a chartered company in North Borneo (1881) and a Residency in fragmented Brunei (1905).[24]

A CENTURY OF ANGLO-CHINESE CONFUSION

Lord Macartney's embassy to China in 1793 was probably the most costly embassy ever sent out from Britain. It achieved nothing. Emperor Ch'ien-Lung issued an edict to King George III telling him quite bluntly that it was impossible to grant the British request for the appointment of a permanent ambassador, and that his country had not the slightest need of British manufactures. This defined the theoretical basis of Anglo-Chinese relations from the Chinese point of view at least until 1860.[25] British thirst for China tea increased by leaps and bounds, so that the British were not content to leave matters alone. Imports were worth £1.3 million in 1785, but seldom less than £3 million a year by 1815. In 1805, 23.7 million lb of tea were imported, but by 1833 the East India Company imported about 30 to 35 million lb of China tea annually.[26] (There was at this date no such commodity as Indian tea). After the abolition of the Company's monopoly in 1833 private traders came to dominate the Canton trade, and friction increased. Tea was mainly paid for in opium grown in India. In 1839 commissioner Lin Tse-hsü ordered the British superintendent at Canton to seize all opium. Lin destroyed

£2,400,000-worth of opium and beseiged the British residents in Canton. This brought the whole China trade to a standstill. The merchants were at last able to persuade the British government that stronger action was required on their behalf, and thus the first Anglo-Chinese war broke out. Although often referred to as the Opium War, the issue developed from the British point of view into one of opening up a total field of commercial operations, and breaking out of the restriction of trading at Canton alone. Palmerston cynically believed that the Chinese objection to opium stemmed from a desire to protect home-grown opium. Perhaps stronger than moral anxiety was the fact that payment for opium contributed to Chinese currency problems by causing a drain of silver from China, which caused a shortage of the circulating medium and the currency in which taxes had to be paid – which in turn had the effect of forcing prices and taxes up alarmingly. The British thought Lin's actions high-handed, violent and unlawful, because the seizures took place before the facts of responsibility were definitely established. [27]

The Chinese found the Europeans uncouth and physically repulsive. Of all the foreign barbarians the British 'red devils' were regarded as 'the most fierce and arrogant' and the most given to 'sharp practice'. One or two of them saw the danger signals of the war, but generally the Chinese remained unimpressed either by the British or by British military victory in 1842. [28]

In May 1841 there took place a famous incident to the north of Canton, just as a truce was being signed. 7,500 armed peasants appeared around the village of San-yüan-li, and in the skirmish which followed, one Briton was killed and 15 were wounded. This peasant militia was mobilised with extraordinary speed into a force of 25,000 from 103 villages. This anti-British peasant corps, based on the rural area around Canton, had been formed among people angry that the 20,000 official troops in Canton had refused to fight a British Indian force of less than 2,000, and then tried to hinder the action of the anti-British militia corps. The army never quite recovered from its disorganisation, and the war diminished the prestige of the Manchu government, exposing its weakness, indecision and ignorance. But a rational answer had been found by the exhilaratingly politicised peasantry, whose leaders no longer feared the foreign barbarian. Instead of the desperate official search for a secret weapon to defeat the barbarians – underwater divers, trained monkeys, bandits – by 1847 an elaborate urban militia was created in Canton. All shops were asked to contribute one month's rent to the cause of self-defence. The weapons of the volunteer militiamen were dispersed among the people. [29]

Although essentially a compromise settlement, the 1842 treaty of Nanking represented the substance of many of the aspirations of the British merchants. Opium was not to be mentioned, although they would have liked its legalisation. Besides indemnity and compensation, duties were reduced; the Chinese Co-hong (or traders guild monopoly) was abolished, Hong Kong was ceded, and five ports were opened 'where the foreign merchants with their

The Chinese Empire

- •Shanghai The 5 Treaty Ports 1842-44
- •Tientsin The 9 additional Ports of 1860s
- ——Northward route of Taipings 1850-53
- ----Taiping Northern Expedition 1853-54
- Area dominated by Taipings
- ▶British leases

0   100   200   300 Miles

Newchwang
Peking
Tientsin
Dairen
Chefoo
WEIHAIWEI 1898
KIAOCHOW
Yellow R.
Craddle area of Nien Rebellion
KIANGSU
Chinkiang
Wusung
ANHWEI
Shanghai
SZECHWAN
Yangtze R.
Hankow
Nanking
Ningpo
Kiukiang
HUNAN
CHEKIANG
KIANGSI
KWEICHOW
FUKIEN
Foochow
KWANGSI
KWANGTUNG
Tamsui
Hsi (West) R.
Canton
Amoy
Taiwanfu
Chin-t'ien
KOWLOON 1860,1898
Swatow
Craddle area of Taiping Rebellion
HONG KONG 1842

families and establishments shall be allowed to reside for the purpose of carrying on their mercantile pursuits without molestation or restraint'. They were shrewdly chosen for their usefulness in commercial penetration. Palmerston thought the treaty very satisfactory: the defeat of the Chinese would without a doubt 'form an epoch in the progress of the civilisation of the human races, [and] must be attended with the most important advantages to the commercial interests of England'.[30]

Between 1850 and 1864 China was afflicted by the Taiping rebellion, a curious mixture of millenarian peasant revolt, anti-Manchu rebellion and religious crusade, which in terms of size, duration and destructiveness was probably the biggest single event in the history of the world known to Europeans in the nineteenth century, the greatest revolt and most disastrous civil war in world history.[31] It was not an isolated event. Other huge rebellions took place concurrently deep in the Chinese interior. The Nien rebellion, less sophisticated than the Taiping and closer to the traditional model of peasant defiance, lasted from 1853 until 1868. It was produced by administrative corruption, by drought and flood leading to famine and refugee problems, and it was directly provoked by the further upheaval resulting from the arrival of the Taipings in the Yangtse valley. Its leader, Chang Lo-hsing, organised salt smuggling on a grand scale.[32] Such turbulence was related to the traditional underground reservoir of secret societies, professional thugs, robbers and pirates. Practically half Kwangsi province was ravaged by bandits and rebel gangs, where a bankrupt peasantry provided a growing source of recruits. Above all there was a population explosion, intense pressure on land resources, and many natural disasters. Between 1766 and 1833 the Chinese population grew from approximately 208 million to 399 million, and to more than 430 million in 1851. The figures are unreliable, but indicate the trend. Meanwhile the cultivated area of land remained to all intents and purposes the same. The population of Kwangtung increased from 16 million in 1787 to 28 million in 1850, and the density per square mile increased from 160 to 284. The equilibrium of traditional society was upset, without any accompanying attempt at technological or institutional change. In the North China famine of 1876 to 1879, 12 or 13 million people died.[33]

The Taipings had their precursors, and roots in dynastic crisis, misgovernment and disillusionment; also in the ethnic feuding caused by the sufferings of the immigrant Hakka people of Kwangtung and Kwangsi. It is, however, almost impossible to deny some connection, extremely important if only indirect, between western influences and the outbreak of the Taiping rebellion. It originated in the hinterland of Canton, where reaction to the foreigner was strongest during the first Anglo-Chinese war, and the main foothold of European influence. As part of the post-war mopping-up operations, the extension of British navigation, and the splitting of the tea trade into five treaty ports, Canton lost nearly half its trade to Shanghai by 1850. Thus, 100,000 inland porters became unemployed and 10,000 boatmen were impoverished; fishermen, opium smugglers and pirates were put out of business and driven up-river into the hinterland where they added to the instability. The trade routes and transport system of the Canton commercial hinterland were thus disrupted by the new competition imposed by the British. The introduction of American food crops may also have been a major contributing factor to the population explosion.[34] The closure of the silver-mines in the 1840s caused further unemployment. Droughts in 1848, 1849 and 1850 were followed by terrible inflation, enabling the Taipings to find much support among the impoverished peasants and vagabonds of the Yangtse valley. The future leader of the Taipings, Hung Hsiu-ch'üan, began to study Christianity while the guns were firing at Canton. Hung was a member of a small commoner land-owning peasant family of declining fortunes and insufficient money, who had repeatedly failed to obtain his first degree; the diminishing chances facing commoners on the 'ladder of success' and their consequent alienation from the old system may well have been an element in unrest at that level.[35]

If western influences affected the origin of the rebellion, they also coloured its nature. Ideologically it rested on pseudo-Christian doctrines received at third hand. The fundamental source was not the Bible but Liang A-fa's *Good Words to Admonish the Age,* based on Robert Morrison's translation of the Authorised Version into Chinese. Liang's work represents less than ten per cent of the Bible. Thus information on Christianity was vague and full of misunderstandings, and Liang was also influenced by other religions. The Taipings upheld, after a fashion, belief in God, Christ, the Atonement, with an apocalyptic vision of a heavenly kingdom on earth. They were iconoclastic towards Confucian, Buddhist and Taoist practice. They held weekly religious services, said grace before meals, knew of the ten commandments; they practised a modified form of baptism, observed the sabbath strictly with prayer, but ignored any form of mass or holy communion. There were no churches or full-time ministers. Apart from the original leader Hung Hsiu-ch'üan, who had suffered a nervous breakdown and seen visions of God, most of the leaders were in fact more influenced by Chinese religions and superstitions than by Christianity and they lacked the true Christian spirit. And a fanatical millenarian strain was introduced by Yang Hsiu-Ch'ing, leader of miners and charcoal burners.[36]

The British anticipated the French and American fact-finding missions and sent out George Bonham to Nanking to report in 1853. He was poorly received but managed to get hold of most of the latest Taiping publications. The Taipings took Nanking in 1853 and made it their capital for 11 years, but their failure to take Peking or get an outlet to the sea was decisive in turning westerners against them. Britain did not wish to be drawn in, particularly after the rise of Louis Napoleon and the outbreak of the Crimean War. All western powers took advantage of the situation to further their own interests. Before 1862 the Taipings did not seriously disrupt trade, but when they began to do so, the westerners finally decided they must be put down, and the West began reluctantly to interfere in internal affairs at Shanghai, creating extra-territorial treaty ports elsewhere, and organising the customs system from 1861, with Chinese government approval in the latter case.

The total loss of population in four provinces alone probably far exceeded the estimated 20 or 30 millions (or more lives than were lost in the First World War). Scores of thousands of Taipings died in Nanking in internecine confhict and again at the 'last stand' in 1864. The suppression of the rebellion was equally devastating; in Canton some 70,000 decapitations took place in 1855 until the rivers were described as clotted with corpses; and perhaps a million people were executed in Kwangtung.[37]

British policy towards the Taipings exhibited many hesitations and uncertainties. Many reports were written, but few were based on knowledge of the interior where conditions might have been more settled. Britain's main concern was not to be forced to choose between having to govern China herself or go without trade altogether. Bowring was most careful to point out in 1854 a parallel: that in India Britain had begun by trading and ended by governing. This could only arouse misgivings in the vast China field. Also discussing the Taipings, the *Chinese Missionary Gleaner,* organ of the China Evangelisation Society, was thoroughly taken in and wrote: 'these men will ultimately prove the pioneers of the greatest work that has been accomplished since the days of the apostles'. By 1861 nearly all reports were unanimous in describing them as destructive. The year 1862 marked a real and decisive change in British policy, neutrality being abandoned in favour of deliberate intervention against the Taipings. The elements of banditry and blasphemy were stressed now. Intervention was on behalf of a supposed future trade rather than an actually existing one, and more important, to protect concessions and preferences. General Charles Gordon assisted the Chinese government in the suppression of the Taipings, but there is no reason to suppose that his contribution was more than marginal.[38] Aid – and aggression, for meanwhile the second China War was fought between 1856 and 1860. It was touched off by an incident involving the lorcha, *Arrow,* flying the British flag. This was the occasion of Palmerston's famous remark that: 'an insolent barbarian, wielding authority at Canton, has violated the British flag, broken the engagement of treaties, offered rewards for the heads of British subjects ... and planned their destruction by murder, assassinations and poisons'. On this issue Palmerston's government won the biggest triumph at a general election since 1832.[39]

The second China War in effect once again arose from the clash between Chinese exclusiveness and British economic expansion, and especially out of Palmerston's realisation that these orientals needed 'a drubbing' once a decade to keep them in order. Clarendon explained that the first aim of the war was to get residence of representatives of foreign powers at the seat of the supreme government in order to redress British grievances; 'next in importance to this is the extension of our commercial intercourse, not only with the sea coast, but also with the interior of China', at least up the major rivers to the great commercial cities. Elgin (plenipotentiary to China during the war) noted that every official who had tried to carry out the provisions of the treaty of 1842 had been disgraced, and rewards and honours showered upon obstructors. Elgin saw the obstinacy of the Peking government in refusing to treat other powers on an equal footing as 'at the root of our differences with that country'.[40] A treaty of Tientsin was negotiated in 1858 by Elgin, who was carried to Tientsin by a gunboat. When Bruce started up the River Peiho to Peking to secure ratification of the treaty his naval escort was repulsed with heavy losses. Elgin returned, never very happy about his China missions. Particularly in the light of the Indian Mutiny, he wondered if he could do anything 'to prevent England from calling down on herself God's curse for brutalities committed on another feeble Oriental race'. Or were his exertions simply 'to result only in the extension of the area over which Englishmen are to exhibit how hollow and superficial are both their civilisation and their Christianity?' He wanted to leave to his successors a reasonable chance of building a relationship with China based on something better than periodic use of force. However, he realised that the idea of 'non-political tea' was impossible: it was nonsense to say that Britain could have tea without political relations with the Chinese, for without them the Chinese would not allow trade at all. Capricious interferences of all kind abounded. Although it was not his idea, Elgin concurred in the military recommendation (made by Sir Hope Grant) to burn the splendid Summer Palace of Yüan-ming Yüan as a spectacular retribution for the treacherous behaviour of their opponents and for the atrocities which had taken place in it. Palmerston was mightily pleased by this demonstration of British indignation, and only wished the Peking palace itself had suffered the same fate.[41]

In 1860 ratification of the Treaty of Tientsin and the Convention of Peking opened more ports (partly excluded from Chinese jurisdiction), gave freedom for Christian missionaries, permitted a permanent British embassy in Peking, and secured the navigation of the Yangtse. Throughout the 1860s Britain adopted, and held other powers to, a basic policy of non-intervention. Foreign private groups were effectively prevented from unduly exploiting the unstable situation. Many changes were made during the T'ung-chih restoration, which, even if they did not effect basic modernisation, helped to moderate British attitudes during the reform period. 'Chinese learning as basis: Western learning for use' was hardly a realistic slogan, since the real obstacle to successful adaption, then as later, was the inherent problem of actually governing so huge and unwieldy a state, and one which could not lead or compel economic development in the face of the political and literary preoccupations of an élite which remained committed to the traditional value system.[42]

Towards the end of the century intervention increased again. The missionary movement tended relentlessly to draw European powers towards greater interference. In 1858 there were 81 Protestant missionaries in China; in 1900 there were 2,818, more than half of them British. They were present in all provinces. The number of mission stations increased from 132 in 1881 to 498 in 1900.[43]

Robert Hart's customs organisation enforced the tariff, collected revenues, completed the charting of the China coast, installed navigational aids, established a postal system, schools and colleges, published analyses of trade and sent educational missions abroad. It had 700 western employees, mostly British; its multifarious functions made it the single most important model of modernisation. Britain controlled 80 per cent of the foreign trade and this promoted a comparatively magisterial attitude at Peking. Until 1870 a large part of British imports of tea and silk were financed directly or indirectly by sales of opium to China via Hong Kong. But the importance of opium declined as new steamship agents, such as J. S. Swire, were in a stronger position to offer alternative sources of credit acceptable to the Chinese dealers. The spread of banks was important, especially the Hong Kong & Shanghai Banking Corporation from 1865. There were banks in the interior of China by 1900. In the mid-1880s the British government seemed to show a growing concern for the fate of British enterprise in China; it helped Jardine Matheson to rise above its foreign rivals, and generally appeared anxious to improve the competitive position of British financiers and industrialists in China, by-passing formal diplomatic channels. By the 1890s British dominance in the Far East was in decline as foreign economic competition increased. Britain could no longer impose a unilateral policy. Increasing rivalries culminated in the scramble for concessions after the Sino-Japanese war, which severely weakened the Manchu regime; in this sense it was the Japanese who brought the foreigners in.[44]

There followed a period of battling for concessions among rival Europeans from 1895, when Britain got a railway concession to connect Burma and Yunnan. In the scramble for naval bases and spheres of influence between 1898 and 1900, Britain obtained 356 square miles adjoining Hong Kong (known as the New Territories); Britain also secured the lease of a naval base at Weihaiwei in north China – not because she really needed either but because they seemed necessary to sustain political influence in China. She also got the largest share of railways and mining concessions, and an assurance that the Yangtse Valley would not be alienated. Russia won the secret concession of mining and railways rights in Manchuria and a special position at Port Arthur and Darien. Germany acquired mining and railway rights in Shantung. In 1898 France secured the lease of Kwangchow Bay in South China and a railway concession.[45] Sovereign rights were exercised through leasehold tenure conferring the substance of territorial authority, together with 'railway zones' attached to them: the Kiaochow lease was for 99 years,

Port Arthur 25; but both Russia and Germany regarded the acquisitions as permanent and China's reversionary rights as merely nominal. There was an anxious air of unreality about all this. In 1901 Lansdowne urged the merits of a scheme by which indemnity demanded from the Boxers should be finally repaid in 1944.[46]

The Boxer catastrophe of 1900 was the culmination of protest against foreign interference, aiming to drive out and 'exterminate the foreign devils'. It was the climax of secret society activity, of the anti-western feeling of the gentry, peasant hostility to the missions, and public indignation at the concessions. It was marked by obvious resistance to modern technology: the Boxers attacked the construction of railways and telegraphs. 32,000 Chinese Christians lost their lives, along with about 200 missionaries. In short, it was a response to the forcible injection of European religion, capital and railways.[47]

The end of the old examination system was decreed in 1901 and became effective from 1905. In 1911 the Manchu dynasty finally collapsed, sinking under the combined influence of foreign intervention, peasant revolts and the assertion by the gentry of control of their own provinces – the pressure for provincial autonomy spread rapidly after 1900, when the court ineffectively represented the gentry interests in dealing with the foreigners: strong central government had become less useful.[48]

THE PATTERN OF BRITISH INFLUENCE IN CHINA

For most of the century Britain's interest in China was purely commercial. Lord Macartney had concluded in 1794 that 'the breaking up of the power of China' was 'no very improbable event', but he did not think that Britain should become the residuary legatee:

> our present interests, our reason, and our humanity equally forbid the thoughts of any offensive measures with regard to the Chinese, whilst a ray of hope remains for succeeding by gentle ones . . .
>
> The project of a territory on the continent of China (which I have heard imputed to the late Lord Clive) is too wild to be seriously mentioned, and especially if all can be quietly got without it, that was expected to be got with it.[49]

Macartney's view proved to be not seriously different from that held by most policy-makers in the nineteenth century. Although Britain dominated the foreign relations of China for most of the century, her commitments remained informal, without any attempts to take territorial control. Nevertheless, the possibility of turning China into 'another India' was repeatedly canvassed in the nineteenth century, and feared by China herself and by Russia. H. Marshall, the American minister to China in 1853, was convinced that Britain was planning a vast coup to unite Taiping South China to the Indian empire.[50] As late as 1868 Sir Charles Dilke, an acute observer, thought an empire in China must come.[51] It was discussed as a serious question by the *Times* in 1875 and in the *Spectator* as late as 1898, though dismissed by both. 'We are not in the mood to undertake the responsibilities of another India', declared the *Times*, whereas the *Spectator* saw the effort of holding it as too burdensome, estimating that it would require a force of 70,000 men.[52] Kipling visited China in 1887–88; in *From Sea to Sea* (1900) he mused that in India they might have conquered the wrong country – 'Let us annex China'.[53]

The definitive policy statement of Clarendon (Palmerston's disciple) made in 1870 stood in fact for the whole century:

> British interests in China are strictly commercial or, at all events, only so far political as they may be for the protection of commerce . . .[54]

Herbert warned in 1859 against further destroying Manchu prestige, 'so plunging the country into a state of anarchy which would be fatal to our trade, the prosecution of which is the object of all our proceedings'.[55] Balfour nearly 30 years later said much the same thing as Clarendon, and Hicks Beach's opinion was typical of many ministers. They did not, he said, regard China as a place suitable for conquest or acquisition by any European or other power, but as the most hopeful place of the future for the commerce of Britain and the commerce of the world at large. The government declared in 1899 when China was being partially divided into spheres of influence and concessions:

> We cannot make the Yangtse valley a province like Shantung or Manchuria, first because it is infinitely larger, and secondly we are not prepared to undertake the immense responsibility of governing what is practically a third of China.[56]

Despite the consistency of these denials, their repetition indicates the issue was very much alive. The chief pressure group in favour of a degree of political control was the 'Old China Hands', the men who had on-the-spot knowledge of trading conditions and vested interests in making profit. Such pressure groups existed in other regions, and several had more success than the Chinese group. Why was this? There are three main reasons for the government's reluctance to take territory. First, it was thought unnecessary since India was already held. Secondly, it was thought to be unjustifiable, because commercially not worthwhile owing to the self-sufficiency of China. Thirdly, it was thought unfeasible and unwise, owing to the turbulence and size of China, and its remoteness from Britain.

'Another India' would have been superfluous; all that could be achieved on behalf of the expansion of trade by some political dominion in the east was in fact being achieved by India. There was no strategic reason for taking territory in China. China was not on the route to anywhere. Furthermore, there was an instinctive dislike of advancing imperial land frontiers beyond the protective reach of British sea power. The widespread aversion to further extension was aptly expressed by Sir William Harcourt. 'We have already as much empire as the nation can carry', he said; 'If you give the heart too much work to do by extending the limbs and frame beyond measure you enfeeble its action and it succumbs'.[57] Men more closely concerned with China saw no reason to make an exception there. Sir Claude Macdonald said in 1899

> British enterprise in China must be independent, individual and self reliant. The moment it ceases to be this and leans too much on state assistance it ceases to be enterprise, indeed I may say that it ceases to be British.[58]

Victorian governments were, however, despite a prevailing preference for informal control, always prepared to support an individual trading interest where injury to that interest might be interpreted as injury to the nation's interest as a whole, defined almost exclusively in political terms. Until the 1870s, it was not the size of the trade as such which was considered important. Beyond securing normal trading conditions for obtaining the maximum quantity of tea and silk, the economic value of China as a market did not justify great exertions to secure it. Despite what Pelcovits calls the 'folklore of the merchants' (the popular belief that China could be the El Dorado of the age), and the persistent optimism of old China hands and other interested persons that improvements were always imminent, the foreign trade of China never amounted to much. There was a great gulf fixed between rhetoric and reality. It mattered little to the Chinese economy: if its fringe activities had entirely ceased altogether this would have had small effect. By the end of the century China's foreign trade did not exceed 1.5 per cent of the world's total. All Chinese trade figures show two main characteristics – stagnation at a comparatively low level, and a British predominance at about 70 per cent of the total foreign commerce and shipping in China. In 1882 Britain sent £29 million exports to India, but only £7½ million to China, that is to say, less to China than to Belgium. In 1894 while India and the Straits Settlements took £20 million of cotton piece-goods of all types from Britain, China and Hong Kong took less than £4 million.[59] China's huge internal trade and considerable domestic industry contributed to a basic self-sufficiency. As Sir Robert Hart observed towards the end of the century:

> the Chinese have the best food in the world, rice; the best drink, tea; and the best clothing, cotton, silk and fur. Possessing these staples and their innumerable ... adjuncts, they do not need to buy a penny's-worth elsewhere.

The peasant could not produce a surplus to spend on consumer goods, and most western products ran counter to the ancient preferences of Chinese taste. Distribution was restricted by bad transport, which was nearly non-existent except for rivers: even the Grand Canal was in disrepair, and almost no attention was paid to roads.[60] There was thus no sound basis for a market. A government report had sounded a warning as early as 1847:

> We must not be led into error by the numerous boats and junks, many of which carry bulky and very valueless articles; one of our moderately laden ships would be an equivalent for a hundred of the largest vessels.

The substance of another report of 1852 was that Chinese self-sufficiency was bound 'to condense the fabulous dream into a relatively meagre reality'.[61] A little later, Elgin upheld this conclusion:

> The expectations held out to British manufacturers at the close of the last war [1842] between Gt. Britain and China, when they were told that a new world was opened to their trade so vast that all the mills of Lancashire could not make stocking stuff ... for one of its provinces, have not been realised, and I am of the opinion that when force and diplomacy shall have done all that they can legitimately effect, the work which has to be accomplished in China will be but at its commencement.

By the mid 1860s the government was firmly convinced that the China trade would never be worth the expense of war and territorial control; that the potentialities had been grossly exaggerated by the old China hands. It therefore proceeded on the assumption that British interests would remain temporary and limited; that commercial interests would always remain particular, even speculative interests, but never territorial ones. The basis of British policy for the rest of the century was a report prepared by Louis Mallet of the board of trade in 1869. He showed that the trade rested on unhealthy and insecure foundations, and had not repaid British exertions, because China had plenty of raw materials, a large labour supply, and impoverished consumers. He concluded that with such poor results after constant efforts and repeated war, 'it is a great question on which side of the national ledger the balance will be found to stand'. Because Indian tea was becoming established, the loss of China tea imports would not now result in one British spindle the less at work, he added; the amount of trade was becoming relatively so small that it could easily be transferred to Ceylon or Brazil in exchange for tobacco or coffee. This kind of reasoning explains the comparative indifference to Chinese affairs even in critical periods. The China trade *was* relatively declining after 1870, and not only as a result of competition from Indian tea, but also from Japanese silk. That the trade was incapable of significant expansion was the conclusion of every successive consular report and intelligence from China after 1852.[62] In 1848 Rutherford Alcock had analysed further powerful checks inhibiting a large and comprehensive development of the British position. Firstly the danger of a disastrous collision between east and west. Secondly the magnitude of British commercial interests in China as lubricating the Indian trade. Thirdly, the risk that foreign powers would follow — Russia, France, America, and even Spain, Portugal and Holland, could all create disturbance if Britain opened the way. A struggle for supremacy in China could embroil all Europe. He also feared the uncertain result of a struggle with a vast empire whose resources were so imperfectly known.[63]

Britain in particular willingly upheld the American doctrine of the 'Open Door', which suited her commercial interests. In fact she had operated the policy before it was formulated. France or Russia in territorial occupation would set up tariff walls — when powers had annexed the peripheral territories they invariably imposed heavy protective duties. The British conclusion was that the existing Chinese Manchu system was less restrictive than the system which European powers might institute; hence Curzon's declaration that 'our policy is and must be to prevent her disruption as long as we can ... '; the maintenance of the integrity and independence of China were always the 'cardinal bases of our policy'.[64] To assert a British territorial dominion at the end of the nineteenth century was out of the question because it would have been opposed by the Dual Alliance, which was nowhere so effective or so certain of German backing as in the Far East; and because the areas were so huge that it was beyond British strength, especially as she had assumed so many similar responsibilities elsewhere.[65] China continued just about to present a united front to the west, and persisted in an overwhelming sense of its own superiority. It was altogether a big, tough nut to crack. Political unity under the Manchu dynasty did not fail in the nineteenth century even at times of greatest weakness. As a result, in every case the west had to fight out issues with a central government, which on the whole was successful in keeping westerners bottled up on the coast. Until the very end of the nineteenth century China had enough organised government to prevent the penetration into the interior of unofficial freebooters in sufficient numbers to drag governments after them.

However lamentably inefficient in dealing with the British coastal invasion — which can only have seemed of peripheral importance to Peking — a regime which successfully put down first the Taiping rebellion and then the Nien was one which clearly had extraordinary powers of resilience. Tseng Kuo-fan and his friends marshalled provincial resources to raise new armies which crushed the rebels without a trace. The Chinese state survived because significant parts of the élite (combining local and state rôles) coalesced in mid-century to identify the dynasty's interests with their own, and to take the lead in suppressing the enemies of the Manchu. The old élite was able to hold together with surprising toughness and flexibility, and effectively to mobilise loosely-articulated militias (local civil and military organisations which had a respectable history as customary, but informal, local associations), assuming co-ordinating functions to meet emergency, and expanding into larger units. These were under the leadership of a remarkable constellation of Hunan gentry, linked by a network of personal loyalties, who activated and financed local defence organisations into the highly professional Hunan army, which was able to campaign beyond its provincial base and make alliances with the élite in other provinces. They were able to form further effective regional armies as part of a formal structure of local government, and began to function as virtually autonomous satrapies. Only 30,000 out of the 80,000 strong Hunan army were disbanded, and the way was open for the emergence of twentieth-century local warlords.[66]

The Mughal civil servants in India lacked initiative, because they were tested by spies in an atmosphere of suspicion – but the Chinese mandarins could often lessen the evil effects of an incompetent emperor and maintain or re-activate local government. In contrast to India, the British could not in China readily discern well-regulated army, police or revenue systems awaiting easy capture and utilisation.[67] Although some Chinese collaborated as 'sepoys' or police (and thus aided British victory in both wars), the British were unable to make full use of potential collaborators: their own manpower was inadequate for so big a problem. It was difficult to incorporate western military technology and command structure into traditional Chinese armies or the locally-based defence associations. At least four times as much revenue was appropriated by local officials as was remitted to the central Chinese exchequer.[68] Local autonomy and secret societies were increasing in strength. Corruption, distress and discontent were deep and widespread, and did not present at all an encouraging prospect to a western invader. The situation in some localities was out of control by the 1830s. The two major waves of unrest unfolded themselves between 1850 and 1870 and between 1895 and 1911: both periods of intense foreign pressure. Quite apart from the Taiping and Nien rebellions already mentioned (and the former at least was well known in Britain), there were two great Muslim rebellions in Yunnan (1853–73) and in the North-west (1863–73), and the Miao rebellion in Kweichow lasted from 1854 to 1872. Between 1856 and 1860 perhaps seven million peasants were involved in revolt. The second wave of peasant unrest from 1895 to 1911 was based on subversive secret societies – thousands of them were active, tirelessly organising stereotyped revolts. There were hundreds of peasant risings all over China between 1909 and 1911: the disintegration was nearly total. This peasant potential explains why Peking gave in to the west on the coast, because the Manchu could never be sure of the stability of the hinterland; the peasants thus contributed to Manchu failure simply by posing a threat. This peasant potential and the Boxer rebellion checked any reviving western plan there might have been for a partition.[69]

There was thus a great apprehension of putting pressure on China. In 1880 one British observer noted 'a kind of fear of attacking China as of attacking an unknown quantity'. Hobson described China a little later as 'a vast repository of incalculable forces'. Trying to open up China while 'the psychology of the Chinese is a terra incognita' was for him 'the crowning instance of irrational government'.[70] China was in short, totally unamenable to the techniques of formal control, and recalcitrant even to those of informal control. In the last resort China was saved from partition not by Britain but by other powers, who stood to lose more than they would gain. 32 treaty ports were open by the 1890s and 48 by 1913, and from 1895 there was freedom to penetrate the river systems. Each treaty port was taken to include a 30-mile radius of territory. The power who most threatened Chinese integrity was Russia, and she was defeated by Japan in 1905. The real plums were Manchuria, Shanghai and the Yangtse valley. If Russia insisted on the former, Britain would insist on the other two. Shanghai handled 40 per cent of the external trade of China — and so all powers except Russia and Japan concluded that partition would be economically damaging to their interests. The indigenous political structure continued to provide an essential framework of order superior to any which it was supposed could be imposed from without.[71]

It would be a mistake to see the western impact on China as deliberately aggressive in all its manifestations. Businessmen did much less harm than missionaries, and the notion of economic exploitation needs qualification. The traditional order was not defenceless in the face of offers of loans and railways, but officials balanced one western firm against another in competition. A study of Jardine Matheson and Co's operations suggests that they were not as aggressive in dealing with Chinese officials as internal conditions would have allowed. At least after 1870 they believed success depended on co-operation, and they aimed to influence the traditional order without weakening it; they firmly believed a progressive Ch'ing government-directed programme of economic development would triumph and they were willing to work closely with Chinese businessmen for mutual profit; in fact the firm could not dictate the terms of the partnership even in the years of China's progressive decline. Between 1870 and 1895 the firm's members generally favoured helping China to help itself towards modernisation. Aggressive views were rarely expressed after 1870. Even between 1842 and 1858, when there were many aggressive statements, these did not amount to a single fixed policy advocating continuous military pressure as apparently supposed by Pelcovits. Other shipping companies and merchant houses, such as Butterfield and Swire, also had a sense of responsibility towards China, contributing generously to the foundation of educational and recreational institutions; they certainly felt that they had made friends rather than enemies. It is not true that western treatment of China immediately before the Boxer uprising was 'devoid of all consideration and all understanding' – the west has for too long been a convenient scapegoat for Chinese unwillingness to face its inability to adapt adequately.[72]

THE OPENING AND MODERNISATION OF JAPAN.[73]

On 8 July 1853 the American Commodore Perry steamed into Yedo Bay harbour with four gunboats and a presidential letter asking the Japanese for trade openings, humane treatment for shipwrecked sailors, and a port where American steamers could obtain coal and provisions. A year later Perry returned with seven American ships and concluded the first nineteenth-century convention between Japan and the outside world. The Treaty of Kanagawa (1858) opened five Japanese ports to foreign trade. Foreign diplomats took up residence in 1859. Japan's two centuries of exclusion to western ships and commerce was over. During that period the only limited trade permitted had been to the Dutch at Nagasaki. Since 1603 Japan had been ruled by a shogun or military governer, whose system of government was known as the Bakufu and exercised by the house of Tokugawa. The Tokugawa regime gave in to America chiefly because it was insolvent. In 1868 the emperor was restored to power and the new Meiji government immediately assumed responsibility for modernising the country.[74]

Britain made no attempt to forestall the Americans, and was not upset by the American initiative. If successful, Britain expected to profit from it, since this would make it easier for Britain to establish trade relations. This, it was thought, would provide some compensation for the British initiative in China from which the Americans had profited. Clearly Japan was not regarded in Britain as important enough to justify international competition. Despite the enthusiasm of Raffles in 1813 for an attempt to open Japan, and despite Palmerston's instruction to Napier in 1834 to explore the possibilities, and even despite vague foreign office plans in the 1840s, Britain did not really move beyond the standpoint that opening and goodwill were desirable in principle but not likely to lead to much commercial reward. There was no deep interest. Although many cabinet ministers in the middle of the century were interested in pressing trade generally, Granville summed up an important reservation in 1852: the government still did not accept the view that 'all considerations of a higher nature ... be sacrificed to the pushing of our manufactures by any means into every possible corner of the globe'. And there was certainly no desire to use force to make Japan do something which might be disagreeable to her. Thus no action was taken by Britain until Perry provided an opportunity to open relations without special risk or expense. Britain made two attempts to follow the American initiative. The first was under rear-admiral Sir James Stirling, who negotiated at Nagasaki in 1854. The second was under Elgin at Edo in 1858. Neither Stirling nor Elgin made any important change in the treaty pattern established by the Americans. Stirling, with the anti-Russian needs of the Crimean War in mind, secured entry to Nagasaki and Hakodate for ships to repair and get supplies. Elgin's treaty of Yedo provided for the opening of Nagasaki, Kanagawa, and Hakodate to British residents and trade, and for two more ports and residence in two more towns by 1863.[75] Elgin obtained no really close understanding of Japanese conditions, but he formed a favourable impression of the people, contrasting them advantageously with the Chinese. They were, he found, 'so anxious to learn, so *prévenants*, with none of the 'stiffness and bigotry of the Chinese'.[76]

Britain's first official representative was Rutherford Alcock, consul-general for Japan, instructed in December 1858 to obtain gradual extension of trade and to watch Russian activities. He was expected to work with the French, the Dutch and the Americans to further their common interests, but not to compete with foreign agents for influence with the Japanese government. These instructions show an obvious attempt by the foreign office to avoid the evils inflicted on China and to deal with Japan without giving cause for offence.[77] However it proved difficult to enforce the treaty of Yedo, and Britain was provoked into wielding the big stick. Admiral Kuper bombarded Kagoshima (capital of Satsuma) on 16 August 1863, an action which was hotly debated by the House of Commons in February 1864. To punish the Chōshū clan for its unprovoked attacks on foreign ships, 17 more gunboats bombarded the Shimonoseki straits in 1864. These actions were followed by a joint display of 12 European warships at Osaka in 1865.

The imposition of unequal treaties by gunboat diplomacy and the end to security from attack produced an upsurge of emotion in Japan greater than that aroused by the domestic shortcomings of the Bakufu. The naval displays were a blow to Japanese pride and were felt as a 'national' dishonour in all areas and at all levels of society. They thereby helped to upset the regional and sociological fragmentation which had been one of the foundations of Tokugawa power, and they had some effect in assisting the shift of power from the ancien régime of the Bakufu to the western clans, a shift which underpinned the Meiji restoration. It was the humiliation at the hands of the west which precipitated the internal Japanese power struggle and controversy over the leadership. The Meiji Restoration saw the redistribution of power within the ruling class, the military elements superintending a restoration of the emperor's authority and the institution of a centralised bureaucratic state. The threat from abroad (coinciding with the internal process of decay and revolt) was utilised by the anti-Bakufu forces as a lever to overturn the shogunate. Resistance was led by Chōshū province, traditionally hostile to the Tokugawa, and a centre of anti-foreign activity. They bought 7,000 rifles from the west and sank their differences with Satsuma in order to bring down the Tokugawa and thus ensure stronger action against the west. The adoption of this western technology enabled Chōshū to defeat the combined Bakufu army in 1866 and enabled Chōshū and Satsuma to triumph over numerically superior Bakufu forces in 1868. Without this technological factor the new government would undoubtedly have been more of a compromise with the old Tokugawa institutions than was actually the case. But the adoption of western technology was possible only because of the strength of Chōshū's traditional society and its adoption was precipitated by the Shimonoseki bombardment.[78] There is little evidence that the shogun's hold could have been so successfully broken without the catalyst of foreign intervention.[79] This is not to imply, however, that Britain or any other power actively incited the anti-Bakufu elements, although Alcock and his successor Parkes surmised that the enemies of the shogun might be better friends to the west. When Parkes was appointed minister plenipotentiary in 1865 he was instructed to remain neutral in the internal conflict. Britain was the first power to recognise the new government, but British sympathy with the *daimyo* cause could not of itself have brought about the overthrow of the shogunate. Parkes became the foremost foreign adviser, and critic, of the Meiji government.[80]

The Meiji Restoration took place at a time when the expansive thrust of the west was at less than full throttle. Britain, preoccupied in China, had no desire to make big exertions. The Americans had become entirely absorbed by their civil strife. French ambitions and intrigues in Japan were checked by the Mexican venture. China in effect acted as a shield for Japan, and thus absorbed some of the thrust which might otherwise have been turned against Japan. A new regime was thus set up able to keep full control of Japanese independence.[81]

Japan's encounter with the west occurred sufficiently late in time for her to be able to plan her response with the experience of others in mind. She was able to keep control over foreign enterprise and make sure it did not attain a dominant position. She never gave railway concessions to foreigners. She displayed a rigorous reluctance to borrow money abroad, despite a desperate need for working capital. She learned specifically from the fate of Egypt and Turkey, and in the nineteenth century contracted only two loans, in 1870 and 1873, both for railways and both in London. The structure of Japanese industry was created by the Japanese themselves.[82]

Japanese freedom of action in modernising herself was also powerfully aided by the comparative absence of religious impediments to educational, technological and other changes.[83] They were determined to learn as much as possible from foreign example. There was first-hand study of European and American institutions and methods, led by the prime minister, Prince Ito. German influence was particularly strong in the later nineteenth century, but the British impact was steady and prolonged.[84] Japan's success in the economic field was based on skilful organisation and good luck. The Japanese showed an unusual talent for corporate action in large-scale enterprises, under facilitating state influence.[85] Their industrial revolution was initially built chiefly on silk exports; fortuitously, European silk-worm disease powerfully aided them in their first assault upon foreign markets.[86]

What was Britain's part in all this? 75 per cent of Japanese imports until the mid-1880s were British in origin,[87] but these represented only the most negligible stake for British world trade. Britain's imports from Japan never reached even one per cent of her total import trade before 1883. Japan was decidedly a minor outpost on the fringe of Britain's commercial empire. Nevertheless it was Britons who led the way in establishing journalism, engineering, banking procedures, naval and railway development, and western medicine. Britain supplied the largest number of foreign employees working for the Japanese government. The breadth and depth of British influence cannot be attributed to any great interest in Japan among politicians and public opinion, but the proximity of Britain's established Chinese and Indian interest led to a natural overspill. Japan also consciously followed the British model in many things. Parkes helped to establish British standards in the running of the imperial naval college at Tokyo, where officers of the royal navy gave instruction between 1873 and 1882. In the last three decades most Japanese battleships were built in British shipyards. It was British effort and technical co-operation which helped the creation of a Japanese navy. Parkes also provided initiative and assistance in the construction of lighthouses, telegraphs and railways. Drainage and roadmaking were also helped, notably by R. H. Brunton, an outstanding engineer. British scientists were prominent in the early development of western techniques. Henry Dyer was first principal of the Meiji government's Engineering College. Two British seismologists, John Milne and James Ewing, introduced the scientific study of earthquakes and invented instruments for recording and measuring their intensity. The small British community in Japan exercised a far-reaching influence, which was remarkable in view of the minor importance of Japan to British interests. Generous assistance was given by leading British diplomats, merchants, teachers and scholars. Jardine Matheson & Co. helped Japanese students to get to Europe, not only providing them with hospitality there, but also aiding the Japanese government in selecting scientists to teach in Japan. Superintending all this early activity was Parkes, noted for his hauteur and air of condescension to the Japanese and for his outbursts of temper; but for all that he was sincerely interested in the development of Japan.[88]

Thus, despite the American lead in opening Japan, it was Britain whose influence was most obvious in the early and systematic modernisation of the Meiji régime. The economic miracle performed by Japan and the self-discipline it involved greatly impressed Britain, and provided the background to the alliance of 1902.[89]

CONCLUSION

13 The End of Empire

In any analysis of British interests 'profit and power ought jointly to be considered', as Sir Josiah Child recognised as long ago as the 1690s. And this is so for the simple reason that the two tend to reinforce one another: trade increases power and power protects trade. One of the things which strategy is designed to secure is economic position, but it can become an end in itself, and there are many instances where territory was acquired for its strategic significance. A problem arises when we try to decide the relative balance between profit and power in explaining British motives for expansion in those historically contentious areas where economic interests were also prominent. The answer, I suggest, is to be found in distinguishing between two *levels* of motive. At the metropolitan, governmental level, the 'official mind' in Whitehall (recruited from aristocratic, academic and professional classes) was preoccupied by political decisions – with the higher questions of adjusting international relations, the mission of spreading 'civilisation', and the duty of protecting the national interest (broadly conceived) by maintaining prestige and strategic security. Disdainful of merely commercial activities, and temperamentally detached from special interest groups of whatever kind, the 'official mind' would nevertheless assist these in so far as they affected the national interest as Whitehall defined it. Grandly independent of any pressures put upon them, ministers decided the needs of commerce for themselves. Then at the local overseas level, the interests of private individuals were decidedly sectional, even selfish: investors, traders and businessmen seeking profit, concessionaires and adventurers seeking fame and aggrandisement, missionaries seeking souls, and nearly everyone seeking sexual satisfaction. Mostly private individuals expected to carry out their activities without government interference. Government ministers in fact saw little reason to promote these local-level interests, although there were exceptions – Glenelg the evangelical and Chamberlain the businessman obviously spring to mind. Whitehall was no more concerned to increase or protect the financial dividends of private individuals than it was their sexual satisfactions. The empire was not run as a bond-holders' empire, any more than as a brothel-hunters', but both, quite incidentally, did well out of the unique framework of opportunity it created. The profit motive, like the sex drive, was fundamental at the local level, but the one was as little likely as the other to impress Whitehall as a guide for policy at the decision-making level. The definitive statement of policy in 1905 was laid down by Lansdowne:

> We are being continually hammered on account of our failure to do more for British commerce and enterprise of all sorts, and our performance is contrasted with that of the foreigners. The public cannot be made to understand that, apart from the objection to embarking public money in doubtful ventures, which prevents us from subsidising British railways in China and elsewhere, we cannot condescend to the methods of our competitors in such matters as orders for ships and artillery. It is something to know that our reputation stands higher in consequence.[1]

Territory could, however, be acquired when the two levels of interest interlocked. Individuals overseas could create circumstances which made an acquisition possible or even probable, usually through their economic endeavour (the role of the missionaries, except in New Zealand and the Pacific, and parts of Central Africa, may be discounted), but they could never ensure or determine it. The actual decision to run up the flag was usually taken by Whitehall, superintending an ever-increasing international rivalry explicable only (in the first instance) by domestic urges to expansion within Europe. Occasionally it was taken by its overseas interpreters, the governors and military officers. These were not of course supposed to take such decisions, but for much of the century there was a small but vital gap between what a really ambitious officer on the spot could do and what his metropolitan masters dared to veto. Thus no explanation of the taking of territory will ever be satisfactory unless it is considered at two levels, the one making final political decisions in a European context and framework of reference, and the other contributing to the creation of preparatory conditions in a non-European context, requiring, but certainly not always obtaining, government control. Where local indigenous régimes were unable to maintain an adequate system of law and order sufficient for the successful operation of European economic activities (as in western India in the eighteenth century, or West Africa in the nineteenth) the government might step in. But it did so chiefly because it believed these chaotic conditions could lead to international conflicts or humanitarian abuses which it was its job to contain as custodian for the peaceful progress of mankind, for the honour and security of the empire as a whole, and the maintenance of Britain as a first-class power in the face of foreign challenge. The government was *never* manipulated by economic pressure groups, which, in any case could never agree among themselves. Indeed, the government can be shown to have ignored trading interests even when their traditional activities were directly concerned in a change of policy, as in Tunis in 1878 or Persia in 1907.[2]

The interlocking of levels did not automatically produce territorial control. Throughout the century, the government occasionally used economic means to buttress threatened informal political positions. Canning did this on a small scale in Latin America, and Palmerston also in a limited way in the Ottoman empire and Afghanistan; and from the late 1880s the foreign office became directly involved (though unhappily) in the battle for concessions in China and Persia, once it realised that other powers had begun to wage the political battle with economic weapons. But as we have already noted, there was a distinct limit beyond which, for the sake of reputation, they would not go. The late nineteenth century was not in any case marked by any real increase in British intervention in other parts of the world, because after 1815 it always was the case that, as a first-class power with a position in five continents, her *very presence is intervention*, as Sir Robert Morier remarked.[3]

Why did men go overseas? – or give themselves to the service of the empire? Again the question ought to be considered at two levels. At the level of the anonymous emigrant, the self-seeking settler, it was often, in Sinclair's words, because of 'bigamy or bankruptcy, disappointment or disgrace' at home, or because of the superior opportunity for making money or exercising talents abroad. India and Egypt provided, for example, far better opportunities for hydraulic and irrigation experts than Britain could; and once the railway system of Britain was complete, railway engineers had to look elsewhere. And then at the level of the administrative élite, although an element of escape could apply here too, the emphasis was heavily on a sense of duty, of mission, or at least on the self-satisfaction of making a good name rather than a lot of money, or of succeeding at work rather than love. For to a greater extent than has been realised, the fundamental dynamic of British expansion was the export of surplus emotional and sexual energy. The ferocious effort put into acquiring and running the empire was directly proportional to the frustrated, repressed and unimaginative love-lives of its heroes. The British were the world's greatest empire-builders: they were also the world's worst lovers. But whether or not the result of sublimation, the sense of duty stands out, and with it, at the governmental level, the prestige motive. It has often been supposed, though sometimes grudgingly, that prestige, 'la gloire' may have something to do with French expansion, but that something more sophisticated (such as the niceties of strategical calculation) is required to explain British expansion. And yet what did that highly successful ambassador Robert Morier say? He agreed with Mallet: as a great power with a great position, Britain had great duties, and life was not worth living without individual and national honour. Morier wrote of 'the great forces of barbarism, which it is our mission to subdue and control'. To do any good international work Britain must keep up her material power and her prestige: and these were ends to which he was prepared to devote his life.

Similar ideas guided Rosebery, Chamberlain and Curzon. Devotion to the empire often represented the transfer of religious emotion to secular purposes. Lugard in Nigeria (according to his wife) nearly killed himself and 'a fair percentage of his staff' with overwork, 'yet they like it'; after all (she added), 'they are working for an idea, and that is more than all men can say'. The ruling élite was often contemptuous of the ordinary Briton overseas not inspired by this sense of mission. The word 'colonial' frequently had pejorative undertones: not merely of convict, but of peasant, adventurer and remittance man. Colonists were always suspect for supposed indifference to the happiness of those among whom they lived. 'East of Suez' especially the members of the ruling élite were continually appalled by the conduct of their compatriots. One opinion must stand as representative. The eighth earl of Elgin wrote from Calcutta in 1857 (just after the Mutiny):

> It is a terrible business . . ., this living among inferior races. I have seldom, from man or woman, since I came to the East, heard a sentence . . . reconcilable with the hypothesis that Christianity had ever come into the world. Detestation, contempt, ferocity, vengeance, whether Chinamen or Indians be the object . . .

As far as servants were concerned:

> one moves among them with perfect indifference, treating them, not as dogs, because in that case one would whistle to them and pat them, but as machines with which one can have no communion or sympathy . . . When the passions of fear and hatred are engrafted on this indifference, the result is frightful . . .

After proceeding on his mission to China, Elgin concluded that he had seen more in the east to disgust him with his fellow-countrymen than ever before in his life. The east he found abominable, not so much in itself, but because 'it is strewed all over with the records of our violence and fraud, and disregard of right': the British had burst through it 'with hideous violence and brutal energy', and done so with 'an absolute callousness' to the suffering they had caused.[4]

At whatever level, expatriate Britons behaved more swaggeringly, more grandly than they could have done at home – and this gave a 'touch of unreality and theatricality' to all their lives. These 'displaced persons' relied increasingly heavily upon a sense of racial superiority as the century wore on: it was their justification and their protection. The empire was, after all, always a curiously hollow affair, dependent in the last resort not so much on force (for there was never enough of that to go round), but on the ability to find, for the imperial purpose, collaborators within the non-European communities.[5] The ability to evoke this co-operation, and to balance conflicting local indigenous interest-groups by a process of 'divide and rule' was part of the quiddity of the white man's magic. It could only work while the white man was found to have something genuine to offer, and while he offered it confidently. In his vanity, he had in fact less to offer than he thought he had in every sphere except the technological, and with its ability to be duped, the rest of the world for long failed to see this. But when the ultimate use of that technology was seen, after 1914, to be the destruction of human life on a terrible scale, in what (to non-European eyes) was a white man's civil war, the hollowness came dangerously close to being unmasked.

The First World War brought in its train a number of shocks, providing widespread evidence of the growing unpopularity of British rule and the imperial connection: a rebellion of Afrikaner generals in 1914 in South Africa, an uprising in Ireland in 1916, and, after the war, an almost general crisis of empire in India, Ireland and Egypt, beginning with 379 Indians shot dead at Amritsar in 1919. These more spectacular manifestations were however in many ways eclipsed by the symbolic Chilembwe episode in Nyasaland, planned in 1914 itself,[6] a gesture of defiance, consciously seeking martyrdom. How much longer could the British go on pretending that all the world loved them?

The end of the empire was protracted. It carried the sentence of death within itself at least from the 1890s, perhaps even from the 1870s, yet immense powers of resilience were repeatedly displayed. A great deal of effective patching-up was achieved between 1900 and 1914. It was said of Asquith that he was equal to every contingency except that of fighting a world war, and in a way that was true of the empire itself. Paradoxically the overriding concern in Europe with the German problem from 1908 to 1948 had the effect of masking and delaying the end. In fact, the aftermath of each world war brought reassertions of the imperial factor. After 1918, ex-German colonies were administered under League of Nations mandates, a Middle East empire was put together, a National Home for the Jewish people was promoted, a stronger colonial service was recruited. But it was a severely over-extended empire, as the Second World War was to show: the fall of Singapore demonstrated that the defence of Britain (as Balfour had feared) was indeed incompatible with the maintenance of an oriental empire. Still the British refused to believe that the empire was dead – and after 1945 fresh exertions were made to build up the east and central African section of the imperial bastion. And yet essentially Britain's imperial century came to an end, if not actually with the shots at Sarajevo in 1914, then in 1915 in the mud of Flanders. If Edward Grey had had a greater breadth of vision he would have realised that it was not only, or even mainly, in Europe that the lamps were going out: it was happening all over the empire too. The post-war world was utterly unlike the pre-war one. The war was won only with American aid, and that fact alone had an incalculable bearing on the decline of the British empire. Unilateral action by Britain was never again really possible, and the tyranny of the telegraph kept her representatives on a tighter rein. Empire had become an unmitigated burden, a serious, even a grim business. The day of the jester was over.

The other main effect of the war was upon the leadership of the empire. As early as 1907 Morley (reflecting on the problem of administering Egypt) had written: 'It often occurs to me that John Bull needs almost more brains than we can command, for the government of this vast and rather haphazard sprawling kind of empire'. And, six months later, he added: 'There is no surplus of brain in the administrative world just now'. If Morley was right, and the manpower shortage for the administration of the empire was becoming a worry even before the war, it was a nightmare after it, when the empire had been further enlarged and the administrative élite was depleted by the war death-roll. Men under the age of 45 were virtually decimated. 745,000 died, nine per cent of all British males under the age of 45, and these by definition (since the majority had volunteered before conscription was introduced) were its bravest and best. The number included 30,000 officers, just the sort whom the empire relied on.[7] Five out of the 12 scholars in College at Eton elected in 1906 (the year of Harold Macmillan, and he was not the ablest of them) lost their lives in the war; one of the survivors recorded that in his diary for the year 1915 'there were almost daily entries of the death in action, or the death after wounds, of Eton and Cambridge friends'. Of 3,100 Old Cliftonians who went to war, 578 died. In one English state grammar school, probably not untypical, nearly half the school-leavers in the decade before the war were killed or wounded, and only two members of the Old Boys Soccer XI of 1914 played again in 1919.[8] A demographic disaster of this magnitude did not merely cause a serious dearth of suitable leaders, but severely shook many of the survivors with doubt and misery. In one way it was a chastening and humanising experience. But Edwardian confidence was irreparably shattered, and the empire depended above all on a confidence which admitted of no doubt. After the war the empire was still one upon which the sun never set, but, with a ruling élite so damaged, this was more of a liability than a boast.

The congregation in Great St Mary's Church, Cambridge on a grey November day in 1932 were asked by F. A. Simpson, the Lady Margaret's Preacher, to remember:

those whose bright dawn no noon awaited here; those who would have been the light and lamp of our own generation, which now halts and stumbles, robbed of its natural leaders, towards its night ... the chief thing to remember about our leaders in the dozen years ahead of us is this: that most of them were not meant to be our leaders at all. They are only the last and worst of our war substitutes. Our true leaders, as well in literature and the arts as in public life – but most of all I think in public life – our true leaders were taken from our head now nearly twenty years ago: when a generation was not decimated but decapitated; not mauled at mere haphazard, but shorn precisely of its grace and glory, of its most ardent, its most generous, its most brave . . . *Our born leaders are dead.*[9]

There is a study to be made of naivety, which seems never to have been undertaken. It is one of the main cogs in the machinery of the world; in fact it is what makes everything run smoothly. What would the world be without dupes?

— Henri de Montherlant

References

ABBREVIATIONS

AHR	*American Historical Review.*
AR	*Annual Register.*
BIHR	*Bulletin of the Institute of Historical Research.*
CEHE	*Cambridge Economic History of Europe.*
CHBE	*Cambridge History of the British Empire.*
CHJ	*Cambridge Historical Journal.*
CHR	*Canadian Historical Review.*
CO	Colonial Office records.
DNB	*Dictionary of national biography.*
EconHR	*Economic History Review* (2nd series unless indicated).
EHR	*English Historical Review.*
FO	Foreign Office records.
HJ	*Historical Journal.*
JAH	*Journal of African History.*
JBS	*Journal of British Studies.*
JEconH	*Journal of Economic History.*
JICH	*Journal of Imperial & Commonwealth History.*
JMH	*Journal of Modern History.*
NCMH	*New Cambridge Modern History.*
PD	*Parliamentary Debates* (preceeding number indicates series).
P&P	*Past & Present.*
PBA	*Proceedings of the British Academy.*
PRO	Public Record Office.
TRHS	*Transactions of the Royal Historical Society* (preceeding number indicates series).
VS	*Victorian Studies.*

The more specialised journals are referred to in full.

1. THE FOUNDATIONS OF POWER 1815–70

1. G. W. Martin 'Was there a British empire?' *HJ* XV (1972) 562, quoting J. A. Roebuck (14 Apr. 37); R. Hyam & G. W. Martin, *Reappraisals in British imperial history* (1975) ch.1, 'Personal & impersonal forces and the continuity of British imperial history'.
2. CO.446/76/46301 Crewe 24 Feb. 09; R. Hyam, *Elgin & Churchill at the Colonial Office 1905–08: the watershed of the Empire-Commonwealth* (1968) 198.
3. Martin, *HJ* XV 562; R. E. Robinson, 'Imperial problems in British politics 1880–95' in *CHBE* III (1959) 132.
4. Martin 563–65; L. C. Duly, *British land policy at the Cape 1795–1844: a study of administrative procedures in the empire* (1968); H. T. Manning, 'Who ran the British empire 1830–50?' *JBS* (1965) 88–121; T. R. H. Davenport & K. Hunt, *The right to the land* (1974) section 1.
5. G. W. Martin, 'Empire federalism & imperial parliamentary union 1820–70' *HJ* XVI (1973) 78; C. C. Eldridge, *England's mission: the imperial idea in the age of Gladstone & Disraeli 1868–80* (1973) 113.
6. Hyam, *Elgin & Churchill* 526; J. Amery, *Joseph Chamberlain & the tariff reform campaign* (*Life* VI, 1969) 601; M. Beloff, *Imperial sunset* I *Britain's liberal empire 1897–1921* (1969) 77.
7. F. S. Oliver, *Alexander Hamilton: an essay on American union* (1906) 20, 447, 452, 457.
8. Adam Smith, *An inquiry into the nature and causes of the wealth of nations* (ed. E. Cannan, 6th edn. 1950) II 432.
9. J. Rosselli, *Lord William Bentinck: the making of a Liberal Imperialist 1774–1839* (1974) 127, 146, 253–54; N. G. Barrier, 'The Punjab disturbances of 1907' *Modern Asian Studies* I (1967); R. Frykenberg, *Guntur District 1788–1848* (1965) 231–41, & 'Village strength in South India' in Frykenberg (ed.), *Land control and social structure in Indian history* (1969) 245–46, & review by Frykenberg in *AHR* 77 (1972) 463–72; E. T. Stokes, 'The first century of British colonial rule in India: social revolution or social stagnation?' *P&P* 58 (1973) 136–60; A. Seal, *The emergence of Indian nationalism: competition & collaboration in the later 19th century* (1968) 351; D. A. Low, *Lion Rampant: essays in the study of British imperialism* (1973) ch.1.
10. R. E. Robinson, 'Non-European foundations of European imperialism: sketch for a theory of collaboration' in R. Owen & R. Sutcliffe, (eds.) *Studies in the theory of imperialism* (1972) ch.v; R. Graham, 'Sepoys & imperialists: techniques of British power in 19th century Brazil' *Inter-American Economic Affairs* XXIII (1969) 23–37; Yen-P'ing Hao, *The comprador in 19th century China: bridge between east & west* (1970); A. G. Hopkins, *An economic history of West Africa* (1973) 109.
11. PRO, Cromer Papers FO.633/8/315 C to Morley 11 Apr. 01 (copy);

F. Warre Cornish, (ed.) *Extracts from the letters & journals of William Cory* (1897) 451, 511.

12. An illustration of this: Charles Kingsley's support for the establishment of a lectureship in American history and institutions at Cambridge, for which money had been given – the dons rejected it. (G. W. Martin, 'The Cambridge lectureship of 1866: false start in American studies' *Jrnl of American Studies* VII (1973) 17–29).

13. Rosselli, *Lord William Bentinck* 193, 199, 223.

14. L. H. Gann & P. Duignan, (eds.) *Colonialism in Africa* II *1914–1960* (1970) 92; *Collected essays, journalism and letters of George Orwell* (ed. S. Orwell & I. Angus 1968) IV *1945–1950* 358; the pigsticking remark is attributed to W. S. Churchill in T. Jones, *Whitehall Diary* (ed. J. Barnes & K. Middlemas) II (1969) 77; Rosselli 87, 274; *Extracts from the letters & journals of William Cory* 306, 523, 532, 546.

15. *Hansard* Commons Debate 9 Dec. 1762, *Parliamentary history of England to 1803* XV *1753–65* (1813) 1265.

16. H. W. Richmond, *National policy and naval strength; and other essays* (1928) 182–83, *The navy in war of 1739–48* (1920) III 50; J. Holland Rose, 'The influence of sea power on Indian history 1746–1802', *J. Indian History* III (1924).

17. G. S. Graham, *The politics of naval supremacy* (1965).

18. R. L. Schuyler, *Fall of the old colonial system: a study in British free trade 1770–1870* (1945) 200: D. A. Farnie, *East & west of Suez: the Suez canal in history 1854–1956* (1969) 23, 36–37, 73–74, 451.

19. Graham, *Politics of naval supremacy* 105 & *Tides of empire* (1973).

20. M. Davidson, *The world, the flesh & myself* (1962) 282.

21. C. J. Bartlett, *Great Britain & seapower* (1963) viii–xi; Judith B. Williams, *British commercial policy & trade expansion 1750–1850* (1972) 425–30.

22. C. J. Bartlett, 'Statecraft, power & influence' in Bartlett (ed.), *Britain pre-eminent: studies of British world influence in the 19th century* (1969) 187; J. Gallagher & R. E. Robinson 'Imperialism of free trade' *EconHR* VI (1953).

23. P. D. Curtin, *The Atlantic slave trade: a census* (1969) 269, & *The image of Africa: British ideas & action 1780–1850* (1965) 298, 303, 444; A. G. Hopkins, *An economic history of West Africa* (1973) 113.

24. K. O. Diké, *Trade and politics in the Niger delta 1830–1885* (1956) 204.

25. Bartlett, *Britain pre-eminent* 184–91.

26. R. E. Robinson in *CHBE* III 'The Empire-Commonwealth 1870–1919' (1959) 128.

27. H. S. Ferns, *Britain & Argentina in 19th century* (1960) 252; G. Blainey, *The tyranny of distance: how distance shaped Australia's history* (1968) 119.

28. L. Girard in *CEHE* VI/2 (1965) ch.iv, 249.

29. Diké, *Trade and politics in Niger delta* 204–07; R. E. Robinson &

J. Gallagher, *Africa and the Victorians: the official mind of imperialism* (1961) 37.

30. Bartlett, *Britain pre-eminent* 191, & *Great Britain & Seapower* 155, 164.

31. B. R. Mitchell & P. Deane, *Abstract of British historical statistics* (1962) 182, 282–83.

32. *CEHE* VI/1 (1965) 53, 353.

33. W. W. Rostow, *British economy in the 19th century* (1948) 23.

34. F. Thistlethwaite, 'Birds of passage: some aspects of the history of migration' (*Reports of 11th international congress of historical sciences* VI (1960) 32–60), 'Migration from Europe overseas' in H. Moller (ed.), *Population movements in modern European history* (1964); K. Sinclair, *A history of New Zealand* (revd. edn. 1969) 313.

35. C. W. Dilke, *Greater Britain* (1868) 390; H. J. M. Johnston, *British emigration policy 1815–30* (1972).

36. B. Thomas, *Migration and economic growth: a study of Great Britain and the Atlantic economy* (1954) 57.

37. Ibid., 204–07; G. Serle, *The golden age: a history of the colony of Victoria 1851–61* (1963) 45–46.

38. H. O. Pappé in A. G. L. Shaw (ed.), *Great Britain and the colonies 1815–65* (1970) 208–09.

39. E. R. Norman, *A history of modern Ireland* (1971) 12.

40. A. J. Youngson in *CEHE* VI/1, 144.

41. W. A. Carrothers, *Emigration from the British Isles* (1929) 112, 171, 182, 212.

42. W. K. Hancock, *Survey of British Commonwealth Affairs* II 'Problems of economic policy 1918–39' Part I (1940) 157.

43. Bartlett *Britain pre-eminent* 3.

44. *NCMH* IX *1793–1830* (1965) 46.

45. Hancock, *Survey of British Commonwealth Affairs* II/i, 168; H. Feis, *Europe, the world's banker* (1930) 23.

46. Feis 88.

47. A. H. Imlah, *Economic elements in the Pax Britannica* (1958) 70–75.

48. M. Simon, 'The pattern of new British portfolio foreign investment 1865–1914' in J. H. Adler, (ed.) *Capital movements & economic development 1865–1914* (1967) 40.

49. D. C. M. Platt, *Latin America & British trade 1806–1914* (1972) 287; P. J. Marshall, *Problems of empire: Britain & India 1757–1813* (1968) 96.

50. B. Thomas, (ed.) *Economics of international migration* (1958) 4; A. K. Cairncross, *Home and foreign investment 1870–1913* (1953) 209; L. H. Jenks, *The migration of British capital to 1875* (1938/1963) 332.

51. Hancock, *Survey* II/1, 183.

52. N. Gash, *Sir Robert Peel: the life of Peel after 1830* (1972) 329.

53. B. Semmel, *The rise of free trade imperialism* (1970) 149–50; PD. LX/279–80 (27 Jan 42) & 1041–42 (16 Feb. 42).

54. *Sunday Times* 1928, quoted in E. T. Stokes, *The English Utilitarians and India* (1959) 43.

55. Schuyler, *Fall of the old colonial system* 146 ff.

56. D. G. Creighton, *The commercial empire of the St Lawrence 1760–1850* (1937) 357–9; J. B. Brebner, *North Atlantic Triangle: the interplay of Canada, the United States, Great Britain* (1945) 151.

57. Schuyler 155, 164.

58. Hancock, II/1, 41–52, 73.

59. V. T. Harlow, *The founding of the second British empire 1763–1793* I *Discovery and Revolution* (1952) 219.

60. Notably C. A. Bodelsen, *Studies in mid-Victorian imperialism* (1924); Hyam & Martin, *Reappraisals in British imperial history* ch. 5 for commentary.

61. K. Bourne, *Britain and the balance of power in North America 1815–1908* (1967) 180.

62. S. R. Stembridge 'Disraeli & the millstones' *JBS* V (1965) 122–39.

63. A distinction elaborated in R. Hyam, 'The Colonial Office mind, 1900–14' in P. Wigley & N. Hillmer (eds.) *Experience of the Commonwealth: essays presented to Nicholas Mansergh* (1976).

64. Goldwin Smith, *Reminiscences* (ed. A. Haultain, 1910) 139; Bodelsen, *Studies in mid-Victorian imperialism* 56.

65. J. S. Mill, *Letters* (ed. H. S. R. Elliot 1910) II 237.

66. W. Denison, *Varieties of vice-regal life* (1870) I, 346–47, II 426.

67. Russell to Grey 19 Aug 49: Hyam & Martin, *Reappraisals* 113–15, and see Martin's chs. 5 & 6 generally, & 'Empire federalism' *HJ* XVI 65–92.

68. Another point I owe to Ged Martin.

69. A. R. M. Lower, 'The evolution of a sentimental idea of empire: a Canadian view' *History* XI (1926/27) 300; E. A. Walker, *The British empire: its structure and spirit 1497–1953* (2nd. edn. 1953) 65.

70. H. E. Egerton & W. L. Grant, *Canadian constitutional development: selected speeches and despatches* (1907) 201–07.

71. W. Molesworth, *Selected speeches on questions relating to colonial policy* (ed. H. E. Egerton, 1903) 391.

72. J. S. Mill, *Considerations on representative government* (1861) 404.

73. T. T. Meadows, *The Chinese and their rebellions* (1856) xxiv, xlvi, 633, 638.

74. *Fraser's Magazine* 1854, quoted in B. A. Knox, 'Rise of colonial federation as an object of British policy 1850–70' *JBS* XI (1971).

75. J. E. Tyler, *The struggle for imperial unity 1868–1895* (1938).

76. J. H. Gleason, *The genesis of Russophobia in Great Britain* (1950) 204.

77. *Fortnightly Review* VII (1870) 164–65; Martin *HJ* XVI 91–92.

78. Mill, *Letters* II 238.

79. Bodleian Library, Bryce Papers, C.2 Merriman to Bryce 15 Feb. 1919.

80. W. K. Hancock, *Colonial self-government* (Cust Foundation lecture

1956); J. M. Ward, *Empire in the Antipodes: the British in Australasia 1840–1860* (1966) 78–87.

81. Earl Grey, *The colonial policy of Lord John Russell's administration* (2nd. edn. 1853) II 286–7.

82. Hancock, *Colonial self-government* 17; Walker, *The British Empire* 71–72.

83. See below, p. 326–28.

84. J. W. Cell, *British colonial administration in the mid-19th century: the policy-making process* (1970) 193–200.

85. J. M. Ward, *Eawzey and the Australian colonies 1846–57: a study of self-government and self-interest* (1958), esp., 1–17, 23, 130, *Empire in the antipodes: the British in Australasia 1840–60* (1966) 79 ff.

86. Denison, *Varieties of vice-regal life* I 262, II 21.

87. Cell, *British colonial administration* 195.

88. Denison II 4.

2. THE MOTIVES & METHODS OF EXPANSION 1815–60

1. G. F. Hudson in R. Dawson (ed) *The Legacy of China* (1964) 359.

2. T. Walrond *Letters & journals of James, 8th earl of Elgin* (1872) 392–93; C. Kingsley *Limits of exact science as applied to history* (1860) 56–60.

3. J. W. Burrow *Evolution and society: a study in Victorian social theory* (1966) 51

4. G. D. Bearce *British attitudes towards India 1784–1858* (1961) 81–3.

5. Stokes *English Utilitarians and India.*

6. James Mill *History of British India* (1817) I, 428 ff.; T. R. Metcalf 'Victorian Liberalism and the Indian empire: the impact of the Mutiny of 1857 on British policy in India' (Ph.D. Harvard 1959), *The aftermath of revolt: India 1857–70* (1965).

7. R. Gavin 'Palmerston's policy towards the east and west coasts of Africa' (Ph.D. Cambridge 1959) 11–12

8. Curtin *Image of Africa* 236.

9. Low *Lion Rampant* 58.

10. Robinson & Gallagher *Africa & the Victorians* 2–3.

11. Mill *History of British India* I, 429, 625.

12. J. S. Mill *Considerations on representative government* ch. 3; Metcalf 'Victorian Liberalism and Indian empire' 8; D. G. Hoskin 'Genesis and significance of the 1886 "Home Rule" split in the Liberal Party' (Ph.D. Cambridge 1964) 29–33.

13. H. C. F. Bell *Lord Palmerston* (1936) II 411, Palmerston to Russell 1864.

14. W. Baring Pemberton *Lord Palmerston* (1954) 99, 112, 249.

15. V. G. Kiernan *The lords of human kind: European attitudes towards the outside world in the imperial age* (1969) 315–16; F. G. Hutchins *The illusion of permanence: British imperialism in India* (1967) 124.

16. G. Murray in F. W. Hirst *et al.* (eds) *Liberalism and the empire* (1900) 155.

17. J. Nehru *An Autobiography* (1936) 500.

18. R. T. Anstey *Atlantic slave trade & British abolition 1760–1810* (1975) & ' "Capitalism & Slavery": a critique' *EconHR* XXI (1968), 'A reinterpretation of the abolition of the British slave trade 1806–7' *EHR* LXXXVII, (1972) 304–32; R. Coupland *British anti-slavery movement* (ed. J. D. Fage, 1964); E. Williams *Capitalism & Slavery* (1944); F. J. Klingberg *The anti-slavery movement in England* (1926). In the attack on Williams' 'economic' explanation it is not always remembered that he deliberately subordinated the humanitarian factor – but, he wrote, 'to disregard it completely, however, would be to commit a grave historical error . . .' (178). For the statistical problem see P. D. Curtin *The Atlantic Slave Trade: a census* (1969). See also an excellent section on the slave trade in A. G. Hopkins *An economic –ory of West Africa* (1973) 99–119.

19. G. R. Mellor *British Imperial trusteeship 1783–1850* (1951) 420.

20. M. Postlethwayt *Britain's commercial interest explained and improved* (1757) II 217–21.

21. F. W. Pitman *The development of the British West Indies 1700–63* (1917) 63.

22. L. J. Ragatz *Fall of the planter class in the British Caribbean 1763–1833* (1928).

23. C. M. MacInnes *England & Slavery* (1934) 136.

24. F. Armytage *Free Port system in British West Indies 1766–1822* (1953) 65–68.

25. H. Temperley *British anti-slavery 1833–70* (1972).

26. J. Gallagher 'Fowell Buxton & the new African policy' *CHJ* X (1950).

27. *PD* LXV/1251–2, 10 Aug 42.

28. Gallagher *CHJ* (1950). See below, pp. 268–69.

29. J. B. Kelly *Britain & the Persian Gulf 1795–1880* (1968) 442–44, 636.

30. I. Schapera, (ed.) *Livingstone's missionary correspondence 1841–56* (1961) 308; R. Coupland, intro. to D. Chamberlin (ed.) *Some letters from Livingstone 1840–72* (1940) xvii.

31. M. Perham, (ed.) *Diaries of Lord Lugard* (1954) I 259–60, III 155.

32. Mellor, *British imperial trusteeship* 249–50; R. E. Robinson, 'The Trust in British Central African policy 1889–1939' (Ph.D. Cambridge 1950) 3–4.

33. Mellor, 251, 283, 290–1, 303, 391.

34. Ward *Empire in the Antipodes* 51.

35. K. Sinclair, *A history of New Zealand* (rev. ed. 1969) 66–69.

36. Robinson & Gallagher, *Africa & the Victorians* 50; G. C. Bolton *Britain's legacy overseas* (1973) 54; O. W. Parnaby, *Britain & the labour trade in the Southwest Pacific* (1964) x.

37. J. S. Galbraith, *Reluctant empire: British policy on the South African frontier 1834–54* (1963); G. C. Bolton, *Britain's legacy overseas* (1973) 37.

38. Temperley, *British anti-slavery* 43.

39. Hyam *Elgin & Churchill* 401–04.

40. J. D. Chambers, *Workshop of the world* (1961); A. Redford, *Manchester merchants and foreign trade* (1934) I 97; D. C. M. Platt, 'The national economy and British imperial expansion before 1914' JICH II (1973) 3–14.

41. H. M. Robertson, '150 years of economic contact between black & white' *S. African J. of Economics* (1934–35) II & III.

42. E. Robinson '18th century commerce & fashion: Matthew Boulton's marketing techniques' *EconHR* XVI (1963) 40.

43. Goldwin Smith, *Reminiscences* 2.

44. N. McKendrick 'Josiah Wedgwood: an 18th century entrepreneur' *EconHR* XII (1960) 426–28.

45. Harlow, *Founding of the second British empire* II (1964) 419–64.

46. G. S. Graham, *Peculiar Interlude: the expansion of England 1815–50* (Wood lecture 1959) 4–6; W. S. Jevons, *The coal question* (1906 edn.) 411.

47. Earl Grey, *Colonial policy of Lord John Russell's administration* II 203, 259.

48. *PD* LXV/1261–2, 10 Aug 42, & LXVI/1073.

49. Gavin, 'Palmerston's policy' 18, 32. Charles Wood's education despatch (1854) echoed these sentiments (Stokes, *English Utilitarians* 252).

50. W. E. Houghton *Victorian frame of mind 1830–70* (1957) 43–4.

51. D. Newsome, *Godliness & good learning: four studies on a Victorian ideal* (1961) 68, 91.

52. T. B. Macaulay *History of England from the accession of James II* (1848, ed. C. H. Firth 1913) 1, 2.

53. A. Briggs, *Age of improvement* (1959) 344, 446.

54. W. B. Pemberton, *Lord Palmerston* 141; also 1, 22, 251.

55. Briggs, *Age of improvement* 344, 402.

56. W. L. Burn, *Age of equipoise* (1964) 49–50, 103.

57. $\frac{1}{2}$. Shannon, *Gladstone & the Bulgarian agitation 1876* (1963) 28; M. Warren, 'The Church Militant abroad: Victorian missionaries' in A. Symondson (ed.) *The Victorian crisis of faith* (1970) 57–70; P. G. R. Brendon, *Hurrell Froude & the Oxford movement* (1974) xiii.

58. G. Kitson Clark, *The making of Victorian England* (1962) 20, 169–72, 284.

59. *Hymns Ancient & Modern* (1st ed. 1859) esp. nos. 358, 359, 361 and in later editions 477 and 586.

60. I. Schapera, (ed.) *Livingstone's African journal 1853–56* (1963) I 57, II 389.

61. K. S. Latourette, *A history of the expansion of Christianity: the great century* (1941) IV 44; M.A. C. Warren, *Missionary movement from Britain in modern history* (1965) 45–53 & 'The Church militant abroad' 66; S. Neill, *A history of Christian missions* (1964) ch. 9.

62. Parkinson *East & West* 218; Ferns, *Britain & Argentina* 46–8;

N. Tarling, *Anglo-Dutch rivalry in the Malay world 1780–1824* (1962) 105.

63. Stokes, *English Utilitarians* 43–4.

64. E. Huxley, *White Man's Country: Lord Delamere & the making of Kenya* (1953 edn.) I 176; Goldwin Smith, *Commonwealth or Empire: a bystander's view of the question* (1902) 69–70.

65. A point not made plain in O. MacDonagh 'The anti-imperialism of free trade' *EconHR* XIV (1962) 489 ff.

66. Dilke, *Greater Britain* (1868) vii–viii, 224; S. Gwynn & G. Tuckwell, *Life of Sir Charles Dilke* (1918) I 68; R. Koebner & H. D. Schmidt, *Imperialism; the story & significance of a political word 1840–1960* (1964) 89.

67. E. G. Wakefield, *A view of the art of colonisation* (1849) x, 17, 104.

68. R. A. Huttenback, *British imperial experience* (1966) 113.

69. H. P. Hughes, *The philanthropy of God* (1890) 97.

70. D. G. Creighton 'Victorians & empire' *CHR* XIX (1938).

71. Pemberton, *Lord Palmerston* 92.

72. Gavin 'Palmerston's policy' 124.

73. Earl of Cromer, *Modern Egypt* (1908) I 92.

74. C. K. Webster, *Foreign policy of Lord Palmerston 1830–41* (1951) II 177.

75. Palmerston's phrase with respect to Turkey: Webster *Foreign policy of Lord Palmerston* II 540.

76. Curtin, *Image of Africa* 252.

77. Mill, *Considerations on representative government* ch. 2.

78. Webster, II 787, Pemberton 62.

79. Stokes, 56–7; T. B. Macaulay, *Speeches* (1853) I, 193–94.

80. Bearce *British attitudes towards India* 141; G. F. Hudson *Far East in world politics* (2nd edn. 1939) 82; R. D. Collison Black *Economic thought and the Irish question 1817–70* (1960) 32, 88, 243.

81. 3 *PD*/LX/618–19, 16 Feb 42, partly quoted in Robinson & Gallagher 2.

82. E. D. Steele 'Irish land reform & English Liberal politics' (Ph.D. Cambridge 1963) 6, & *Irish land & British politics; tenant right & nationality 1865–70* (1974) 37 & ch. 1 generally.

83. R. Cobden *England, Ireland & America* (1835) quoted in F. Thistlethwaite *The Anglo-American connection in the early 19th century* (1959) 167.

84. D. Read, *Cobden & Bright: a Victorian partnership* (1967) 110, 238.

85. R. F. Burton, *The lake regions of Central Africa* (1860) II 419.

86. Low *Lion Rampant* 121; G. C. Moore Smith, (ed.) *The autobiography of Lt-Gen Sir Harry Smith* (1901) II 379–81.

87. Mellor, *British imperial trusteeship* 249–50.

88. *Letters & journals of . . . 8th earl of Elgin* 23.

89. Metcalf, *Aftermath of revolt* 25; P. J. Marshall, *Problems of empire: Britain & India 1757–1813* (1968) 70–71.

90. E. Kedourie *England & the Middle East 1914–21* (1956) 13.

91. H. A. C. Cairns, *Prelude to imperialism: British reactions to Central African society 1840–90* (1965) 201.

92. D. Southgate, *The passing of the Whigs 1832–86* (1962) 158.

93. J. Vincent *The formation of the Liberal Party 1857–68* (1966) 158.

94. J. Bastin, *Native policies of Sir Stamford Raffles in Java & Sumatra* (1957) 140.

95. C. Bruce, *The Broad Stone of empire: problems of Crown Colony administration* (1910) I 134.

96. T. G. P. Spear, 'Bentinck & education' *CHJ* VI (1938) 78–100, 'Lord Wm Bentinck' *Jrnl. Indian Hist* 19 (1940) 109–10, G. D. Bearce, 'Lord Wm Bentinck: the application of liberalism to India' *JMH* 28 (1956) 236; Rosselli *Lord William Bentinck* 208–25.

97. Stokes 46, 252.

98. Bearce *Attitudes* 62; W. J. MacPherson, 'Investment in Indian railways 1845–75' *EconHR* VIII (1955) 177; Rosselli, *Lord William Bentinck* 275, 285–92.

99. Low, *Lion Rampant* 53.

100. Kiernan, *Lords of human kind*, 116.

101. *Letters & journals of . . . Elgin* 446.

102. *Last Journals* (ed. H. Waller 1874) II 215; Mackenzie quoted in V. Purcell *The Boxer Uprising* (1963) 115–16.

103. J. K. Fairbank, *The United States & China* (rev. edn. 1962) 119 n.

104. J. F. A. Ajayi, *Christian missons in Nigeria 1841–91* (1965) 14, 65.

105. *Autobiography of . . . Harry Smith* II 90, 381–2.

106. Stokes, xiv: C. N. Parkinson, *British intervention in Malaya 1867–77* (1960) xiii.

107. S. W. Baker, *The Albert N'yanza* (1866) I xxiii.

108. *Livingstone's missionary correspondence 1841–56* 183–84, 301.

109. *Livingstone's African journal 1853–56* I xix, II 244, 304.

110. Ajayi, *Christian missions in Nigeria* 18–19.

111. W. B. Campbell, 'The South African frontier 1865–85: a study in expansion' *Archives Yearbook for S. African History* (1959), I 36; Ramm, *Sir Robert Morier . . . 1876–93* (1973) 81.

112. O. Furley in Bartlett (ed.) *Britain pre-eminent* 133.

113. *The life of Frederick Denison Maurice by his son F. Maurice* (1885) II 482, 1 Jul 64.

114. O. Omosini 'Origins of British methods of tropical development in West African dependencies 1880–1906' (Ph.D. Cambridge 1968) 52–64.

115. D. Pike, *Paradise of dissent: South Australia 1829–57* (2nd edn. 1967) 95.

116. See for example the dedication in R. M. Martin *China: political, commercial & social* (1847).

117. Kedourie *England & the Middle East* 15.

118. Hancock, *Survey of British Commonwealth Affairs* 11/2 (1942) 314.

119. L. Robbins, *The theory of economic policy in English classical political economy* (1952) 11, 57; Collison Black, *Economic thought & the Irish question* 39, 108, 166–67, 194; Smith *Wealth of nations* I, 421.

120. S. Smiles, *Self-Help* (1958 centenary edn.) 35; W. G. Beasley, *The modern history of Japan* (1963) 153.

121. Hoskin, 'Genesis & significance of 1886 "Home Rule" split' 124.

122. M. C. Wright, *The last stand of Chinese conservatism: the T'ung-Chih restoration 1862–74* (1957) 251, 280–1.

123. Bearce, *British attitudes* 265.

124. K. Ballhatchet, *Social policy & social change in Western India 1817–30* (1957) 248.

125. Stokes 45–46, Macaulay to his father 12 Oct 36.

126. Grey, *Colonial policy of Lord John Russell's administration* II 281; Gavin 355.

127. A. P. Thornton, for example, finds it difficult to accept Palmerston as a promoter of free trade (*For the file on empire* 256).

128. Webster, *Foreign policy of Palmerston* II 540; F. S. Rodkey 'Lord Palmerston's policy for the rejuvenation of Turkey 1839–41' 4 *TRHS* XII (1929) 171; J. B. Williams *British commercial policy & trade expansion* 427–37; D.C.M. Platt, *Cinderella Service* (1971).

129. J. L. Cranmer-Byng (ed.) *An embassy to China: Lord Macartney's journal 1793–94* (1962) 3.

130. Li Chien-Nung, *The political history of China 1840–1928* (transl. & ed. S.-Y. Teng & J. Ingalls, 1956) 19.

131. *PD* LXV/1254, 10 Aug 42; F. R. Flournoy, *British policy towards Morocco . . . 1830–65* (1935) 252–56; Curtin *Image* 465–68.

132. Webster II 751.

133. Diké, *Trade & politics* 175–76; Gavin 27.

134. Stokes 46–7; G. O. Trevelyan, *Competition wallah* (1864) 422.

135. Grey *Colonial policy* II 181.

136. *Papers relating to the rebellion in China and trade in the Yang Tse-Kiang River* 3–8, 56–58; *Further papers relating to the rebellion in China* 20–21 (*Parliamentary Accounts and Papers* (1862) LXIII); J. F. Cady, *Roots of French imperialism in Eastern Asia* (1954)) 108.

137. O. Lattimore, *From China looking outward* (Inaugural lecture 1964) 20; W. J. Hail *Tsêng Kuo-Fan & the Taiping Rebellion* (1927).

138. D. Southgate, *'The Most English Minister'* . . . *the policies & politics of Palmerston* (1966) 146.

139. J. K. Fairbank, *Trade & diplomacy on the China coast 1842–54* (1953) I 380.

140. Bourne, *Britain & balance of power in North America* 182.

141. Southgate, *'The Most English Minister'* 143; Robinson & Gallagher 4.

142. Pemberton 95: Gavin 231, 347.

143. G. Douglas, Duke of Argyll *Autobiography & Memoirs* (1906) II 148–50.
144. Pemberton 99.
145. Gavin 12, 26.
146. Stokes 178.
147. Metcalf 8–13.
148. J. Rutherford *Sir George Grey 1812–1898: a study in colonial government* (1961) 207–09, 262, 655.
149. Asa Briggs chose extremely aptly the title *The age of improvement* for his book on the period 1780–1865.
150. In what follows I draw heavily upon D. C. M. Platt 'Further objections to an "Imperialism of free trade" 1830–60' *EconHR* XXVI (1973) 77–91, esp. 83; see also F. Wakeman jnr. *Strangers at the gate: South China 1839–61* (1966) 15; A. G. Hopkins *An economic history of West Africa* (1973) 48–50. There was no appreciable increase in cotton exports to Nigeria 1891–1938 because British manufacturers could not compete with local industry – see M. Johnson 'Cotton imperialism in West Africa' *African Affairs* 73 (1974) 178–87.
151. J. J. Eddy, *Britain & the Australian colonies 1818–31: the technique of government* (1969) xvi.
152. *Extracts from the letters & journals of William Cory* 376.

3. THE DECLINE OF BRITISH PRE-EMINENCE 1855–1914

1. J. Morley, *Life of Richard Cobden* (1883 edn.) 395–405.
2. G. Alder 'India & the Crimean War' *JICH* II (1973) 15–37; Martin, 'Empire Federalism' *HJ* XVI (1973) 77–78.
3. E. Grierson, *Imperial Dream* (1972) 84.
4. Field Marshal Viscount Wolseley, *The story of a soldier's life* (1903) I 253.
5. C. H. Stuart, 'The Prince Consort & ministerial politics 1856–59' in H. R. Trevor Roper (ed.) *Essays in British history presented to Sir Keith Feiling* (1964).
6. Rutherford, *Sir George Grey* 373–74.
7. D. Hurd, *The Arrow War; an Anglo-Chinese confusion 1856–60* (1967) 99.
8. E. Fitzmaurice, *The life of . . . 2nd earl Granville 1815–91* (1905) I 244.
9. C. C. F. Greville, *The Greville Memoirs, 3rd Part: a journal of the reign of Queen Victoria from 1852 to 1860* (1887) II 112–153.
10. Goldwin Smith, *Reminiscences* 203–04.
11. *The Life of F. D. Maurice* II 313.
12. J. Sturgis, *John Bright & the empire* (1969) 44–45.
13. Morley, *Cobden* 431–8.
14. F. E. Kingsley, *Charles Kingsley: his letters & memories of his life* II 34–35.